The Facility Management Handbook
Second Edition

The Facility Management Handbook
Second Edition

David G. Cotts

AMACOM

American Management Association

New York • Atlanta • Boston • Chicago • Kansas City • San Francisco • Washington, D.C.
Brussels • Mexico City • Tokyo • Toronto

Library of Congress Cataloging-in-Publication Data

Cotts, David G.
    The facility management handbook / David G. Cotts. — 2nd ed.
        p.   cm.
    Includes index.
    ISBN 0-8144-0380-8
    1. Real estate management.   2. Building management.   I. Title.
HD1394.C68   1998
658.2—dc21   98-12400
                                                                CIP

To:
Stephen Coite Eller
Brendan Eric Cotts
Meaghan Maria Cotts
Lauren Diane Eller

Contents

Preface to the
Second Edition

Two things led me to revise *The Facility Management Handbook*. The first stems from my observations of between 100 and 150 facility management departments annually through my consulting practice and teaching for George Mason University, the University of Manitoba, and the International Facility Management Association (IFMA). The practice of facility management is changing dramatically, accelerated by the changes in the way that both private- and public-sector business is conducted. Chapter 1 discusses these changes at length. Most facility departments have been through total quality management, rightsizing, reengineering, and outsourcing since *The Handbook* first appeared. Many facility managers are reeling and staffing down and organizations have been shattered and budgets slashed dramatically. This new edition reflects these changed conditions. Conversely, a large number of facility managers have broken into the $100,000–150,000 salary range. Salaries at that level were extremely rare when I wrote the first edition in 1992, but this fact shows the opportunities available for good facility managers. This book deals with those opportunities.

Second, in the spring of 1996, I participated in a National Academy of Science symposium, *Federal Facilities Beyond the 1990s* (the symposium report is available from the National Academy Press, Washington, D.C.). It represented to me the good, the bad, and the ugly of the current state of facility management. There, alongside the reports of continuing efforts to improve bureaucratic procedures, were some real management jewels. Instead of the usual citing of better project management, proper construction management, and better design (all of which are important but have been emphasized for years), several speakers articulated the real keys to effective facility management:

1. We need to recognize facility management as a business function and the facility manager as a business manager.
2. We need to produce a quality service defined not by us but by our customers.
3. We need to implement best practices.

These conclusions illustrate that some of the presenters and attendees at that symposium had the word; others no doubt will continue to present solutions to problems that were solved years ago or are irrelevant to the modern facility manager.

Moreover, the professional organizations for facility managers have finally realized that their real mission is to serve the facility management customer. In fact, World Workplace now has become not just the IFMA annual conference but also the preeminent educational conference for facility managers, sponsored by eleven different professional, trade, and public interest associations. The professional associations are moving toward specialization and referring customers to the research source or educational effort that meets their needs, regardless of who gets the credit. There are still too many professional associations, but short of their unlikely mergers, this cooperation—referred to as "co-opetition"—is encouraging.

What matters most to facility managers is how their organizations and bosses view them and their performance. In 1997, IFMA conducted a survey, *Views from the Top . . . Executives Evaluate the Facility Management Function*, which confirms several important perceptions of facility management. Even more important, it illustrates a perception gap between what facility managers think is important in their jobs and what their bosses view as important. Finally, this survey indicates that facility managers need to be better salespeople, both for what they do and for the importance of their department's support of the corporate mission. These are themes that will recur throughout this book.

The Facility Management Handbook has been the most widely used book in degree-granting and certificate facility management programs throughout the world. Consequently, I have retained the basic structure of the book, since it fosters good instruction.

I have added a chapter on quality management (Chapter 18). Where it is applicable, substantial material on outsourcing, partnering, and benchmarking has been added throughout the book. I consistently stress viewing facility management as a business function and customer service. I have upgraded the Glossary and added sections on commonly used Internet numbers and a facility manager's tool kit of reference books that should be at the elbow of every facility manager.

I have retained the popular "pulse points" at the start of each chapter. In the interest of space, I have reduced the backup documents that related to space definition. For economic reasons, the definitions of space have become quite contentious. The American Society for Testing and Materials is taking the lead in defining space through its standards program. I think that is the right approach, but space users need to understand that in signing leases, it is caveat emptor until the standard is promulgated and accepted.

Please note three conventions I use in the book. At times I use *FM* as an abbreviation for both *facility management* and *facility manager*. Second, I realize that this book will be read by both public- and private-sector facility managers, so when I say *company*, I mean company or agency, unless I draw a distinction between the public and private sector. Also, as in the original, I use *he* when referring to facility managers to avoid the awkward *he/she* pronoun construction.

Acknowledgments

Acknowledgments always present a problem because they are by nature exclusive, whereas a book like this is the product of the knowledge and expertise of fellow facility managers, vendors and contractors, colleagues and bosses, and educators to whom I will be forever indebted. Where documentation was available, their contribution has been attributed, but I am sure that the ideas of others have so permeated my own that even I do not remember who first showed me the light in some areas. I have chosen to acknowledge two individuals and certain facility management (FM) educators.

Peter Kimmel is the founder and driving force behind FMLink, the online facility management service, and president of Peter S. Kimmel & Associates in Bethesda, Maryland. While others contemplated the idea of FM on the Internet or sought corporate backing, Peter fielded FMLink and provided a new resource to facility managers, educators, researchers, and authors worldwide.

Education of facility managers has always been a difficult task. At any one time, it seems that as many programs are disappearing as are entering the field.

- I want to recognize the FM program at Cornell University, particularly one of my mentors, Bill Sims. He has not only influenced a generation of facility managers, but has guided the educational efforts of the professional associations to an extent that no one else has. As other programs have come and gone, the Cornell program has only gotten better.
- I acknowledge the Faculty of Architecture at the University of Manitoba in its attempt to field a master's in facility management through distance education. As an active participant in the program, I appreciate both the challenge and the potential benefits.
- I especially want to recognize Keith Alexander, a real educational pioneer with his FM program at the University of Strathclyde. He is a mover and a shaker at a time when facility management is just becoming recognized as a profession in Europe.
- The final education program that I want to acknowledge is the professional certificate program at George Mason University, the faculty, who make the program so successful, Kitty Hoover, who keeps it running and in the black,

and Terry Ryan, who is always stretching our vision as we work to meet the professional needs of facility managers in the Washington, D.C., area.

Professor Victoria Hardy of Ferris State University and her 1997–98 students in facility management merit special appreciation for their suggestions for improvements in this book as a textbook. I hope Professor Hardy and her students will see the results of their criticism reflected in the final product.

The Glossary section of this book deserves its own acknowledgments. My special thanks go to Gerald Davis and Francoise Szigeti of the Centre for Facility Management, who have worked tirelessly for better definitions and standardization within facility management. (The professional associations need to continue to press for greater standardization of terms. Efforts to date have been marginal, and the shortcomings in standardization create problems for the profession, particularly in research and education.) I also acknowledge the contributions of the BOMI Institute and Doug Sherman, Tom Northam, Mike Croskery, Dan Hightower, Ed Rondeau, Robert Kevin Brown, and Paul Lapides, whose favorite definitions are included here.

Finally, I want to express my gratitude to that greatest of all editors and copyreaders, Linda Willard Cotts, who also happens to be the greatest wife and friend that a guy could ever have.

Section I

Background and Organization

This opening section of *The Facility Management Handbook, Second Edition* deals with the nature of facility management and focuses on change created by the business environment. I emphasize the need for the facility manager to be a business leader and discuss various aspects of that leadership. I discuss what organizations and executives expect of facility managers and give a profile of success for facility managers. Finally, I look at organizations that can be adapted to meet the requirements of various organizations and discuss staffing issues to fill those organizations.

1

The Nature of Facility Management

Pulse Points

- *Both the organization and the facility manager should have a specific philosophy about facilities.*
- *Facility management is an essential business function; the facility manager is a business manager.*
- *Different types of organizations require different approaches to facility management.*
- *Facility management needs better basic research, particularly to support claims of increasing worker productivity.*

Facility management, commonly abbreviated as FM, is a fairly new business and management discipline. Widespread use of the term dates from the creation of the Facility Management Institute at Ann Arbor, Michigan, in 1979 and the founding of the National (later International) Facility Management Association in 1980. However, facility management of large and diverse facilities has long been practiced by the military, government, and North American college and university campus officials, usually under the name of postengineering, public works, or plant administration. In the private sector, commercial owners and developers have practiced property management, or managing properties for a profit.

The common definition of *facility management* is "the practice of coordinating the physical workplace with the people and work of the organization; integrates the principles of business administration, architecture, and the behavioral and engineering sciences." It is often simplified to mean that facility managers integrate the *people* of an organization with its *purpose* (work) and *place* (facilities).* Exhibit 1-1 defines FM in terms of the commonly performed functions and subfunctions.

---

*Credit for this concept goes to the former Facility Management Institute, which simplified and defined the concept as three interlocking rings (purpose, place, people) whose common area represents the integrative nature of facility management.

Exhibit 1-1. Common functions of facility management.

Management of the Organization
- Planning
- Organizing
    - By function, organization, or building
    - Centralized versus user driven
- Staffing
    - Personnel management
    - Evaluation of mix of staff, consultants, and contractors
    - Training
- Directing
    - Work scheduling
    - Work coordination
    - Policy and procedure development
- Controlling
    - Work reception
    - Standards establishment (dollar range, quality, quantity, time to deliver)
    - Scheduling
    - Use of management information systems and basic computer literacy
    - Contract administration
    - Policy and procedure execution
- Evaluating
    - Design
    - Punch-list preparation and execution
    - Postoccupancy evaluation
    - Program analysis
    - Contractor evaluation

Facility Planning and Forecasting
- Five- to ten-year plan
- Three- to five-year plan
- Eighteen-month to three-year plan
- Space forecasting (macrolevel organizationwide)
- Macrolevel programming (organizationwide)
- Financial forecasting and macrolevel estimating (organizationwide)
- Capital program development

Lease Administration
- Outleasing (as owner)
- Lease administration (as owner or lessee)
- Property management (as lessee)

Space Planning, Allocation, and Management
- Space allocation
- Space inventory

- Space forecasting (microlevel, one location)
- Space management

Architectural/Engineering Planning and Design
- Macrolevel programming (one location)
- Building planning
- Architectural design
- Engineering design of major systems
- Macrolevel estimating (one location)
- "As-built" maintenance
- Disaster-recovery planning
- Design documents
- Code compliance
- Traffic engineering
- Zoning compliance

Workplace Planning, Allocation, and Management
- Workplace planning
- Workplace design
- Furniture specification
- Equipment specification
- Furnishing specification
- Estimating
- "As-built" maintenance
- Code compliance
- Art program management

Budgeting, Accounting, and Economic Justification
- Programming (2–3 years)
- Work plan preparation
- Types of budget (1–2 years)
  — Administrative
  — Capital
  — Operations and maintenance
  — Chargeback
- Economic justifications
- Financial forecasting (1–2 years)
- Budget formulation
- Budget execution

Real Estate Acquisition and Disposal
- Site selection and acquisition
- Building purchase
- Building lease
- Real estate disposal

(continues)

Exhibit 1-1. (continued)

Construction Project Management
- Project management
- Construction management
- Procurement management
- Procurement (to construct)
- Preparation of "as-builts"

Alteration, Renovation, and Workplace Installation
- Alteration management
- Renovation management
- Furniture installation
- Datacom installation
- Voice installation
- Provision of furnishings
- Equipping
- Relocation moving
- Procurement (to alter, renovate, and install)
- Preparation of "as-builts"
- Project management

Operations, Maintenance, and Repair
- Exterior maintenance (roofs, shell, and window systems)
- Preventive maintenance
- Breakdown maintenance
- Cyclic maintenance
- Grounds maintenance
- Road maintenance
- Custodial maintenance
- Pest and rodent control
- Trash removal
- Hazardous waste management
- Energy management
- Inventory
- Maintenance projects
- Repair projects
- Correction of hazards (asbestos, bad air quality, radon, underground leaks, PCBs, etc.)
- Disaster recovery
- Procurement (operations, maintenance, and repair supplies and services)

Telecommunications, Datacommunications, Wire, and Network Management
- Operations
- Maintenance
- Central voice operations
- Data system reconfiguration

- Network management
- "As-built" maintenance

Security and Life-Safety Management
- Code compliance
- Operations
- Criminal investigation

General Administrative Services
- Food services
- Reprographics
- Mail and messenger management
- Transportation and vehicle maintenance
- Property disposal
- Moving services
- Procurement (as a function)
- Health and fitness program management
- Day care center management

Facility management embraces the concepts of cost-effectiveness, productivity improvement, efficiency, and employee quality of life. In practice, these concepts often seem to be in conflict. For example, many facility managers find themselves sinking in the quicksand of diminishing white-collar productivity, placed at the precipice of office air-quality problems, or embroiled in waste-management issues that predate their employment. Research in many of these areas is nonexistent or has produced conflicting results. Government guidelines often do not exist, or else they are vague. Employee expectations and concerns almost always come before clearcut technical solutions. Often there are no set answers—only management decisions that must be made.

Some say Murphy (of Murphy's law) was a facility manager. Every good facility manager is a good *reactive* manager because reaction is a fact of life in delivering services. Unfortunately that situation can downplay planning, even though planning is the key to cost-effectiveness and the proper reaction to multiple needs. You probably will not agree with all of our facilities management philosophy. However, a facility manager who does not have a philosophy regarding his position, his department, and the facilities cannot provide the leadership needed by the company.

The Development of Facility Management

The management of very large and complex facilities is not new to some people. Many municipal public works directors, corporate facility managers, or collegiate plant administrators were formerly military post engineers, public works officers, or base civil engineers.

The American Institute of Plant Engineers (AIPE), since renamed The Association for Facilities Engineering (AFE), and the Association of Physical Plant Administrators (APPA) (now named the Association of Higher Education Facilities Officers) were among the first to organize disparate professionals with diverse backgrounds but common goals. And early in the 1980s two things happened. First, the term *facility management* started to appear in the trade and popular press, and companies started to recruit *facility managers*. Second, the Facility Management Institute (FMI) was founded as a focal point for training and research. During an early seminar at FMI, approximately forty public and corporate facility managers founded the National Facility Management Association (NFMA).

Although NFMA did not represent all facility managers, its growth was a gauge of interest in facility management. Early on, Canadian interest led NFMA to become the International Facility Management Association (IFMA), which, in 1997, has grown to almost 15,000 members. In addition, IFMA encouraged the development of FM organizations throughout the world and the founding of Global FM, for which it provides the secretariat. There are now separate FM organizations in five countries outside North America, while IFMA continues to accept both membership and chapters throughout the world.

AFE, APPA, the BOMI Institute, IFMA, IREM, ISFE, and NACORE all provide membership, educational, and research services to facility managers. It is unfortunate, though, that the professional organizations cannot unite into a single organization; professionals and their bosses would be much less confused. A major step toward unity and better service to facility managers occurred in 1995 when the first World Workplace was held in Miami. World Workplace has become the premier educational opportunity and trade show for facility managers. In 1997 fifteen professional, trade, and educational organizations participated. Although facility management has come a long way, the profession also faces major challenges.

Often facility managers, in both the public and private sectors, either do not realize or fail to understand how they are perceived within their companies—a major problem for the profession and for individual facility managers. Historically facility managers and their departments have been viewed as shown here:

- Caretakers
- Naysayers
- Advocates for employee welfare
- Controllers
- Employee efficiency multipliers
- Heavy reliers on the Purchasing Department
- Service providers
- Producers of voluminous policies and regulations
- Project handlers

Not all of these attributes are bad, but the business and government worlds have changed, and so must we. Here are the important business and cultural trends that have radically changed the private and public sectors:

Business Trends	*Cultural Trends*
• Rise of the chief financial officer	• Generational perceptions
• Focus on cost reduction and shareholder value	• Demographics
	• Increasingly diverse workforce

Business Trends	*Cultural Trends*
• Internationalization	• Concerns with the environment
• Rise of information management	• Lack of faith in institutions
• Payoff in investment in automation	• Libertarianism
• The quality movement	
• Flattening of organizations	
• Emphasis on speed of delivery	

A new facility manager profile emerges based on these trends. The facility manager moves from a narrow technical focus where his language is "FMspeak" to the expanded viewpoint of a business leader who helps the company take a strategic view of its facilities and their impact on productivity. Here are the characteristics of a facility manager who is successful in today's business environment:

• Business leader	• Networker
• Mentor	• Survivor
• Strategic business planner and implementer	• Spokesperson
• Environmentalist	• Agile purchaser, lessor, and contractor
• Resource obtainer	• Innovator
• Financial manager	• Information manager

As I view a broad assortment of facility managers, it is obvious that facility managers who have not just survived but thrived have shed the role of technician and have adopted the characteristics shown in the above list. Yet in a recent trade publication, an experienced facility manager decried the experts who are telling the profession, "Think strategic, not tactical," and "Be more of a business strategist than the traditional facilities manager."[1] How sad! Keeping to that line of reactionary thinking will relegate facility managers to a life of misery and reaction—*if* they are able to retain their positions at all.

Views from the Top . . . Executives Evaluate the Facility Management Function, a recent IFMA survey of 252 senior business and government managers, speaks to facility managers directly. Company executives indicated that 60 percent of them viewed facilities as "a cost of doing business that enables our organization to function," and 37 percent viewed facilities as "a resource that can provide a competitive edge." Nine of ten executives felt financial and project management skills were paramount for their facility managers.[2] There is a two-edged message here for the profession. First, bosses want facility managers to be good businesspeople. Second, facility managers still have a long way to go to sell their message that facilities are a strategic advantage for companies. The facility manager who is most successful in conveying that message must have his own mission and philosophy clearly in mind.

In this chapter, I discuss the themes that shape the facility management philosophy I espouse: They are as follows:

Facility Management Philosophy

- View facility management as a business function.
- Safety is always the first concern; legality is tied for second with customer service.
- Someone should be directly responsible for every physical asset and function.
- There is a cost of ownership of facilities; it is the facility manager's task to ensure that management understands that cost.
- The facility manager's responsibility to management is well known; he should concentrate on responsibility to employees.
- The facility manager should be cost-effective in everything he does and capture all costs in his analyses.
- If something looks like a good idea, try it. If it doesn't work, change it.
- A good, commonsense decision beats "paralysis by analysis." Avoid excessive dependence on quantitative measurement.
- A budget is a management tool. Put effort into its preparation and format, and then monitor its execution.
- Every physical asset should be under life-cycle maintenance.
- When an outside consultant is used, requirements must be defined.
- As the design-construct cycle proceeds, changes become costlier and less effective. The facility manager must retain control of the design-construct cycle.
- In the planning of major projects, engineering requirements are nearly always understated.
- Plan for flexibility and redundancy in building systems.
- Plan with care, and always retain the capability to react.
- Cultivate long-term relationships. Remember that the successful facility management organization is a team (staff, suppliers, contractors, consultants).
- Remember that the customer—and the customer alone—defines service. The facility manager's responsibility is to find out how his customer rates his services.
- The facility manager must regularly measure both the effectiveness and the efficiency of the department.
- The facility manager must be active in public relations outside the department. If he doesn't promote his department, it will not be promoted.
- The best way to save money is to participate in facility business planning. A facility business plan should support every company business plan.
- The facility manager should prioritize the development of a facility management information system with the budget as a base document.

When all facility managers adopt these elements of a philosophy, or if they adopt their own, the practice of FM will improve immensely. My observation is that too often facility managers view themselves as victims or are so bogged down in their day-to-day work that they fail to grasp the truly important aspects of success. Not every point in the list is equally applicable to every organization, but facility managers who have a philosophy of leading are those who lead best, and I have drawn each of the points from a successful FM leader.

There are eight major actions that every facility manager should take to manage the facilities and his department successfully. I call them the Big Eight, and they appear as Exhibit 1-2. These are all concrete things to do. When the Big Eight are complete, the facility manager has the tools to exhibit his leadership. Without them, there will be gaps in funding, staff, service assessment, or information. Some of the Big Eight are duplicative of items in the philosophy I already stated; actually, all of them are an outgrowth of that philosophy. If you have accomplished all of these eight tasks or are working on them, you probably have a good handle on your position and department. Your success will then depend on your ability as a leader because the basic building blocks of success are in place.

FM as a Business Function

Corporate facilities, as confirmed by Harvard and MIT studies in 1981 and 1987, respectively, have been undermanaged.[3] For reasons that are not totally clear, both the public and the private sectors have been slow to realize the business nature of facility management—for example:

- Facilities management is often big business. The Department of Defense is estimated to have over 2 billion square feet of facilities under its management.[4]
- After payroll, facilities are usually the greatest component of a company's administrative expense.
- Some facility departments have saved or even avoided costs in the 30 to 35

Exhibit 1-2. Big Eight.

---

1. Conduct and regularly update an assessment of both physical facilities and operations.
2. Get your reorganization right. Too many of us are handicapped by bad organizations. Don't confuse staffing and organization.
3. Institute a customer-based quality program.
4. Determine the information you need to manage and then develop automation to produce it for you. Your facility management information system should be budget based.
5. Institute facility business planning even if you are initially rebuffed by company planners.
6. Show results! Companies don't pay off for good intentions and plans.
7. Have a public relations plan each year that targets each of your target constituencies.
8. Get management commitment to good facility management. You, and you alone, can obtain it. It is worth the effort.

---

percent range, with no diminution of services, by applying sound principles of planning, lease management, and energy management.

Yet most facility managers are viewed narrowly as technical facility managers, not as business managers. Most M.B.A. candidates are not even exposed to the subject. But this situation is changing as increasing numbers of companies recognize the value of FM.

Facility management is the quintessential business function, affecting not only revenues and costs but production, quality of life for employees, health and safety, the work environment, and, increasingly, areas such as the ability to recruit and hold employees. When facility management is practiced properly, the following benefits accrue to the company:

- Facility plans match company plans.
- Space is available when and where it is needed.
- Capital expenditures are planned and controlled.
- Employee productivity is maximized.
- Costs are minimized, sometimes avoided, and always predicted.

Survey results, particularly comparative results, are always interesting. In late 1996, *Facilities Manager*, the journal of APPA, the professional association of the facility managers of colleges and universities, asked readers which topics in the magazine they were most interested in. The results are listed below:

Topics of Greatest Interest	*Topics of Least Interest*
• Best practices	• Privatization
• Improving communications with campus constituencies	• Marketing of facilities
• New technologies	• Facilities financing
• Leadership	• Diversity
• Staffing guidelines	• Rightsizing
• Preventive maintenance	
• Custodial services	
• Benchmarking	
• Maintenance management	
• Training	

Source: *Readership Survey Results, Facilities Manager* (Alexandria, Va.: APPA, 1997), p. 1.

I find this list interesting but not particularly surprising. Typical of facility managers, five of the ten hot topics are technical ones. I suspect that the five least interesting topics are those that facility managers have tired of; they certainly are still pertinent.

Compare this survey of interest in topics with the 1996 survey of company executives mentioned early. Of those executives, 60 percent were concerned about the business aspects of facility management. Executives are most concerned with receiving accurate and timely cost information from their facility staff. Nine of ten said that financial management and project management were the most important factors in evaluating their facility managers. Seven of ten executives looked to their facility managers for planning and communications skills. The top four skills that executives thought needed to be fostered in the future were an ability to demonstrate a positive financial impact, a proactive approach to jobs, more emphasis on long-range planning, and skills beyond vendor management and day-to-day operations.[5] The differences in perceptions and interests between facility managers and their bosses are troubling. It is also interesting to note that the bosses' interest in the business aspects of the facility department has changed radically in less than ten years; in 1988, they were more interested in day-to-day activities than the average facility manager.[6] My sense is that those business executives are reading the business climate better than facility managers, to the detriment of the latter.

Particularly with the rise of benchmarking, facility managers often want to know how they measure up. A 1994 IFMA survey of facility managers produced the following profile of the typical facility manager:

> Forty-four years old, 20 years full-time experience with about 10 of those directly involved in facility management. Past 10 years have been with service sector employer and has held current job for past four.
>
> Responsible for areas totalling 500,000 square feet, 75 percent of which is office space. Has one level of supervisors reporting directly with a total staff of 12 plus contracted labor. Current position has multiple management responsibilities with subordinates assigned specialty work. Experience prior to facility management included job in other corporate departments.
>
> Holds a bachelor's degree in business and total compensation last year was $58,000. Feels facility management work offers good compensation, job security and recognition for performance when compared to other departments, but advancement opportunities may be more restricted. Within five to 10 years hopes to be promoted to higher management position that includes functions in addition to facility management.[7]

It is interesting to compare IFMA profiles of facility managers from 1984 and 1994. During those ten years, the average amount of space was reduced by 80 percent while the average salary went up 48 percent.[8] Actually, both of those facts probably indicate a greater appreciation of facility management by companies. More facility managers responded to the survey in 1993 than were members of IFMA in 1984.

Facility managers' purchasing power continues to be substantial. In 1994, IFMA found that the combined purchasing power of its U.S. and Canadian members was $42 billion (in U.S. dollars).[9] In the same year, APPA found that the average reader of *Facilities Manager* had an average budget of $3.44 million and that 97 percent of those facility managers were involved in purchasing decisions.

In both surveys, services were the category of purchased products most influenced by facility managers.[10] Perhaps the most important fact from all of these survey data is that the FM department remains a multifunctional one that controls large resources, is more recognized now than ever before, and deserves a vital business leader. Much progress has been made, but much more is needed.

Major Themes of Facility Management

Certain FM themes run through this book:

- *The cost of ownership.* There are initial and ongoing costs to the ownership of facilities. Management must understand and provide for those costs, from planning through disposal.
- *Life-cycle costing.* As a general rule, all economic analyses and comparisons should be based on life-cycle costs. Bad decisions are often made when only capital or initial costs are considered.
- *Integration of services.* Good management means integrating different services (e.g., design and operations).
- *Design for operations and maintenance.* Operators and maintainers, even if they are contractors, must be actively involved in the design review process.
- *Delegated responsibility.* FM functions should be grouped into budget programs, with a manager responsible and accountable for each.
- *Cost-effectiveness.* The key is to identify and compare costs, and make those comparisons regularly over time.
- *Efficiency improvement.* Efficiency should be judged constantly through comparators, user feedback, and management by walking around.
- *Quality of life.* The facility manager must actively promote and protect the employee quality of life. A safe workplace is the minimum; a workplace where the facility promotes individual and group productivity should be the goal.
- *Integration of elements.* The facility manager is the company's expert on facilities (the place), those factors which determine the success of work (the process), and the employees (the people), and how the three come together.
- *Redundancy and flexibility.* Because the nature of this work is always partly reactive, the facility manager must build redundancy and flexibility into the facilities.
- *Facilities as assets.* The facilities should be viewed as a valued asset that contribute in numerous ways to the company mission.
- *FM as a business function.* The facilities deserve to be managed in a businesslike manner. Facilities must be developed in parallel with the company's business and planned to the same degree.
- *FM as a continuum.* FM is a continuum, from planning through disposal. It is not a series of discrete projects.
- *Service.* FM provides only one product: service. The nature of FM is likely to emphasize control and compliance, whereas it should be flexibility and

service. A quality program is based on how service is perceived by the customer. A successful quality program depends on long-term relationships and commitment at all levels.

The Facility Management Life Cycle

Exhibit 1-3 depicts the life cycle of any facility requirement. The only variables are scale and complexity. For smaller facility departments, the landlord meets all or most of its space, build-out, operations, maintenance, and repair needs through terms agreed on in the lease. In owned facilities (normally associated with larger facility departments), functions like design, construction, or alterations may be done by outsiders, but control is resident in the facility manager.

Eventually a facility is occupied, operated, maintained, and repaired. Sometimes it is altered to a use beyond its original. (Adaptive reuse was popular in the 1980s. Churches, abandoned schools, and former manufacturing facilities have become houses, offices, and apartments).

A facility is probably evaluated several times during its lifetime. Does it fit its original intent? Is it worth renovating? Is an upgrade economical? Such evaluations may lead to renewed life through alteration or to a decision to dispose of the facility through sale or demolition. Gerald Davis at the International Centre for Facilities has been a pioneer in developing a rating scheme for comparing the serviceability of buildings.

Types of Organizations

Every organization has its unique personality, and the facility department is a reflection of that personality. All facility managers share some common characteristics in management style; however, the emphasis varies with the type of organization.

There is an almost infinite number of cultures that we could examine. In the total universe of facility managers, there is a great deal of diversity (too much, in my opinion) of organization, policy, and procedures. In this chapter we discuss only major cultures in which most facility managers operate. The technical environment in which the facility manager and the department must operate, together with this corporate climate, dictates the envelope in which the facility manager functions.

FM in the Public Sector

No facility manager handles as diverse a facility, with as consistently inadequate resources, as a municipal, state, or federal manager.[11]

The public sector has a culture overwhelmingly shaped by bureaucracy. That

Exhibit 1-3. Facility management life cycle.

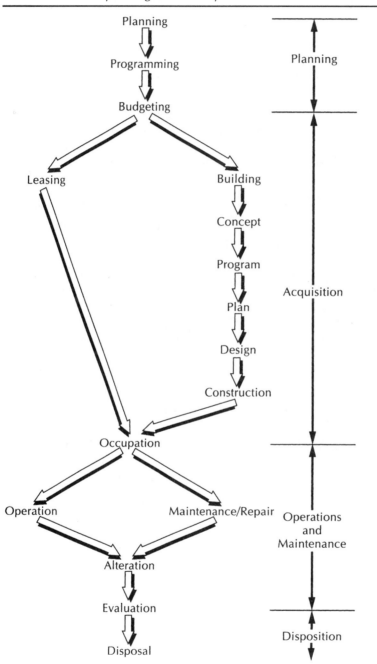

is not a derogation; it is a fact. Nearly every action is governed by a regulation. Also, except for capital construction, public-sector programs are subject to the vagaries of short-term budgets. Change is difficult, particularly if it depends on another department, because there is little incentive for cooperation.

Two particularly difficult areas are procurement and personnel. Public-sector procurement policies are thick with detail. Thus, the facility manager often is at the mercy of a purchasing or contracting officer, whose priorities are not necessarily coincident. Other seemingly inevitable conflicts involve sole-sourcing vendors and products and contract negotiation. Though directed (sole-source) procurements are at the heart of standardization programs, they are generally opposed or made bureaucratically difficult by public-sector purchasing departments. Similarly, many public-sector procurements, particularly extensions of existing contracts, are made more difficult because the purchasing department views negotiation as procurement with very limited applicability and to be avoided. Both of these situations arise because most public-sector purchasing departments (1) are overregulated by their legislative body, (2) are overworked and truly underpaid, and (3) have a low-bid mentality. (As explained later in this book, competitive bidding has its place, but its effectiveness generally is overstated. Also, it almost inevitably ratchets down the quality of service provided with each rebid.) These inflexible procurement approaches greatly influence the climate in which the public sector facility manager must function.

There never seems to be enough money to accomplish the annual work plan in the public sector.[12] Almost all North American public-sector facility managers face an ever-increasing backlog of work. When this backlog is presented to the appropriate legislative body, the reaction has been to shoot the messenger by attacking the credibility of the facility manager. Capital projects, though, tend to have long planning cycles and to fare better in legislatures because they bring pork to the legislative districts. Thus, managing shortages of resources is a fact of life for the public-sector facility manager.

Maintaining a quality workforce is a particular problem in public life. Despite what people say, it is generally difficult to eliminate an unneeded position, especially if the position is filled, or to create a new position. Many facility managers saddled with this system have contracted out many functions just to achieve some management flexibility. Unfortunately, most public-sector facility managers' actions are bound by a rigid human resources system.

The public-sector facility manager must also be a particularly good reactor, since he may have been forced to backlog proactive programs to eliminate crises. And he must be cost conscious, since funds in the public sector tend to come in specified pipelines. It means knowing the system so that funds can be shifted from one account to another at the right time—legally. Also, it is a challenge to ensure that all funds are used on meaningful work items, even though some might not be top departmental priorities. Finally, the facility manager must have *do-able* work that can soak up funds from other departments' excess money in the last thirty days of a fiscal year.

Public-sector facility management is framed in regulation. No one will remember who upgraded the electrical system, but everyone will remember who misallocated funds, even if done unwittingly. A public-sector facility manager needs to be legally smart and conscious of the do's and don'ts.

Finally, the public-sector facility manager needs to maintain a special relationship with the mayor, county manager, or governor. The facility department's budget is often the second largest administrative cost in the agency (only personnel is larger), so the chief executive needs to know that the facility manager is doing the best he can with limited resources. For his part, the facility manager needs to know that he's on the administration's wavelength. If such a climate does not exist, it's time to do some active job searching.

Legislators have so overregulated the public sector that change is difficult. If this description seems bleak, it is not intended to be. A public-sector facility department can be stable, dedicated, with a great sense of mission. On the plus side, public-sector facility managers often have better organized departments, more effective standards, excellent written procedures, and a more philosophical approach to their jobs than do private-sector facility managers.

Educational Facilities

Whether public or private, educational institutions tend to follow the public-sector model. This is particularly true of resources. In fact, annual funding for college facilities in the United States has reached crisis proportions.[13]

The facility manager at a college or a university should not only be technically competent but might want to consider an advanced academic degree for credibility. This is because university staff expect decisions to be made in a collegial fashion. Even such decisions as a setback of thermostats for energy management can become the subject of extended discussion. That is particularly true of decisions regarding aesthetics, the workplace, and historic preservation. And because there is so much consensus decision making in educational institutions, it is important that the facility manager be somewhat politically savvy in order to sell a program.

The facility manager faces other problems too. There are no more diverse facilities than those found on a university campus. Many institutions cannot effectively maintain and operate their existing facilities even while building more.[14] Also, the management climate has all the problems of large bureaucracies, plus the oversight of a board of regents or trustees. There will be more help than desired from the academic department heads of architecture, engineering, and design. In short, this is no job for a novice. A large educational facility needs an experienced facility manager.

Private Sector

Although no two private companies are alike, and corporate cultures vary widely, it is still possible to draw some conclusions regarding facility management in the private sector. For example, private-sector organizations are much more flexible than those in the public sector and can be changed relatively easily. All administrative functions and personnel tend to be tied closely to the product or service they support. Because facilities costs tend to be the second highest administrative cost, there is often pressure on the facilities manager to reduce staff and costs.

Also, since most of the facility department's managers tend to be middle management, they are susceptible to downsizing. Thus, although the private sector offers greater flexibility, the manager is subject to more staffing instability.

Because companies are driven by the need to provide service or product at a profit, private-sector managers are expected to make those changes necessary to manage their department effectively and efficiently. Thus, procurement is less bureaucratic, with more emphasis on long-term relationships, negotiations, and rapid response, and leasing is done quickly. Private-sector facility departments place great emphasis on design, perhaps because their managers feel that they can increase productivity through better facility design. Perhaps economic justification for design changes has more influence in an environment controlled by profitability than by budget.

Costs are yet another difference. For example, the private-sector facility manager is less likely to expend funds on end-of-the-year, suboptimal projects. The emphasis is on reducing costs rather than staying within budget.

A private-sector facility manager must be a particularly good communicator. Often his very existence depends on an ability to sell the department to upper management; this is particularly true if he charges back his services.

Private-sector facility managers are ultimately judged on how service oriented and cost conscious they are. If they do not measure up, someone else will be found who will. They must be comfortable with quantitative measurements and evaluation, since they will be measured frequently as managers, and they must be capable of evaluating leases, capital project justifications, life-cycle analyses, and ratios.

Finally, they must have a business sense and an ability to speak in terms other managers in the company will understand. Perhaps experience is a little less important in the private sector; an experienced deputy can be hired, if necessary. While it is perhaps an overstatement to say that private-sector facility managers should run their departments like a company within a company, that certainly is not a bad approach.

International Organizations

Increasingly, many of us are being employed by companies that are truly international. That has accelerated in the 1990s and will continue to accelerate well into the next century. Because facilities are always, to some degree, a manifestation of the occupying company, managing facilities in an international or multicultural organization has unique characteristics.

For example, decision making is often done by consensus and therefore takes longer. Also, once made, decisions are subject to constant review. In many cultures, those who provide services are treated like servants; service-oriented facility managers may find that their managerial expertise is neither sought nor appreciated. That same cultural bias is reflected in the approach to user maintenance. Some cultures feel no obligation to keep their facilities clean or well maintained, or to participate in facility management by reporting deficiencies or problems.

Contrarily, other cultures, especially northern European, have higher expectations for their facilities. Many items that North Americans normally regulate by company policy, procedure, or standards are fixed by law. Four common areas of contention are access to light, subterranean officing, locked windows, and workstation dimensions.

In each of these situations, the facility manager must be sensitive to multicultural concerns. Laws must be followed. Also, all employees are subject to company policy. But with little effort and relatively few exceptions, everyone's needs can be met if the facility manager works at it.

Other Situations

A facility manager in a company that is highly decentralized will find himself acting almost as an entrepreneur. That approach is much different from the facility manager in a highly centralized corporation. Concern there is on control, documentation, standards, and published policy and procedures.

Company attitudes toward facilities standards fall into three groups: controlling companies have published standards; flexible companies neither have nor see a need for standards; and companies in the middle have standards that are unpublished. The management style of the facility manager enforcing those standards must be generally congruent with the attitude of the company, or he will find himself continually in conflict with both management and his customers. Standards can be changed over time or at moments of major physical change (a new building or major renovation).

Conclusion

I end this chapter with a word of caution. I am optimistic about facility management, facility managers, and the professional associations that support them. Having said that, I am concerned about the often noted attitude, "We facility managers aren't respected." We must realize that we are not core business and are under special scrutiny by management, and that makes our job more difficult. However, many facility managers view themselves as innovative, entrepreneurial, and good businesspeople. They articulate the successes of their department and are not only respected but highly sought after.

Finally, I worry that we sometimes get too complacent as a profession. In a summary of a building performance summit in Washington, D.C., attendees quoted huge savings for companies through innovative building construction, design, and operation. Unfortunately, that summary contained no reference to research to back up what has been achieved, referring only to what could be achieved.[15] This problem has been with us since I entered the profession. No widely accepted research exits that quantifies increases in productivity with better facility management, particularly in the office environment. We lag in basic research in our profession. Along with the failure to publicize and implement best practices, the failure to support, publish, and implement solid research remains the Achilles' heel of the FM profession.

Notes

1. Letters to the editor, *Facilities Design and Management* (March 1996): 11.
2. *Views from the Top . . . Executives Evaluate the Facility Management Function* (Houston: IFMA, 1997), pp. 1–4.
3. Peter R. Veale, *Managing Corporate Real Estate Assets* (Cambridge, Mass.: MIT Laboratory of Architecture and Planning, 1987), p. 1.
4. Personal communication with the Office of the Deputy Under Secretary of Defense for Industrial Affairs and Installations, May 15, 1998.
5. *Views from the Top.*
6. *Centercore Survey: A Summary* (Plainfield, N.J.: Centercore, 1988), pp. 1–4.
7. *Profiles '94* (Houston: IFMA, 1994), p. 8.
8. Ibid., p. 8; *IFMA Report 1* (Houston: IFMA, 1984), pp. 8, 10.
9. "Survey Results Profile Practitioners, Purchasing Power," *IFMA News* (July 1996): 7.
10. Ibid.; *Purchasing Power* (Alexandria, Va.: APPA, October 1994), p. 1.
11. Building Research Board, *Committing to the Cost of Ownership* (Washington, D.C.: National Academy Press, 1990), p. xi.
12. *The Decaying American Campus: A Ticking Time Bomb* (Alexandria, Va.: APPA, 1986).
13. Ibid., p. 2.
14. Building Research Board, *Committing,* p. 2.
15. "National Summit Research Indicates Companies Can Achieve Billions in Employee Productivity Improvements," press release, Washington, D.C.: Building Performance Consortium, 1997, pp. 1–4.

2

Organizing the Department

Pulse Points

- *Outsourcing is a staffing issue, not an organizational one.*
- *When contracting out, retain control of all functions.*
- *Someone should be directly responsible for every asset and function.*
- *The facility manager organizes his way out of 90 to 95 percent of FM problems. He centrally controls those functions with the greatest financial impact on the business.*
- *The facility manager is most effective when ranked two levels below the chief executive of an organization.*
- *The basis of facility management organization is separate functions for planning and design and operations and maintenance.*
- *Communications planning, design, and engineering are facilities functions.*
- *Engineering should be given as much design attention as architecture and interior design.*
- *The optimal organization is a mixture of staff, consultants, and contractors.*

It is not my intent to explore all the various theories of organization. I do believe, however, that there are better ways and poorer ways to organize.

Considerations for Organizing a Department

The facilities department must reflect the needs of the parent organization. Too often, facilities departments reflect an organization's short-term resources rather than its long-term needs. While I am well aware that most departments develop along with the parent company, and that the organization of the department is always resource constrained, nevertheless, good departmental organization aids accomplishing the facilities mission.

There are many considerations in organizing for the facilities mission, such as the size of the department, whether there are single or multiple locations, and whether the business wants standardized versus user-driven services. You must consider how best to provide services cost-effectively and efficiently before you can organize properly. Often how you have organized is not as important as having thought through the known organizational considerations and problems.

The size of a facility management department varies from one individual to hundreds of people. Size and its corollary, span of control, certainly are major determinants in how the department is organized. But all facility managers must perform the same basic functions for their companies. Also, both very large and very small organizations tend to have a lot in common in their approach to problem solving. For example, both tend to use consultants often. Small organizations use consultants owing to lack of staff; large organizations use them to assist in special projects and to limit the size of their staff.

The facility manager's place in the corporate structure is important. Given the fact that corporate titles vary, if the facility manager's title is Director, then he will not have vice-presidential responsibilities. In midsize to large organizations, the facility manager must be highly placed to be truly effective. I recommend placement at two organizational levels below the chief executive officer (CEO). That balances necessary access against organizational reality in all organizations.

There is a vast difference between managing a corporate headquarters in one location and facilities in 500 or more locations worldwide. Multiple locations, even if in the same city, lead to different organizations. For example, a company that operates internationally has a different organizational model from one that operates in one country.

An increasingly important factor in organization is the growing use of contractual services—contracting out.

Since the mid-1980s, it has been popular to downgrade organizational structure. First downsizing and then rightsizing hit most companies, particularly the administrative departments. Much of this staff reduction has been accomplished by increasingly contracting out functions. As long as you maintain control of essential functions, this need not be a major concern. What could be done with staff can also be done with contractors. There are appropriate organizational models for all sizes of organization. With the correct model, 90 to 95 percent of FM problems can be solved in a routine manner, allowing you to concentrate on less routine problems.

Several of these organizational factors are control issues. One excellent rule is to control centrally those aspects that have the greatest impact financially (e.g., real estate, major construction) and control the rest through development and oversight of policy.

Unfortunately, some organizations are able to staff only to the degree that they can expect to be reimbursed for their services by the operating agencies of the corporation. This practice is commonly called a *chargeback system*. It can be an organizational problem in that there is uncertainty of resources year-to-year, although pure chargeback situations seldom exist.

One of the most important decisions is whether facility services will be on a centralized or decentralized basis. Often this decision is closely equated to the geographic considerations. For example, an organization with branch offices spread across a state has to give each office some autonomy in facility matters or run the risk of paralysis through centralization, even though the latter generally is the most cost-effective way to organize. Another decision is whether facility services will be highly standardized, or if there will be effort to meet unique user needs. Generally standardization and cost-effectiveness go hand in hand.

The difference between a line (management) and a staff function is an important one in organizing. In larger organizations, FM functions that would ordinarily be considered staff functions in a small organization become line functions, with line managers assigned to manage them. This occurs, for instance, in companies that have international design and real estate functions.

Finally, there are substantial organizational differences when companies choose to own their facilities rather than lease them. The former have staff and managers; the latter emphasize contracts and lease administration. Most midsized to large organizations both own and lease property, and their staffing must reflect those requirements.

Little of this is new, yet I am often struck by the most elemental errors in organization, caused apparently by a failure to understand the nature of facility management and the nature of organizing. Some organizations have grown like Topsy, with no view of how the department should be organized best to perform the facilities mission. The most common failures are these:

1. Treating all work as projects and trying to apply the principles and organizational structure of project management.
2. Failing to provide an organizational element to integrate and coordinate all work.
3. Mixing the planning and design functions with the operations, maintenance, and repair functions.
4. Forming an outside group to accomplish a major capital project, with no integration of that group into the organization providing the ongoing services.
5. Allowing communications installation to be accomplished by a work unit outside the department. Communications functions, including planning and design, should be accomplished in the facilities department.
6. Failing to provide engineering services to match the planning and design services in the department.

Because organizations are so complex, these problems never appear singly. There is always a long list of considerations. All organizations are compromises, and the factors intertwine with politics and resource constraints to produce an almost infinite variety of facility organizations. However, there are several organizational models that can serve as guides during the inevitable reorganizations.

Organizational Models

There could be many models—one to fit every situation—but my experience shows that about five models are sufficient. These models can be called, in order of increased staffing:

1. Office manager model
2. One-location, one-site model
3. One-location, multiple-sites model
4. Multiple-locations, strong-regional, or divisional-headquarters model
5. Fully international model

In all models, I examine the facility department structure at the corporate headquarters. Also, I present the facility department as an institutionally funded, primarily centralized business function. In most models, the organization at a subordinate office is one of the other models. It is relatively unimportant, from a theoretical standpoint, whether one of the boxes on an organizational chart represents staff, consultant, or contractor.

In the models shown in Exhibits 2-1 to 2-5, the level immediately above the facility manager is included in order to illustrate to whom the facility manager typically reports. Note that there are sometimes different titles for the facility manager. The models also show the positions ordinarily at the same level of responsibility as the facility manager and any position with which he closely coordinates. In addition, I list the facility department functions typically performed by each organizational unit.

Office Manager Model

The office manager model (see Exhibit 2-1) is applicable to companies that reside primarily in one leased building. It is heavily dependent on consultants and contractors, primarily because the company does not want to devote human resources for facility management; it prefers to buy the service. Only the following functions are actually performed by company staff: (1) management of the organization; (2) lease administration; (3) budgeting, accounting, and economic justification; and (4) procurement.

Control of facility management is executed primarily through administration of leases (building, vehicles, and office equipment), service contracts, and consulting contracts. Management ultimately rests with the office manager (and perhaps one assistant and a secretary). The model displays the day-to-day mechanics of each function.

Exhibit 2-1 shows a typical model. Some alternative placement of functions might be:

Exhibit 2-1. Office manager model.

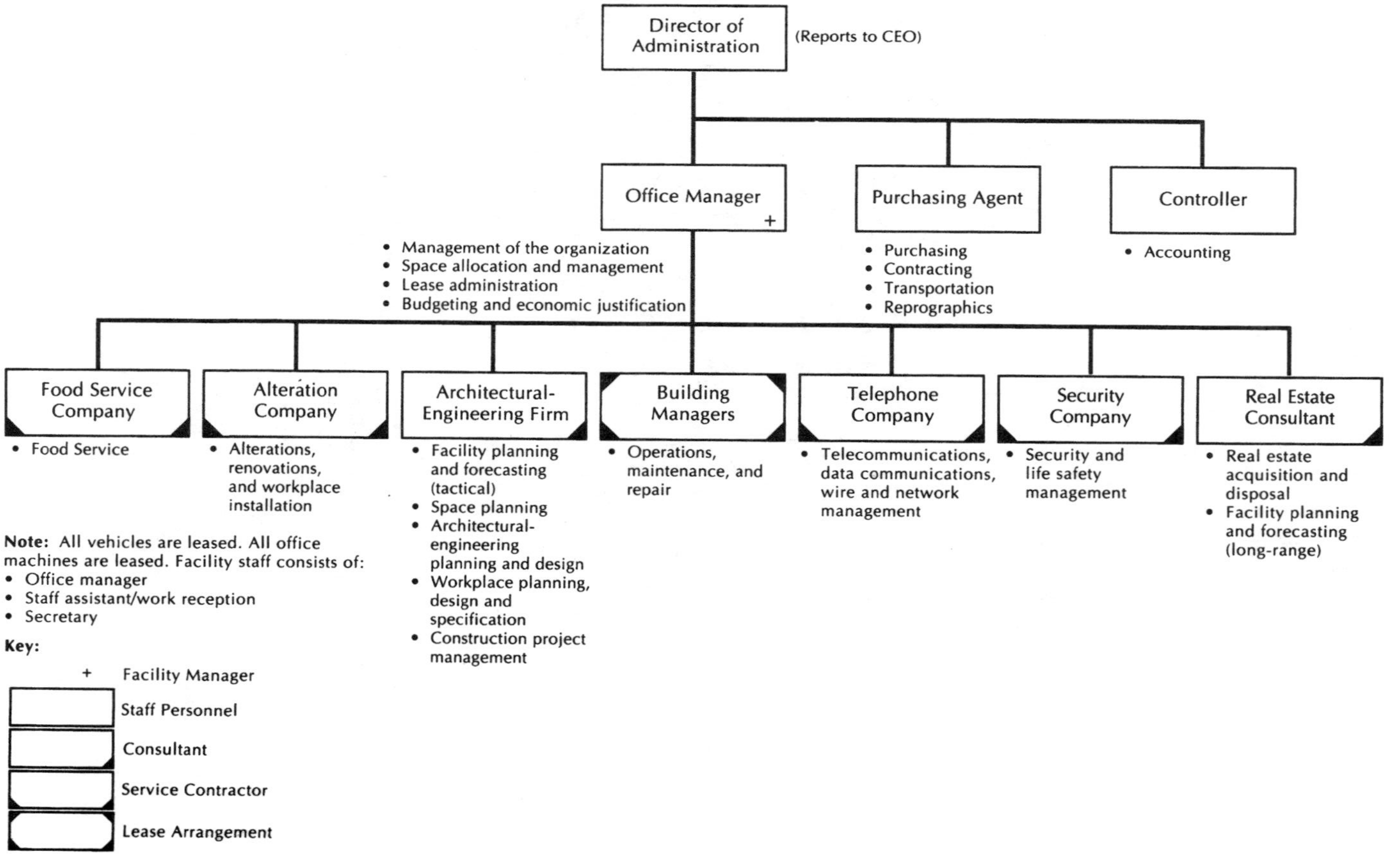

Director of Administration

(Reports to CEO)

Office Manager +
- Management of the organization
- Space allocation and management
- Lease administration
- Budgeting and economic justification

Purchasing Agent
- Purchasing
- Contracting
- Transportation
- Reprographics

Controller
- Accounting

Food Service Company
- Food Service

Alteration Company
- Alterations, renovations, and workplace installation

Architectural-Engineering Firm
- Facility planning and forecasting (tactical)
- Space planning
- Architectural-engineering planning and design
- Workplace planning, design and specification
- Construction project management

Building Managers
- Operations, maintenance, and repair

Telephone Company
- Telecommunications, data communications, wire and network management

Security Company
- Security and life safety management

Real Estate Consultant
- Real estate acquisition and disposal
- Facility planning and forecasting (long-range)

Note: All vehicles are leased. All office machines are leased. Facility staff consists of:
- Office manager
- Staff assistant/work reception
- Secretary

Key:

+ Facility Manager

Staff Personnel

Consultant

Service Contractor

Lease Arrangement

Function	From	To
Lease administration	Office manager	Purchasing agent
Space allocation and management	Office manager	Architectural/ engineering firm
Economic justification	Office manager	Controller
Transportation or repro-graphics	Purchasing agent	Appropriate service companies
Food service	Food service company	Building manager
Security and life-safety management	Security company	Building manager
Real estate acquisition and disposal	Real estate consultant	Office manager
Facility planning and forecasting (long range)	Real estate consultant	Office manager
Alterations, renovations, and workplace instal-lation	Alterations company	Building manager

Of course, other contractors or consultants could be used—estimators, value engineers, brokers—but most essential services can be provided by those shown, or else they are highly specialized and infrequently used.

The extent to which a certain contractor or consultant is used largely depends on two factors: (1) the frequency of the function and (2) the magnitude of the function. A permanent arrangement for either staff or contract should be established for functions that occur frequently or in high volume.

One-Location, One-Site Model

In many ways the one-location, one-site model, shown in Exhibit 2-2, is the simplest setup for a full-service facility department. It occurs in companies that are large enough to have a facility division or department, but are located at one location and one major site in a major building or buildings that are owned. It illustrates several of the following principles:

1. Presence of an organizational unit to coordinate and integrate work
2. Management for both ongoing work and project work
3. Integration of communications
4. Adequate engineering
5. Balance between planning and design and operations and maintenance

This model is heavily weighted toward the use of in-house human resources, both as a contrast to the office manager model and because research has shown that such is likely to be the case.[1] It displays more organizational units than most companies will fund, but alternative functional placements or contractual ar-

Exhibit 2-2. One-location, one-site model.

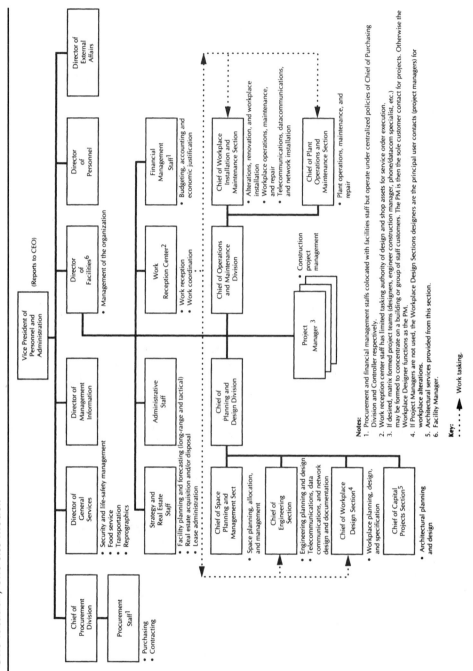

Vice President of Personnel and Administration

(Reports to CEO)

Chief of Procurement Division
- **Procurement Staff[1]**
  - Purchasing
  - Contracting

Director of General Services
- Security and life-safety management
- Food service
- Transportation
- Reprographics

Director of Management Information

Director of Facilities[6]
- Management of the organization

Director of Personnel

Director of External Affairs

Administrative Staff

Strategy and Real Estate Staff
- Facility planning and forecasting (long-range and tactical)
- Real estate acquisition and/or disposal
- Lease administration

Chief of Planning and Design Division

Work Reception Center[2]
- Work reception
- Work coordination

Financial Management Staff[1]
- Budgeting, accounting and economic justification

Chief of Space Planning and Management Sect
- Space planning, allocation, and management

Chief of Engineering Section
- Engineering planning and design
- Telecommunications, data communications, and network design and documentation

Chief of Workplace Design Section[4]
- Workplace planning, design, and specification

Chief of Capital Projects Section[5]
- Architectural planning and design

Chief of Operations and Maintenance Division

Project Manager[3]
- Construction project management

Chief of Workplace Installation and Maintenance Section
- Alterations, renovation, and workplace installation
- Workplace operations, maintenance, and repair
- Telecommunications, datacommunications, and network installation

Chief of Plant Operations and Maintenance Section
- Plant operations, maintenance, and repair

Notes:

1. Procurement and financial management staffs colocated with facilities staff but operate under centralized policies of Chief of Purchasing Division and Controller respectively.
2. Work reception center staff has limited tasking authority of design and shop assets for service order execution.
3. If desired, matrix formed project teams (designers, engineer construction manager, phone/datacom specialist, etc.) may be formed to concentrate on a building or group of staff customers. The PM is then the sole customer contact for projects. Otherwise the Workplace Designer functions as the PM.
4. If Project Managers are not used, the Workplace Design Sections designers are the principal user contacts (project managers) for workplace alterations.
5. Architectural services provided from this section.
6. Facility Manager.

Key:

····▶ Work tasking.

rangements are noted. Consultants, in particular, could be used to assist in staffing.

The figure is a typical model. Some logical alternatives for placement of functions might be:

Function	From	To
Life-safety management	Director of general services	Supervisor engineering
Those listed under	Director of general services	Units under supervisor, operations, and maintenance division
Tactical planning and forecasting	Strategy and real estate staff	Supervisor, space planning and management
Architectural planning and design	Manager, capital projects section	Supervisor, workplace design
Construction project management	Project manager	Supervisor, workplace installation

In this model, contractors or consultants are most frequently used to provide a unique skill or to handle peak loads.

One-Location, Multiple-Sites Model

The next model, shown in Exhibit 2-3, is typically a headquarters with major operational elements (labs, branches, plants) located in the same county or metropolitan area. Homogeneous facilities at any one location fit the model in Exhibit 2-2 better than this model.

One of the concepts developed here for the first time is the gathering, consolidation, and evaluation (and possible decentralized execution) of requirements. This can be done in one of two ways:

1. Decentralize certain operational elements to operate within set limitations. Larger, prescreened requirements are passed upward.
2. Have an administrator at each location aggregate and screen requirements.

Complete decentralization under this model is not economically justifiable. If complete decentralization appears to be a solution (one of the satellite sites is as complex as the headquarters, for example), the model in Exhibit 2-4 is probably more appropriate.

This model is between the first two in the number of consultants and contractors used, acknowledging that additional resources are needed to compensate for time-distance factors. The more decentralized the organization is, the more probable it is that consultants and contractors will be used. Each of the remote sites is likely to be organized for facility management as shown in Exhibits 2-1 or 2-2, with ties back to the headquarters that are financial and reporting in nature,

Exhibit 2-3. One-location, multiple-sites model.

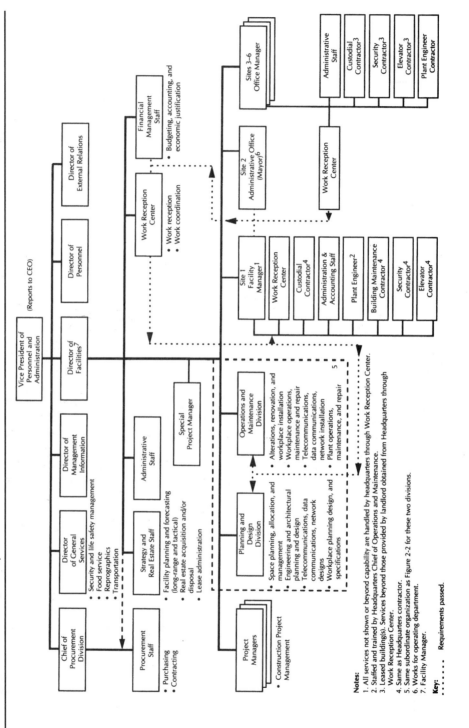

Notes:
1. All services not shown or beyond capability are handled by headquarters through Work Reception Center.
2. Staffed and trained by Headquarters Chief of Operations and Maintenance.
3. Leased building(s). Services beyond those provided by landlord obtained from Headquarters through Work Reception Center.
4. Same as Headquarters contractor.
5. Same subordinate organization as Figure 2-2 for these two divisions.
6. Works for operating department.
7. Facility Manager.

Key: .... Requirements passed.

or for passing requirements. In all cases, the headquarters organization provides policy, oversight, budget control, and technical assistance. Many combinations of staff, consultants, leases, and contractors can be used to provide services to remote sites, but generally only facility operations and maintenance taskings are passed down for execution. In this model, design assets must be strengthened, as must the lease management, financial management, project management, and work reception and coordination functions.

Multiple-Locations, Strong-Regional, or Divisional-Headquarters Model

With the fourth model, shown in Exhibit 2-4, I start to discuss large organizations that operate in widely separated geographic regions, probably nationally. Subordinate regional or divisional headquarters have facility departments similar to those shown in Exhibits 2-2 or 2-3. Operational issues are deemphasized except within the headquarters itself. The principal functions are allocating resources, tactical and strategic planning, real estate acquisition and disposal, policy and standards setting, technical assistance, macrolevel space planning and management, and oversight. In this and the international model, headquarters performs primarily policy and oversight functions.

In this model, the facility department is almost entirely staff. The facility manager has no direct responsibility for any of the general administrative services. It is not necessary that all the professional staff shown (counsel, for example) be directly assigned to the facility manager, but neither would it be unusual. The principal staff are directors with directive authority within their areas of functional expertise. The regions or groups have their direct line to the "boss" through their liaison officer at the headquarters.

Consultants and contractors, especially those who operate nationwide, are used extensively, particularly for real estate, planning, design, and construction. Legal issues are a daily matter, and a law firm versed in facility matters is on retainer, or staff lawyers work directly within the vice presidency (similar to procurement specialists in the earlier models). Both very small (office manager model) and very large (this model) organizations rely extensively on consultants.

Fully International Model

The fifth model, shown in Exhibit 2-5, is another way to reorganize a very large facility department and could be used (totally or in part) interchangeably with the model in Exhibit 2-4. In both models, the headquarters functions as overseer, policymaker, problem solver, and resource allocator. The work of the organization is done by the regional or national offices or directorates.

These regional or national units can function primarily under their individual business unit with only technical FM direction from headquarters. I prefer this approach, but the field facility units could take their principal direction from headquarters, commonly called a *pipeline approach*. The company depicted is large enough that it has invested in a training academy to assist in standardizing policy and procedures. This is both extremely effective and extremely costly.

Exhibit 2-4. Multiple-locations, strong regional or divisional headquarters model.

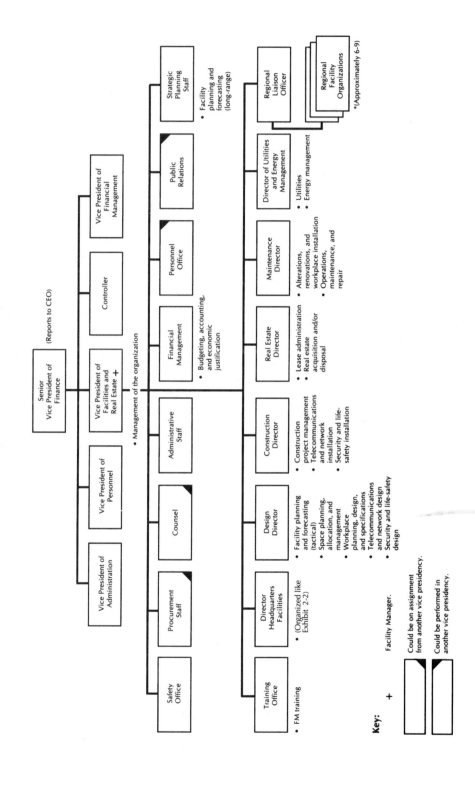

Senior Vice President of Finance (Reports to CEO)

Vice President of Administration | Vice President of Personnel | Vice President of Facilities and Real Estate + | Controller | Vice President of Financial Management

- Management of the organization

Procurement Staff | Counsel | Administrative Staff | Financial Management | Personnel Office | Public Relations | Strategic Planning Staff

Safety Office

- Budgeting, accounting, and economic justification

- Facility planning and forecasting (long-range)

Director Headquarters Facilities | Design Director | Construction Director | Real Estate Director | Maintenance Director | Director of Utilities and Energy Management | Regional Liaison Officer

Training Office

- FM training

- (Organized like Exhibit 2-2)

Design Director:
- Facility planning and forecasting (tactical)
- Space planning, allocation, and management
- Workplace planning, design, and specifications
- Telecommunications and network design
- Security and life-safety design

Construction Director:
- Construction project management
- Telecommunications and network installation
- Security and life-safety installation

Real Estate Director:
- Lease administration
- Real estate acquisition and/or disposal

Maintenance Director:
- Alterations, renovations, and workplace installation
- Operations, maintenance, and repair

Director of Utilities and Energy Management:
- Utilities
- Energy management

Regional Facility Organizations
*(Approximately 6–9)

Key:

+ Facility Manager.

◥ Could be on assignment from another vice presidency.

◤ Could be performed in another vice presidency.

Exhibit 2-5. Fully international model.

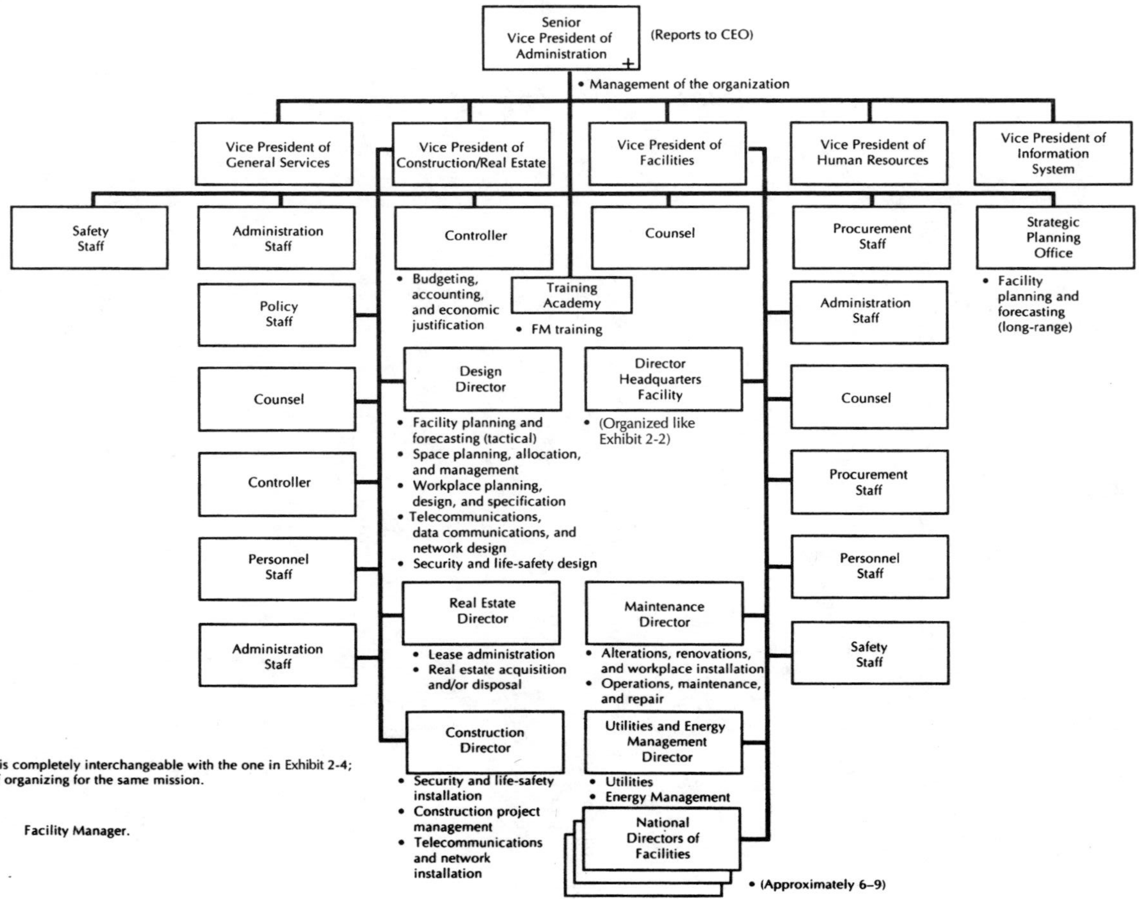

Senior Vice President of Administration (Reports to CEO)
+
• Management of the organization

Vice President of General Services
Vice President of Construction/Real Estate
Vice President of Facilities
Vice President of Human Resources
Vice President of Information System

Safety Staff
Administration Staff
Controller
Counsel
Procurement Staff
Strategic Planning Office
• Facility planning and forecasting (long-range)

Policy Staff
Training Academy
• FM training

Counsel

Design Director
• Facility planning and forecasting (tactical)
• Space planning, allocation, and management
• Workplace planning, design, and specification
• Telecommunications, data communications, and network design
• Security and life-safety design

Director Headquarters Facility
(Organized like Exhibit 2-2)

Administration Staff

Controller

Real Estate Director
• Lease administration
• Real estate acquisition and/or disposal

Maintenance Director
• Alterations, renovations, and workplace installation
• Operations, maintenance, and repair

Counsel

Personnel Staff

Budgeting, accounting, and economic justification

Personnel Staff

Administration Staff

Construction Director
• Security and life-safety installation
• Construction project management
• Telecommunications and network installation

Utilities and Energy Management Director
• Utilities
• Energy Management

Procurement Staff

Safety Staff

National Directors of Facilities

• (Approximately 6–9)

Note:
This model is completely interchangeable with the one in Exhibit 2-4; two ways of organizing for the same mission.

Key:
+   Facility Manager.

In both of the very large organizational models (Exhibits 2-4 and 2-5), the elements shown at the headquarters all serve primarily staff functions but at two levels. The true staff services the headquarters; the directorates are oriented on the field organization. There is no magic formula, for example, to determine whether legal advice should be provided outside the department, from within the directorates, in the field units, or all of these. Counsel should be placed where needed. Whether counsel needs strong technical control (pipeline) or close management ties within the facilities department depends on the philosophy of the company regarding its legal resources. As a rule, the first level of authority to buy or lease real estate needs direct access to counsel.

Model Wrap-Up

There is a tendency to look at these models and conclude that with so many blocks on a page, there is a need for a huge bureaucracy. Nothing could be less true. Nevertheless, the facility manager must be provided with a staff and line organization that allows him to manage efficiently and effectively. Contractors and consultants can be used effectively. Corporate staff (human resources, procurement, controller, public relations) can often be shared effectively; co-locating corporate staff with the facility staff often works very well. However, at some point, the facility staff must grow as the company grows and will eventually reflect other business units with full line and staff organizations. Organization remains the stepchild of good facility management. A facility manager should solve 95 percent of his problems by organizing properly.

Staffing

No other aspect of facility management has been as neglected as organization, probably because until recently there has been little to think, speak, or write about. Nevertheless, there are unique staffing problems in facility departments, and it is helpful to understand their nature. Particularly in large corporations, the facility department's human resources needs are often both minor and unique compared to those of the main business elements. That means the facility manager's skilled human resources needs—quantitatively and qualitatively—are often not properly understood. This problem can be solved only by having direct access to personnel specialists knowledgeable about administrative staffing. Only in very large organizations will the facility manager actually have an assigned personnel department. In medium-sized organizations, a human resources team, operating under the central human resources policies, is successfully co-located with the facility staff.

Most experienced facility managers are already employed, and only a few universities currently offer degrees in entry-level facility management. The pool of qualified facility managers is not large. There are, however, some solutions to placement:

1. *Grow your own.* Large organizations, in particular, can develop a succession plan for functional managers to move through the organization.
2. *Hire retiring or resigning military personnel with facility management experience.* The Reserve Officers Association and Society of American Military Engineers are good sources of leads. The Non-Commissioned Officers Association is a superior source of support personnel.
3. *Use graduates of the universities.* Gain familiarity with those programs by employing their students as interns. Be particularly alert for the development of other programs; many universities worldwide are considering FM degree programs or provide associate degrees or areas of concentration in facility management.
4. *Look to the professional associations.* Both the International Facility Management Association (IFMA) and the Association of Higher Education Facilities Officers assist in personnel placement.
5. *Hire from other companies.* Many competent managers and technical specialists are dead-ended in their current organizations; they would be grateful for the opportunity for advancement.
6. FM Link (www.FMLink.com), the Friday Group, and the FM Knowledge Center (www.FMKC.com) all can assist in recruiting experienced facility managers.

There are some staffing problems resulting from the imprecision of job titles. Facility managers themselves are called many things. What some people call an interior designer is a space planner in other agencies. When working with an agency unfamiliar with facility management, these inconsistencies make it very difficult to hire and properly grade people. A placement specialist once told me that I had to hire a research assistant when what I needed was a space planner because "that's the closest job title that we have in our inventory of titles." The professional associations should take the lead here to standardize job titles.

As is the case in many other administrative service areas, some competent people will find themselves dead-ended in facility management organizations long before their work life is over. The relatively small number of positions make this inevitable. For example, consider a director of construction, at age 45, working for a vice president three years her junior. These situations happen in organizations where FM skills are not the predominant skills of the business units of the company. Therefore, hiring from other companies or retired or resigned physical plant administrators and military personnel is a practical solution to the proper distribution of skilled personnel at one location. The professional associations, through their local chapters, can serve as catalysts in this process.

One problem is the lack of skilled technicians (engineers, maintenance mechanics, supervisors) that prevails for many reasons (poor vocational education programs, lack of pay and prestige, the demise of apprenticeships). The situation is, in fact, becoming critical. Elevator mechanics are becoming extinct. Meanwhile the systems (elevator, air quality, life safety, security) are becoming more and more complex. By extensive use of manufacturers' training (to include paying for contractor or consultant training), facility managers are holding their own, but the base of trainable personnel has diminished noticeably.

One of the greatest staffing issues is the use of consultants and contractors (sometimes humorously called the in-house versus out-house debate). The great impetus to farm out facilities services came from a desire to eliminate staff positions. In the federal government it was a major Office of Management and Budget initiative; in the private sector it occurred as organizations tried to eliminate middle management.

I believe in making maximum use of consultants and contractors. The ideal organization is flexible, with a mix of in-house staff, consultants, and contractors. Consultants meet short-term, highly specialized needs; contractors provide the same flexibility for a longer term. Ideally, the solution is to use skill-oriented, body-shop contracts where the contractor provides personnel and first-line supervision that the facility manager organizes, directs, and evaluates. In all, the facility manager must retain the ability to set policy, maintain oversight, and develop requirements. Consultants can even suggest policy and help gather requirements, but in-house staff must approve both. A facility manager who abrogates those functions has lost control.

Also, before the facility manager enters into extensive consultant or contractual arrangements, he must have the right to select the appropriate contractor or properly skilled consultant. If all he has to tie his contractor or consultant to him is a least-cost contract, he is in trouble!

I am very suspicious of contracting out solely to reduce costs. Too often studies that claim cost savings do not analyze all costs (looking at only one budget, for example) or fail to compare them over time. Service contract rates normally increase every time the contract is rebid. So what appears to be a saving by contracting out may, by the second or third rebid, become more costly than in-house staffing. My general analysis is that contracting out to save money is fiction. If there is savings, it tends to be in the area of benefit costs, in that most contractors have lower benefits costs than an in-house workforce. The real benefits come from having flexibility and, to a lesser degree, being able to hire expertise.

There has not been a broad-based, comprehensive study of FM department organizational structure since 1986, although APPA regularly recommends ideal organizational structures for colleges and universities. Partly this neglect seems to stem from the fact that facility managers and their companies have confused staffing and organization. As outsourcing became more and more prevalent, facility managers seemed to feel that it lessened the need for proper organization. Outsourcing essentially is a staffing issue. Whether the positions are filled by in-house staff, consultants, or contract staff, it is important to get the organization correct to meet customer needs. We have spent too little time on this issue.

Typical staffing (of all types) across a broad range of FM organizations is as follows:[2]

Area in Gross Square Feet (gsf)	Staff Served/FM Employee (all sources)
Less than 100,000	27
100,000–200,000	38
200,000–500,000	47
500,000–1,000,000	59
Greater than 1,000,000	87

Although some variance from these guidelines is understandable, it is difficult to rationalize how there could be a variance of over 220 percent between the smallest FM organization's staffing and the largest if the services provided are similar. Geographic dispersal will drive up the staff needed, but not by 200 percent. We obviously need to do benchmarking in this area and develop best practices. My experience is that medium to large organizations operating at one location need 1 facilities staff per 50 to 60 staff served.

More and more, effective FM organizations combine staff, contractors, and consultants. It is the facility manager's job to minimize the divisions among these elements and to meld them into a facilities team. That will not automatically happen. Some staff will be jealous of others' status. Procurement will say it cannot be done; human resources will say it should not be done. Before deciding to contract out, the facility manager must have management's support for your plan. A facilities department must be an integrated team; an "us versus them" attitude is fatal. For a final look at staffing, refer to Exhibit 2-6, which shows a typical facility management department.

Outsourcing

As someone who has personally managed an organization where all supervisors and skilled workers were contractors, I think that most facility managers are needlessly concerned about the effects of outsourcing. I doubt that we ever saved much money by contracting out, but we had an organization that was extremely flexible, enough to meet the changing requirements placed on us. Also, if one of the supervisors or technicians was not performing well or if his behavior was unacceptable, I simply asked his company to replace him.

I prefer to use small to medium-size contracting firms to which my department is an important customer. I also believe strongly in "body-shop" contracting, where the contractor provides the skills and supervision and we provide the management. In our contract documents and all discussions with the contractor's management, I am frank and honest and encourage the contractor to be the same with me. There is no doubt that I am demanding, but I also am careful to be fair.

We partnered before partnering was a common concept. One of the things that both I and the contractor try to ensure is that there are no surprises in our relationship. We try to warn the contractor of upcoming expansions or contractions of the workforce; the contractor never removes a key person without consul-

Exhibit 2-6. Typical facility management department.

Space managed	400,000 gsf (59% office)	
Workforce supported	695	
Internal staff	38	
Percentage change in size or employees in the last year	0%	
Reports to:		
Administration	34%	
Operations	23%	
Senior management	19%	
Finance	16%	
Human resources	8%	

Functional Management	*In-House*	*Contracted*
Maintenance		
Furniture	42%	49%
Custodial	20	67
Landscape	17	63
Administrative Services		
Mail	43	11
Security	28	43
Telecommunications	28	25
Reprographics	28	16
Space Planning and Design		
Inventory	83	7
Forecasting	76	6
Major redesign	40	51
Move management	34	58
Architecture and Engineering		
Design	10	73
Building systems	26	58
Code compliance	45	43
Real Estate		
Leasing	44	23
Acquisition/disposal	29	22
Subleasing	9	43
Facility Business Planning		
Operational planning	79	7
Strategic planning	69	7
Emergency planning	70	13
Financial Management		
Operational budgeting	91	3
Capital budgeting	82	3
Major financing	29	8

Health and Safety		
Energy management	55	24
Ergonomics	60	14
Recycling	37	46
Solid waste management	17	65
Churn rate 25%		
Chargebacks used	Yes	No
Facility overhead	57	43
Facility services	64	36

Source: *Facility Management Practices, 1996* (Houston: IFMA, 1996), pp. 7–30.

tation. One of the best methods to keep the contractor working well with us is to ensure that payment is made within days of submission of an invoice.

Every function requires a slightly different approach when outsourcing. I am opposed to using large contractors that bundle all services, from food service through security through custodial to reprographics. There are two reasons. First, these tend to be too large; your contract is just one more account. Second, as in so many other things, companies that do everything tend not to do anything well. It is my experience that a full-service facility department should have at least the following contracts if it makes a decision to outsource:

Administrative Services	*Building Services*
Food service	Architecture, engineering, and interior
Security	design
Data communications and telecommu-	Operations and maintenance
nications	Moving and asset management
Mail, messenger, and reprographics	Project management and estimating

It may be wise to divide the work further by contracting subfunctions. The general rule is that the more finite that you define a function as you contract it, the more expertise you will obtain through contracting. There is, however, a trade-off between the ability to contract and administrate those contracts versus the marginal advantages of further subdividing those functions.

One of the real experts in the field, Joe Incognito, lists the following questions that an organization should ask before it decides to outsource:

1. Has the organization successfully utilized the concept of outsourcing in the past?
2. Has the organization outsourced a business function in the past and realized less-than-expected results?
3. Does the culture of the organization allow for the outsourcing concept?
4. Does the need to rightsize the organization create a need to outsource?[3]

Remember that you hired the contractor or consultant for his expertise and his initiative; you must allow him to display it. Get comfortable with your outsourcer before you sign the contract with him, and then trust him to help you improve your operation. That is one of the reasons that you hired him.

I would be reluctant to hire any outsourcing firm that did not have a quality management program that was compatible with my own or could not be adapted to our situation. Second, outsourcing contracts are ideal for partnering arrangements. The facility manager should work with the purchasing department to build partnering into the contractual arrangement. The outsourcer needs to make the facility manager a hero; the facility manager wants to ensure that the outsourcer is successful. Any facility manager not skilled in contract administration needs to get training. Increasingly the job of the facility manager will be determined by the ability to contract for and manage services successfully rather than to supervise them directly.

Personality and Skills of Facility Personnel

Too much perhaps can be made of the type of individuals who succeed in facility management. You look for the same characteristics in facility management candidates as all managers look for: managerial capability for managers and technical competence for specialists. Nevertheless, my experience does emphasize the following:

1. Academic degrees are given less weight than practical experience because currently academic programs, except for the university degree programs, do not produce managers or technicians skilled in facility management. This will change as more degree-granted experienced facility managers become available.

Customers' Top Ten Complaints to Facility Managers

1. It's too cold!
2. It's too hot!
3. There are not enough conference rooms.
4. This office isn't clean.
5. There's never enough filing/storage space in my workstation.
6. I always have computer problems.
7. The office is too stuffy.
8. There's never enough parking.
9. There's no privacy in my workstation/office.
10. The smokers outside the building are offensive.

Source: *1997 International Facility Management Association Survey*, as quoted in *Facilities Design and Management*, October 1997.

---

2. A facility manager must be comfortable with a certain amount of reactive management.
3. Staff, consultants, and contractors must truly be committed to service.
4. Facility management is not brain surgery. Take a team player over a brilliant individualist if there is a choice.
5. Facility managers should be comfortable about being measured quantitatively and should make their staff equally comfortable.
6. Specialists who have not worked in a corporate environment should rarely be placed on staff. As an example, the motivating factors are different between a competitive design firm and an in-house design staff.

Thorny Issues in Organization

The issue of line versus staff functions is always contentious. In very small organizations there is little need for staff support; if needed, it comes from consultants. In very large organizations almost all activities at headquarters are staff in nature; line functions are in the regions. In midsize organizations, staff versus line becomes less clear. Planning and design are ordinarily staff functions, but in most midsize organizations, that kind of activity is so prevalent that often a line planning and design organization is formed.

The proper placement of the *real estate function* is often controversial. In small or midsize departments, the real estate and long-range planning functions are combined in one staff element, perhaps a consultant, because at that level the functions are intertwined. Real estate becomes a line function when a company occupies multiple, leased locations and is both a lessor and lessee.

Except in the smallest organizations where the facility manager does it, *strategic planning* is a function deserving special organizational consideration. In midsize organizations, it can be placed in a staff office with real estate. In very large national and international organizations, strategic planning is a constant activity and should have its own staff office.

It is puzzling that *engineering* should be an organizational problem, but it is. Time after time, companies fail to staff properly to meet their engineering challenges. Engineering problems in general are costlier than others and have the greatest potential for employer liability, yet many employers do not hire enough engineering consultants or staff to match their interior planning and design assets. Consultants can do the job well, but oversight, policy setting, and requirements framing must be done by knowledgeable staff.

Almost as a corollary to the engineering issue is the failure to ensure that facilities are properly documented clearly and uniformly. In my own practice and consultant practices, I have observed a common failure to provide proper documentation in what are commonly called as-built drawings. I believe that this is a *design function* (though others certainly have a role). Companies would never try to build a new building without detailed and correct drawings, yet they rebuild their facilities every three to six years without correct drawings because they have never provided for staff to maintain them properly.

Where to place *project management* in an organization is a major issue. Project management, within an existing framework, implies a matrix organization and is very appealing in midsize and large organizations in two cases: (1) special projects, like building a major new plant, or (2) providing operational managers a single facility's department contact to coordinate design, construction, moving, and communications for all work in that department.

Theoretically, a project management unit should report directly to the facility manager. This works quite well for the first case, the special project. Such a case is displayed in the organizational model shown in Exhibit 2-3. For the day-to-day projects (typically 250 to 500 annually, ranging from $2,500 to $500,000 each, in an active midsize facility department), the facility manager normally does not desire to be directly involved in each project (as shown in Exhibit 2-3) and often forms a project management unit under the planning and design manager.

A long-standing issue is where to assign responsibility for installed equipment. Kitchen equipment is a classic example. Generally I favor the facilities department's being organized and staffed to maintain all installed equipment, but I realize that often exceptions make sense (a credit union ATM machine, for example).

Many of us who have been frustrated in our facility plans by "those guys in purchasing" have longed to have the *procurement function* placed under us. However, there are two good reasons not to do so: (1) Although the facilities department tends to be a large customer of the procurement division by transaction, that division has other customers (and other problems) better not put on the facility plate; and (2) the facilities department is better protected by having its procurements conducted and reviewed by another unit.

At the same time, the facility manager must make it clear, and the purchasing manager may well support it, that facility procurements are unique. In midsize organizations, it has often been successful to co-locate two or three procurement officers (one contracting officer and one to two procurement specialists) in the facilities department operating under centralized procurement policies and procedures. These officers must be treated as full team members. (I strongly feel that contracts for consultant firms should be handled through the procurement department; for individuals, through the human resources department.)

The issue of meeting *user requirements* has several organizational aspects:

• There are two ways for users to communicate their facility requirements to the appropriate individual in the facility department:
  1. Unlimited access
  2. Screening by the administrative officer of each business unit or by the "mayor" of a building

• Whether to provide services centrally according to a priority system or to ensure that everyone gets something every year by decentralizing funding expenditures early in the budget year.

I strongly support some screening of user requirements and a system—a priority-setting board for major requirements—that establishes the application of resources against requirements, with some user input.

An FM organization on a *chargeback system* will be organized and staffed somewhat differently from one that is institutionally funded. A chargeback department has more financial personnel devoted to calculating and collecting charges. The department will probably be more contractor or consultant oriented to allow for the peaks and valleys of a noninsured level of fund resources. There will be particular emphasis on a small cadre of project managers; unfortunately, there will also be an overemphasis on functions that can be defined as projects and therefore charged back.

If the facility manager does not have responsibility for *security,* several functions can be troublesome if they are not thought out carefully; this is particularly true as security and life-safety systems become increasingly automated. Typically, security operates and tests the systems and facilities operates and maintains them, but neither can function without the other. Typical issues that need to be considered are proper placement of the fire marshal, locksmithing and key control, testing of fire and life-safety systems, and maintenance and repair of security, fire, and life-safety systems, particularly emergency repair.

A completely integrated CAFM (computer-assisted facility management) system is now feasible. At least initially, CAFM should have a system manager (maybe a consultant) who should report to the facility manager. Other subsystems that may require separate system managers are computer-aided design and space planning, work management, and management information systems financial management.

Key Relationships for the Facility Manager

Functioning successfully in a bureaucracy requires establishing and maintaining relationships. Some of them are set in the organization chart; all of them depend as much on the personality of the individual as on their position. However, experience indicates that you should be especially aware of your relationships with the following individuals ex officio:

- Information resources manager, particularly if this person is responsible for communications, networking, or a major computing facility
- Procurement manager. Relationships need to be established at least one level deeper into this organization
- Counsel
- Human resources manager
- General services manager (or food services manager and security manager, if these functions are separately managed)

Position Descriptions

Because of numerous variables, no two facility management organizations are ever exactly alike. However, we have learned enough about facility departments that models have been developed and can be used for guiding specific company organizations. There are better ways to staff and organize; you should capitalize on them.

Unfortunately, too much organizational discussion since the 1980s has concentrated on eliminating positions. Even *rightsizing* is often a euphemism for reducing staff. This has clouded the matter of organizations. A "letter" in the *Harvard Business Review*, from its editor, said it well: "Two great challenges lie increasingly ahead for the modern organization to have the requisite types and numbers of knowledge workers . . . and to have an organization in which they will thrive and with which they will want to remain."[4]

Notes

1. "Demographics and Trends," *IFMA Report 2* (Houston: International Facility Management Association, 1986), p. 16.
2. "Facility Management Practices," *IFMA Report 16* (Houston: International Facility Management Association, 1996), p. 34.
3. *Conference Proceedings of the Fifteenth Annual Conference of the International Facility Management Association, 1994* (Houston: International Facility Management Association: 1994), pp. 3–6.
4. Theodore Levitt, "From the Editor: Management and Knowledge," *Harvard Business Review* (May–June 1989): 8.

3

Facility Management Leadership

Pulse Points

- *Be a business leader within your company.*
- *Concentrate on your responsibility to your employees; your responsibility to management is known.*
- *Don't become paralyzed by lack of analysis; make timely, commonsense decisions.*
- *Hire well, keep a loose rein, and manage by walking around.*
- *Set the tone for quality.*
- *Develop a network of expert advice; learn how to use it effectively.*
- *You alone must sell your department.*

Leadership in a facility department is vital. Departments that run well and are well respected are managed by strong leaders. Although there is little research on the subject of FM leadership, five things are evident:

1. The skills and traits that traditionally have been characteristic of successful facility managers (technical knowledge, for example) are no longer enough. Both new and changed skills are needed today.
2. Those inside the department often have a different view of the role of a successful facility manager than those outside the department.
3. The requirements of a FM department are substantial—in most cases, meeting expanding requirements and customer expectations with decreasing resources.
4. Business acumen and a sense of public relations are increasingly important for facility managers.
5. By their nature and education, most facility managers do not fit the profile for success.

When I speak to facility management groups, I tell them that facility management is a contact sport, and only dynamic leaders will ever be truly successful. In this chapter, I discuss the implications of each of the Pulse Points and profile a successful facility manager.

I am committed to the development of good leadership because no facilities team can function without it. Although this book is not exclusively on leadership, in this chapter I concentrate on those aspects of leadership considered unique to facility management.

Leadership Philosophy

There is obviously no one way to lead, but there are principles applicable at all levels. Whether the facility manager is titled Officer Manager or Vice President, the following apply:

1. The leader serves at least two constituencies: the external, which is business-oriented and normally political; and the internal, with a results-oriented, technical orientation. The leader must bridge these needs and demands.

2. The leader is an activist if facilities are truly to be managed correctly.
   - Resources will never (or will never be perceived to) be adequate to accomplish all administrative programs.
   - The facilities, unlike personnel, cannot speak. They need an advocate.
   - Facility management is so new that it is neither understood nor accepted. It needs to be explained and promoted.

3. The leader integrates diverse technical functions and demands teamwork.

4. The leader of the facilities team hires well, uses the loose-rein technique, evaluates through numbers, and manages by walking around.

5. The leader sets the tone for quality service.

6. The leader simultaneously prepares for the future and reacts to today's crisis. There will always be a significant reactive component to the leader's job; a FM leader must be reactive without being reactionary.

Too many facility managers simply try to be the best traditional facility manager. But it is no longer acceptable to be simply the best caretaker, maintainer, policy writer, operator, and maintainer. Companies now expect those attributes as the *minimum* skills to hold the job. Instead, the successful facility manager must be a business leader, a superb service provider as defined by customers, and an expert in public relations. For those with primarily technical skills and training, acquiring those new skills can be a real challenge. It is encouraging to note that by 1994, an increasing number of facility managers (41 percent) had degrees in business rather than the traditional ones of engineering, architecture, or interior design. Equally noteworthy was that only 3 percent of facility managers had degrees in facility management.[1]

Leaders and Leadership

Facility managers today must be business leaders. They must know the business they support, know their own business, run the department like a business, and be able to speak the language of business. How businesslike the facility manager is will largely determine how he is viewed outside the department, particularly by upper management.

But because he is managing a technical staff, a facility manager must also be comfortable with the technical aspects of his job. Every facility manager needs to be comfortable with quantitative analysis, specifically using numbers to measure operational effectiveness and efficiency. Unfortunately, too many facility managers, probably due to their education, tend to overemphasize their role as a technical manager. A quick review of Exhibit 1-1 indicates that no one person can expect to be expert in all FM functions. Therefore, it is important that the facility manager hone his ability to manage technical experts—often contractors or consultants— manage from a customer service perspective, and strengthen his job knowledge and skills as a business leader.

There is always a danger in stating that a certain type of leader or a particular management style will be successful in a given environment or position. However, there are certain leadership traits that are more likely to lead to success. For instance, such a person should possess good management skills, be knowledgeable about facilities, and be comfortable managing experts in design, engineering, technology, finance, law, food service, and so on.

This is basic. In addition, a good facilities manager must be capable of simultaneously handling problems that require immediate resolution and those that are long range. He deals with questions for which there are no absolute answers and often that are emotionally charged. Some responses will require rapid reaction as well as strategic insight. And there needs to be the ability to allocate shortages as well as resources.

The facilities manager must be comfortable saying no (and diplomatically), be absolutely committed to providing service, be capable of allowing subordinates their independence within common objectives, and be readily available and recognizable. Be aware, however, that facility managers have a reputation as naysayers, not a characteristic valued in business leaders.

Leading in facility management sometimes seems impossible because these organizations are so diverse and the demands so great. The diversity of functions, the level of activity, the active interest of employees in their work environment (the social status inherent in the size and shape of offices, for example), and the normal lack of adequate resources make the facility manager highly visible. Systems and standards handle 90 to 95 percent of the problems, but the facility manager must be personally available and visible to do the following:

- Tend to the other 5 to 10 percent of the problems.
- Handle exceptions.
- Promote department as a concerned, cost-conscious service provider.
- Reinforce and motivate subordinates.

Because facility management is so diverse, the leader will never be knowledgeable in everything. That means he must have a system to produce expert advice at an appropriate time and the wisdom and judgment to sort through often conflicting opinions to decide on a course of action. Developing a network of experts and knowing how to use experts effectively are skills that must be developed. Unfortunately, these skills sometimes are short-circuited by the need to heed the lowest bidder. (Remember the fallibility of numbers. George Hotsopolous, *Inc.* magazine's 1989 Entrepreneur of the Year, perhaps put it best: "People can always cheat on numbers, intuition is better."[2] My experience is that people not only can cheat on numbers but do so because competition overwhelms their judgment. Leaders who do not verify the validity of numbers with personal experience often make bad decisions.)

There is a place for bureaucracy in any large organization. If structured correctly, bureaucracy allows the day-to-day work of the department to proceed without crisis. However, bureaucracy is also the principal maintainer of the status quo and an enemy of creative change. The leader must be willing to oppose the bureaucracy, promote change, or to seek exceptions.

Finally, management by walking around is an excellent leadership technique. It allows for frank, nonstructured discussion and observation. If nothing else, it verifies or denies the statistics in reports. For those who feel this is too unstructured, consider the fact that a study of managers shows that, according to Henry Mintzberg, "managers' activities are characterized by brevity, variety, and discontinuity. . . . They get their information almost randomly, favoring inefficient face-to-face meetings over a systematic paper flow."[3] It is doubtful that a management style stressing written communication, voluminous analysis, total reliance on quantitative factors, and a reclusive personal style will be successful in facility management.

I have observed many good facility managers. They have the following characteristics:

1. Business-oriented
2. Technically competent
3. Capable of good oral and written communication
4. Comfortable with reaction
5. Customer service oriented
6. Cost conscious
7. Outgoing, even politically savvy
8. Decisive
9. Slightly legalistic
10. Capable of concurrent problem solving
11. Comfortable with and capable of quantitative measurement
12. Action-oriented
13. Able to deal well with people
14. Experienced

Unfortunately, the final characteristic—experience—can be gained only by successful performance at smaller facilities or in a technical specialty.

As a facility manager, you must be a persuasive advocate for your department. You must know how to exercise the formal and informal chain of authority and communications lines, both internal and external. Your relationships with other key leaders and staff are particularly critical to the department. You must be not only an effective informal communicator but a skilled writer.

Since so many decisions involve major expenditures of funds, increasingly facility managers are expected to be able to make sophisticated economic arguments. While the numbers crunching can be done by staff, you must understand the context and methodology of net present value analyses, cost-benefit ratios, payback periods, return on investment, and so on. I call this "speaking the language of business."

Let's explore two leadership scenarios of facility management: forming the facilities team and taking charge.

The Facilities Team

A major challenge for the facility manager is forming a facilities team and getting it to function as a team. Unfortunately, many factors in a company work counter to a team approach, which is why a facility manager must be a leader, not simply a manager.

Almost all facility departments are a composite of staff, consultants, and contractors. This allows for both maximization of skills and flexibility to meet peak workloads. Yet all members of the team, regardless of employment status, must feel that they are important. This is true even of one-time contractors. In some organizations, even though it makes sense, a staff member would never be placed in a position subordinate to a consultant. Bureaucratic personnel policies or traditions that preclude such assignments often run contrary to effective team building and require an aggressive leader to get them modified.

Unfortunately, some supposedly good management techniques often run contrary to good teamwork. Excessive dependence on quantitative measurement, particularly measuring one work unit against another, often leads to cutting corners, bickering, and even sabotage. Quantitative measurements always must be evaluated in context and used as indicators for discussion, not as the final word. Likewise, subordinate objectives must reinforce departmental goals. Subordinates who stress an understanding and support of the entire organization must be rewarded.

A classic example of a lack of teamwork is using a special team, responsible to top management, to construct a building. Typically the team has two goals: finish the construction on time (often at the expense of good workmanship) and within the capital budget (even though that often ensures that life-cycle costs for energy management and maintainability are suboptimized). The operational side of the facilities team is excluded from design and review, almost ensuring later problems. Facility department leaders must insist that this does not happen. Special-purpose groups have a place, but their ties to the facility team must be delineated and enforced.

Many typical procurement processes also run contrary to facility team building; probably none is as consistently destructive as low-bid contracting. In one case, a custodial contractor performing adequately lost a low-bid contract by $13,000 on a $3 million base contract. The result was almost predictable. The new contractor was terminated for nonperformance after a year, and the disruption cost hundreds of thousands of dollars. What suffered most was the facilities team concept. Because the custodial contractor covered nearly every square foot of the facility daily, it had been trained to be the eyes and ears of the facilities staff, reporting not only custodial problems but broken furniture, inoperable plumbing, malfunctioning elevators, and so on. The low-bid contractor never "joined" the team, and inadequately reported or failed to report these deficiencies. The leader needs to identify procurement rules that detract from his facilities team, and work to change or modify them.

There is no single professional experience more rewarding than forming the facilities team. But the effort cannot end there. The leader must plan and direct that team for the long run as staff members retire, contracts terminate, and new requirements surface. Managing a facility organization is managing a continuum of interrelated events. The team will change and must have both substitutes and built-in depth if it is to survive. No one, including the leader, should be irreplaceable. When all of these factors come together, a synergism is created, and the facility department functions in a manner that is truly greater than the sum of its parts.

Taking Charge

No other situation is as challenging as taking charge of a facility department, whether by founding one or by assuming the reins from someone else. Most of my comments apply to a midsize organization, but they are applicable to large or small organizations, and to ones staffed primarily with either in-house people or independent contractors. I examine here the first year of taking charge. (There's an excellent discussion of this also in *Leaders: The Strategies for Taking Charge* by Warren Bennis and Burt Nanus.[4] Particularly pertinent is the section entitled "The Context of Leadership.")

When taking charge of a facility department, the facility manager should gain perspective on what the parent organization desires. From his boss he should obtain a reasonably detailed statement of both objectives and probable resourcing through mid-term. At the same time he should have an indication of the true level of support to be expected. Concurrently he should assess the department by all available quantitative means and by talking, in depth, to the subordinate groups in open forums. Finally, he needs to gather customer comments for the past two years and, in addition, talk to user groups for their perceptions of the timeliness and quality of services. Senior administrative personnel or senior occupants form a good sample. User groups may need a form or format (questionnaire, telephone survey) to familiarize them with the services provided. The new leader actively seeks and heeds comments from the security chief, chief of communications, and procurement chief.

When the leader has a good overall picture of the present status of the department, he needs to establish a game plan to keep the organization operating while ensuring the needed improvements. Here are the steps:

1. Use the ink-blot approach to implement physical change. Start small; use your organization's work areas as testing laboratories. Try a division or department test on items like wall covering, furniture, and carpet before standardizing or distributing items companywide.

2. Unless satisfied, take action immediately (within the first year) in the following areas:
   - Concentrate on operational matters first. Establish policy, procedures, and standards. If possible, run a pilot on each. Insist that changes are implemented; set up feedback mechanisms.
   - Establish an efficient services reception and work coordination center.

3. Establish, as soon as possible, organizational and procedural distinctions between planning and design, and operations and maintenance.

4. Study the organizational chart. Sharpen the lines of responsibility and authority. Ensure that someone, by job title, is responsible for each function in the department.

5. Make personnel moves while on your honeymoon. Be fair, but get the right team. (We do not agree with the philosophy of making wide-sweeping personnel changes, because that is seldom needed. At the same time, rid yourself of dead weight or those who cannot adapt to your approach.)

6. Expend the effort to explain all changes that affect your staff, the staff at large, your boss, and other service providers. This is a tremendously time-consuming task. Use a multimedia approach. Share this task with trusted subordinates once they are on board.

7. Launch a public relations campaign. Put someone in charge of public relations—yourself if necessary.
   - Internal efforts: Give awards, publicize, sell to your boss.
   - External efforts: Promote your department by saying, "Here's what we can do for you"; use the current administrative network; use the company newspaper or newsletter—stress public interest stories featuring your department; develop a professional departmental briefing and seek out opportunities to use it.

8. If something does not work, do not be afraid to change it, but ensure that it was properly implemented and supported, and understand why it went wrong. There is a fine line between strength of conviction and stubbornness.

9. Establish a system of collecting user service evaluation. Make yourself visible and readily available to your customers to explain what you are trying to do, your constraints, and to answer questions.

10. Develop and execute at least one project where tangible cost savings can be realized. Publicize it!

11. Do several visible projects. A great deal of goodwill can be created with paint and carpet in office areas and cafeteria remodeling.

12. Whether you can afford it immediately or not, plan to get every part of the facility, including furniture, furnishings, and equipment, under life-cycle management. Implement what you can as fast as you can.

13. Initiate a preventive maintenance program in all interior areas that emphasize furnishings, furniture, finishes, and general appearance. Priority should go to public areas, executive areas, and general work space, and finally to garages, storage rooms, and closets.

14. Develop maintenance cycles consistent with need and political importance. This is very important because it determines one major portion of your budget.

15. Assess your design, planning, and consulting needs—both quantitatively and qualitatively.

16. Inject yourself into the company's business planning. For every company business plan, there should be a facility business plan. Personally direct (if only for the first year) the preparation of an annual work plan, an annual budget, and the capital budget. You have to go through the cycle once to understand every aspect of these documents in order to direct their execution.

17. Learn in detail the paperwork flow from your submission of a request for goods or services until the vendor is paid. This chain of events is fraught with pitfalls. You cannot control the process unless you understand it.

18. Personally review all existing service contracts and supply agreements.

19. Develop all comparators and management indicators that you want to use. Put systems in place to gather the data.

20. Write, or have written, an organization and functions manual for the department. If you can write functions clearly and sensibly, they probably are properly assigned.

21. Adopt programmatic budgeting. Working with your financial managers, reformat your budget so that it directly feeds your management information systems. For example, if one of the management indicators that you desire to track is maintenance and repair costs for a facility on a square footage basis, one line of your budget should be for maintenance and repair costs by facility without complicated factoring, additions, and corrections.

22. Develop a system, perhaps individual business luncheons, with your operational colleagues to discuss how you might support the business units of your company better. Do not forget important administrative players like the heads of human relations, information systems, and purchasing. You should be meeting with these individuals quarterly—or at least semiannually.

23. Start to develop an image for your department. Perhaps you want the department to be viewed as the environmental leader, or perhaps as the risk mitigator. Perhaps you want to emphasize its contributions to company productivity—and hence the bottom line. Maybe emphasizing your ergonomic efforts will get the attention of top management. *It is not enough to simply do a good job; that is*

expected. The challenge is to position the department so that it is viewed as an invaluable part of the business, not simply a cost center.

Of the twenty-three items above, some will be resisted internally, and many will have to be sold outside the department. That is why taking charge is such a leadership challenge. Founding a department or assuming leadership in a comatose one is a sixty-hour-a-week (maybe eighty at budget time) job for the first eighteen to twenty-four months. After that, it can be accomplished within normal hours—provided you have set up things correctly.

As the first year comes to an end, the new leader should be putting in place, or at least actively planning, the department audit. This major activity will set the tone and substance for the department for at least a decade. Although there is no standard format for this audit, a good department audit consists of the following:

1. An organizational audit of mission, functions, organization, relationships, staffing, and grading
2. A physical facilities audit, to obtain a level of documentation you need for planning and design decisions; and a condition assessment that will allow you to make knowledgeable decisions for maintenance, repair, and capital improvement
3. A comprehensive energy audit
4. A way-finding and location system that will permit proper signage despite churn rates up to 30 percent annually
5. An automated work management system that provides a crossover from work plan execution to the budget
6. A company space plan, for at least five years, including both lease requirements and a capital investment plan
7. Standards for all facilities and services
8. A furniture, furnishings, and art audit that ensures standards, control, inventory, and security can be maintained over time
9. A facility management information system that ties all the above together in a common database accessible to all managers

This audit should be completed within eighteen to twenty-four months except for the automation aspects. During this time the greatest leadership challenges are to retain management interest and support, to retain funding, and to stay on schedule. However, by project's end, both the facility manager and all departmental managers should have the tools necessary to manage effectively and efficiently for the long term.

Leadership Style

Leadership style and personality are highly individualized. (For example, I like to manage by empowerment using metrics to provide accountability. But that is not everyone's style.) Unfortunately, not much research has been done in this area. Martha Whitaker and Cecil Williams of the Facility Management Institute administered the Meyers-Briggs personality test to attendees, primarily facility managers, at their seminars, and found that most facility managers were judgmental. (Judging types enjoy decision making and do it with ease.) The facility managers exhibited slightly more than the average sensing dimension—that is, they focus on data and objects, and have a today orientation.[5]

However, it is obvious that social changes are influencing leadership practices. For example, the authoritarian model is waning because a highly educated, skilled workforce rebels against it. Some management writers have struck a sympathetic chord: Peter Drucker, for his philosophical approach to management; Tom Peters, for his observations on common traits of excellence; James Kouzes and Barry Posner, for their expectations of those led; W. Edwards Deming, for a commitment to quality and quantitative evaluation; and Ken Blanchard, for personal style.

In this chapter, I have posed the most important questions. Too much in facility management is merely a reaction to short-term problems, since so much of the job is reactive. With that in mind, each facility manager must adopt a philosophy of leadership so that decisions are made in a context beyond more than the moment. I hope this chapter will assist you in formulating or crystallizing that leadership philosophy, because, as Rosabeth Moss Kanter, the well-known management consultant and author, has said: "The individual may still be the ultimate actor, but the actions often stem from the context in which the individual operates. Leadership therefore consists increasingly of the design of settings which provide tools for and stimulate constructive, productive individual actions."[6]

Notes

1. *Research Report* 12 (Houston: IFMA, 1994), p. 13.

2. "The Master Entrepreneur," *Inc.* (January 1990): 50.

3. *Washington Post,* April 12, 1988, p. D4.

4. Warren Bennis and Burt Nanus, *Leaders: The Strategy for Taking Charge* (New York: Harper & Row, 1985).

5. Martha Whitaker, personal note, August 14, 1989.

6. *Facilities Management Leadership* (Grand Rapids, Mich.: Steelcase, 1988), p. 4.

Section II

Planning, Programming, and Budgeting

A good business manager plans so that actions are proactive, not always reactive. In this section, I explore three aspects of planning from the facilities vantage point: strategic and annual planning to determine priorities and goals, space planning because space is the lingua franca of facility management, and financial planning to anticipate costs and expenditures to accomplish the organization's goals.

The state of facility management is not good because too often it has been confused with project or space planning. Facility planning must not only cover all facility functions but must be closely tied to the company's business plan.

For every company or agency plan (strategic, midterm, ad hoc, work, or other), there should be a corresponding facility plan. These facility plans should be organized around the manager's selected programs.

Within the facility department, there should be a logical sequence established from planning through budgeting. Not only should there be a horizontal flow from strategic planning through the work plan to the budget, but there should also be a vertical flow. Strategic plans feed subsequent iterations (e.g., this year's budget inputs next year's).

Good facility management offers the greatest single source of cost savings and avoidances.

4

Strategic and Annual Planning

Pulse Points

- *Facility programs, the building blocks of planning and budgeting, should be consistent and trackable over time.*
- *The work plan is a specific manifestation of the programs in the strategic plan.*
- *There should be a facilities business plan to support every company business plan.*
- *Facility management functions should be grouped into budget programs with a manager responsible and accountable for each.*
- *Use life-cycle costing for all analysis of projects over $100,000.*
- *At least one person in the facility department should be focused on planning.*
- *Planning is the facility manager's entree into the business of the company.*
- *Prioritization panels, with user participation, can assist the facility manager in aligning oversubscribed programs.*
- *Prepare an annual work plan 5 to 15 percent in excess of the anticipated budget.*

The role of planning in facility management has special significance. First, it directly interfaces with the business aspects of the company. Second, it clearly exhibits how far from the boiler room the profession has come. Third, it substantially reduces costs and has a high relative return. Despite the emphasis on planning in modern management, it is astounding how few people and companies really buy into planning. "Our company is too dynamic [or complex or screwed up] to plan" is a common belief. That attitude is unfortunate, and probably derives from the fact that business writers have oversold the concept of planning and have failed to articulate exactly what it is.*

---

*As in many areas of facility management, good research on facility business planning is lacking. The best discussion of the topic is *Strategic Planning; Best FM Practices* by Jon Ryburg, available from the Facility Performance Group, Ann Arbor, Michigan, 1995.

Think of a plan as a map of an unexplored area into which you are moving. The nearest portion is reasonably detailed—the major obstacles are shown, and the map provides rough guidance for everyday activities. But as you get farther into the unknown, the map is vaguer and provides only general direction. Like Lewis and Clark, however, you should be updating as you go along, so that the next map is more detailed and more useful. This is why annual plan reviews and rolling planning are so necessary. Planning, particularly strategic planning, has come under criticism, some of that justified because U.S. businesses do not have a good record of planning strategically. However, failure to plan for facilities use is to be a prisoner of reaction.

Planning should be cost-effective. The military has the right idea. In most major headquarters, there is a staff devoted to operations and another devoted to planning. When the stakes are death or survival, there is a strong commitment to planning. Private businesses should learn from that. As our colleague Tom Kvan, who has done much to bring company business and facility planning together, says about strategic planning, "As much as anything, we plan [in order] to avoid disaster."[1]

In my experience, the problem is not planning but implementation. Here are some common mistakes:

- Plans are prepared entirely by consultants, without commitment from managers.
- Plans are prepared and then put on the shelf because (1) the goal is to *have* a plan, not to *use* the plan, and (2) the plan is not updated.
- Plans are 90 percent form and 10 percent substance.

Quite often a plan is nothing more than assurance that a consultant will get wealthier and the department has to start from scratch as each version is implemented. Likewise, many plans try to do too much too soon and thus lose credibility. Or they fail to tie strategic to annual planning, and annual planning to programming and budgeting. If this concept is alien, or if there is more than a 30 percent information void as you move step by step through these loops, then both the process and the planner deserve a hard look.

Facility planning, like most other business endeavors, is only as effective as a facility manager wants to make it. Good planning accelerates response time, improves coordination of major expenditures, and coordinates short-term activities with long-term goals.[2] Both the advantages of good planning and the risks of bad planning are apparent. It will be done well only if it is viewed as significant.

Types of Planning

There are two types of facility planning: strategic or long-range and short or mid-range (see Exhibit 4-1). A well-functioning facility department uses both.

Planning should be done in the context of the company business plan. It is important to understand the relationship that exists among the company's busi-

Exhibit 4-1. Differences between short- and long-term facility planning.

Consideration	Short Term	Long Term
Time line	Less than three years	More than three years
Clarity of future	Reasonably clear	Not clear
Purpose of planning	To provide facilities	To provide infrastructure; to permit future short-range plans to be made more easily
Planning pressures	Lost business, laws and regulations, suddenly recognized need	Doubts and uncertainties, long-term savings, locating of highly fixed assets
Basis of projecting needs	Specific input information	Probable likelihoods
Techniques of planning	Space layout	Top down—bottom up
Nature of plans	Definite and specific	General and conceptual
Capital investment and budgets	Budget, cash-flow analysis	Investment analysis

Source: Richard S. Tryce, unpublished manuscript, June 14, 1988.

ness plan, the facility management plan, and the department's budgeting. It is also important to understand the concept of *facility programs,* the building blocks of each plan. These facility programs are the basic building blocks of facility management plans and budgets. They are those activities that you desire to plan, budget, resource, and manage directly. Exhibit 4-2 shows a list of suggested programs for a complete plan. These are appropriate programs for a midsize organization. A larger organization might use more categories, whereas a smaller company might use fewer. In general, the mid-range plan for an organization contains a consolidation of categories, the long-range plan fewer. Design and engineering can be absorbed in each project cost. You might choose other programs, but whichever ones make up your plan, they should be consistent and trackable from year to year.

The level of detail varies with both the plan and the size of the organization. Since there is no standardization of planning or planning cycles, the model in Exhibit 4-2 may require extensive modification to meet your particular needs. Nevertheless, the basic system here is workable.

How often does a department prepare a plan? Both long- and short-range plans are linked to the department's budget. The budgets should be prepared annually, with a term of one year. All managers are likely to be involved in three budgets in any one fiscal year; budget closeout, execution of the current budget, and development of the follow-up budget. Similarly, facility managers will be involved with two annual work plans—the one in execution and the one in preparation.

Exhibit 4-2. Facility department annual work plan.

1. Capital Costs
   Construction
   Alteration
   Major repair
   Replacement
   Equipment purchase
   Furniture purchase
   Design and engineering

2. Annually Funded Costs (Nondiscretionary)
   Utilities
   Operations
   Maintenance and repair
   • Preventive maintenance
   • Corrective maintenance
   • Special maintenance
   • Minor repair
   • Major repair
   • Design and engineering
   Custodial
   Moving

3. Annually Funded Costs (Discretionary)
   Alterations
   Maintenance
   Repair
   Moving
   Design and engineering

4. Lease Costs
   Space
   Utilities
   Alterations
   Equipment
   Furniture
   Design and engineering

5. Lease Holding Income

6. Overhead Costs
   Personnel
   • Regular staff salaries and benefits (positions by category)
   • Supplementary staff (temporaries, nondesign consultants, etc., by category)
   • Training
   • Travel

Office equipment
Vehicles
Design and engineering

7. Space Needs Projections
Owned
Leased

The department's budget should flow directly from an annual work plan, which is simply an orderly presentation of the amount of work, arranged by program, that the department can expect to accomplish in a year. The items are grouped by program to correspond to the programs in the plan. Unfortunately, too often one of two things sometimes happens: (1) the work plan is developed after the budget is approved, or (2) during the budget process the work plan is not updated, so there is a huge discrepancy between the approved budget and the approved work plan. To solve these problems, it is essential to manage the planning and budgeting processes, perhaps, in a midsize organization, with a full-time planner or consultant. Work plans prepared annually with a twelve-month term are adequate. However, some planners desire a fifteen- or even eighteen-month horizon, for the following two reasons:

1. They ensure that there is continuity of purpose during the end-of-year period.
2. They maximize the productive use of any excess funds that sometimes appear in the last days of a fiscal year.

My purpose is to eliminate the sometimes exasperating funding of noncritical year-end projects simply because they require little time to design and execute. The longer-term work plan helps promote an important concept: the series of work plans as spaces on a continuum rather than discrete entities. Changes in priorities can be made by periodic reviews, not because something has already been designed or requires no approval from the corporate office.

I am committed to good midrange planning. I feel the ideal length is eighteen to thirty-six months, and that the first draft of each annual work plan derives from the mid-range plan. At least 70 percent of the mid-range plan should be translatable into an annual work plan once the planning process is mature. If facility planning is to be successful, it will reap its greatest rewards in mid-range planning. A sample format for both mid-range and strategic plans is given in Exhibit 4-3. The difference is only in the regard to specificity of assumptions and degree of detail.

If the department can plan in a truly meaningful way beyond five years, and the strategic planning document is actually used, great! But for purposes of this book, I consider strategic facility planning to be three to five years.

Tom Kvan provides interesting insight when he calls strategic planning descriptive and annual planning prescriptive. He feels that any company unable to plan beyond five years is blind in the area of facility management, particularly in

Exhibit 4-3. Mid- or long-range facility plan.

I. Introduction

II. Environment

III. Assumptions[1]

IV. Constraints[1]

V. Discussion
   A. Presentation of scenarios
   B. Impact on/of programs for each scenario
      1. Capital
      2. Annually funded nondiscretionary
      3. Annually funded discretionary
      4. Lease costs
      5. Lease holding incomes
      6. Overhead costs
      7. Space need projections
   C. Discussion of most probable scenario (highlight critical deviations from other scenarios which could affect the facility department and/or business significantly; include risk and sensitivity analyses, if possible)

VI. Conclusions

VII. Recommendations

VIII. Appendixes
   A. Time-phased list of events to implement most probable scenario
   B. Capital[2]
      1. Environment[3]
      2. Assumptions[3]
      3. Constraints[3]
      4. Impacts on program
      5. New initiatives required[4]
   C. Annually funded nondiscretionary costs
   D. Annually funded discretionary costs
   E. Lease costs
   F. Lease holding income
   G. Overhead costs
   H. Personnel projection
   I. Space needs projection
   J. Organization chart for departmental structure

[1]Derived from business plan plus best input of facilities staff.
[2]Other program appendixes similarly organized.
[3]Only those applicable from main plan.
[4]Described up to one paragraph with programmatic estimates of start date, duration, and costs.

an international environment. He says that each plan should describe not only what the facilities will look like but what facility department structure will be required to implement needed changes.[3]

Planning Techniques

Since entire books are written on planning techniques, I confine myself here to a general discussion, applying to both business planning and facility planning.

Often planning is done by a single person or a small group. This maximizes the possibility that the resulting plan will be followed and best ensures continuity. On the downside, the input for the plan largely depends on the opinions of a small group, not necessarily reflecting the needs of the company. This limited-perspective approach is typical of a consultant-prepared plan; I call it OMOM, or one man on a mountain.

Top-down planning is similar to OMOM, but the one man or small group is the agency head or company president. It has the same advantages and drawbacks, but can be effective for an initial plan or for a small company. The old saw that "two heads [or three or five or seven] are better than one" is generally accurate for planning.

Another technique is AGIR—a gang in a room. Commonly known as brainstorming, this approach better ensures that various views and aspects are represented, particularly if the individuals are chosen well. The downside is too much input, some of it ego laden, which may yield inconsistent, even contradictory results. A good leader can control the process, maximizing the benefits.

Yet another technique is to bubble up information. By including managers from all echelons for input, you encourage them to buy in to the plan. The disadvantage is again the inconsistency of input unless there's guidance.

For midsize or larger organizations, the optimal planning cycle is depicted in Exhibit 4-4. Critical to this procedure is the need for top management to involve itself in framing and approving. (This procedure is applicable for budget and work plan preparation.)

The adequacy of planning is directly related to the availability of good data. Because of lack of data, it is often three annual planning cycles before the facility business plans are both accurate and useful. There are three major sources of facility data that are invaluable for facility business planning; site master plans, building audits, and serviceability evaluations.

As used in this book, and I wish in the profession, a *master plan* is the technical plan for an individual site; it shows all current and planned development on that site. A master plan is not a facility business plan, though people often confuse the terms. A company that expects to remain at an owned site should plan the future best use of that site through the master planning process. A twenty-year master plan is common.

A *building audit* both describes the current condition of all buildings and provides major projections of operational costs, maintenance costs, major repairs, and capital improvements. Most major architectural and engineering firms offer

Exhibit 4-4. Suggested planning cycle.

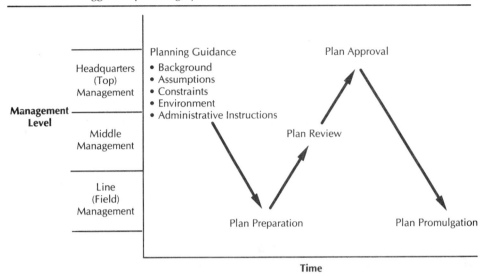

building audits as a service; some large FM departments have the capability in-house. Although the focus of this discussion is on planning, it's worth mentioning that a building audit can also be helpful after construction, to ensure that programming goals and/or contractual requirements were met.

The newest tool for good facility business planning is the *serviceability evaluation*. Gerald Davis and Francoise Szigeti of the International Center for Facilities have been instrumental in refining serviceability tools and methods for buildings, which were recently recognized as an American Society for Testing and Materials standard. One major use of serviceability standards is to allow companies to evaluate current buildings or proposed leases or acquisitions against the needs of the organization. Those data can be invaluable for good facility business planning. Together with historical files, master plans, and building audits, a serviceability evaluation gives the facility manager good data for planning.

The Annual Work Plan

The annual work plan should flow from the mid-range plan. It should have the following qualities:

1. *Present a clear message.* The boss and facility employees should clearly understand the goals, objectives, and priorities when they read the facility work plan.

2. *Be clearly structured.* There should be direct parallelism between the format of long- and midrange plans, the work plan, and the budget.

3. *Be maintainable.* The work plan will probably need to be updated at least at midyear. It should be a tool, not an administrative burden. KISS—Keep It Simple, Stupid.

Gathering the requirements for the work plan is relatively simple. Up to 70 percent of the requirements will be specified in the midrange plan. The remainder of the work involves bringing in unplanned requirements and molding them into an effective document. Exhibit 4-5 is a matrix for gathering the final 30 percent of the requirements annually and integrating them into the plan.

One important planning consideration is timing. No item can be placed in the work plan unless a working cost estimate has been prepared. For work on a capital project, obtaining such an estimate can require a 10 to 30 percent design effort and at least gross estimating. That can take two to three months, even longer, so the procedure for gathering requirements must include this time.

It is recommended that capital project requirements be gathered separately from annual requirements. Because of the investment in capital projects and the need to develop them substantially before they can be estimated and analyzed for cost-effectiveness, the capital requirements and their justification should be in

Exhibit 4-5. Gathering work plan requirements.

Program	Responsible for Developing Requirement	Responsible for Prioritizing Requirement	How Cost Is Estimated
Capital	User/Facility management department	Facility management department	Estimated from conceptual design
Annually funded nondiscretionary	Facility management department	Facility management department	Extrapolated from historical data
Annually funded discretionary	User/Facility management department	Facility management department	Application of unit costs
Lease costs/income	Facility management department	Higher management	Derived from existing leases
Overheads	Facility management department	Higher management	Application of planning factors and historical data
Space needs	User/Facility management department	Facility management department	N/A

some detail. Normally a set of concept drawings is included with each submission. Gather the capital requirements annually, typically about a month before the capital budget is reviewed by management. Also consider forming a prioritization board to align the work plan requirements with the capital plan. Often, the work plan is a rolling one, with unfulfilled requirements rolled over to the next fiscal year, to be prioritized along with needs. In some companies, a midyear review of priorities may be appropriate.

The requirements for utilities, operations, service orders, preventive maintenance, leases, and most overhead costs should flow directly from the midrange plan or should be calculated in-house. These figures represent the nondiscretionary part of the work plan, so there is little need to prioritize: they are all priority 1. The facility department management information system should readily produce data that, with extrapolation, will allow highly accurate work estimates.

For alterations, minor (noncapital) construction, and maintenance and repair projects, gather and prioritize the requirements in much the same way as for capital projects. There may or may not be a need for an elaborate justification document. Costs are usually estimated using unit costs (e.g., dollars per square foot, dollars per people relocated). Because the requirements for this type of work often are double the funds available, a prioritization panel should both prepare the initial submission and conduct the midyear review.

In general, it is best to oversubscribe the work plan by 5 to 15 percent by category. This is because some projects will be unexecutable during the year and because a prudent facility manager always has substantive projects ready for execution in the final months of a fiscal year, should there be a windfall in the facility account.

The preferred format for a work plan is shown in Exhibit 4-2. Some items—preventive maintenance, for example—take no more than one line. Others require a prioritized list, and still others are a list with each item having a separate backup justification sheet.

There is some controversy about how widely the work plan should be distributed. One approach is to limit the document to the facility department, lest a user, seeing his project in print, will never be dissuaded should some problem arise. The other approach is full disclosure, particularly if users have participated in the prioritizing. Explaining why a project needs to be raised or lowered in its priority rank—or even cancelled—is one of the chores of management. If you cannot explain your action, maybe it was not correct.

Mid- and Long-Range Plans

A 1988 survey of real estate practices showed that although real estate accounts for one-fourth of the assets of U.S. companies, only 40 percent of those companies clearly and consistently evaluate the performance of their real estate.[4] We believe that this practice must be changed. Evaluating and utilizing a company's real property assets demands effective planning.

The format given in Exhibit 4-3 is applicable for both mid- and long-range facility plans. However, the relative importance of each program varies with time, as depicted in Exhibit 4-6. This graph is representative only; the actual weighting of each program is highly situation dependent. Nevertheless, several conclusions are apparent:

1. If good mid- and long-range planning can be done on space, leasing, and capital programs, there will be more effort left for planning annual programs when these peak in years 1 and 2.

2. In the long term, space forecasting and build-vs-lease planning are preeminent. If building is an option, considerable effort must be expended in midrange planning. However, some level of activity in those programs most closely associated with annual planning (operations, maintenance, utilities, structure, position levels) is important even in the out-years of strategic planning.

3. In the near term (years 1 and 2), when the emphasis is on implementation, macrolevel planning of all programs continues.

It is important to realize that this is a snapshot of one ten-year period. As each year passes, the process rolls—that is, one year of the midrange plan becomes an annual plan for the next fiscal year. There is a rhythm and a continuity to this process.

Planning Input

The principle inputs for the mid- and long-range facility plans are the complementary company business plans. Particularly important are the sections re-

Exhibit 4-6. Relative importance of planning facility programs.

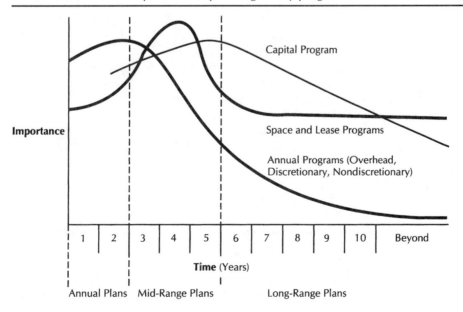

garding environment, assumptions, constraints, and conclusions. If the facility manager has been part of the business planning group or if the facility plan is developed concurrently with the business plan, little other input will be required. If, however, the facility plan is being developed in a vacuum, it is worthwhile reviewing the company plan with the principal managers, and perhaps even holding a brainstorming session among key persons. The facility manager can act as a facilitator for the session or hire a consultant to do so.

It is, of course, preferable for the facility plan to bubble up from the managers responsible for the programs. This means that they must be exposed to the business plan. Those managers will perform best if they are familiar with the business plan and are provided guidance on the facility plan, particularly if the facility manager feels strongly about one particular program. Planning, to be good, must be an iterative process. Particularly for a first effort, it could take three to five rewrites to get a plan correct. Remember that before any basic assumptions or constraints of the business plan can be changed, approval must come from the company planner. Ultimately, the facility manager is responsible that (1) the facility plan supports the business plan, and (2) that the facility plan is integrated and complete.

Planning Tools

The facility manager's ability to plan is in direct proportion to his staff's knowledge of its facilities and policies that allow for meaningful extrapolation and forecasting. There are many planning tools, but the following are the minimum a company expects its facility manager to bring to the planning table.[5]

- Facility inventory
- Facility utilization information
- Facility costs (unit costs for every program element to include overhead and design)
- Cost indexes applicable to local labor, material, utility, and lease costs
- Agreed-on growth (or reduction) factors
- Standards, particularly for space and furniture
- Applicable utility information
- Input from the master plan, if available
- A typical cost slice for common types of services (for example, the typical design cost for a common alteration project as a percentage of total project cost)
- Personnel needs and mix

Since most new facility departments do not have these data, the facility manager's first efforts at planning may be less than successful. That is why planning must be viewed as an iterative process. It is extremely important to produce the first of each type of plan (annual, midrange, and long range) so that subsequent plans can adjust from those baselines, rather than be zero based. To this extent, the most valuable tools for preparing a facility plan are (1) last year's applicable facility plan and (2) the last two years' business plans.

Some facility managers who manage large, complex facilities whose companies own the properties and intend to retain them for an extended period (at least ten years) will prepare a master plan for such locations. This is common among U.S. colleges and universities and with the U.S. Department of Defense.

A master plan may have any format but commonly includes the following categories:

- Assumptions and constraints
- Summary of, or reference to, standards
- Facilities inventory by category, by condition
- Summary of applicable zoning and other restrictions, if any
- Visual depiction of fully developed facility (often various elements—housing, utilities, etc.—are shown separately and color-coded when combined)
- Time-phased schedule of facility changes
- Time-phased cost projections

If a master plan exists, it is valuable input for the facility plan.

Both the facilities plan and the master plan must comply with local codes and zoning. For national and international companies, it is strongly recommended that a planning organization familiar with local codes be hired to assist. This allows the facility manager to evaluate a local company for possible implementation consulting, shows local authorities that the company is interested in their concerns, and provides expertise until a decision is made as to whether to staff locally.

Plan Format

From both research and personal experience, I have learned how little has been done to standardize facility planning. Each planner uses a different set of procedures and formats, and sometimes these change from plan to plan or year to year—an undesirable situation. If planning is to be effective, last year's plan should be comparable to this year's. If there is more than a 30 percent deviation from year to year, you need to review the planning process.) A common format can be a major aid in this process of comparison.

In practice, there is commonality in annual planning. Most companies, if they prepare a work plan, construct it as a prioritized project listing by program. However, there is less commonality in formats for mid- and long-range plans. Exhibit 4-3 shows my suggested format. This format dictates some degree of uniformity in procedures also. But let's take a section-by-section look at the facility plan.

1. *Introduction.* The introduction sets the stage and tone. Commonly there is a purpose statement and some bridge material to the corresponding business

plan, from which the facility plan has evolved or to other plans based on this document.

2. *Environment.* The planning team extracts from the business plan pertinent environmental considerations that will affect facilities. For example, this section might include a prediction of high interest rates affecting both leasing and construction costs. But not every environmental factor in the business plan is pertinent to facilities planning. On the other hand, factors here might be general comments regarding utility rate trends, local labor rate projections, or changing company attitudes toward administrative expenses.

It is unrealistic to expect company planners to supply all the environmental factors important to the facility plan. For example, in the late 1980s, construction material costs tended to remain higher than the consumer price index. That fact was known in facilities departments but probably not by company business planners. These types of environmental considerations should be included here because it is important to help company planners and management put the facility plan in context. In fact, the facilities plan will concentrate more on internal company environment than does the business plan.

3. *Assumptions.* As you look further into the future, you must make certain assumptions in order to plan. These assumptions can be generated by knowledgeable individuals extrapolating current data, or consultants can be used. Sometimes it is helpful to ask the question, "What information do I need to prepare a facility plan for five or ten years hence?" Once answered, the response can be compared to the currently available facts. The information gap must be closed with assumptions—ideally, knowledgeable ones.

Assumptions can be so many and so varied that you must limit them to only those truly pertinent. Some assumptions applicable to the facility plan relate to standards, lease or build strategies, and in-house versus contracted services.

4. *Constraints.* Sometimes for emphasis, constraints on the plan's effectiveness are listed separately. However, often the environment, assumptions, and constraints are combined and handled as either introductory material or as assumptions. My preference is that each appear separately. Constraints should be stated only to the extent that they exist. Here are two typical constraint statements:

> During years 5 through 7, the overhead budget is limited to zero absolute growth; growth in years 7 through 10 is limited to that determined by the consumer price index.

> No additional leased space will be allowed in Hartford for years 1 through 3.

Constraints, as applicable, can come from the company business plan. They are an effective way to shape the planning process, but should be used only when you are certain they are supported and supportable.

5. *Discussion.* Although preparation is more difficult, and the plan becomes more voluminous, you should include multiple scenarios. By showing a range of values, the plan more appropriately represents its degree of accuracy. Also, scenarios insulate you best from failure. Which scenarios to consider varies. Here are some common approaches:

- *Fiscal.* The budget or facilities department designates a high, low, and mid- or most probable budget value for each program for each year.
- *Projected.* Current budgets are projected into the out-years using a most favorable, least favorable, and average or most probable multiplier.
- *Rational.* Using assumptions and constraints specific to each year in the plan, three work plans are developed each year. If quantitative data are desired, the values for each work plan are calculated by program.

Once the method of selecting scenarios is determined, you can move to the heart of the plan—the impact of the programs. The principle function of this section is to present each program in each scenario, along with explanatory material and the impact of each scenario on the total plan. When you display all the programs in each of three scenarios, you can suggest modifications. This is the section that truly requires your input and attention, because judgment is crucial. The most probable scenario will undoubtedly be the most developed.

Explain major program highlights (e.g., bringing a new building on line) regardless of the scenario in which they occur. Put special emphasis on areas that could put the facility department at risk, since the principal role of a plan is to insulate against catastrophe.

Finally, designate and explain the most probable scenario. If the department has the ability to do so, perform sensitivity analyses on the scenario selected as most likely. What would happen, for example, if the funds available for leases in year 5 were reduced 5 percent? What would happen if space needs in year 3 exceed projections by 10 percent?

6. *Conclusions.* Present, in simple terms, your major conclusions for supporting the company business plan. In addition, address, in general terms, the impact of other scenarios and sensitivity analyses. In particular, your conclusions should highlight any situation where a facility issue could affect the company business plan.

7. *Recommendations.* In this section, you recommend the preferred course of action for the facilities of the corporation.

8. *Appendixes.* Include appendixes to the degree that they support the conclusions and recommendation. Typical appendixes include financial displays, list of events, personnel projections, space projections, and/or organizational charts.

Reviews and Updates

Once plans are in place, it is easier to adjust annually using the plan as a baseline, unless assumptions and constraints have changed radically. All facility plans should be reviewed annually by departmental managers. Each three to five years, the mid- and long-range plans should be zero based, under the direction of the department's planner.

It is extremely important that someone manage the total planning process. The output of long-range planning feeds and frames the midrange plan. The near-year portion of the plan, in turn, rolls over to become the basis of the annual work plan. Once developed, the process is logical and easy to administer.

At the same time, it is possible to concentrate on goals for six years hence or anticipate utility costs three years into the future.

There's often legitimate concern about the difficulty of dealing with uncertainty; however, uncertainty should not preclude planning—it only complicates it. Rather than develop point estimates for the future, develop scenarios. The company is best protected when a best-case, worst-case, and most-likely-case scenario are projected. Also, the envelope of certainty broadens as the horizon widens.

Formulating the initial facility plan will require great effort. It is quite likely that the first efforts will be suboptimal, even frustrating. It is not uncommon for it to take up to three years for you to feel really good about the final product. But don't get discouraged or stop the planning. The key is to get the initial plan published.[6]

There are synergistic effects from compiling and publishing your first facility plan. Managers in your department will have to become familiar with the company's business plan. Also, they will have to coordinate with each other to plan, and this will carry over to operations. By the time you are comfortable with your planning efforts, your department will be operating more effectively also.

Notes

1. Thomas Kvan, personal interview, March 16, 1989.

2. William Joseph, *Facilities Strategic Planning,* Occasional Paper, 1989, p. 2.

3. Kvan interview.

4. "Real Estate Industry Survey," Harvard Business School, in Richard S. Tryce, manuscript.

5. For some of these suggestions, we credit William Adams, *Developing a Long-Range Facilities Forecast,* occasional paper (Houston: International Facility Management Association, 1986).

6. Charles J. Bodenstab, "Directional Signals," *Inc.* (March 1989): 141.

5

Financial Management

Pulse Points

- *The most successful facility managers view themselves as business managers.*
- *All economic analyses and comparisons should be based on life-cycle costs and should consider the cost of ownership.*
- *Know your company's rules for capitalization, and follow them carefully. Don't cheat.*
- *Manage carefully the depreciation charges for your capital program in your annual budget.*
- *The facility manager must have a working knowledge of capital evaluation tools.*
- *Whenever possible, use life-cycle costs for cost comparisons.*
- *Vendor-supplied cost analyses are not dependable.*
- *Use a landlord mentality when developing and implementing allocations and rules for chargeback.*

In small organizations, financial forecasting and macrolevel estimating are used sporadically, primarily in planning and budget preparation. In large organizations, specialists work full time preparing financial forecasts and cost estimates in support of various programs or projects. The importance of financial forecasting and macrolevel forecasting can best be appreciated by the facility manager who finds a capital project approved but is unable to start because of an inadequate budget made many years before. Another example is the facility manager who leaves $5 million on the table at the end of a fiscal year because the staff misforecast the department's ability to commit funds. These horrors occur because the skills required for macrolevel estimates are not normally those required for construction estimates and financial analysts normally are ill equipped to provide facility financial forecasts.

Life-Cycle Costing

One of the most important economic concepts for a facility manager to understand is *life-cycle costing.* Properly conducted, life-cycle costing allows a comparison of two different options of different expected lives or the total cost of one option over its expected life. It can be used to compare the benefits of retaining a service in-house or outsourcing that service or to compare two different choices for a piece of equipment to accomplish the same task or to determine whether to replace or repair existing equipment.

Unfortunately, life-cycle costing is more often mentioned than practiced. Applied to facility management, life-cycle costing acknowledges that the company buys into a chain of costs when it buys a building—the cost of ownership. The life cycle of costs (in constant-year dollars) could be used to evaluate two options for meeting the same requirement—to build in the suburbs versus lease in the city, for example. At the project level, life-cycle costing would determine the wisdom of installing a rub-rail on conference room walls versus the expenditures required in the future to repair and paint those same walls.

Proper life-cycle costing allows a comparison of actions having different life expectancies and to account for the time value of money. Savings for proposed projects or products can be hard to recognize, harder to quantify, and hardest yet to document. It often takes a joint effort between an experienced facility department staff person and a financial analyst or economist to quantify future costs or savings. These skills can be hired outside, but a facility department with an ongoing capital program should develop an in-house capability to do life-cycle costing. *Major FM decisions made solely on first costs are never good decisions and are more likely wrong than right.* Life-cycle costing is one of those best practices that the profession should embrace as a standard.

Financial Forecasting

Financial forecasts are one of the bridges that allow the financial resources of a plan to be assessed and plans to be converted to budgets. The primary purpose of a financial forecast is financial planning. The forecast may lead to a budget or a project estimate, but it is primarily concerned with planning. When preparing a budget, the facility manager uses a variety of forecasting techniques to obtain a total budget figure. It is very important to understand whether the budget is to be in "constant" or "then year" dollars, particularly in a time of inflation. Failure to account for an increase or decrease in value over time can seriously affect your budget estimates.

A number of sophisticated forecasting techniques have been developed and are in common use:

- Regression analysis
- Moving averages
- Econometric modeling
- Exponential smoothing
- Delphi method
- Simple projection

Each company has its own method of forecasting. Since a capital budget consists of discrete projects, it is the sum of individual estimates. On the other hand, the budget for operations and maintenance requires different forecasting techniques for each program. The different techniques are summarized in Exhibit 5-1. In a dynamic organization, the financial forecast is a combination of historical extrapolation plus increments for increases or decreases caused by new requirements times a unit cost, which itself may be subject to inflation.

Macrolevel Estimating

Forecasts, as they apply to projects, are called *estimates*. Early in any large project, it is necessary to determine what it will cost. Often some estimate is needed soon after the project is conceived, in order to line up board or executive approval. This occurs before there's an architect—before there's a conceptual design, in some cases.

Later, other macrolevel estimates may be necessary to secure administrative approval or to complete a project budget based on a design. This kind of microlevel estimating normally is possible only after the design is approximately 30 percent developed. Similarly, facility managers often have so many small projects on their agenda that making a detailed construction estimate for each is impractical and unnecessary. What's really needed is a budget figure to control each project so that the sum of all projects does not exceed the overall budget. Those project budget figures are often best arrived at by macrolevel estimating.

There are three different types of macrolevel estimates. The *informal estimate* may well be called "intuitive" or "experiential." It's most often done from the barest of information, which means it can be done quickly. Such words or phrases as *blue sky, ballpark, guesstimate, seat of the pants,* and *approximate* come to mind.

The purpose of the informal estimate is to determine whether to allocate resources to research or study the feasibility of a project. The reliability of informal estimates is questionable and depends on the experience and skill of the estimator. Unfortunately, the informal estimate often is remembered by top management as if it were a more sophisticated and reliable estimate, especially when expectations are high. Qualifying footnotes always seem to get separated from the estimate at the earliest opportunity, so don't count on them. Most facility managers avoid being judged on the basis of informal estimates.

The *generic estimate* is formulated by consulting a database that offers standardized costs and duration for detailed aspects of a project or function. This budget is prepared by specifying each item and tabulating a total for all items. Indexes may be available to adjust for specific variances, such as between organizational types or geographic locations. Most macrolevel estimates are informal or generic.

The *comprehensive estimate* is the most reliable primary estimate. This type provides information on materials as well as processes or procedures. It is more effective in that there is attention to variations in how projects are to be completed

Exhibit 5-1. Forecasting operations, maintenance, and administrative programs.

Program	Forecasting Method
Personnel	Determine by extrapolation or the addition of increments/decrements the number of authorized personnel in each personnel category. Multiply each category times an average salary plus benefits increment for each category.
Utilities	Extrapolate historical usage based on square footage or cost per staff member. Increase or decrease if a known facility is added to the inventory or released. Utility companies now have extremely sophisticated analyses; if you are metered properly, they will produce highly accurate forecasts to account for anticipated weather abnormalities, rate increases, and other changes.
Breakdown maintenance	The number of service orders by category can best be extrapolated in a straight-line manner plus an increment/decrement if major facilities are to be acquired/released. The budget figure is then calculated by multiplying by the unit cost per category.
Preventive maintenance	The cost of preventive maintenance is nearly always driven by the labor cost. Determine the crew size for each preventive maintenance function. Multiply by the annual rate per craft, and add a historically derived cost of materials.
Repair projects	Obtain an estimate, in-house or based on a proposal for each project planned. Keep a 15 to 25 percent contingency for emergencies.
Alteration projects	If these projects are funded from the operations and maintenance budget and not capitalized or charged back, they can be estimated based on the number of staff to be moved or the number of feet to be altered multiplied by the appropriate unit cost. I try to retain a 25 to 33 percent contingency in this account but seldom succeed.
Furniture (noncapital)	If you know the exact pieces to be purchased, your vendors can help you do your forecast. My experience is that noncapital furniture purchases are consistent (at least in dollar volume) from year to year, so extrapolation from historical data should be adequate for your forecast.

Note: All extrapolated forecasts should be increased or decreased incrementally for known requirements increases or decreases. All funding forecasts should be adjusted for anticipated inflation or deflation if then-year dollars are to be used. These two concepts are commonly known as *volume increases* (decreases) and *price increases* (decreases).

under specific conditions, not just simple costs and durations from generic standards.

Considerations in Making Estimates

Most construction estimators will tell you that their skill is equal parts art and science. Macrolevel estimating is perhaps more of an art. A skilled construction estimator is not necessarily good at macrolevel estimating. In fact, I once lost a good construction estimator because he was frustrated at the pace and at what he saw as imprecision in our estimating needs.

Organizations that operate internationally but macroestimate centrally almost always use indexes to fine-tune their figures for local application. The *Engineering News Record* index, for example, is often used for construction.* In fact, many organizations have found it worthwhile to publish their data for estimating other programs.

Whereas construction estimators have reference books (e.g., Means and Richardson) to refer to, macrolevel estimators are most successful when using local data.† You should collect the following data for forecasting and estimating purposes:

Personnel costs:	• Costs by category • Benefits costs • Personnel positions
Utilities:	• Utilities rates by utility • Degree days • Usage data by utility
Maintenance costs:	• Costs per square feet or staff member (by location or facility) —Preventive maintenance —Custodial • Shop costs —Unit cost per product —Annual cost • Annual cost of repair projects
Space:	• Amount (by category, by location or facility, by occupant) —Owned —Leased • Leasing rate

---

ENR Index, published by *Engineering News Record*, is an internationally accepted index for "moving" known construction estimates from one locale and applying them to another.
†Means and Richardson are common sources of construction, renovation, and facility costs. These references are used in the absence of company-unique data and are updated annually.

Alteration projects:
- Number of projects
- Unit costs (by location or facility)
  —Per square feet
  —Per linear foot of wall
  —Per employee

Furniture:
- Items purchased by type
- Prices

Indexes (for organizations
at multiple locations):
- Construction
- Maintenance

Grounds—unit cost per acre

Roads:
- Amount by category
- Unit costs by category
  —Repair
  —Replace

This is a representative list. Needs vary greatly, depending on the true requirements of the organization.

Macrolevel estimates are by their nature imprecise. Normally managers are comfortable with and expect an accuracy of +5 percent, but will accept +10 percent or −5 percent. Updating estimates at least annually is a problem for facility managers who have broad responsibilities, however. For example, the U.S. Army often has such a backlog of major construction projects that some take more than ten years from concept to approval. If the macrolevel estimate is not kept up to date, you'll find that approved funds are grossly inadequate. In periods of even moderate inflation, the absolute value of funds requested can depreciate by 20 percent in three years—a significant amount on a large project. Thus, at the conclusion of a project or at the end of a fiscal year, one of the principal purposes of evaluation should be to update the estimating database.

Capital Programs

Capitalization is an orderly and intelligent way to meet major new facility needs. The facility manager should actively participate in developing the requirements, prioritizing the competing needs, and managing the execution of a capital development program. To do this, he must not only understand the rules but follow them closely.

The costs associated with long-lived assets are sometimes referred to as *capitalized costs*.[1] These costs are often met by capital expenditures, which can be used to expand or modernize a company. The amounts spent annually are substantial. Gross, private, nonresidential investment in structures in 1994 exceed $180 billion in the United States.[2] Thus it is important that you know the basics of capital budgeting.

Capital Budgeting

Capital needs flow from a business analysis. With regard to facility management, total space needs must be assessed first. Then the company must determine whether it is in its best interest to lease, build, or make more efficient use of existing space through renovation. If the decision is to renovate or construct, capital funds are normally used.

Determining what can or cannot be capitalized is normally the province of the controller. Often the rules are a combination of two factors: the existing tax code, which determines what can be depreciated over what period, and company rules, which usually set a floor below which a single purchase cannot be capitalized. Some fees associated with a capital project obviously can be capitalized; others cannot. Renovations and replacement projects both raise questions as to proper allocation of costs. Bill Agnello, a capable, knowledgeable facility manager who works extensively in this arena, is a foremost advocate of knowing and understanding the company's rules.[3]

New Capital Projects

As most experienced facility managers realize, capital projects are extremely popular because of the following beliefs:

- They are the first material evidence of a new company initiative.
- They often help project the company image.
- They are sometimes the solution to company problems.
- They involve high expenditure over a short period of time, and therefore they are highly visible.

Some of these perceptions are only marginally correct, yet a facility manager must learn to deal with their results. For example, often there is substantial competition for limited capital dollars in any one budget year.

There are several ways to prepare a capital budget:

1. Based on a funding target from the budget department, gather your requirements.
2. Analyze the requirements, justifications, and numbers using some form of quantification to determine rank order.
3. Conduct a screening and prioritization session using a board that will then make a recommendation.

In smaller firms, capital funding may be extremely limited and expenditures may be dictated by the chief executive officer (CEO) or board. For larger organizations, these steps ensure a well-received submission for capital funds.

Step 1: Gathering the Requirements

Because there can be substantial expense in preparing a capital submission, a good facility manager limits submissions to a probable funding target plus 20 to 30 percent. Requirements should be submitted in a standardized format and forwarded over the signature of an appropriate line manager. Suggested information for such a submission includes the following:

- Fiscal year
- Location
- Project title
- Program and category code (if applicable)
- Project number
- Project cost
- Cost estimate (by major project phases): phase, unit measure, quantity, unit cost, and total cost of phase
- Project description
- Project justification
- Decision device (net present value, for example)
- Concept drawing or rendering

An excellent example of a capital project requirements document is DD Form 1391, available from the Government Printing Office.

Usually several members of the facility department assist in generating this information. Some designs are often needed so that at least a working cost estimate can be initiated, defining the project enough so that it can be considered. Be sure you have annual funds to do this type of preparatory work.

Step 2: Rank-Order the Projects

One of the most difficult tasks is to rank-order the projects based on criteria that are rational, discriminating, and meaningful to the company. Many such devices exist, but the most common ones are annual return on investment (ROI), cash payback system, discounted cash flow, net present value (NPV), internal rate of return, and benefit-cost ratios. An excellent discussion of the first five of these devices is contained in *Accounting Principles* by Weygandt, Kieso, and Kell. Whole books have been written on assessing costs and benefits for the BCR. NPV analyses or IRR are the current favorites for this type of analysis.

Some of these analyses can become quite sophisticated and difficult. Seek help (normally from the budget analyst or controller), but again, a word of advice from Bill Agnello is appropriate: "The facility planner and manager must take *personal* and *professional* responsibility for understanding and accepting the numbers game because your clients (internal or external) will be better served."[4]*

---

*For an excellent commonsense description of the use of basic financial management in FM and the use of spreadsheets, see Mike Hoots, "Dr. Spreadsheet or How I Learned to Stop Worrying and Love Financial Analysis," *Facility Management Journal*, January–February 1998, pp. 10–17.

Step 3: Present to the Capital Project Board

The purpose of the board is to review all submissions, rank-order them using the appropriate decision device, and develop the department's capital budget request. If you are on the board, the board's recommendation should be final. In some cases, however, policy or politics may require capital project approval at the chief financial officer (CFO) or CEO level. If the board merely prepares a recommendation, normally the facility manager is at most a nonvoting chairperson or secretary.

Depreciation Expense

Some companies use a braking device called a *depreciation expense* to ensure that capitalization is not overused. The depreciation expense in your annual operating budget is the sum of the annual depreciation for that year for each outstanding capital project. Because most annual operating budgets are relatively fixed, if the depreciation expense reaches 8 to 10 percent of the total budget, you may be robbing Peter to pay Paul.

Controlling Capital Projects

Because capital projects have a classic peak-and-valley nature, many facility managers form a special team to manage them. Unfortunately, commonly the company project manager (particularly for the new headquarters) is a retiring executive or someone else who just happens to be available. But managing a major capital project is a challenging task. You should control the appointment of each capital project manager. In addition, the facility manager needs to ensure that, in addition to the design and construction team, each project manager has access to the following, either in-house or from a consultant:

- Legal counsel, preferably someone knowledgeable in construction contracting
- Construction accountant
- Value engineer
- Budget expert

Initial costs are always a major concern. However, you need to put those costs in perspective when considering a building design. Over the life of any building, 92 percent of the life-cycle costs of that facility will be the salaries of the occupants. The cost of operating and maintaining that building will be 6 percent, while the original design and construction is but 2 percent. Thus, prudent initial investments for operational efficiency and maintainability will leverage themselves over the life of the building.

Cost Justification

The ability to justify projects economically is an important skill. Companies set requirements for funds use far in excess of what is available in any one year. Two basic approaches have been developed to quantify the economic benefits of particular projects and to prioritize them. For instance, with the *accept-reject approach*, everything over a certain benchmark (benefit-cost ratio = 3.5, for example) is selected, and anything under it is rejected. Or the highest-ranking projects (rank-ordered by IRR, for example) up to the funds available are included in the budget; this is the *ranking approach*. Facility managers should be familiar with these analytical tools and should be aware of their strengths and limitations.

Cost justification is the term used for making decisions between competing proposed projects or go/no-go choices on specific proposed projects. Although the technique is most applicable to capital projects, it can be used whenever there is some degree of freedom to select among competing projects and the analytical time can be cost-justified.

Cost justification has these objectives:

1. Selecting the project with the highest potential for reward
2. Selecting the project that limits or minimizes financial risk
3. Prioritizing the projects competing for limited resources

The factors brought together to evaluate investment alternatives include the net amount of the investment required for a project, the returns or cash flows expected from an investment in the project, and the company's lowest acceptable rate of return on investment, or its cost of capital. The actual cost-evaluation tools we consider here are these:

- Average payback period
- Actual payback period
- Net present value
- Internal rate of return
- Benefit-cost ratio

The first two methods of evaluating investment alternatives are listed to provide a concept only—the idea that an investment must pay back over a period of time to be justified. Payback, however, is overly simplistic, and I do not recommend that anyone use it for making capital decisions.

Average Payback Period

Calculating an average payback period is a method for making an accept/reject decision or to select one project against a standard set by management:

$$\text{Average payback period (years)} = \frac{\text{Net investment}}{\text{Average annual cash inflow}}$$

	Advantages	*Disadvantages*

Advantages	*Disadvantages*
• Simple to use • Considers cash flows • A measure of risk	• Does not fully consider time value of money • Does not consider subsequent cash flow • Cash inflows can be subjective

To use this device, select the project that meets or beats the predetermined maximum average payback period or best average payback period of alternative projects. See Exhibit 5-2 for an example.

Actual Payback Period

This method uses the same data as the average payback period analysis but calculates an actual payback time. Actual payback is when the sum of prior cash inflow exactly equals the initial investment. The payback period is the time it takes to recover the cost of the investment through the net cash flow. The net cash flow consists of the after-tax value of savings generated by the project, and the tax write-off resulting from depreciation expense. To calculate the payback period, divide the annual net cash flow into the cost of the investment. A shorter payback period will be the investment alternative of choice with this method. A major drawback of the payback method is that ongoing long-term profitability is not included in evaluating the investment alternatives.

Advantages	*Disadvantages*
• Measures risk • Simple to use • Considers timing of cash flows	• Does not fully consider time value of money • Does not consider subsequent cash flow

To use the device, select the project that meets or beats the predetermined maximum payback period, or the shortest actual payback period among the alternatives.

Net Present Value

This analytic tool determines the dollar value, at time zero, of some future series of cash flows, discounted at the company's cost of capital. It measures expected

Exhibit 5-2. Payback period.

	Investment A	*Investment B*
Cost	$3,000	$7,000
Net annual cash flow	1,000	2,000
Payback period	3 years	3.5 years
Preferred investment:	Investment A	

future benefits (cash flows) against initial investment. The NPV method recognizes the time value of money. All the cash flows over the life of the investment are converted to present value. The present values of both cash inflows and the outflows are netted. If the NPV is positive, the investment alternative is not good. If comparing two investment alternatives, choose the alternative with the higher NPV or lower negative NPV.

$$NPV = \text{Present value of future cash flows} - \text{net investment}$$

To calculate an NPV, you must know the initial net investment, the company's cost of capital, and future cash flows

Advantages	*Disadvantages*
• Gives consideration to the time value of money	• Makes assumptions as to the cost of capital
• Considers all relevant cash flows	• More difficult to calculate; needs table of discount factors
• Commonly used and understood	

To use the device, select the project that has the highest positive NPV, or the smallest negative NPV from alternative projects. See Exhibit 5-3 for an example. The discounted cash flow can be complicated when you must take into consideration any salvage value of the investment and the annual depreciation amounts. Salvage value should be included as a cash inflow and converted to present value. Depreciation is not a cash expense; however, it does affect the tax expense by reducing the tax owed. So depreciation times the tax rate is a "cash inflow" to be converted to present value for each year depreciation is taken.

Internal Rate of Return

The IRR is the discount rate assuming an NPV of zero:

$$IRR = NPV = 0$$

To calculate the IRR of a project, you must know the initial net investment and future cash inflows. To make an accept/reject decision, you must know the company's cost of capital.

Advantages	*Disadvantages*
• Gives consideration to the time value of money	• Difficult to calculate without a good financial calculator
• Considers all relevant cash flows	• Less understood by nonfinancial managers
	• Assumes that all intermediate cash flows are reinvested at company's IRR

Exhibit 5-3. Net present value.

Example:

	Investment A	Investment B
Cost	$10,000	$11,000
Savings each year	$ 2,000	$ 4,000
Number of years with savings	4 years	4 years

(The discount rate is 10%.)

	Cost	Present Value Factor— P.V. of Inflow	Net Cash
Investment A	$10,000	$2,000 × 3.1699* = $ 6,340	($3,660)
Investment B	11,000	4,000 × 3.1699* = 12,680	1,680

Preferred Investment: Investment B

Present Value of $1 at Compound Interest

Periods Hence	4½%	5%	6%	7%	8%	9%	10%	12%	14%	16%
1	0.9569	0.9524	0.9434	0.9346	0.9259	0.9174	0.9091	0.8929	0.8772	0.8621
2	0.9157	0.9070	0.8900	0.8734	0.8573	0.8417	0.8265	0.7972	0.7695	0.7432
3	0.8763	0.8638	0.8396	0.8163	0.7938	0.7722	0.7513	0.7118	0.6750	0.6407
4	0.8386	0.8227	0.7921	0.7629	0.7350	0.7084	0.6830	0.6355	0.5921	0.5523
5	0.8025	0.7835	0.7473	0.7130	0.6806	0.6499	0.6209	0.5675	0.5194	0.4761
6	0.7679	0.7462	0.7050	0.6663	0.6302	0.5963	0.5645	0.5066	0.4556	0.4104
7	0.7348	0.7107	0.6651	0.6228	0.5835	0.5470	0.5132	0.4524	0.3996	0.3538
8	0.7032	0.6768	0.6274	0.5820	0.5403	0.5019	0.4665	0.4039	0.3506	0.3050
9	0.6729	0.6446	0.5919	0.5439	0.5003	0.4604	0.4241	0.3606	0.3075	0.2630
10	0.6439	0.6139	0.5584	0.5084	0.4632	0.4224	0.3855	0.3220	0.2697	0.2267
11	0.6162	0.5847	0.5268	0.4751	0.4289	0.3875	0.3505	0.2875	0.2366	0.1954
12	0.5897	0.5568	0.4970	0.4440	0.3971	0.3555	0.3186	0.2567	0.2076	0.1685
13	0.5643	0.5303	0.4688	0.4150	0.3677	0.3262	0.2897	0.2292	0.1821	0.1452
14	0.5100	0.5051	0.4423	0.3878	0.3405	0.2993	0.2633	0.2046	0.1597	0.1252
15	0.5167	0.4810	0.4173	0.3625	0.3152	0.2745	0.2394	0.1827	0.1401	0.1079
16	0.4945	0.4581	0.3937	0.3387	0.2919	0.2519	0.2176	0.1631	0.1229	0.0930
17	0.4732	0.4363	0.3714	0.3166	0.2703	0.2311	0.1978	0.1456	0.1078	0.0802
18	0.4528	0.4155	0.3503	0.2959	0.2503	0.2120	0.1799	0.1300	0.0946	0.0691
19	0.4333	0.3957	0.3305	0.2765	0.2317	0.1945	0.1635	0.1161	0.0830	0.0596
20	0.4146	0.3769	0.3118	0.2584	0.2146	0.1784	0.1486	0.1037	0.0728	0.0514

*The sum of the first four entries in the 10 percent interest column. Why?

Once the IRR has been calculated for all competing projects, select the project that has an IRR greater than or equal to the company's cost of capital.

Benefit-Cost Ratio

For very large projects, one way to reach an accept/reject decision is to calculate the BCR.

$$BCR = \frac{\text{Value of benefits of the project}}{\text{Costs of the project}}$$

Both benefits and costs are stated in constant-year dollars.

Implicit in such an analysis is that a wide variety of costs and benefits can be calculated. Ordinarily, calculating costs is much more straightforward than calculating benefits. As a minimum, a sophisticated economics staff is required to calculate benefits and costs. Which benefits and costs can be included is often stated in law or policy.

After the BCR for the project in question is calculated, the project is accepted based on whether the BCR exceeds a certain value fixed by policy. Seldom is a project with a BCR lower than 1.0 undertaken.[5]

Preparing Financial Analyses

As noted in the descriptions of the cost-justification tools, there is considerable room for interpretation in obtaining or calculating costs, benefits, inflows, and incomes, compounded by the fact that the data are often incomplete. Because so much judgment is involved, you need to control the process carefully. If the calculations are done by an accountant or budget department analyst, then you must be prepared to live with the results. The issue is not one of honesty; it is one of balanced judgment. For example, carpet *can* last twelve to fifteen years, but my experience is that tolerance for it wears out after six years. No matter which analytical tool you use, the results will be dramatically different when six rather than twelve years is estimated for new carpet.

In their enthusiasm to purchase a new product, some facility managers rely on the vendor to furnish economic justification or perform the analysis in the company's format. This is frequently done to justify the higher initial cost of carpet tile over broadloom, for example. But there are a couple of risks to that action. First, it may not be possible to support those numbers to management when they are challenged. Second, the calculations might not be supportable at a specific location and situation.

Chargebacks

Charging business units for facility services is widely accepted in both the private and the public sectors. In a 1996 survey, 57 percent of all respondents reported some type of expense chargeback system in use for their services.[6] There are three systems in place for administering the chargeback system.

1. Charge the actual cost of services plus perhaps an overhead charge.
2. Charge an allocation based on factors like space occupied or the number of employees.
3. A combination of the first two systems.

The rationale for chargeback is the belief that if line managers have to pay the cost of facility services, they will be more cost conscious. But often the allocation rules are so bizarre, the chargebacks are so removed from normal operations, and so much time is spent on internally administrating chargebacks that many are questioning their value.

Because chargebacks are rapidly expanding, it is discouraging that the process is not being implemented well. Two methods seem to be most successful and are best practices. In the first, common facility services are contained in a *base rent*, which is calculated using gross square feet occupied. Services over and above the base package are charged at actual cost plus a markup for overhead. In the second method, the facility department develops a detailed model for all space and all services, and organizations are charged according to their impact on facility costs. Alan D. Wilson developed an excellent example of such a model for allocating costs at the Thomas J. Watson Research Center of IBM.[7] No matter which method is used, it is important for facility managers to determine the actual costs of every service that they provide (normally different for owned and leased space) and to understand their overhead cost structure and keep it updated at least quarterly. My experience is that facility managers have never really calculated their costs of doing business by service, to the extent needed for good chargebacks. This is relatively easy to do with modern automated systems provided that budget categories are set up in a way to provide the cost information readily.

If a company chooses to use chargebacks, it should use them properly and as a management tool. Otherwise they simply are a nonproductive administrative burden.

Tax Considerations

In the United States, the Congress has used depreciation and tax law as incentives to businesses to invest in depreciable property. All facility managers need to understand depreciation and its effect on the company and on their department. Facility departments tend to be the managers of the majority of depreciable assets for the company. As a minimum, the facility manager should understand the basis for each asset class managed, depreciation methods applicable to each class, when property was put in service and its appreciable life, and the difference between appreciable and nondepreciable property. Because there are value judgments and tax court precedents in many of these areas, the facility manager should not place himself in the role of rule maker for depreciation. He should seek the counsel of the legal and finance departments. Once the rules are set, he should follow them scrupulously. There are consultants, normally called tax engineers, who will assess property and recommend construction procedures to allow achievement of a more favorable tax status for buildings.

Notes

1. Jerry J. Weygandt, Donald E. Kieso, and Walter G. Kell, *Accounting Principles* (New York: Wiley, 1987), p. 504. Copyright 1987 John Wiley & Sons, Inc. Reprinted by permission of John Wiley & Sons, Inc.

2. Personal phone call to Bureau of Economic Analysis, Department of Commerce, May 20, 1997.

3. William Agnello, "Capital Budgeting," Occasional paper presented at IFMA meeting, Houston, 1986.

4. Ibid.

5. "Cost Justification Tools for Managers," seminar notes prepared by the Minneapolis/St. Paul Chapter, IFMA, March 5, 1986, pp. iii–1.

6. *Research Report 16* (Houston: International Facility Management Association, 1996), p. 22.

7. Alan D. Wilson, *Proceedings, IFMA Best Practices Forum, February 22–23, 1995* (Houston: International Facility Management Association, 1995), pp. 193–211.

6

Space Planning and Management

Pulse Points

- *Management must have a space strategy that supports the organization's objectives and reflects its culture.*
- *Good space planning proceeds from a good business plan.*
- *Space use must be managed.*
- *Space standards are needed for good space management.*
- *Ownership of space should be established, or you will never be able to manage it.*
- *The space inventory should be managed by function, organization, and architectural use.*
- *Space planning and management are important but are not the totality of facility management.*

According to Stephen Binder, vice president of facility planning for Citibank, space is the frontier of facilities management.[1] Each facility manager is responsible for at least one facility with definite dimensions within which at least one productive activity takes place. The physical dimensions of a facility (the space) is the special context within which the manager executes his responsibilities. Therefore, the forecasting, planning, allocation, and management of space are important components of the facility manager's degree of success.

Planning in this context usually relates to growth, or the need for more space. Space growth has at least four potential components. First, there is growth in the industry or field—for example, retirement facilities are growing in size. Company growth, the second component, often reflects growth in the field but occurs on a schedule that might be different from industry growth—for example, a company in a growing field that has made a technological breakthrough. Third, internal programs or social trends (flextime, work at home) can result in employee growth different from the company's growth. Fourth, an organization's desire to accommodate individual needs translates into increased space needs. The complexity

89

of these issues and the nonsequential nature of the requirements complicate the forecasting of space requirements and highlight the need for a good forecasting method.

Forecasting is predicting something as a result of rational study and analysis of pertinent data. It is the link between planning and programming. Space forecasting involves both identifying new space requirements and projecting the need for reallocation or disposal of unneeded space. This is the method most applicable to large international companies; it doesn't really exist in small companies.

Methods of Forecasting Space Needs

A company must have a space strategy that frames the way it handles space needs. This strategy should both support the business objectives of the company and reflect the culture of the organization. There are two basic strategies possible:

1. Occupy owned space, which permits maximum control
2. Occupy leased space, which permits maximum flexibility

Most companies operate somewhere between these two extremes, with substrategies such as overleasing or overbuilding in order to have space for future growth. I am often asked whether it is best to own or lease space. In fact, there is no right answer because the situation depends on the company. In almost all cases, a mix is desirable, determined by whether control or flexibility is more important. We discuss this matter further in Chapter 7.

Because the cost of space is so great, a company's strategy must be clear. For example, shortly after deregulation of the telecommunications industry, an employee of one of the emerging long-distance companies was sent on the road to rent space for business centers in every U.S. city with a population greater than 500,000, plus certain other selected cities. After over six months of site selection and negotiation, he returned to his headquarters, where he was told to cancel most of those leases because the new strategy was to operate through nine regional centers. Many leases were canceled at substantial financial cost because the company's strategy for space forecasting was not well developed before taking action. One objective of downsizing was to free up expensive space for disposal.

Once the company's space strategy is clear, there are two principal ways to forecast space needs. The first is to have space needs be an output of the business planning of the company. In the long run, this method is the only acceptable one. But if the company does not have an adequate business planning process, then space forecasting must be done periodically, using some survey technique. For either situation, you must have analytic tools in order to analyze the projected needs against the current inventory.

Macrolevel space forecasts are company- or corporate-wide forecasts (e.g., a new plant in Madrid, the expansion of a regional headquarters in Denver, or the closing of an R&D lab). These are best derived from the company's business plan and must be done with enough time to implement buy or lease decisions. Since the facility manager identifies the major space needs, a strategic or midrange facility plan almost ensures that this macrolevel space forecasting is accomplished adequately. However, on at least two occasions that I know about, midsize companies that had no midrange facility plan used a survey of top executives followed up by in-depth interviews to forecast their major space needs. These executives had an amazingly realistic and accurate view of their organization's space needs. A side benefit was that the interviews helped gather political support for upcoming changes. Having said that, I cannot overemphasize the importance of having space planning flow from facility business planning.

Facility managers tend to arrive at space forecasts by expedient estimating techniques. In practice, standard allocations (square feet per staff) are multiplied by the appropriate unit (number of staff) to produce a planning figure. The more details you know about the prospective occupants, the more accurate the macrolevel estimate can be. The Department of Defense has excellent tools for macrolevel forecasting. Each facility category has a category code; each category code has a space standard. Once these data are automated, the facility planner can determine whether a particular location can accommodate a particular unit, or whether more or less space is needed at a specific location. "Best-fit" exercises can easily be run. Crucial to success, however, are agreed-on standards that allow projections to be made quickly and accurately. In almost all cases, the feasibility portion is completed and the options narrowed purely on a space-available versus space-needs basis.

A trend I see emerging is that companies are basing fewer decisions on the initial cost of space. The American Society for Testing and Materials (ASTM) standard on serviceability will allow proposed new space for its ability to meet business needs. This approach, comparing the characteristics of a facility to the needs of an organization, is a step beyond macrolevel forecasting and, when it is developed, will permit more knowledgeable buy-lease decisions.

Often a location is not "saleable" within the company, even though the facility department might think it suitable or even desirable. Preparing a forecast for a suburban headquarters when only an urban location is politically feasible is a waste of time and effort. Location is not truly a space issue, but it does create a context for space forecasts. In a similar manner, preparing a forecast for a location where rental costs are beyond what the company will tolerate is unwise. While costing moves you into the area of budgeting, a prudent space forecast requires that costs be kept in the ballpark.

Although the entire subject of space forecasting is replete with policy implications, several issues stand out. For example, the organization needs to decide how to handle *swing space*—the space available to house units during renovation, alterations, and realignments—and *growth space*—space contiguous to operational units to allow for their planned growth. In some organizations, growth space is released to the unit manager; in others, the facility manager controls the space and releases it periodically.

It is my experience that annual swing space required is 2 to 3 percent in large organizations and 5 to 7 percent in small organizations. Growth space should be based on planned growth. A work unit—departmental or higher—should be provided three to five years' growth space. If the rate of growth is unknown but the organization is growing, as a general rule, give units 10 percent excess for growth upon relocation or renovation. If the extra space is properly managed, it is almost always more economical to provide for growth up front. When using these simple rules, however, do not forget that such growth is compounded (i.e., 121 percent at the end of two years, not 120 percent). In very large companies, compounded growth is significant.

Growth is also compounded in patterns of communication and interfacing. Whenever more employees are added to an activity, each potential interface also multiplies. For example, if an activity requires networking among twenty employees, the addition of a single employee changes the potential number of interfaces from 400 to 441, or a factor of 10 percent. A highly dynamic department may experience a growth rate of 30 to 50 percent per year. In that situation, the twenty-person activity would grow at least to twenty-six and increase the complexity of communication possibilities by a factor of 69 percent. (These figures do not take into account the potential that each new employee may also interface with individuals in other activity units.)

Space is not the only commodity that grows when a company is expanding. Activities that occur within that space, and must be planned for, grow also, but at differing rates. Some activities seem to grow phenomenally fast; others, more slowly. Whenever there are highly dynamic activities, there is usually a high churn rate. The emerging pattern ultimately usurps space designed for other activities and concurrently reduces the productivity of those activities. Whenever a significant imbalance might occur, you must anticipate expansion needs for the most dynamic activity, even at the expense of nondesignated space or a poor initial employee-to-space utilization ratio.

Some activities carry weighted factors in their growth. For example, activities that require exceptional support furniture or equipment for each employee require larger amounts of expansion potential, even when growing at the same rate as other activities.

Flexibility is different from growth. Growth requires additional space; flexibility requires that each space be constructed so as to permit and support a variety of different activities effectively, with minimal loss of productivity for any specific activity. Flexibility may include provision for intermediate stages of activity growth; an example is when a dynamic activity requires additional space contiguous to its current occupied space, and moving the entire activity to a more desirable location is planned for the distant future. The activity would grow into the flexible space and utilize that space until the move occurred; then it would relinquish the flexible space to some other prioritized activity. The 1990s have accentuated the need for flexible space planning. Companies and agencies radically changed the way they work, and who has a need for space.

Many of these considerations are difficult to quantify, though experienced facility managers know they exist. That's why in a growth environment you should err on the side of a high forecast if there is a judgment to be made.

Programming Your Space Requirements

Programming is the analysis of a specific function that contributes to the improved execution of that function. According to William Pena, who is a leading facility programmer, in essence it is "the problem-seeking process that precedes problem-solving."[2] It varies from forecasting in that programming is focused on a particular problem.

Programming and design are distinct functions. Good programming must precede good design.

At least initially, the program is an unconstrained statement of space requirements. (The constraints are added during the budget process.) I have already mentioned that it is unwise to develop a space program that is not affordable, or politically saleable, or at the wrong location.

Space programming is applicable only to companies that have large space needs and holdings. When I speak of macrolevel space programming, I mean programming of whole facilities, or even complexes or locations. For small companies, this programming is done normally at the project level. Customarily there are several steps.

Establishing Goals

Perhaps the most important step of the space programming process is to determine the goal—what is to be accomplished. It is also important that the reason for the goal is understood, even if not stated. A possible goal statement might be: "We desire to acquire sufficient production and administrative space in Spain to meet our European production needs through the year 2005."

A clearly stated goal frames the space programming process. Therefore, it is important that the goal be developed with and approved by the applicable line managers and by top management.

In hindsight, it is obvious that some companies, anxious to imprint their corporate image on facilities, trapped themselves into buildings that no one really wanted after downsizing made them expendable.

Gathering Facts and Input

In some ways, gathering facts is the easiest part of the programming process. Two major facts can be obtained by answering these questions: What is desired? and When is it needed? The former is normally quantifiable; the latter can be tough to ascertain unless there is an existing plan or forecast. Other important facts are gained by answering other pertinent questions: What people and functions must be accommodated? When will the space become available and at what price? When is occupancy available? Throughout, consider how your facts are to be analyzed, coordinated with concepts, and compiled to produce a well-rounded, well-stated requirement.

Gathering input for the space program is similar to that required for the space forecast. As with the forecast, the quality of program will be much higher if it flows from the business plan. Also, the facility manager can determine needs much more quickly if the company has already set standards. If a survey technique must be used, he should place emphasis on input from line managers and workers.

Developing Basic Concepts and Determining Needs

How a company wants to operate at a particular location will influence the amount, cost, and quality of space required. Will robotics alter substantially the space requirement for a new manufacturing plant? If an office building is involved, will it be planned to utilize open-space planning? What are the administration and logistics schema?

Using goals, facts, and concepts, the facility manager can produce a comprehensive needs statement. He can determine how much space of what quality is required, where, and by when. When determining needs he should look at scenarios so that he has considered what's needed in a negative future as well as an upside scenario.

Presenting the Program

Before an ambitious space program is presented, the facility manager of a rapidly growing company must be sure that he either has in hand or has programmed for adequate resources to turn the programmed space into usable space. Increases in facility staff tend to trail the expansion in a company. And failure to manage facility growth properly can be a major problem, seriously damaging your credibility.

The result of space programming should outline the clearly defined space requirements, measured against the available resources. The facility manager needs to assess the cost of the space, the time to obtain the space, and the quality of the space obtained. Thus, through programming, the space forecast is converted to specific requirements, to which costs can be assigned.

Space Accounting and Management

This chapter has already stressed the importance of space forecasting and programming. But in many instances the space problems are not a matter of forecasting so much as management of existing space. Part of the problem is that space is not well accounted for.

Accounting for space depends on good definitions. Although there is an ASTM standard definition, it is not as widely used as it should be.

Facility management will never be successful unless it is clear who controls the space. There are basically two possibilities: ownership by the line manager or ownership by the facility department. The extensive use of chargebacks strengthens the concept of line management's responsibility for its space.

When line managers own the space, the company holds that manager responsible, and charging back for space can be an effective control mechanism. The downside of this approach is that the facility manager has little or no control over the asset that most determines how he is viewed and evaluated.

When the facility manager controls the space, the common good is best served. The facility manager can adjudicate space disputes and assign space to the extent of his political clout. The disadvantage is that line units, as "renters," feel less responsible for the care and appearance of the facilities.

Some organizations have worked out a compromise. The approach I favor has space accounting the responsibility of the facility manager, who also recommends space standards as company policy. When business purposes or other reasons necessitate assignment or reallocation of space, the facility manager, as the technical expert, plans the action and "sells" it to the line managers involved. If that is impossible, the dispute is adjudicated one management level above the facility manager, as are exceptions to space standards.

Space Planning for Management Accountability

There are certain procedures related to management accountability of all space owned or leased. The first step to ensure proper management accountability is to obtain floor plans that reflect the current structure. Some method of differentiating among departments is advisable; shading is one method to accomplish this. In addition, core and common areas can be treated as company overhead or allocated to departments by predetermined rules. Operational costs of support areas can then be charged back to individual departments as a percentage of employee utilization to total employee base, or as a percentage of departmental space to total space. Unless departments are about the same size (in space and employees), do not suggest an equal division of operational costs among departments.

The second step is to seek departmental approval of the space for which each is accountable. Official drawings, sometimes called *key plans,* can indicate occupancy by each department. Some companies require that departmental managers sign off in agreement that they are actually using the space for which they are accountable. Any subsequent changes in departmental utilization must be reflected in an updated key plan. All circulation space is normally charged back to a specific department for purposes of accounting. Unassigned or unassignable space is either carried by the facility department or allocated to user departments on a pro rata basis.

A facility manager of a large company usually has blocs of unoccupied space that must be charged to some account in order to satisfy 100 percent of operating costs. At the same time, that space must be controlled, or it will disappear. Large blocks of unused space should be controlled, even to the point of locking them up. Small blocks should be assigned to local managers for growth space, if possible, before going under central control. If all space is charged back, all departments will have to share in costs for unallocated space, just as they do for unassignable space.

Proper allocation of space is important because facility expenses are often apportioned according to space allocation. Inequitable allocation among departments may be deliberate or an obvious error by the facility manager. Regardless, it is a fiscal and political problem. Allocation is an extremely complex process that requires excellent cost accounting, a good allocation process, and constant reevaluation. For an example of an excellent but extremely complex space allocation system see Alan D. Wilson's description of his best practice at IBM's Watson Research Center.[3]

Space Management Planning

There are basic planning elements that contribute to the facility manager's ability to manage space effectively within existing parameters and to forecast efficient utilization. The basic considerations are:

1. The amount of space available and the time frame for the availability.
2. The type of space available and the general condition and limitations of the architecture or construction.
3. Configurations of the space (dimensions, square footage, volume, shape and/or location).
4. Utilization of the space, including specific activities and necessary support functions. The utilization section discusses techniques of organizational analysis and adequate adjacencies.

How much space. Perhaps the least difficult of all considerations is that of how much space is needed. There are only two alternatives: Either there is existing space to which the scope of activities must conform, or the scope of activities will dictate the type, configuration, and utilization of a space yet defined. Allocating space to work units on a gross basis is extremely dangerous, whereas using gross space for companywide allocations can be quite acceptable.

Type of space. The utilization of space dictates the alterations, construction, and renovations necessary to existing conditions. Extensive demolition and new construction may be required to accommodate the specified utilization criteria, or alterations may suffice. In almost every situation where construction and renovation of existing facilities is compared with new construction, the costs of renovation are less.

There may be hidden liabilities to the renovation. For example, renovations may require relocation of employees, expose employees to dust and airborne contaminants, or cause excessive noise and distractions. Renovation projects usually include major compromises on efficient arrangements of activities or employees (adjacencies), and frequently offer fewer alternatives or less flexibility than new construction. The age of a structure may require that structural elements and the roof be evaluated carefully. Often the power supply and telecommunication support are inadequate and inefficient as well.

Configuration of space. Without launching the actual design process, the facility manager must often determine that certain space is more appropriate for one department than for another. Existing structures usually conform to a normative sizing according to the time when the structure was built and its location; that affects the space available for allocation. For example, ceiling heights have changed from higher to lower in recent years. Column placements are getting wider, and columns are growing large again. Many modern designs are based on an assumption of infinite open areas, and they suffer greatly when applied to older buildings. While there may be a certain charm in dealing with older structures, that charm may not be a suitable substitute for organizational needs.

New office planning concepts introduced in the early 1980s provided for increased functional density of workers in an open environment. By the mid-1980s, many departments downsized to individual workstations. And, according to the Steelcase Office Environment Index, there was a tendency toward larger individual workstations by the end of the decade.[4] Many older office buildings have construction features that will not facilitate larger workstations, especially closely spaced columns.

Changes in the workforce and the way that we work in the 1990s affect not only how we plan and program for space but how we provide workplaces themselves. Alternative office solutions have become so prevalent that lines of furniture and equipment have been designed solely to meet those needs. Many authors have characterized these new standard and alternative workplace solutions, but my favorite is Jon Ryburg's because he lists best practices:[5]

- Home-based and shared offices
- Just-in-time spaces
- Free address
- Flexspace
- Shared/assigned space
- Floating office

Other employees are working from home or in satellite offices, and those who are working in a central location are more often doing so in a team mode. The programming and planning response to each of these alternatives is different and puts an unprecedented emphasis on space planning, programming, and management. Also, due to outsourcing and downsizing, many facility managers are becoming much more expert in consolidating space and planning for space disposal.

Obviously, the utilization criteria determine how efficiently a specific activity may be accomplished within a given space. Some sizes, shapes, or volumes of space lend themselves to certain kinds of activities. In general, the more dynamic an organization, the more important is flexibility; thus, large expanses of uninterrupted space are preferred. Existing architectural and design features prove most appropriate for companies with a less dynamic character. Older structures usually exhibit the least favorable square-foot occupancy ratios.

Locations of activities within specific spaces are important for greater productivity. Many times adjacencies may not be available on the same floor. Under those circumstances, you must determine whether connectivity with another floor in the same building is appropriate, or if the same floor in an adjacent building is better.

Utilization of space. Several techniques can be applied to specific activities programmed into a space. Sophisticated space planning systems are now accomplished by computer. In fact, computers have been instrumental in applying programming techniques to unaffected space without resorting to the "intuitive" process that Jean Cousin, a leading thinker in space planning, alludes to in his book.[6] Cousin refers to a "topological" approach for special organizations. *Topology* is primarily a mathematical term but relates to special organization in the sense of statistical relativity. Cousin thinks that we will ultimately arrive at a time when it will be possible to program activities and requirements into a computer, and the computer will arrange the activities within a special context effectively and efficiently. Cousin concedes that technology has not arrived at that point yet. It is interesting, however, that visionaries have been considering the possibility since the 1970s.[7]

There is no lack of literature on theoretical approaches to space planning. Several authors come to mind. Richard Muther offers a recipe for layout planning. He provides forms that can be used to gather data on flow of materials, activity relationships, and space relationships. Muther refers to his process as Systematic Layout Planning, and applies it also to the white-collar workplace, even though much of his book deals with manufacturing facility.[8]

A third method for utilizing space is proposed by Roger Brauer, in his book *Facilities Planning.* Brauer's primary agenda is to define and manage "user requirements," offering programming techniques that prioritize individuals performing activities within a space. Conformities of space and construction are an extension of user needs, according to Brauer. His book also provides standard forms and examples of matrix development activities.[9]

Space planners Michael Saphier and Lila Shoshkes orient their thoughts toward equipment and the special displacement requirements of office workers. Their space planner model involves interviewing each employee and identifying the furniture support items. By the simple process of inventory application and activity adjacency, a place is found for all items—thus space is planned.[10] The space planner is likely to place less importance on overall productivity than is the facility manager utilizing either the Muther or Brauer models.

Other Planning Considerations

Universal planning is the response by Gensler & Associates, a giant among interior design firms, to the high costs of relocation in response to churn. Most conventional planning responses consider furniture configuration and communications matrices in relation to employee needs. The universal planning concept provides for a percentage of effectiveness (or ineffectiveness) by placing furniture permanently and moving employees.[11]

Universal planning provides an apparent savings in relocation expenses when there are high churn rates. There may be few overall advantages, however, when employee productivity figures are included in a long-term model or when strong communications links are essential. It is also likely that there will be some employee resistance, owing to the impersonal nature of the process.

I have always emphasized the need for flexibility in space planning. Flexibility, universality of design, and an allowance for growth can materially reduce the nearly constant renovation of space caused by churn in most modern corporations. In addition, most companies need to optimize their modern communications technology, for which they have paid a premium, to reduce the price of churn. Fellow workers no longer need to be seated contiguously for good internal communications.

Prioritizing the Space

Space is prioritized only when there is an intrinsic value to the space. Status is sometimes implied in a space or is seen so in its relationship to other space. Many times proximity to top management receives high priority. Value is often placed on nearness of windows, or panoramic vistas, or closeness to the top of a building. Mostly you will have little to do with the valuing process, although you can help establish policies that may determine the priority of activities taking place within the space.

Be aware that most middle managers who identify their responsibility with a specific activity will be on constant vigil to protect and expand their area. There is constant debate concerning the value of certain activities and their existing resources.

Space Accounting Systems and Inventories

I once noted that my organization's space for office workers seemed to be disappearing. Since our organization was already rapidly growing, the space loss (estimated at 6 percent of the inventory annually) soon became a matter of great concern. We confirmed that the company's space needed to be managed and that good space management depended on good space accounting. The specific problem was an overload of paper storage—in a supposedly "paperless" office with a computer on every desk. The local paper storage ate up office space. The solution was to implement a space accounting system. This system defines all space, assigns it to a responsible manager, and carefully tracks additions, deletions, and conversions. I recommend three different space accounting systems. In all but the largest companies, you can account for the three systems both by building and in the aggregate.

The first system accounts for space for architectural and design purposes. The best categories are based on area measurement terms, which are most valuable to the design team.

The second system is based on functional categories (e.g., warehousing, shops, office space). The size of holdings obviously dictates the degree of detail to which category codes are assigned and the space is accounted. International organizations may have eighty to a hundred category codes, a corporate head-quarters eight to ten.

The third system accounts for space by occupant (user). Some facility managers prefer to account by occupant and category code. This system has broad application but is the information most often shared with users.

The facility space inventory should be reviewed annually. For inventories under 10 million square feet, I favor a formal review twice a year: once at annual planning time and once six months later. The review should concentrate on trends, standards compliance, and equitableness between occupants. One question that might be asked, for example, is, Do we really want to devote 76,000 square feet of downtown office space to paper storage? Another might be, Are we really making the best use of our conference space?

In the last few years, a combination of technologies has produced true facility management systems. For years I was highly critical of many technology vendors who advertised space management systems as computer-assisted facility management (CAFM). Now, however, we truly have CAFM systems, and superb space management modules are part of that system. These systems are now computer based and affordable to all facility managers who manage over 100,000 square feet. Using bar coding, a relational database, a geographic information system, and a good computer-assisted design and drawing system, the manager of a large facility can manage workplace information that will make him a powerful player in the business. Space management systems now have capabilities and information that business managers need in their work. Facility managers should leverage that capability for a seat in the inner circle of their companies.

Once you have your system in place, each time you allocate or reallocate space, be sure to capture that information. Too often space management is hampered by an out-of-date inventory or is based on crash inventories. Keep your database current.

And just before the company planning cycle begins, I suggest producing a three- to five-year space plan. That plan should consist of a detailed move schema and revised space inventory for year 1. The year 1 components should have management concurrence prior to their use in the company annual business planning cycle. For small to medium companies, include a block diagram. Years 2 to 5 should be represented by revised space inventory projections and block diagrams, if appropriate.

Conclusion

A recent *Fortune* survey of facility executives concluded that many facility executives feel that their companies are doing a good job of optimizing the use of their space, and they have an intuitive feeling that the workplace is important to employee productivity. At the same time, they are more reticent in agreeing that there is a link between the physical environment and significant productivity gains.[12] Until facility managers develop better research, they will remain at a disadvantage in managing space as well as in proving their business worth to their companies.

Notes

1. Stephen Binder, *Corporate Facility Planning* (New York: McGraw-Hill, 1989).
2. Jo Heinz, "Space Planning/Programming and Building Analysis," *IFMA Conference Proceedings* (Houston: IFMA, 1988), p. 326.
3. Alan D. Wilson, "Distribution and Measurement of Laboratory and Office Space Costs," *IFMA Best Practices Proceedings, Winter 1995* (Houston: IFMA, 1995), pp. 193–211.
4. Louis Harris and Associates, *Office Environment Index, 1980* (Grand Rapids, Mich.: Steelcase, Inc., 1981).
5. Jon Ryburg, *Emerging Work Patterns: Best FM Practices* (Ann Arbor, Mich.: Facility Performance Group, 1995), pp. 16–19.
6. Jean Cousin, *Organisation topologique de l'espace architectural/Topological Organization of Architectural Space* (Montreal: University of Montreal Press, 1970), pp. 9–10.
7. Ibid., p. 10.
8. Richard Muther, *Systematic Layout Planning* (Boston: Cahners Books, 1974), pp. 1-1–2-8.
9. Roger L. Brauer, *Facilities Planning*, 2d ed. (New York: AMACOM, 1992), pp. 1–10.
10. Michael Saphier, *Office Planning and Design* (New York: McGraw-Hill, 1968), pp. 68–72, and Lila Shoshkes, *Space Planning* (New York: Architectural Record Books, 1976), pp. 44–48.
11. William Joseph, "The Need to Design for Change," *IFMA Conference Proceedings* (Houston: IFMA, 1988), pp. 7–22.
12. *Facilities and Real Estate Strategies* (New York: Fortune Marketing, 1996), pp. 3–4.

Section III

Real Estate

All facility managers are in the real estate business. As a minimum, the company leases its space. Some facility managers have full-blown real estate divisions or departments in their organizations.

In this section, I look at standard options for a growing organization: buying or leasing and at what site. Also, I look at the considerations of becoming a lessor. Since many facility managers have some property management responsibilities, I also discuss that function.

7

Real Estate Options

Pulse Points

- *The facility manager must coordinate the user, legal, and financial requirements for good purchase-lease decisions.*
- *The facility manager should actively participate in site evaluation and acquisition.*
- *The facility manager should have an active plan to manage the inevitable politics of site selection.*
- *The facility manager should learn as much as possible about any site to be acquired, but enter all negotiations knowing that he probably knows less than the current owner.*
- *When considering a real estate acquisition, the facility manager must also think about an exit strategy.*

The decision to purchase or lease real estate goes to the very heart of a company—its culture, investment strategy, and desire for control. It is important for decision makers to identify the opportunity costs for each option, in present value terms, but the final decision may just as likely be made for subjective reasons. Nevertheless, in this chapter I discuss the factors that go into this decision as they relate to facility management, including the consequent responsibility of site selection, should that be within the manager's realm.

Purchase or Lease?

Although there are two major applications of the lease versus purchase process—the acquisition of major properties and sites, or major equipment—this chapter deals with the lease or purchase of real estate. The lease versus purchase analysis is a capital budgeting analysis that compares the pertinent costs of each method on an equal basis. Most facility managers need help in making these decisions. Joseph Horowitz, the director of administration for CBS, Inc., discusses user requirements and provides a predecision checklist for real estate decisions.[1] In addition, building assessment is a fledgling technique that helps managers match an organization's needs to a proper building. For the financial aspects of this decision, there are accepted accounting principles regulated by the Financial Accounting Standards Board.[2] But to begin, let's look at the factors to be considered in the lease versus purchase question.

The Buy-Lease Analysis

In theory, the analysis is quite simple. The net present value (NPV) of the cash outflow associated with the lease option is compared to that for the buy option. The lesser value is the preferred option.

Most companies have a financial analyst or accounting firm capable of computing cash outlays and NPVs for each option. You'll need the following information:

- The company's cost of capital
- All lease terms having a financial impact, especially the lease payment
- The purchase price of the real estate or equipment plus any other financial terms related to the purchase
- The company's incremental cost of borrowing

Answers to the following questions must be obtained, compared, and analyzed to make an appropriate decision:

1. Has there been an appropriate in-house evaluation?
2. Has there been an independent evaluation?
3. Is the primary issue least-cost financing?
4. Is the purchase or lease decision to be treated as an independent project?
5. Is the lease to be considered a financial or an operating lease?
6. Have options been maximized?
7. Will the value of the property decline at least 75 percent over the term of the lease?
8. Have Internal Revenue Service (IRS) guidelines been checked?
9. Will the lessor absorb operating or maintenance charges?
10. Who will receive the investment tax credits?
11. How much equity is available from expendable property?
12. Will additional property be required to make this project operational?
13. What is the estimated productive life of the property?
14. What is the inflation trend?
15. What is the trend of interest rates?
16. Have state and federal legislative agenda been checked for pending legislation?
17. What are the additional expenses chargeable to this project?
18. What is the marginal tax rate?
19. If the real estate is purchased, how will the project be financed? (term and rate)

20. If the property is leased, how will the project be paid? (term, rate, options, and taxes)

Risk is a major criterion in a number of lease versus purchase decisions. Ideally, there should be no significant difference between the risk of owning and of leasing the same property. However, management's perception of the company's strengths and weaknesses, the economic climate, and governmental constraints may drive the decision.

Based on cash flow, each project should be evaluated independently. Items such as investment tax credits, other accrual items, return on assets, effect on working capital ratios, and effect on debt-equity ratios must be considered when analyzing a buy situation.

The asset will definitely become part of the business, but it must be determined how that will happen. Should the business pay rent, or should the business purchase the asset? There are benefits to both situations. Therefore, a financial analysis will be a present value comparison of cash flows resulting from purchasing an asset on the one hand or leasing the same asset on the other hand. The objective is to select the particular action that minimizes the present value of cash outflows.

The following information is required to perform a buy/lease analysis:

1. Purchase price of the asset
2. Other terms of the purchase option
3. Company's incremental borrowing rate
4. Lease payment
5. Other terms of the lease, including buyout costs, cancellation costs, and length
6. Company's cost of capital

A buy/lease analysis requires finding the cash outflows associated with the lease option, determining the cash outflows associated with the purchase option, and computing and then comparing the net present values of the cash flows. For an example, see Exhibit 7-1.[3]

Whether purchase or leasing is preferred varies also according to the investment capability and philosophy of the company. For instance, certain government agencies are regularly either owners or lessors. Manufacturing companies are more likely than service companies to choose ownership.

Advantages of Purchasing

Although it is seldom stated, most arguments for buying are emotional, political ones. Companies like the control inherent in purchasing, particularly real estate. For organizations that want to convey a high standard or a unique look, the purchase option greatly enhances that. In fact, the desire for control is so strong—

Exhibit 7-1. Buy versus lease.

Your company's lease is coming due next year and you need to decide whether you will remain at your current address and sign a new lease or move to a building that your company would then purchase. The cost of capital is 10 percent. The tax rate is 40 percent. The building would be depreciated using straight line with a $800,000 salvage value. Current IRS law requires a building to be depreciated 31½ years, but for purposes of this example, the building will be depreciated only 5 years.

Alternative A: Sign a five-year lease with annual lease payments of $700,000. Your company is currently in this building and will not need any major modifications to the building.

Alternative B: Purchase a building for $2,000,000 and spend another $600,000 in renovations for your company's needs.

Alternative A

Years	0	1	2	3	4	5
Lease payments	(700)	(700)	(700)	(700)	(700)	
Tax shield	280	280	280	280	280	
Net cash flow	(420)	(420)	(420)	(420)	(420)	
Discounted cash	(420)	(382)	(347)	(316)	(287)	
Cumulative	(420)	(802)	(1,149)	(1,465)	(1,752)	(1,752)

Alternative B

Years	0	1	2	3	4	5
Buy building	(2,000)					
Renovation cost	(600)					
Depreciation		(360)	(360)	(360)	(360)	(360)
tax shield		144	144	144	144	144
Salvage value						800
Net cash flow	(2,600)	144	144	144	144	944
Discounted cash	(2,600)	131	119	108	98	586
cumulative	(2,600)	(2,469)	(2,350)	(2,242)	(2,144)	(1,558)

Preferred Alternative: Alternative B. Your company should move into the new building and make the purchase.

Source: Heidi Lord Butler, notes from IFMA "Facility Accounting" seminar, Seattle, November 1989.

particularly in large, well-established companies or smaller companies greatly concerned about their image—that "doing the numbers" is often a waste of time.

Other advantages of purchasing are that property appreciates in value over its life; in fact, some view purchase as a good hedge against inflation. Also, life-cycle costs are normally less, property has a disposal value at the end of its use, property can be a source of later financing, and annual depreciation can be written off. Finally, expansion and alterations at an existing site can usually be accomplished more rapidly.

Advantages of Leasing

Leasing certainly has its advocates. For a young company, leasing its space may be the only real option. If a company cannot resource at least a minimal facility department, leasing may be the only solution. Even some major companies have policies that expansion, at least initially, is accomplished through leasing. Almost all companies lease some property for unexpected new requirements, to meet temporary needs, or for initial expansion. In the current business environment, companies use a balance of owned and leased space to provide them business flexibility.

The other advantages of leasing are the tax deductibility of lease payments, accelerated if not immediate delivery, the opportunity to have state-of-the-art buildings and less risk of obsolescence, a predictable cash flow during the initial term of the lease, the lack of a large initial capital outlay, and maintenance with the lease.

Perhaps the most negative characteristic of leases is the inability to predict and control costs. Even a tightly negotiated lease leaves option year costs contingent on some type of index. At renewal, the company can face substantial increased costs or the option of moving elsewhere.

Sale-Leaseback

A method that combines the features of real estate ownership and leasing is sale-leaseback. If applied correctly, this maximizes the value of the company's real estate assets by reducing occupancy costs while permitting the company to maintain long-term control.

In a sale-leaseback, the corporation sells one or more of its properties to a limited partnership and simultaneously leases back the real estate for long-term use. The typical transaction has three participants: the seller or lessee, the purchaser or lessor, and the lenders. Sale-leasebacks offer many benefits, including:[4]

- Raising funds for 100 percent of the property's value
- Long-term, fixed-rate capital
- Long-term control
- Off-balance-sheet treatment
- Earnings improvements
- Cash flow

The Negotiating Process

When negotiating a lease, an entirely different set of considerations must be made. The extent to which the lessee may be favorably accommodated is strongly affected by both financial considerations and other factors. For example:

• *Size of organization.* Large organizations always ask for and receive more favorable lease terms than smaller organizations. If your size or the nature of your organization makes you a prestigious tenant, strengthen your position during lease negotiation.

• *Stage of building construction.* During the early stages of building construction, a lessee can get the most favorable lease considerations.

• *Part of building occupied.* Generally the highest floors with the best views afford the fewest leasing concessions. Accepting lower-status space offers the greatest opportunity for other concessions.

• *Availability of space in the area.* In overbuilt cities (vacancy rates of 10 percent or more) leasing organizations are much more likely to be accommodating. In cities where the vacancy rate exceeds 15 percent, it is not uncommon to ask for and receive up to one-third of the term of the lease in free rent, in addition to special furnishings and other concessions. It is reasonably common for a lease to be written at "net zero" or just for the lessor's operating expenses under these conditions.

• *Term length.* Most leases for commercial spaces are for five or seven years. The facility manager in search of space should remember that lease terms may be written to accommodate the lessee, and different lengths may be better for the organization. A lease with a term of five years will leave the organization that is growing rapidly with a burden of inflexibility years before the lease expires. It might be better to negotiate an original lease of three years with options to absorb additional space at a fixed rate at the end of the three years. Options to expand into suitable space (which may afford, for example, a better view, more status, or greater accessibility to interfacing departments) are also possible.

• *Operating expenses.* Operating expenses and parking are issues of some importance and may also be negotiated according to the relative strength of the market, position of the lessor, and priorities of the lessee.

The advantage of a lease decision over purchase may depend greatly on specific negotiable items in the agreement. For instance, cash benefits may accrue to the lessee if terms require little or no down payment and balloon payments after one or more years. The organization is then able to apply 100 percent of its income to operating expenses and keep its cash flow liquid.

It is important to negotiate the proper kind of lease (e.g., operating, financial, maintenance, leveraged) and be certain that the IRS recognizes the agreement as a true lease, not a rental-purchase agreement. (The rental-purchase agreement is treated as ownership by the IRS.) It may be an advantage to ensure that the lease does not affect the debt-equity ratio of the organization, since the IRS requires that most bank loans have debt accounted against equity.

It may be advisable to negotiate a varying cash flow. For instance, balloon payments can be scheduled to coincide with cash-rich periods within the fiscal year and avoid periods of cash drought.

In negotiating, understand the position of the lessor. Often the lessor is willing to offer lower rates if he retains investment tax credits and rights to depreciation tax credits. A fluctuating taxable income may affect the lessor's willingness to grant advantageous fixed-rate terms, or he may be willing to offer variable-rate terms that are satisfactory.

Site Selection and Acquisition

Facility managers in companies that acquire and dispose of facilities routinely have a real estate division and financial, legal, architectural, and engineering experts well equipped to handle the acquisition and disposal of real estate. For most facility managers, however, site selection and acquisition can be the initial step on a major capital project that could be the highlight of their career. For that reason, it should be done with care, discretion, and prudent use of expertise to obtain the best deal for the best dollar on the schedule expected.

For the majority of facility managers, site selection and acquisition is so infrequent that it takes on a life of its own. There are always political aspects to site selection, for example. A common saying in the corporate world is that the headquarters relocation will always reduce the CEO's commute. It is not possible to eliminate politics totally, but you can take several steps to make site selection as objective as possible.

1. Establish a confidentiality policy and restrict access to those having a need to know, including administrative personnel.

2. Ensure that in-house personnel are objective and have broad-based knowledge of the company's requirements. Often a consultant is needed for focus and to do the legwork and analysis.

3. The criteria for selection must be credible and truly the most important factors. They must be developed within the corporation, and used to judge all sites. This is a substantial effort, and a consultant can be used here well.

4. The acquisition team should identify those individuals and groups who will be winners or losers in the various options or who will try to influence the decision. An internal relations campaign should be launched both to strengthen the voice of supporters and to minimize the detractors. Make sure everyone supports what the team decides because it is best for the company.

Given the importance of site selection, internal politics are inevitable. Fortunately in large firms, site selection is almost routine, thus less politically charged.[5]

Site Selection Team

The first task in selecting a site is to put together a team or committee to determine who the decision maker is and to set the criteria for selection. But if the decision is political, or if the chief executive officer (CEO) or chairman has predetermined the location, admit it up front and do not waste time on a search. That sounds simple, but when the matter isn't viewed realistically, there's often much wasted time and energy.

In either case, prepare detailed cost comparisons for all sites or locations. Be sure that no single individual or department analyzes all the information, so that you obtain an adequate range of options and negate personal bias. It may be the final responsibility of one individual or department to propose the site or property; however, the team should offer its combined expertise.

Whether the team is all in-house personnel or includes an outside consultant depends on your personnel and their familiarity with the local market. A consultant is often used because most companies acquire sites so seldom that the staff cannot provide adequate advice, and large companies that operate internationally are not versed in local market conditions.

The consultant to use is a matter of personal preference. A new type of consultant—the relocation adviser—has emerged in all major U.S. cities to provide a technical and fee alternative to brokers. But your relationship with the consultant is more important than the type of consultant hired, particularly since brokers' fees can be negotiated. Also, it is not unusual for a company to augment the site selection team with an architect, a builder, legal counsel, and a financial analyst.

Decision Making

The factors or decision matrix used to organize the decision making may be simple or complex. Typical factors are given in Exhibit 7-2. However, each acquisition is unique and depends on the type of facility to be located and the work to be performed there. The more sophisticated decision models weigh factors according to their predetermined importance.

Undoubtedly cost is a factor in site selection, so the cost factors must be quantified. Typical cost factors are presented in Exhibit 7-3. Most facility managers prefer a rule of thumb approach to solving problems whenever possible. But facility managers with strong mathematical backgrounds might prefer to use mathematical modeling. *Facilities Locations, Models and Methods,* by Robert F. Love, James G. Morris, and George O. Wesolosky, discusses mathematical modeling for facility location.

The list of sites to be considered can be generated by the consultant, based on confidential general criteria set by the company. If no consultant is used, ascertain site availability from in-house data or a local guide to locations, available in most localities without charge and without unnecessarily exciting the real estate market.

The site search and evaluation should be as confidential as possible, but relocation searches are about as hush-hush as the Super Bowl and often take on characteristics of that event. Despite these limiting aspects of the process, the company and the facility manager must ensure that the final decision is credible, transparent, equitable, and comprehensive.

Acquisition

The line between site selection and acquisition is a fuzzy one. The acquisition process starts when the requirements and criteria for the site have been devel-

Exhibit 7-2. Major factors in location searches.

Access to Markets/Distribution Centers
    Cost of serving markets
    Trends in sales by areas
    Ability to penetrate local market by plant presence

Access to Supplies/Resources
    Cost of transporting supplies
    Trends in supplier by area

Community/Government Aspects
    Ambience
    Cost of living
    Cooperation with established local industry
    Community pride (appearance, activity, citizen views)
    Housing (availability, pricing)
    Schools, cultural and recreation programs
    Colleges, graduate programs
    Churches, civic groups

Competitive Considerations
    Location of competitors
    Likely reaction to this new site

Environmental Considerations

Interaction With the Remainder of the Corporation
    Is this supposed to be a satellite plant?
    Supplied by or supplier to other company plants?
    Extent of engineering/management assistance from headquarters

Labor
    Prevailing wage rates
    Extent and militancy of unions in the area
    Productivity
    Availability
    Skill levels available

Site Itself
    Area of site—layout of structure
    Price of site structures
    Construction/remodeling costs—insurance
    Condition

Taxes and Financing
    State income tax
    Local property and income taxes
    Unemployment and workman's compensation premiums
    Tax incentive/concessions
    Industrial/pollution control revenue bonds

(continues)

Exhibit 7-2. (continued)

Transportation
  Trucking services
  Rail services
  Air freight services
Utilities/Services
  Availability, quality, price of water, sewage, electric, and natural gas services
  Quality of roads, police, fire, medical, and similar services

Source: Bruce N. Wardrep, "Factors Which Play Major Roles in Location Decision," in McKinley Conway and Linda L. Liston, eds., *Facility Planning Technology* (Norcross, Ga.: Conway Data, 1987), p. 322.

oped. Acquisition without a real estate professional, particularly one familiar with the local area and its political jurisdiction, is not recommended. If a real estate professional is not on staff, then hire a consultant because acquisition can be a snake pit without one. The seller will always know the property better than you. Consequently, try to learn as much about the site as possible. Don't overlook critical sources of information. Exhibit 7-4 is a listing of possible sources. The time spent finding this information translates into a firmer position during acquisition and can help avoid embarrassment.

If time and finances permit, use a team composed of yourself; an operations person; structural, mechanical, and electrical engineers; a communications specialist; and a security, fire, and life safety expert to prepare a property assessment. This assessment will focus on hard costs for the final acquisition decision and highlight factors that might block acquisition.

One of the best practical discussions of real estate strategies is the HOK consulting report, *Exit Strategies.* An exit strategy is a methodology for explicitly ad-

Exhibit 7-3. Quantifiable location factors.

Site and preparation costs
Construction (renovation) costs
Equipment costs
Labor and fringe benefit costs
Start-up costs (e.g., training)
Working capital requirements (e.g., inventories)
Freight (in and/or out) expense
Property taxes
Workman's compensation premiums
Unemployment compensation premiums
Relocation expenses
Revenue forecast

Source: Bruce N. Wardrep, "Factors Which Play Major Roles in Location Decision," in McKinley Conway and Linda L. Liston, eds., *Facility Planning Technology* (Norcross, Ga.: Conway Data, 1987), p. 322.

Exhibit 7-4. Sources of site information.

Federal and State Agencies
    U.S. Geological Survey maps
    Army Corps of Engineers' or state floodplain studies
    Soil conservation maps
    Regional land planning studies
    Environmental protection requirements

City and County Authorities
    City and county records
    Zoning ordinances and maps
    Property tax assessment records
    Planning abstracts or surveys

Documents of Public Record
    Mortgage history
    Liens or other financial encumbrances
    Long-term leases
    Easements, covenants, equitable servitudes
    Reversionary and remainder interests, rights of entry, power of termination (rare)

Other Local Informational Sources
    Previous or comparable sales
    Accessibility consideration; rights-of-way and availability of required modes of transportation

Site-Specific Data
    Building permits
    Building blueprints and specifications

Interviews
    Planning consultants or other counselors
    Real estate appraisers
    Economic development agencies
    Present and prior owner

Source: Bruce N. Wardrep, "Factors Which Play Major Roles in Location Decision," in McKinley Conway and Linda L. Liston, eds., *Facility Planning Technology* (Norcross, Ga.: Conway Data, 1987), p. 322.

dressing factors that affect real estate risk and for accommodating the many changes that confront facility managers every day. Here are some of the considerations for exit strategies:[6]

- You have fewer options when downsizing. Downsizing companies should concentrate on leasing versus buying.
- A rapidly growing company should refrain from owning real estate until it has the cash that can be diverted to building ownership. Once cash is committed to bricks and mortar, it becomes nonliquid.
- High-volatility companies need to spend the most time in planning their real estate strategy and any individual real estate action.

- Alternative work strategies may assist or alleviate the impacts of exit strategies. Some of these alternative work strategies have implementation costs.
- The facility manager can provide the most value by giving good advice on controllable risk. A market-based partner may help in reaching good decisions.
- Before building or leasing, particularly the former, evaluate the market attractiveness for future sale, lease, or sublease. This is particularly important when considering building or renovating unique facilities with substantial mechanical or electrical infrastructure. Single-purpose facilities can be very difficult to dispose of.
- International acquisitions emphasize the need for thoughtful exit strategies.
- We can't always change our mind later; our decisions to build are, in fact, cast in stone.
- Orderly acquisition and disposition tends to be the most cost-effective.
- When negotiating a lease, ask for all of the rights that you can get that won't cost anything to obtain.
- Early lease renewals can result in more favorable rates.
- Facility managers should prepare multiple scenarios for business units so that their managers can choose among options. Never underestimate the time for decision making. Cost estimates need to consider both this deliberation time and that, once a decision is made, implementation will take time, particularly if leases have not expired.
- Never neglect the impact of business interruption.
- Downsizing often frees up small pockets of space. That space often can't be marketed until consolidated. There is a cost to that consolidation.
- Make sure that costs for an acquisition are in line with other speculative space in the area.
- Don't tailor the building for one tenant; plan it so that it can be used by multiple tenants.

The company counsel and a real estate professional can guide you around the potential pitfalls in negotiating the sale and closure. With their guidance approach the acquisition with three rules in mind:

1. Create the time envelope for the acquisition process and control it.
2. Negotiate with the principal owner.
3. Maximize leverage with the initial offer.[7]

The process of selecting a new site or property is only one phase of the strategic process of managing assets of the organization. You can attempt to influence top management to include relevant facility data in the formal decision making by offering specific information that significantly skews the financial projects, derived from your site-selection process.

The site and property selection process, when combined with the strategic planning process, offers greater visibility and credibility to the facility manager within the company than most other functions do. Therefore, upper management will tend to judge the facility manager disproportionately on the quality of the site selection process.

Notes

1. Joseph Horowitz, "A Facility Manager Looks at Office Leases," *IFMA Conference Proceedings* (Houston: IFMA, 1988), pp. 125–138.

2. Bruce N. Wardrep, "GAAP Considerations of Lease versus Purchase Analysis," in McKinley Conway and Linda L. Liston, eds., *Facility Planning Technology* (Norcross, Ga.: Conway Data, 1987), p. 266.

3. Heidi Lord Butler, notes from IFMA "Facility Accounting" seminar, Seattle, November 1989.

4. John E. Jamerson, Michael J. Leahy, Peter M. Bradley, and Andrea D. Terzi, "The Sale-Leaseback, in *Facility Planning Technology*, p. 176.

5. Based on Charles F. Harding, "Company Politics in Plant Locations," in *Facility Planning Technology*, p. 354.

6. *Exit Strategies* (St. Louis: HOK Consulting, 1996), pp. 2–19.

7. H. Basil Hallquist, "The Fundamentals of Acquiring Corporate Real Estate," in *Facility Planning Technology*, p. 202.

8

Lease Administration and Property Management

Pulse Points

- *A company with multiple facilities requires careful lease management.*
- *The facility manager needs to be familiar with the principles of property management.*
- *When real estate development is the organization's goal, the facility manager should be part of the corporate development team.*
- *Properties should be disposed of when they are no longer of value to the organization.*
- *Development projects that are designed specifically for investment or resale purposes may severely inhibit the flexibility of the facility to respond to the productivity support needs of the workforce.*
- *Public sector facility managers must be politically astute in disposing of major public facilities.*

Regardless of a company's preference, at some time it almost inevitably is a lessor. For that reason, it is desirable to have at least a rudimentary knowledge of lease administration. And since many corporations choose purchase over leasing, it behooves facility managers to understand property management, including when to develop and when to dispose of real estate.

Lease Administration

When a company or agency, for whatever reason, decides to become a lessor, certain changes in management and attitude are necessary. Someone must be in charge of administering the lease (lease management) and in meeting tenant needs and ensuring they comply with the lease (property management). Additionally, at least part of the facilities department must reorient itself from a tenant

118

to a landlord perspective, while taking on both different types of legal and financial obligations.

The joint BOMA-BOMI* document entitled "Leasing Concepts" is a guide to
leasing from the lessor's point of view, presenting a "know your enemy" strategy.
Another approach is Michael Stack's "Lease Negotiations," available from IFMA.
My personal favorite is *Managing Corporate Real Estate* by Robert Kevin Brown,
Paul D. Lapidos, and Edmond P. Rondeau.

The Corporate Owner as Landlord

I have two disturbing observations on corporate real estate and lease management. First, too many large companies fragment their real estate management
function from operations and maintenance (the same companies mistakenly separate design and construction also). The result is disjointed, suboptimal management of facilities. Second, too many companies turn the management of leases
over to unqualified people, often as a secondary assignment. Real estate transactions are highly complex and require specialized financial, legal, and market
knowledge. When there is no real estate professional on staff, get a partner to
help. A knowledgeable professional is a hedge against a bad deal with long-term
consequences.

In general, corporate owners are not good landlords unless they maintain a
real estate staff, either in-house or a consultant. This is perhaps even truer in the
public sector. There certainly are marvelous success stories of universities' financing their expansion by leveraging their endowment in the real estate market, particularly if some of the endowment consisted of real estate.[1] That is commendable,
but the portfolio must be managed toward a set objective, the organization must
be willing to accept a new level of liability, and the function must be properly
resourced.

In Chapter 7, I discussed strategies for determining the proper mix of owned
and leased facilities. In general, companies are using leasing much more extensively than in the past because leases provide the flexibility needed until rapid,
short-term growth can be consolidated into assured cash flow or during periods
of downsizing.

For most public agencies and corporations, the better policy is to own or
lease only that space required for planned growth—that is, three years if planning
is for three years, five years for five-year planning. There are some who disagree
however. Alfred Behrens of Volkswagen, one of the first companies to manage
real estate for other than corporate needs, states, "By the nature of our . . . industry we are also in the real estate business, and we might just as well make the best
of it."[2] However, since facility management is already a daunting prospect, we
recommend only those challenges of your own choosing.

Organization and Documentation

In medium and large companies, a small staff office is assigned the responsibility
of lease administration. This staff reports directly to the facility manager (see Ex-

---

*BOMI is the Building Owners and Managers Institute: BOMA, the Building Owners and
Managers Association.

hibits 2-2 and 2-3). Since leased space is often a short-term solution for space problems, this same staff often is also charged with strategic planning. If the company cannot spare an individual exclusively for lease administration, then this function is best given to the individual with planning responsibility. Because it requires contact with people outside the company, one individual should be the lease manager. In its most recent survey, the International Facility Management Association (IFMA) found that over 70 percent of facility managers serve in the role of lessee, fewer than 30 percent as lessor.[3] But whoever is responsible for leasing operations must rely on counsel—either a staff attorney or outside counsel specializing in lease law.

You need a systematic method of organizing the company's leases. Once the number of leases reaches the double digits, move to a computer-based system.

Your automated system should provide pertinent information (options, termination dates, lease increases, etc.) at the time when it should be acted on. Ed Rondeau, director of consulting, Johnson Controls, lists the following benefits of a tracking system:[4]

1. Saves time.
2. Identifies opportunities to reduce real estate expenses.
3. Increases accuracy and reduces records duplication.
4. Provides reports and real estate analyses.
5. Efficiently transfers correct information to appropriate levels of the corporation.
6. Aids real estate strategy formulation.

The Lease Agreement

The lessor writes the lease and thus controls the leasing situation. Assuming that you have competent legal counsel, there should be few problems, but some areas require special attention if you are the lessor:

- With office technology increasingly entering the workplace, the lease should address how the cost of substantial electrical and HVAC (heating, ventilation, and air-conditioning systems) load increases will be handled. A major user, for example, could force the landlord to install a new electrical riser.
- The lease should specify proper installation and apportioning of costs for supplemental HVAC.
- The lease should certify that the space is free of PCBs, asbestos, lead in the drinking water, and common air pollutants.
- The agreement should be clear about special-purpose space, which varies substantially from common use, of the facilities. An example could be file rooms (high floor loads) and computer rooms (high HVAC, fire safety, and electrical loads).
- There must be adequate access and egress for material and debris, particularly for facilities that do not have freight elevators or loading docks.

• The lease must specify the use of tenant material handling devices inside the facilities.

IFMA has studied but has still not approved the best boilerplate lease for facility managers as lessees. Until such time, the following should be of particular concern when you enter into a lease as the lessee:

• Escalation clauses
• The building standard or "work letter"
• Tenant allowance and their applicability against extra work
• Signage
• Approval of tenant's extra work
• Access by lessee's contractor
• Weekend HVAC
• Division of costs for:
  —Operations
  —Major building alteration
  —Landlord repairs
  —Building services
• Subleases
• Appurtenances (parking, toilets, storage space, etc.)
• Rules
• Renewal options

Leasing can be mystifying, frustrating, and worrisome because it is fraught with legalism and seemingly biased toward the landlord. Nevertheless, if you are willing to learn the basics of lease negotiations, you will more effectively employ your counsel, broker, or consultant.

Trends in Lease Management

The nature of work is changing, and the real estate market shifts constantly. So you need to be aware of developments in lease management and anticipate changes. For example, tenants are seeking different kinds of buildings. This has produced the following trends.[5]

• Companies seek flexible buildings capable of housing research, laboratories, office space, warehousing, and support space—all in an attractive setting with increased amenities.

• Lessors are shifting as much risk as possible to tenants.

• Tenants are becoming more sophisticated in stating their requirements and in selecting buildings to fit their needs.

• More tenants are considering becoming developers and/or owners.

It has been said that capital costs come and go but rent is forever. However, the financial impact (cost or income) is only one aspect of lease administration.

Equally important are issues of liability and legalities. This is an area requiring both expertise and management. Whether you function as a lessor, a lessee, or both, you must bring those skills to the table.

Property Management

Property management is managing a facility to maximize profit. There is no negative connotation to the word *profit*. In fact, several large property management companies could give management lessons to facility managers. With a certain type and class of property, customer-oriented property management makes good business sense. Nevertheless, the bottom line is maximizing profit from those properties. Since many corporate facility managers also serve as property managers, it is worthwhile to discuss good property management. While there are many similarities, the facility manager should keep in mind the basic difference between himself and the property manager. The approach to a common problem may, in fact, be quite different.

Organization and Documentation

Normally the on-premises property management staff is smaller than for a corporate facility manager. Service and response are spelled out in the lease. Services over and above that are provided only if specially funded and in good time. This is because building services are primarily contracted out, with instantaneous reaction only for emergencies or life-threatening situations. Exhibit 8-1 represents a typical property management organization of a midtown, midrise office building.

The property manager is an exceptionally important individual to the tenants. Increasingly, it is the custom not to have a resident manager and, in some cases, not even an engineer or handyman on the premises. The property is serviced on an as-needed basis by on-call or roving personnel, with one manager managing four or five properties.

Certainly there is a break-even point for the size property that justifies a resident property manager. However, the following benefits to the tenants accrue when a property manager is resident:

1. Rules and regulations are enforced, and violations are discovered before they become serious.
2. Contractual services are performed to a higher standard.
3. Small problems are solved before they become crises.
4. There is less physical abuse of the facility.
5. Tenants have a visible presence for complaints, suggestions, and praise.

All of these result in a better-run building and a happier tenant. That should be reflected in higher renewals and the ability to charge top dollar for well-run space. I am extremely reluctant to rent in properties that do not have a resident manager, particularly office space.

Exhibit 8-1. On-premises property management organization.

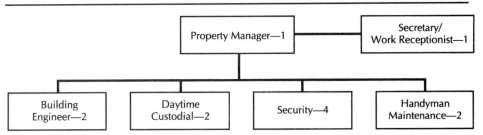

Other contracted services (not on premises)

Alterations
Electrical
Communications
Custodial
Window washing
Pest and rodent control
Signage
Plants and grounds
Elevator maintenance
Supplemental plant engineering and plumbing
Elevator maintenance

All (or any part of these) services could be provided by a property management firm. The handling of communications is dependent upon who owns the switch.

The same arguments for a managerial-level person on-site apply to a resident engineer or handyman. There is no greater insurance policy. A flood because no one knew where to find the shut-off valve, or the closest handyman was thirty minutes away when the main broke, will more than offset several years salary saved for an on-site handyman. However, it is important that this technical person have a sense of proprietorship in the building and be customer oriented. A lead engineer, skilled in the building's systems and in customer service, can serve the building and the tenants well.

Since profit maximization is the raison d'être for leasing a building, it is important that leases be systematically controlled. A proper lease management system has four characteristics:[6]

1. It is a real property database.
2. It is an action-reporting system.
3. It is a management-reporting mechanism.
4. It is a tool for real estate planning.

Services

Property managers should be interested in how their services are being rendered and how they are perceived by the tenants. There are many inexpensive ways to gain this knowledge—for example, by:

- Monitoring work requests for timeliness and completeness—by trade and by building location
- Quizzing the work receptionist or having him keep statistics or conduct short surveys
- Following up all or a percentage of service requests for satisfaction, with phone calls or with a brief questionnaire
- Having a tenant advisory council meeting, perhaps quarterly

It is extremely important that once this information is gathered, you take action and communicate your response back to the tenants.

Trends in Property Management

The changes in lessor-lessee relationships that were noted for lease management earlier in this chapter apply to property management as well. It is recommended that facility managers who also serve as property managers keep current with these trends and anticipate change.

Property Development

I admit a certain ambivalence toward facility managers' becoming property developers. Some argue that it shows how far facility managers have come; others say that the facility manager already has enough on his plate without taking on another major task; yet others are concerned that even before facility management is defined, it is merging into property management, where there's a different philosophy. The considerations are similar to those regarding ownership or leasing of property: Stay out of the development business but also realize that some of your colleagues will become developers by default. So if development is to be done, it deserves to be done well. And by "doing well," I mean that the shareholders receive a competitive return on their investment.

The Development Process

The process of development usually connotes a transition of function and improvement of a property. In Chapter 7 I urged the facility management department to work closely with finance, counsel, and top management in the lease versus purchase decision. I also suggested developing a comprehensive real-property database. Those suggestions are even more appropriate when considering property development.

The major difference between developmental activities and site selection or acquisition is that site selection is part of a process, the results of which are concerned with greater productivity. Development implies that improvement of a property will return a profit outside the organization. In other words, in site selection the facility manager offers advice that can optimize profits from internal activities; in development, the advice is tempered with considerations affecting the future leasing and resale of the property. The significant criteria for maximizing internal activities were considered in the previous section. Here, I focus on the factors affecting return on investment as it relates to property acquisition and improvement planning for the leasing and eventual resale of the property. As implied in a quote from Alfred Behrens earlier in this chapter, a site selected to meet a corporate need may well offer opportunities for development as well.

Development Constraints and Considerations

A facility manager may be able to control most of the factors related to internal activities, but a developer develops sites to meet the needs of potential clients as well.

In property selection, attempt to persuade top management to consider properties in terms of employee and vendor access, or for their transportation capabilities. Investment properties may be better suited at locations that will service other clients. A facility manager is concerned that stacking plans (how departments relate to each other in a multifloor building) are consistent with communications needs and work flow. That same building, viewed as an investment property, should be developed according to the needs of potential clients.

A dynamic organization planning a building program may wish to construct a number of buildings that afford a panoramic vista. But when vistas are not available, lakes, rivers, or fountains can be constructed instead; this makes the total site desirable to others and promotes further development.

When developed for a particular company, the architecture for a building is integrated, and access to amenities is universal. However, when a building is constructed for outside clients, the architecture may be varied, and each will demand amenities not to be shared by others. Heterogeneous architecture presents considerable problems with regard to grounds keeping, traffic control, security, and features such as walking paths, jogging trails, food service, and emergency preparedness.

One concern of great interest to investors is the potential for efficient expansion. By their nature, some investment properties may not have the flexibility to respond to certain renters' specific needs. For example, an urban site, despite a favorable location, may not be appealing to a think tank desiring tranquility and a scenic view for its headquarters.

Among the factors inhibiting development flexibility are the following:

- Specific state regulations, zoning, or community demands
- Limited access to major streets
- Limited air rights
- Wildlife preserves and permanent open space
- Quiet zones
- Limits on land reclamation
- Inadequate public transportation
- Limited-capacity sewage and waste disposal
- Limited water and power access

- Historic preservation covenants
- Public housing dictums
- Public amenities dictums

If a facility manager becomes a developer, he must be equally concerned about his ability to dispose of the property to meet company business plans. Many of the factors listed above are equally applicable in a disposal scenario. Two other considerations are the extent that there might be regulatory time bombs on the property (e.g., submerged, leaking tanks or contaminated waste) or that the facilities are so uniquely engineered or so closely identified with a single company that no other organization wants to occupy them. Both factors can be deal breakers and make properties difficult, if not impossible, to sell.

The Development Team

From the facility manager's perspective, there is little to recommend the acquisition of a property for investment purposes. There are few advantages and many potential headaches. Nonetheless, the property may be acquired. The chief financial officer (CFO) will have a major interest in the development project, but it is the facility manager who must control the development team.

Although each development project is a unique challenge, the makeup of the team is fairly standard:

1. The facility manager
2. A land-use consultant
3. A concept designer
4. Counsel with local land-use expertise
5. An internal client representative (if one is involved)

The sole purpose of this team is to develop a project that will best meet company needs within available resources. They must sell the project to the necessary board or other decision-making body.

Your CFO can assist in determining what an adequate return is. The primary determinant is the cost of capital. However, the question then becomes one of choosing among potential investments. John Dues, of Mead Land Services, suggests the following:[7]

1. Manage the allocation of capital or cash resources to business units selectively.
2. Ascertain or confirm the long-term viability of each investment in its business.
3. Determine the overall performance objectives of the units.
4. Facilitate identifying critical threats and opportunities facing the business units.
5. Provide a baseline for measurement and control of performance during the planning horizon.

Exhibit 8-2. Forms of development ownership.

	Advantages	*Disadvantages*
Leasehold control	• No building management • Less administrative cost • Minimum front-end investment • Cost expensed immediately for taxes	• Lowest appreciation potential • Generates no leverage
Fee simple	• Fullest range of financial options • Considerable tax benefits	• "In-house" management attention needed • Up-front investment high • High administrative costs
Joint venture	• "Off-balance sheet" financing • Minimum contribution • Risk minimization • Flexibility	• Can be complicated

Source: Peter Haverkampf and Gary Salton, "Real Estate as a Corporate Reservoir," in McKinley Conway and Linda L. Liston, eds., *Facility Planning Technology* (Norcross, Ga.: Conway Data, 1987), pp. 18–19.

These criteria help the team judge whether an investment fits the strategic planning objectives of the business. If it is compatible, then it is probably a proper investment, and the project can be assessed further, using primarily capital investment evaluation techniques.

The facility manager contributes information to the team effort regarding probable operating expenses, leasing information, engineering and architectural attributes of the project, maintenance programs, and costs for office building or industrial property developments.

By its composition, the development team should have the proper technical, financial, and political expertise to prepare whatever decision-making document is used by the company or agency. When that is done, the necessary groundwork should already be in place to ensure that board approval will be achieved, and the team can disband.

Ownership and Financing

The form of ownership a company chooses for its development project depends on both its financial commitment and development philosophy. The advantages and disadvantages of the three major types of ownership are shown in Exhibit 8-2.

Having chosen an ownership form, the company then often wants to select a development partner. Five criteria are important for selecting that partner:[8]

1. *Integrity.* Choose a firm with which you are comfortable.
2. *Financial strength.* Have the resources to fund the project without constant concern.
3. *Experience.* Have a similar project completed.
4. *Appropriateness to the scope.* Select a firm appropriate to the type of financing you are envisioning.
5. *Familiarity with the location.* Both partners will feel more comfortable if the development partner knows local conditions.

To structure the financing of the development project, the facility manager, in conjunction with the CFO, must be aware of the aspects of real estate that translate into assets and that can be traded for cash. They must both also be aware of the possible objectives of lenders, equity investors, and developers. And they must realize the actual financing means peculiar to real estate, which reconcile the inherent attributes of property with the objectives of money suppliers.[9]

Furthermore, the financial plan for the company should identify the cheapest sources of money, create investment incentives to replace high cash returns, and use devices that defer to the greatest extent the need for cash. Some options that meet these criteria are (1) structuring the development as a tax shelter, (2) using tax-exempt financing, (3) choosing land leaseback, and (4) engaging in joint ventures with institutions.[10] The facility manager will have internal financial and legal advice during the development of the financial plan to support a development project. However, it is necessary at this point to reflect on responsibility. If midway through the project the finances (or any other aspect) goes sour, it is the facility manager who is on the line. For that reason, the facility manager should rightly challenge every aspect of the project development as it proceeds. Internal experts and consultants need to make the facility manager comfortable, or no aspect should proceed.

One last note of caution: Most companies that lost a lot of money in development ventures did not understand the true extent of their risks.[11] One of the principal roles of the facility manager is to ensure that company management is aware of not only the opportunities of development, but the downside risk. Admittedly, in the enthusiasm of a major development project, those risks are not popular, but they must be presented.

Successful development requires both a company devoted to that business and also a change of philosophy of the facility manager toward at least a portion of the facilities for which he is responsible. That cannot be done without careful thought and planning and complete commitment.

Property Disposal

Property disposal has become a much more complicated process than when decisions were made simply on market factors like price and location. No one will buy a property without conducting extensive due diligence investigations to ensure that no legal and environmental problems exist. Sometimes the mere whiff of an environmental problem can scare off a potential buyer, because whoever is holding the environmental problem at the time that it is discovered tends to be liable for the solution to that problem.

A facility manager must be as sensitive to excess real property as to purchase and development. Often, however, timely disposal seems almost an afterthought. And as important as disposal can be, the literature is noticeably silent on this topic. The ultimate horror story in this regard is the company paying rent on a facility it already owned. That facility should obviously have been a candidate for disposal.

How does real estate become excess to the needs of an organization? It can be obsolete. The company can be downsizing or changing products or services. An example can be found in the public sector, where changing demographics have closed many schools. Also, the organization may have relocated.

Leland Smith, a senior vice president at Grubbs and Belli's Commercial Accounts, in his inimitable style, lists the five traditional ways to dispose of excess facilities:[12]

1. Unload this turkey on another operating division as an internal transfer of assets at full book value.
2. Put your widget plant on the market as a widget plant and try to get its full replacement value as a ready-to-operate facility. Hire a broker and tell your boss it is his fault if you can't sell it.
3. Redeploy or auction the equipment, then put the land and buildings on the market as an ideal facility for any conceivable use.
4. Sell it to whoever will take it off your hands and hope to get its depreciated value. Tell your treasurer you've done the company a favor by minimizing the tax consequences of the sale.
5. Donate it to charity, take the tax write-off, and give yourself a plaque for being a good corporate citizen.

Unfortunately, this is typical of the standard approach to property disposal. However, there is another view: The excess property might represent planned excess capacity, obtained at a favorable market rate for future expansion. Surplus real estate is not, in and of itself, good or bad. It is part of the life of a facility, and it deserves to be managed like all real property assets. Most often the problems occur when property becomes excess unexpectedly and it remains excess and becomes a burden, normally financial.

As a general rule, there can be hidden costs in excess property, so only property that has been planned as excess to an organization's need should be retained. There is the old saying, "Hang on to land; it is under all and they are not going to make any more of it." The reciprocal is, "Value is generated by earning power." Vacant, nonproductive land is not a liquid asset; at current interest rates, and considering the cost of management and taxes, land must double in value every four to five years to be an outstanding investment.[13]

Methods of Disposal

The best discussion I've seen of disposal options for facility managers with excess property is by Robert E. Baird. He cites the following as alternative disposal methods:[14]

1. Sale and partial lease-back
2. Subdivision
3. Raze and redevelop
4. Tax-free exchange
5. Short-term financing
6. Short-term lease with purchase option
7. Donations

An alternative to disposal is adaptive reuse. I have several excellent examples in my own Washington, D.C., neighborhood: An excess school has been converted to administrative space for the school district. A former but inadequate police station is now a full-service, one-stop human services center. For adaptive reuse to work, the company must be comfortable with the function for the new use.

Disposal Process

Disposal of real estate requires the same close coordination as purchase or leasing. Imagine the embarrassment of the facility manager who has just sold the headquarters of a subsidiary in Chicago, only to find that the headquarters for a new service product in another subsidiary will be needed there in six months. Hard as it is to believe, some organizations lack a real-property information system to identify property as excess to their needs. And of three corporate real estate databases that I reviewed, only one had the capability of identifying upcoming excess property or cataloging surplus property.

The facility manager should follow a detailed procedure for shopping around excess property for an appropriate period in all parts of the company. Most public sector agencies have such procedures. Once they are cleared through operations, the facility manager must develop a game plan with the finance department to maximize the profit or minimize the loss. With the plan in hand, he can then go forward with that popular partner, the company counsel, and a broker if one is appropriate. Each potential disposal property should be carefully evaluated, inspected thoroughly, and its features categorized according to potential buyer types and needs.

Each disposal situation requires an understanding of equity in the property. Many times equity exists in the property, but often it may be enhanced by unused or deferred tax deductions or allowances. There may also be taxes that are due at the time of disposal of a property. Potential buyers will be interested in the property's present cash value as well as its capitalization rate. They will also want to know the amortization rate and how much depreciation they can expect, at what rate, and the financial leverage possible.[15]

Prospective buyers should also be informed regarding the property valuations and assessments for similar properties in the region.[16] They will ask about any special exemptions or tax relief inherent in the property. For instance, sometimes prior agreements with state or local authorities include tax abatements or special considerations that can be passed on to new owners.

In the Public Sector

One of the more interesting aspects of my public service life was my involvement in military base closures. Several of these facilities were declared in excess of the military's needs or were proposed for new missions or funding cuts. An elaborate bureaucratic system had been agreed upon with Congress, and it included the following for each site:

- A mission analysis
- A financial analysis
- An environmental impact statement to include the impact on the local economy
- An assessment of national historic significance
- A public hearing

The system was so elaborate, the analysis so detailed, and the environment so political that no bases were ever closed if the closure was contested. The analyses were so complex and contained so much subjective data that they could easily be challenged or returned for further analysis. Public-sector facility managers in particular must be politically astute if they plan to dispose of major facilities.

Congress and the president realized these problems were serious and nearly impossible to overcome if politics was to be the principal driver for base closures. Therefore, to determine the bases to be closed to match the 1990s downsizing of the Department of Defense, they established a commission of experts who prepared an impartial list of base closures based on the analyses listed above. Congress then had to pass or not pass the recommended package in toto. Politics was not completely eliminated from this process, but the country was able to close most of the bases necessary.

Notes

1. Jane H. Lehman, "Many Universities Getting Real Estate Lessons," *Washington Post*, June 3, 1989, pp. E1, E19.

2. Alfred H. Behrens, "Managing Corporate Real Estate as a Profit Center," in McKinley Conway and Linda L. Liston, eds., *Facility Planning Technology* (Norcross, Ga.: Conway Data, 1987), p. 118.

3. Benchmarks II, 1994 (Houston: IFMA, 1994), p. 10.

4. Edmond P. Rondeau, "Contel Finds Great Way to Manage Real Estate," *IFMA Journal* (April 1989), 28.

5. Arthur M. Delmhorst, "Why Tenant-Landlord Relations Are Changing," in *Facility Planning Technology*, p. 150.

6. John D. Mac Eachron, "Managing Real Property Assets," in *Facility Planning Technology*, p. 291.

7. John J. Dues, "Real Estate Management and the Corporate Planning Process," in *Facility Planning Technology*, p. 11.

8. Peter Haverkampf and Gary Salton, "Real Estate as a Corporate Reservoir," in *Facility Planning Technology*, pp. 18–19.

9. Howart T. Slayen, "Financing Corporate Real Estate Acquisitions," in *Facility Planning Technology*, p. 82.

10. Ibid., pp. 83–84.

11. Robert A. Sigafoos, *Corporate Real Estate Development* (Lexington, Mass.: Lexington Books, 1976), pp. 157–158.

12. Leland F. Smith, "Turning Obsolete Buildings Into Income," in *Facility Planning Technology*, p. 254.

13. H. Basil Hallquist, "The Fundamentals of Acquiring Corporate Real Estate," in *Facility Planning Technology*, p. 203.

14. Robert E. Baird, "More Innovative Approaches for Surplus Properties," in *Facility Planning Technology*, pp. 250–253.

15. Charles F. Floyd, *Real Estate Principles* (Chicago: Longman Financial Services Publishing, 1990), p. 2.

16. Ibid., pp. 271–275.

Section IV
The Design-Build Cycle

How many facility managers understand how a large architectural-engineering firm designs a major project? How many understand, from a builder's perspective, how a manufacturing facility is constructed? Unless you have a working knowledge of these dynamics, you will continue to get suboptimum projects, even from the most reputable of firms. As the industry has become increasingly specialized, the facility manager must take a more active role to ensure a satisfactory final product.

Perhaps more than any other facility management function, the design-build cycle has been studied, codified, and automated. Facility projects are planned, programmed, designed, reviewed, constructed, and evaluated similarily, whether they involve a new manufacturing site or an alteration.

I start this section with a discussion of project management, then proceed sequentially through the life of a project, including evaluation.

9

Project Management

Pulse Points

- *Project management is not facility management.*
- *The facility manager must control, if not manage, all large capital projects for which he will become responsible.*
- *Life-cycle costing should be used for project decisions.*
- *Partnering provides an opportunity to avoid litigation during major projects.*

In general terms, *project management* means managing a distinct piece of work to be completed on time and within budget. For the facility manager, project management means taking a project through the design-build schedule to ensure that operational requirements are met within the budget and on schedule.

Often projects are defined by a dollar value ($5,000 being a good line of demarcation), by the level of effort required (one man-day per trade not to exceed two man-days total, for example), or whether they require planning or design effort. In those ways, projects are differentiated from routine work and preventive maintenance. In fact, the management of projects is but one function of facility management. Yet one common failing is a tendency to view all facility management activities as separate projects, each justified at set costs with discrete start and end dates. This is the situation that causes walls to be demolished for alterations only a week after they were painted for maintenance. This mind-set builds a facility at the least capital cost that makes the project manager look good, but has increased operating and maintenance costs over the life of the facility. As I say many times in this book, the essence of facility management is cost-effectiveness, quality of service, and operational efficiency for the life of the facility. Project management, improperly applied and with the wrong incentive and evaluation system, can be extremely harmful to good facility management.

Unfortunately, because capital projects are so visible, there is always great pressure to minimize initial costs and bring the project in at the earliest possible date. Often this almost ensures suboptimizing the life-cycle costs, which typically are three times the capital costs. Annual budget pressures ("The money disappears on September 30") cause the same type of costly thinking on smaller projects. Many governmental facility managers have their favorite story of poor-quality projects funded in an end-of-the-year spending binge.

There certainly is a place for project management in facility management. Capital projects, discretionary annual projects, and repair projects are programs best managed in a project mode. (Project management is inappropriate for utilities, custodial work, leasing, preventive maintenance, and administration.) As a general rule, nonroutine services, those that require high user contact or discretion, and those that coordinate multiple functions are candidates for project management.

Definition and Organization

In most organizations, capital expenditures—with the exception of furniture and furnishings—are developed, justified, and executed as projects. Within the annual budget, however, only certain work, with these characteristics, is handled as projects:

- Largely discretionary (or could be delayed)
- Design is involved
- Cost exceeds a floor cost ($5,000, for example)
- Multidisciplinary
- Requires high user involvement

As a facility department moves to midsize, it is essential to define (normally in coordination with the budget department) what work will be handled as projects.

Large capital projects, particularly if they are rarely done, are often handled by a separate project team whose manager reports to the facility manager. When the capital project is run out of the chief executive officer's (CEO) or chairman's office, there is a built-in propensity for long-term disaster. Unfortunately it is also common to appoint a retiring or "spare" vice president as project manager. The project manager for a major capital project must not only be competent. He must also have the trust of and be compatible with the facility manager. The facility manager must control, if not manage, all capital projects.

When faced with managing a major project, the facility department can manage the project itself, hire its own project team, or hire a development team. If a department manages the project itself, at least in theory, it controls the project. This approach probably has the lowest overhead. However, most organizations do not have the depth or breadth of skills to manage a large project. Even when both design and construction services are contracted, a large project is incredibly time-consuming. Someone must be a full-time project manager. In addition, it will probably be necessary to dedicate one full-time contracting officer, one architect, one engineer, one interior designer, and one project accountant to the project for its duration. Few facility managers can spare these people from their normal departmental duties. Specialized support, like legal support during permitting, will have to be sought from an outside source. Finally, this approach represents the greatest technical risk if the department is not used to managing major projects.

If individuals are hired to form a project team, it should be possible to get a team that is both technically proficient and loyal to the department. The extent to which individuals feel that they are a member of the facility department team is directly proportional to the degree to which they are welcomed and trained. Initially, the team will not be used to working with one another or with the department, and there may well be difficulty assessing how this situation is developing until it is too late. The success of this approach is highly dependent on the project manager's being able to pull the team together. Finally, the cost of the project team has to be funded out of project costs.

Hiring an already assembled project team should make it possible to have a team with all of the skills and with team members who are used to working with one another. They may even have worked on a similar project. This team should be able to hit the ground running. Although this approach presents the least technical risk of the approaches mentioned, it is also the highest cost because the department is paying a management fee to the employer. Choosing the development firm can get political; everyone has a favorite developer. It is still probably desirable to have an internal project manager to work with the team since the facility manager tends to be the most distant from daily happenings on the project under this approach.

Most organizations accept the need for using a design-build team (architect, engineers, interior architects, consultants, and builder), but companies commencing large capital projects should also consider augmenting their internal facilities, legal, accounting, and purchasing staffs with the following:

- Construction accountant
- Estimator
- Construction procurement specialist
- Inspectors
- Scheduler

Before contacting consultants, however, the facility manager should organize the internal staff so it can control the design-build team. Especially critical are procedures to establish requirements and formal reviews by in-house experts.

The Design Phase

Crucial to completing any project on time and within budget are the proper program, plan, and design. These are developed during the design process (see Chapter 11). These aspects of a project set the tone and fix the available resources as well as its form and function. Too often facility managers neglect design. It's unclear whether this is out of deference to architects or because they are unaware of the design cycle or how design firms work. Perhaps it's because large projects are often handled outside the department, and by the time the facility manager takes control, the project has been designed.

Devote special attention to the project management organization—both the project management team and the committees for user and technical input or communication with users and management.

Chapter 11 discusses the selection of an outside design team and the proper relationship between the facility manager and the design team. The team should not only bring technical competence to the project but also mesh well with the facility department.

During the design phase, look not just at the architect's work but also the work of major consultants. Participate in major design decisions.

Experienced facility managers soon learn the importance of good estimators to the design process. Without a reliable estimate at every step of design, the project cannot be properly controlled.

Also, extensively and rigorously review the schedule at each stage of design.

The Construction Phase

The contracting and construction of a building can be managed in many ways. This is perhaps why, of all portions of the design-build cycle, construction is the most studied and the aspect about which we know the most. Exhibit 9-1 shows the advantages and disadvantages of four common ways of contracting for construction.

If possible, the design firm and the project manager should help select the builder. However, if the contracting method is construction management, then select the construction manager first and have him assist in selecting the design firm. (Caution: In some markets, architectural-engineering (A-E) firms and builders are so tightly linked that impartiality may not be possible.) Also, though certainly not required, it is preferable to use local builders, particularly in areas with complicated codes and permit processes. In some ways, the developer is a captive of the system, but fighting local codes, permit offices, and customs with a "foreign" builder is likely to cause both grief and delay.

Anyone who has been involved with the project approval process appreciates the complexity of issues and frequent frustration involved in obtaining the necessary permits and approvals from local government. This is such a prevalent problem in some jurisdictions that some law firms have developed a reputation as expediters to ensure relatively fast permit approvals. Silicon Valley facility managers, many of whom were faced with fast-track projects to meet the business needs of booming technology companies, met with local government officials to develop permit streamlining practices, programs, and policies. The result is a set of guidelines that should be emulated across the profession.[1]

Direction and control of major projects is best exercised on two different levels. Policy issues are decided by a *policy commitee* composed of a responsible vice president or chairman, a facility manager, a project manager, a design team project manager (or construction manager), legal counsel, and a controller representa-

Exhibit 9-1. Contracting construction methods.

Lump Sum—Sequential Design and Construction	Construction Management or Cost-Plus-Fixed-Fee	Guaranteed Maximum Price	Turnkey
Advantages			
Complete plans for bidding available.	Impact of escalation reduced.	Complete plans not necessary.	Complete plans not necessary.
	Foundations and structure can be bid in advance.	Foundations and structure can be bid in advance.	Foundations and structure can be bid in advance.
Fixed price at start of construction.	Impact of escalation reduced.	Maximum price known during design process.	Price fixed at start of project.
		Escalation impact reduced.	Impact of escalation reduced.
Single responsibility of contractor.	Construction manager working as owner's agent, not in adversary position with owner, designer.		
Quality and O&M aspects of design under control of owner.	Quality and O&M aspects of design under control of owner.	Quality and O&M aspects of design under control of owner.	
	Advice of contractor available during design period.	Advice of contractor available during design period.	
	Design-construct period reduced.	Design-construct period reduced.	Design-construct period reduced.
	Changes to plans discouraged due to telescoped design period.	Changes to plans discouraged due to telescoped design period.	Changes to plans discouraged owing to telescoped design period.
Disadvantages			
Lengthiest process.			
Length of design period encourages modifications.	Total cost of job not known until after foundations and frame underway and plans complete and bid.	Any owner changes affect guaranteed price.	Ability of owner to make changes severely restricted.
Advice of contractor for effecting economies not available during design.			
Impact of escalation most severe.			
Contractor placed in adversary position with respect to owner and designer.		Contractor placed in adversary position with respect to owner and designer.	Contractor placed in adversary position with respect to owner.
Contractor may seek change orders and loopholes.	Extra costs may arise from modifications needed after plans are completed.		Aesthetic and O&M quality of design may be questionable because they are not directly under control of owner.
Contingency and profit factors higher than CM/cost-plus-fixed-fee method.		Contingency and profit factors much higher than for lump-sum and CM/cost-plus-fixed-fee methods due to great risk involved.	Contingency and profit factors higher than CM/cost-plus-fixed-fee and guaranteed maximum price. Total cost may be highest of all methods.

tive. This committee normally meets monthly but may meet as often as weekly. In addition to policy, the committee considers and approves all major changes, communicates to the CEO and board, and takes under advisement issues forwarded by the experts committee.

The *experts committee* closely approximates the design-build team and makes the day-to-day decisions that keep the project on time and within budget. Committee members typically are the project manager, the design team project manager, the builder's project manager, an in-house design chief, in-house engineering chief, in-house operations chief, project accountant, legal counsel, chief inspector, a staff representative or line manager, and a security or safety representative. Of these, the project accountant, legal counsel, chief inspector, and design team project manager are nonvoting. This committee usually meets weekly with an agenda approved by the chairman. Members of the design-build team make presentations, the team reviews the progress, they resolve the problems, and the team recommends issues for the policy committee.

In large projects, the project manager spends an inordinate amount of time in meetings. This must be both realized and appreciated. The team builds the project while the project manager is concerned with these issues:

- Managing the team
- Keeping management informed and transmitting policy to the design-build team
- Keeping the design-build experts "tuned in and turned on" to organizational requirements and perceptions
- Handling public relations

This seems as if I am advocating management by committee, and to a certain extent I am. Large construction projects are, by their nature, collaborative. The project manager must be skilled in guiding the project through these committees.

These two committees should not steamroll issues, but majority membership should ensure that the project manager controls the truly critical issues. Particularly on the policy committee, he should have done his homework so that there are no surprises at meetings.

The project manager prepares an agenda and distributes it for each meeting. A good format has these items:

1. Update
2. Comparison to budget and schedule
3. "Get back to ya's" from the project manager
4. Old business
5. Other problems
6. New business
7. Review of tasks assigned

There is a different emphasis on these items in either committee.

The agenda should be circulated at least twenty-four hours in advance, and it should be reviewed by the project manager personally. Meeting minutes should be circulated within forty-eight hours of the meeting, with corrections required within an additional forty-eight hours.

Preparing for and going to meetings is the single greatest demand on a project manager's time. The successful project manager knows how to manage these activities.

Common Pitfalls

Major construction projects are, by their nature, complex. However, there are truly outstanding designers, architects, engineers, and builders to assist. Thousands of things can go wrong; some problems will crop up despite your best efforts. That is why it is important to have a strong team. Once the mistake is found, the team can correct it quickly and cheaply.

The number of problems can be lessened or minimized by avoiding the following pitfalls:

- Not contracting with an experienced A-E firm; using the chairman's favorite architect.
- Failing to provide the design team with important requirements.
- Allowing the A-E firm to pick its own consultants without your review or approval.
- Hiring a builder who has never built in the market.
- Failing to have work inspected or operational tests performed.
- Failing to establish a budget, fiscal controls, or proper construction accounting.
- Approving changes before they are designed and costed.
- Failing to schedule fixed reviews or progress meetings.
- Not observing the work of the builder's subcontractors.
- Failing to agree on procedures for punch list, operational tests, beneficial occupancy, training, warranties, and project turnover.
- Failing to define documentation (type, quantity, and format) required at turnover.
- Failing to budget for contingencies.

Partnering

I have never participated in a project where partnering was used. However, my observation of two projects and a review of research indicate that partnering is a concept that needs to be developed.[2] There is too much litigation in major construction; some projects end with everyone suing everyone else. Facility managers, as the consumers of construction services, pay for this litigation, so it is to their advantage to seek ways to minimize it.

There are many definitions for partnering, and, in practice, it tends to vary from project to project. Partnering is a structured process that obligates the partners (hopefully all members of the design-build team) to foster innovation, teamwork, continuous quality improvement, and team problem solving. The following characteristics of a partnering agreement are common:

- Clarifying the role of each partner in the process.
- A commitment to information sharing with the establishment and a procedure to do so consistently.
- The sharing of lessons learned and formalized postmortems of major or repeating events.
- Formalized trust building and training.
- Establishing common goals, objectives, and priorities for the project.
- Defining risks and establishing procedures to manage them.
- Fostering innovation.
- Establishing ways to measure success.
- Developing mechanisms to resolve differences quickly.

These elements are often placed into a single document, called the *partnering charter*, which all major decision makers on the project sign.

Does partnering work? In one study, the U.S. Army Corps of Engineers, Kansas City District, found that partnering reduced modifications by 39 percent, time growth by 55 percent, and cost growth by 38 percent.[3] Not everyone is enthralled with partnering. The breaking down of some of the "firewalls" in normal contracting by which adversarial relationships kept the various parties honest disturbs some traditionalists. However, it appears that partnering can offer savings to all concerned where there is a genuine desire to cooperate and all parties are roughly equal in experience and political power. Traditional project management has been so rancorous and litigious that any process that goes counter to that tradition is welcome.

Large and Small Projects

Most facility departments handle work over a certain dollar value (such as $5,000 each requirement), or which requires substantial design input but is small and is part of an annual project program. Often projects are broken down into move projects, maintenance and repair projects, or other alterations.

Some large organizations accomplish 200 to 250 of these projects annually, averaging one start-up and one close-out each working day. The scale of work projects can be daunting. Requirements, therefore, are gathered by project managers assigned regularly to work with certain customers or in particular geographic areas. In smaller organizations, project designers gather the requirements and manage the process from beginning to end.

After the requirements are costed, they are prioritized and met according to priority. Often the priority list is reviewed semiannually. Because these projects are so popular, there is almost never enough funds to do all the work. Large organizations often institute steps to control and prioritize the funds. There are three ways to do this:

1. Establish administrative approval levels for varying levels of projects (e.g., $10K, manager; $50K, director, $250K, VP).
2. Delineate between new work (construction, alterations) and maintenance and repair, and put a ceiling on the amount that can be used for new construction.
3. Establish a joint user-facility department review committee to set priorities for project accomplishment and then review those priorities at midyear.

In small organizations, definitions and approval levels are less of an issue because the volume of work is much smaller. Even fairly small projects (less than $10,000) are well known to company management before even planning is set in motion.

The difficulty in managing small projects is gathering requirements and costing the projects early enough so that the facility manager can submit his estimated budget. This can best be accomplished by having an annual requirements-gathering process with a midyear review to pick up changes. Management then approves this list, in aggregate for design and construction.

Highly sophisticated project management systems have been developed, many of them within the U.S. Department of Defense. And now computers have automated almost all of these systems. Using software such as Microsoft Project, the facility manager has a project management tool formerly available only to project management firms. There are systems for mainframes as well as PCs. There are systems for handling multiple small projects. No other function of facility management has been as well developed as project management.

Some of the more common project management methods are:

1. Critical path method (CPM)
2. Program Evaluation Review Technique (PERT)
3. GANTT charts
4. Precedence method (PM)
5. Resource constrained scheduling

Critical to all these methods is the ability to estimate time and resource use accurately. A quality estimator or estimating team is extremely important because these estimates must be made initially, when only a project estimate exists. Both CPM and PERT use "not more than and not later than" estimates to help set realistic budgets and schedules.

Because a change in one project—especially the need for additional resources—can affect other department resources and programs, the facility manager must carefully assess these changes before they are made. It is not enough to view how the changes will affect the particular program budget or schedule, but how they will influence leasing needs, maintenance and repair programs, and the like. This is one of the major factors that separates facility management from project management. The facility manager must understand the total picture. Any failure to do so puts both the project and the department in jeopardy. In conclusion, I recommend two books on project management: Steve Binder's *Corporate Facility Planning,* which places project management in a corporate context, and Carole Farren's *Planning and Managing Interior Projects,* which discusses in detail the kind of project management performed by most facility managers.

Notes

1. *Permit Streamlining* (Santa Clara, Calif.: Santa Clara County Manufacturing Group Facility Managers Committee, 1994), pp. 1–13).

2. Jeffrey W. Hills, "Partnering: Does It Work?" *The Military Engineer* (December 1995): 45–47. By permission of The Society of American Military Engineers (SAME).

3. Ibid., p. 45.

10

Programming and Project Development

Pulse Points

- *Planning for major projects nearly always understates engineering requirements.*
- *The facility manager should program for maintainability as well as functionality, and place special emphasis on support areas.*
- *Project planning integrates information from the facility plan with requirements gathered through programming.*
- *The facility manager plans with care but always retains flexibility.*

The project programming process involves gathering the requirements for a specific project and examining the relationships of individual tasks. The program is a tool for managing the project and a guide to anticipated results. Its essence is (1) an understanding of what is needed and expected by the user and (2) the establishment of performance expectations at specific time intervals.

It is not possible to develop an aesthetically pleasing or functional work environment without first defining the overall objective for the space to be used. Many textbooks regard the establishment of project objectives as the first stage in the design-build cycle. For example, Manuel Marti, a prominent theoretical space planner, indicates that the overall organizational framework shapes the entire process.[1] I interpret this more literally to mean that the structure, culture, and philosophy of the parent organization establish the parameters within which any project is identified, prioritized, and executed. The organization's philosophy may be modified by circumstances that develop during the design-build cycle; however, the initial assumptions and resource allocations are always determined by corporate philosophy.

Often, the only stated objective is the number of individuals to occupy a specific space. The planner then is asked to offer solutions within the constraints of that space and budget. In such circumstances planning activities are likely to be suboptimal. The project can be accomplished, but not necessarily as effectively or efficiently as it could have been. But if complete requirements are collected and analyzed, the results can be more than satisfactory. This is what programming can and should do.

The project programming process involves gathering the requirements for a specific project and examining the relationships of individual tasks. The program is a tool for managing the project and a guide to anticipated results. Its essence is (1) an understanding of what is needed and expected by the user and (2) the establishment of performance expectations at specific time intervals. We discussed macrolevel space programming in Chapter 5; in this chapter, we apply the programming process to define and gather the requirements for a specific project.

Aspects of Programming

The task definition stage of programming defines the project expectations. It is a statement of what should be able to happen as a direct result of successful completion. One of my favorite sayings describes the results when this step is not properly performed: "If you always do what you've always done, you will always get what you've always got." Don't validate obsolescence.

The feasibility analysis stage of any project is conceptual. In general, programming means that the company has determined that the overall project is feasible. However, as requirements are gathered, solutions will come to mind, and the feasibility needs to be verified. Feasibility analysis should go deeply enough to ensure reliability of expenditure and profitability projections. A fully developed program permits the facility manager to plan effectively and eliminate unwanted surprises. The following specifics should be included in the feasibility analysis:

1. *Technological feasibility*, including employee training and organizational resources such as machinery, equipment, computers. In planning major projects, don't understate engineering requirements; later deficiencies are costly to correct.
2. *Operational aspects*, such as employee morale, adaptability, organizational policy changes, modifications to facility, and anticipated success.
3. *Economic aspects*, to determine whether the completed project will return a greater dollar benefit than the expenditure in staff and resources.
4. *Communications aspects*, which give insight into both needed communications links and contiguity of location for various units. The Quickborner organization, pioneers in the concept of the office landscape, is normally credited with looking at organizations as dynamic entities, particularly at how units within the organization communicate with each other.

Political considerations are an important part of any program. Senior executives should be consulted early to determine their "hot buttons," those program aspects that either must be in the project or that can't be in the project. Identify those issues early on. They often form the performance envelope within which all other programming is done.

Also, a maintainability program should be developed. This is not commonly done, because in-house and consultant programmers appear to have little interest in the subject. By carrying out good maintenance programming, not only can the life-cycle costs of a building be reduced substantially but maintenance can be made easier.

Sources and Methods

The depth and breadth of the programming effort varies somewhat. Exhibit 10-1 is a list of possible areas. It goes beyond the normal areas of programming investigation but may be a good model as companies concern themselves not only with adequate and safe workplaces but ones that allow for individual expression and a sense of control. It is important to realize that some requirements will be in direct conflict with other requirements. For example, the organization may want to maximize productivity by expecting specific behaviors from its workers, but workers may not be perceive that behavior in their best interest. Under such circumstances, you may find yourself having to advocate a specific strategy to management.

A program is likely to establish expectations on the part of top management and might be used, at least, in part, to judge the effectiveness of the facility manager. It is in your best interests to use the most reliable information possible. If there's faulty information, disastrous results may follow. If top management's expectations are overly ambitious, that may be equally damaging. A program may also be expected to assist in the planning for contingencies as well as in the normal management of a project.

There are at least four sources to query for requirements for a major renovation or new facility:

1. Top management
2. Operating staff
3. Support staff
4. Regulations and codes

The requirements of top management often need to be gathered before a decision can be made to go ahead on a project, so this step may already be complete before you start programming. For example, a 1997 National Construction and Development Survey by the International Association of Corporate Real Estate Executives (NACORE) states that 46 percent of building decisions are made by CEOs.[2] These are the most political of requirements; thus, this initial level of programming is extremely important and cannot be assigned to an inexperienced architectural programmer. I favor the facility manager's either doing the interviews personally or controlling the participating consultant. In either case, there should be agreement on the questions to be asked.

Typically interviewed are the chief executive officer (CEO), chairman of the board, all senior vice presidents, the budget director, and the vice presidents of affected units. Their comments must be treated individually, no matter who gath-

Exhibit 10-1. Possible areas for programming.

Natural Compliances
- Site
- Surroundings
- Region
- Urban location
- Functional placement
- Accessibility
- Natural conditions
- Elements
- Weather
- Seasons
- Energy and resources

Environmental Compliances
- Temperature
- Light
- Sonic conditions
- Shelter
- Environmental impact
- Preservation
- Pollution

Functional Compliances
- Purpose
- Activities
- Movement
- Flexibility
- Scale
- Use
- Manpower

Physical Compliances
- Measurement and scale
- Sex
- Health
- Hygiene
- Security
- Hazards
- Disability
- Comfort

Psychological Compliances
- Ego
- Privacy
- Authority
- Aesthetics
- Style
- Scale
- Habits
- Phobias
- Status
- Image
- Character
- Individuality
- Impact
- Isolation
- Behavior
- Territory
- Personalization

Sociological Compliances
- Culture
- Creed
- Race
- Demography
- Economic status
- Class
- Impact

Regulatory Compliances
- Government
- Private policies and systems
- Legal and contractual conditions
- Codes
- Related agencies
- Commissions
- Associations
- Special interest groups
- Violations
- Variances

Economic Compliances
- Quality
- Cost
- Purpose (function)
- Investment
- Return
- Interest
- Depreciation
- Capital plan
- Economic trends
- Projection
- Operating costs
- Maintenance
- Marketing
- Sales
- Budget
- Land acquisition
- Taxation

Temporal Compliances
- Historic value
- Preservation
- Schedules
- Change
- Growth

Source: Manuel Marti, Jr., *Space Operational Analysis* (West Lafayette, Ind.: PDA Publishers, 1981).

ers them. If those interviewed express concerns or state strong positions, the issues must be addressed (not necessarily validated) and the results conveyed back to the individuals. When you ask questions of this group, you must deal with the answers.

Gathering requirements from operating staff depends on two basic issues. If standards are in place, less programming needs to be done. Normally, interviewing every employee is unnecessary. In large companies a 10 percent sample, subject to some minimum level and distribution, is more than adequate. Also, if management will not fund workplace functionality, there is no sense expending the effort to accommodate it.

Usually the requirements of support departments are not systematically and uniformly well gathered. Exhibit 10-2 is a list of functional areas that should be investigated. In developer-originated buildings, there may be a rationale for skimping on support facilities. In corporate or public buildings, this skimping is an invitation to both higher operating and higher maintenance costs. Most design firms are unable to program for support facilities, and too often the support managers cannot realistically state their requirements. Frequently the use of an industrial design consultant can prove helpful in getting this information into your programming.

Programming implies a series of projects within a time frame.[3] All the information gathering and problem identification in the world will not make a program. Thus the programming must also establish schedules. Completion schedules, along with project criteria and quality controls, will differ from project to project, but you should not lose sight of the fact that they are essential to the success of the project.

When the information gathering is completed, the results of all surveys and data should be combined, interpreted, and approved before they are passed on to the design team. The gathered data can also be used to start a facility database. Data definitely should be retained as the base document for a postoccupancy evaluation.

Annually one program should be the subject of an intense review by the facility manager. The questions asked are:

1. What is the mission of this program? The goals? The objectives? How well are they being met? Is change needed?
2. Is the program adequately resourced? If not, how can this requirement be accomplished?
3. How effective is the program? How cost-effective? How did the units produced measure against historical production figures?
4. How is the program perceived? By the manager? By the facility manager? By the users?

It is readily apparent that data are needed in order to perform an adequate evaluation. The facility manager should be conscious of future program evaluation requirements and structure the program monitoring systems so that they will provide those data.

Exhibit 10-2. Support activities to be considered in programming.

Shipping and Receiving

- Loading dock space
- Temporary storage
- Secure storage
- Berthing space
- Access to dumpster
- Centrality
- Proximity to freight elevators
- Proximity to primary users

Security

- Operations center location
- Guard posts
- Personnel access system
- Vehicular access system
- Executive access system
- Access by visitors and nonsecure personnel

Mail and Distribution

- Access to national mail system
- Distribution/collection schema
- Secure storage
- Access by external messengers

Motor Vehicle Pool

- Overnight storage
- Daytime parking
- Pick-up/drop-off points

Shops

- Access to materials
- Sizing
- Access to freight elevators
- Locker room
- Security

Food Service

- Layout
- Access to staff
- Centralized or decentralized coffee bar
- Access for foodstuffs
- Egress for garbage
- Locker room
- Vending locations

Conference Services

- Stage
- Audiovisual requirements
- Acoustics
- Lighting and lighting controls
- Recording capability
- Seating (fixed or movable)

Vertical and Horizontal Transportation

- Personnel elevators
- Freight or service elevators
- Escalators
- People movers
- Robots
- Location
- Access by people and goods
- Access to garages and roofs
- Security

Miscellaneous

- On-site furniture storage
- Custodial closets

Communications

- Closets
- Duct systems
- Location of file servers and network command elements

Benefits of Programming

Since programming is an orderly and systematic process, it would appear logical that facility managers would embrace it enthusiastically. That's not always true. The reluctance seems to stem from the following reasons:

1. Lack of familiarity with the programming process.
2. A view of programming as a luxury or an unneeded design cost.
3. Impatience to get to a design solution.
4. Time pressure to complete the project.

Every manager probably has his favorite programming horror story, but Doug Lowe of 3D International has a great one: A dramatic, award-winning head-quarters for a new business segment of an international corporation was ineffective almost immediately because there was no programming to detect the flexibility necessary for this new, rapidly expanding business. Therefore, a unique floor plan suitable for a mature company with little growth and few moves was designed. The building was obsolescent when built.[4]

Some interesting results come out of programming. My organization found that its population did not fit the anthropometric model (a model of the average office worker, used to design commercial furniture). To meet specific needs, furniture was designed for greater adjustability.[5]

Doug Lowe offers this argument regarding the value of programming:[6]

1. Programming is a logical process that works.
2. Programming is separate from other services offered by architectural-engineering (A-E) firms.
3. The FM can use a good programmer to lead the A-E and wind up with a project that meets his needs.
4. A good program will cause a building to be designed from inside out.
5. The FM can use a good programmer to take control of the decision-making process.
6. The FM and programmer will probably become allies, further strengthening the FM's position in the information chain.
7. A good programmer can help the FM set up procedures to deal with repetitive or other types of data that are better processed in-house.
8. A good programmer will produce a program that will be truly usable by all of its targeted audience.
9. A good programmer will develop a procedure to update the program, thus incorporating future changes.
10. Programming has many uses, and a facility manager has many uses for programming.

Project Planning

Project planning is the next step in the seamless progression that turns a set of requirements into a useful, productive facility. It is the bridge between the program and the design. Like the other steps in the design-build cycle, there is some spillover during planning. Some requirements will become modified or sharpened during planning; some elements of design may even need to be predetermined. The end result of planning, however it is done, is a project schedule and budget that the project team, particularly the project manager, can accept so that design can proceed with confidence.

The planning process for facility projects requires identifying a problem and then applying the resources necessary to solve it. In his book *Problem Finding and Problem Solving*, Alfred Schoennauer outlines techniques for two kinds of problem solving: after-the-fact and before-the-fact.[7] Many problems fall into that after-the-fact category, and these must be attended to daily.

A facility manager must plan effectively so that the operations of the company can proceed with few interruptions regardless of any emergency. The planning must consider available resources, specific aspects of a potential disaster, and corporate culture. Alas, the average facility manager reacts to things rather than anticipates them because it is not possible to make FM a continuum of before-the-fact processes. The balance of this chapter deals with aspects of the interior planning process, which represents a nearly perfect example of before-the-fact problem solving.

Most projects should evolve from the midrange facility plan, or at least from the annual work plan. That implies that some planning—perhaps a concept and a preliminary cost estimate—has already been done. Realistically, however, probably one third of even major projects will arise ad hoc. With luck, there will still be enough time to plan so that before-the-fact processes can be applied.

Once the company commits to a project, the programming will have defined the company's needs and identified the physical and resource requirements to meet those needs. Now the company will expect the facilities manager to meet those stated requirements (the program) within available resources and according to schedule. This is where the planning process steps in.

Planning involves determining the general design-and-build solutions and general sequence of the design-build cycle so that the following is possible:

1. It can be determined that the project is feasible.
2. A schedule can be developed.
3. A not-to-exceed budget can be developed.

Although it can be very detailed, planning is generally that last low-cost (staff) step before costly design, purchasing, and construction processes begin. As such, good planning has great potential for magnifying cost savings.

Establish Purpose and Scope

Like most other human endeavor, and certainly most all facility department efforts, a project is best achieved when there is focus on purpose and scope. The first step in planning is reviewing the project's purpose. The *purpose* clearly states the goal of the project and perhaps the problem it will solve. The *scope* describes the limits (financial, spatial, functional, and time) of the project. Spend time and effort now to ensure that you share an understanding of the scope and purpose with management. After all, it will be your task to transmit that understanding to the project team.

Organizing the Plan

The single common element when planning a white-collar work environment is the space to be occupied by the workers. That space may be owned by the company or leased. It may be divided, decorated, pierced, shared, filled with objects, heated, cooled, powered, illuminated. Stephen Binder calls space "the first frontier" for facility managers.[8]

In our business, planning most often is driven by space and funds, so an assessment of each is necessary. Planning is frequently formatted in terms of space, with the costs an output of the plan.

Resources and Methods

In facilities projects, the planner normally does not lack for information resources. Many projects have had a former life, and information should be available. As a minimum, the following should be available:

- The midrange facility plan
- The annual work plan
- Facility standards
- The program
- Information on like projects done recently
- For capital projects, the project evaluation calculations
- Information on how space needs will be met—for example, by leasing, building, altering, or renovating
- Concept design
- Concept budget
- Concept schedule
- Serviceability study

Depending on the size of the project, the last three items may be provided or you may be asked to proceed without them. Most planners do better-quality work if they are not totally unconstrained. Conversely, the best planner in the world cannot do well if necessary information is not forthcoming.

In Chapter 9, I listed several planning methods (e.g., critical path method, GANTT charts). All of these methods are good planning tools, so it is a matter of picking the proper tool for the project. For example, because our company did so many small interior alteration projects in a year, most of which had a life of from one to four weeks, we used a manual management system that tracked only four events per project. For large projects, we favor automated systems that calculate minimum and maximum values for completion dates and can budget for each event.

It is important to have an organizational database that can produce design and construction unit costs for planning (see Chapter 6). Any organization altering over 50,000 square feet, doing over ten projects, or moving over 100 staff annually should have a database of unit costs that is constantly being updated. If a small to medium facility department cannot invest in a planning or estimating staff, it should consider hiring a cost or estimating consultant to keep applicable unit costs updated. Initially the consultant can provide typical costs for the work the department plans, designs, and executes. Eventually, this will build a unique database for the facility manager.

At the risk of beating a dead horse, I reiterate the importance of standards to cost-effective planning and design. By using standards, and assuming that the design team will use them, the facility manager can reduce planning complexity and time by 50 to 70 percent. I suspect that this is why many facility departments have standards even though they are not officially accepted. Allow the facility designer to plan and design the vast majority of any project quickly (this is accelerated when standards for space and furniture can be fed into a computer-assisted design and drawing system) so that design time and effort can concentrate on unique spaces.

Fiscal Matters

It is very difficult to state hard and fast rules for the fiscal portion of project planning, but if possible, have a finance representative participate in the project planning. If, during the planning process, you exceed the budget used to calculate the projects' net present value or internal rate of return, you should report that to the chief financial officer (CFO). Other than that, it is difficult to provide specific guidance. While a not-to-exceed figure arrived at too early or too arbitrarily may preclude planning and design options, it's unrealistic to think there will be no fiscal constraints.

While there is always concern that overstating the front-end costs will kill the project, be conservative in your estimates until at least 70 percent of the design is complete. Provide a range for the project estimates at the planning stage and state clearly a contingency based on the final probable cost. As always, use life-cycle costing when making decisions about various aspects of the project.

Approval

Within the department, three staff functions must buy in to the plan: the planner, the project manager, and the facility manager. In some cases, all of these functions may be performed by the same individual. A CFO representative should be a party to all major project planning, as should an appropriate business unit representative and the design manager. Ultimately, you must either approve the plan or recommend it to the level having the proper approval authority so that design can commence.

Notes

1. Manuel Marti, Jr., *Space Operational Analysis* (West Lafayette, Ind.: PDA Publishers, 1981).

2. National Construction and Development Survey 2000 as quoted in "Survey Shows Growth in Building, Outsourcing, and the Dakotas," *Facilities Design and Management*, December 1997, p. 10.

3. Douglas H. Lowe, "Why You Should Find a Good Architectural Programmer," in *Facility Management—Meeting the Need of Tomorrow* (Houston: IFMA, 1988), p. 204.

4. Ibid., pp. 211–212.

5. Maree Simmons-Forbes, "J" building mockup and staff demographic results for The World Bank, undated.

6. Lowe, "Why You Should Find," pp. 211–212.

7. Alfred Schoennauer, *Problem Finding and Problem Solving* (Chicago: Nelson Hall, 1981).

8. Stephen Binder, *Corporate Facility Planning* (New York: McGraw-Hill, 1989).

11

The Design Process

Pulse Points

- *Even when design is outsourced, the facility manager must control the design process.*
- *Good design starts with a good concept and a good program.*
- *Complex projects are best designed by a team.*

In this chapter we progress to the point where others in the company see drawings, renderings, perhaps even a model. Because these are the first tangible portions of their project, it is commonly believed that a project begins with design. Nothing is further from the truth; good design must be based on good programming and project planning (Chapter 10). However, those functions remain either hidden or are misunderstood by others in the company, so the expectation level at the design stage is high.

Fortunately, design expertise is a common quality, in North America at least. Local licensing and membership in major professional organizations (e.g., American Institute of Architects, multiple engineering associations and societies, American Society of Interior Designers) ensure a high standard among design professionals. The metropolitan Washington, D.C., Yellow Pages alone has over 300 architectural and 250 interior design listings. That means that any facility manager, whether or not his department has an interior design capability, has access to competent design. It's merely a matter of finding the correct fit among the facility manager, the company, and the design team. There is growing awareness that the best designs are a collaborative effort,[1] but the facility manager and project manager must remain firmly in charge.

The Design Scene

Design firms of all types have accepted facility managers as their principal contacts with companies and agencies to a much greater degree than was true ten years ago. I think that is a sign of the maturity of the FM profession and that the relationships among designers, builders, and facility managers are becoming better defined. The instances where the chief executive officer's (CEO's) golfing buddy becomes the architect for the new headquarters facility seem to be occurring less and less.

First, a word to people on both sides of the user-designer equation. Certain business restrictions and contracts define the envelope within which both parties can operate. There must, however, be more than a contractual relationship. I strongly advocate a team approach with open and frank discussion. Time is better spent discussing design options than maneuvering for a better position. I rarely enter into a contract with a firm that I cannot treat as part of a team. If the fit is not good, both parties are probably better off not doing business together.

Facility managers need design firms (architects, interior architects and designers, engineers and special consultants). No facility manager does 100 percent of the design in-house, 100 percent of the time. Design, in fact, is the most frequently outsourced FM service.[2] Facility managers at small organizations in particular need the skills of contracting with and managing design firms. Therefore, the designer must demonstrate that his firm is unique and best suited to a company's needs. I admit to a bias for full-service firms, in that the design project manager manages all design elements on his side of the table while all user requirements and owner input are funneled through the facility manager. That way the facility manager can use a design firm to its best advantage.

The good facility manager knows the capability of local design firms and tries to match the design resources to the project. He maintains a file of potential firms for small, medium, and large projects. Unfortunately, some companies with strong, centralized purchasing departments take a dim view of negotiated or directed procurement of design services, and therefore make matching difficult.

The design firm's project manager must realize that the facility manager has internal clients who must be satisfied. The facility manager is responsible to his management, to see that the project is completed on time and within budget. The company's employees look to the facility manager to safeguard their health, provide a productive environment, and maintain facilities that are efficient and economical. In essence, the facility manager must live with and operate the building long after the design firm has moved on. A good design firm understands that environment and helps the facility manager with those internal considerations.

Selecting a Firm

In medium and large companies, design teams are selected by an evaluation committee of knowledgeable, in-house experts. The committee should be structured—or packed, if you will—so that the facility manager controls final selection; but committee experts in security, telecommunications, networking, life and safety, and building operations add significantly to the facility manager's ability to select the right design firm for the project. A typical evaluation schema (two-step) is shown in Exhibit 11-1. Other desirable members on the evaluation panel are:

- The corporation's project manager (chairman)
- In-house design representative
- In-house engineering representative
- In-house security or safety representative
- In-house communications representative
- User representative
- Purchasing agent (nonvoting secretary)

Although there are drawbacks to the beauty-contest aspects of evaluation panels, there is a great advantage in having a wide range of expertise and corporate political views. Further, there is a balance to be struck between objectivity of selection and the need for a firm that is a good team player. One of the tenets of the quality management movement is that corporations establish long-term relationships with organizations like design firms.

Perhaps the most difficult factor to evaluate in a design firm is its cooperativeness. Experience and technical capability are readily verifiable, but the fit on the project team is difficult to assess. In an ongoing relationship, of course, this is a known quality.

Some facility managers may be restricted by corporate procurement regulations in their selection of the design team. This is most often to the detriment of good team selection because it bureaucratizes what should be a personal process. A facility manager should work hard in the organization to establish rapport with in-house experts so that the experts will give their technical evaluation without insisting on hiring only "name" firms.

While there may be disincentives, it is essential that the design firm attempt to assess corporate decision-making procedures of potential clients before submit-

Exhibit 11-1. Design firm selection criteria.

Phase I (Determining Short List)

	Percentage Allotted
Project management qualifications	25
Qualifications of key staff	20
Like project experience	25
Approach to request for proposal	15
Financial and insurance capability	15

Phase II (Evaluating Short List)

	Percentage Allotted
Project manager qualifications	25
Qualifications of key staff	20
Like project experience	25
Approach to request for proposal	10
Presentation	20

ting a proposal. Also, designers should talk in depth to the operators of current buildings where the client resides and to the operators of similar buildings. These investigations contribute greatly to a firm's ability to submit a knowledgeable proposal. Some firms flounder because they fail to understand the politics in an organization. While a good project manager can and should expedite decision making, he is no guarantor for all corporate decisions—or their timeliness. A wise design firm reinforces the information capability of the project manager and helps him solve internal decision-making problems.

If possible, and if the project is large enough to justify it, the facility manager should visit a similar project that the proposed design project manager has managed or that the design firm has done. He should talk to the project manager and facility manager alone, asking what the design firm considers good design and seeking examples.

The facility manager should also require designers to prove that they understand designing to maintain, asking them to show examples. No other concept has had so much lip-service (except perhaps life-cycle costing). Finally, the facility manager should pay special attention to engineering. For many reasons, poor engineering design causes great problems, many of which can be mitigated only after the fact. In golf, you drive for show and putt for dough. In design, engineering is like putting; the inadequacies can be extremely costly in both operational and corrective costs.

Select the design firm for its expertise, experience, and demonstrated cooperativeness. Creativity and awards are not necessarily criteria for selection unless those are objectives of the project. Facility projects usually go much smoother when creative egos are not present and when the project objectives are the motivation for *all* participants.

If these suggestions are followed, project execution will be both productive and well controlled. As the design firm commences the design process, the facility manager must ensure that the personnel he was promised are actually on the job. The design firm should design and the project manager should control the management of the total project. The facility manager must ensure that user decisions are available to the design team at the proper time. This, of course, can be a problem in multilayered bureaucracies or when decision making is fragmented.

Design Reviews and Presentations

Early on, formal design reviews should be established. Normally, these reviews are conducted:

1. The feasibility study, if conducted
2. The concept, if done by the design firm
3. The program (if done by the design firm), with user sign-off
4. At 25 to 35 percent developed design (last chance for substantive revision)
5. At 80 to 85 percent developed design (still time for those finishing touches)
6. The final design (before the release for procurement)

On fast-track projects these reviews may be combined, but each time the process is fragmented, the facility manager assumes greater risk for the workability of the total product.

A presentation to senior management is a must, even if not requested. If possible, include the CEO, the senior occupant of the newly designed space, and your boss. It is best if the facility manager or project manager does the presentation, but whoever does so must be well rehearsed. The presentation sells the project.

For projects introducing new concepts or technology, use a mockup. They are expensive, but they can be invaluable for design evaluation and for selling new systems and technologies—or, for that matter, to discover that great ideas won't fly. Vendors do an outstanding job of supplying mockups, which should help reduce costs.

Documentation and Follow-Through

The key to good facility management is documentation. The design firm should be more than willing to update all documentation into a common format at a reasonable price.

It's a good idea to write several important end-of-project procedures into contracts and specifications. They vary from organization to organization, so you must guide the design firm in what should be included. As a minimum, include the following:

- Recommendation on amount and storage of attic stock
- Punch list procedures
- Operational testing procedures
- Documentation
- Furnishing and finish boards
- Training on equipment
- Warranty turnover
- Instruction book turnover

It is now possible for the facility manager to obtain drawings, warranties, and instructions in automated form.

During construction, you will have to ensure that the design team stays involved. How involved the designer will remain is not only a contractual matter but varies widely among design firms. It is likely you will frequently need interpretations of design intent, best given by the designer. How well the firm will support you during construction and how well it will provide pertinent information to make project decisions is a major factor in determining further work with the firm.

Finally, both you and the design team should assess how well the project works three to six months after occupancy. The postoccupancy evaluation should address only those items you are willing and able to correct on-site or as part of downstream projects. Also, the evaluation is not done for academic purposes; the study should fit the size and complexity of the project (see Chapter 12).

Design Practices and Considerations

I do not attempt to provide a design manual. For excellent treatment of the details of interior design projects, I recommend Carol Farren's *Planning and Managing Interior Projects*.[3] However, facility managers need to understand the design process so they can control the process. I also include here some rules of thumb.

Design Outputs

Until good design is put in a form and format where it is useful to contractors, it remains simply a good idea. Historically, a hierarchy of plans for transmitting design into construction has been developed. Each project has unique needs, but some plans are common to most projects.

The *base plan* is a scaled drawing of a specific floor of a building that indicates all permanent and/or structural aspects of that floor. Usually found on the base plan are such items as the building core, lavatories, exits, fenestrations (doors and windows), and support columns. Almost all subsequent plans may be overlaid on the base plan to provide adequate information for each floor without replicating the structural information on each plan. When used in a computer-assisted design and drawing (CADD) situation, all plan-view drawings can be viewed as layers stacked on top of each other. Hard-copy prints (blue line, black line, etc.) may be plotted individually or as a single overlayed plan.

The *demolition plan* is a scaled drawing of a specific floor of a building that indicates the removal of particular walls or partitions, plumbing, telephone and electrical units, and custom fabrications (cabinets, etc.). Demolition plans are used only when remodeling or renovating.

The *installation plan* is in plan view and also in scale with other drawings. This plan identifies the location of modular panels, and indicates the location of sources of power for each series of connected panels (panel runs). Also indicated are individual panels that offer electrical outlets and power, which are not powered and which require power to be passed through to other panels. Individual power circuits are located and noted on this plan too. The plan is used to coordinate the work of furniture manufacturers and installers to ensure proper specification and installation at a later date.

The *component plan* is a scaled drawing related to a specific floor of a building and is a second overlay to the installation plan. On this plan, the components are noted that will be "hung" on the panels shown on the installation plan. Locations of hinges and cabinet door swings are also on this plan, as are indications of lighting specific for each workstation (task lighting).

The *floor plan* (furniture plan) indicates the remaining furniture to be placed on a specific floor. It is completed in the same scale as the drawings of panels and components. Noteworthy in this plan are the files, shared equipment, and seating.

This drawing is often a single sheet, but may be a third overlay, merely adding to the installation and component plans.

The *reflected ceiling plan* (lighting) is a scaled drawing produced from the perspective of looking down on the ceiling from above. This view is the opposite of the view from the floor looking upward in the actual space—thus, the term *reflected ceiling*. The lighting depicted on this plan generally is suspended in a ceiling of acoustic panels (tile) with access openings noted. The lighting is intended to supply an overall lighting condition in the space, sometimes called ambient lighting.

The *telecom/datacom plan* is a scaled drawing of a specific floor, often combining a diagram of placement of data and telephone sources and wires when they utilize structural aspects of the building as avenues of supply. Specific notes are required to identify sources or wiring when plenum or surface supply conditions exist.

The *floor covering plan* is another scaled drawing of a specific floor that indicates the kinds and extent of floor covering to be used in each space. Often this plan is simply a schedule or note.

The *wall covering/finish plan* is a scaled drawing of a specific floor drawn in plan-view, indicating the extent of coverage of a specific paint or wall covering in the space. Often this plan does not completely represent an intended coverage and will require additional information in the form of elevations of specific spaces located on the floor. (The information often is covered by a schedule rather than a drawing.)

Each of these plans requires notations *(schedules)* that refer to additional information found elsewhere in the plans. The schedules may represent a specific piece of information such as color, size, or performance or may be a specific set of instructions or specifications. Common types of schedules found in plan sets include panel size, finish and power capability, lighting, materials and finishes, floor covering, acoustical material, and furniture.

Details and *joinery plans* represent specific, unique circumstances. These plans vary in scale and in information presented. Some common conditions that require special instructions include cabinetry; custom details in ceiling, walls, and windows; or unusual conditions that occur when two dissimilar plans connect or converge.

Perspectives and/or *renderings* are not necessarily to scale. They are not intended to present exact instructions to installers or builders. Rather, these drawings are an opportunity to view an enclosed space in three dimensions. The view captures all furniture and architectural elements in relationship to each other, something that cannot be accomplished in two-dimensional representation. Perspective drawings show space as the user will view it and represent all color and textural aspects that further describe the relationships within the space. Renderings are more expensive to produce than scaled drawings and normally are used to help top management and users understand the intended final product.

Before the design process can begin, it is essential that a facility manager understand the rules of design. Those rules may be divided into three categories:

1. Identification of systems and subsystems
2. Development of standards
3. Regulations and constraints

Systems and Standards

Every project that is interior related must address one or more systems. These systems for interior projects include:

- Building systems
- Floor systems
- Wall systems
- Ceiling systems
- Fenestration systems
- Furniture systems

The systems, to varying degrees, dictate to the designer what can be designed in a particular space. The degree to which these are written standards for various design factors is shown in Exhibit 11-2. Interestingly the data indicate an across-the-board increase in policy writing.

Managers whose major function is to lease space usually develop a set of building standard allowances. That is, each prospective tenant is automatically provided with materials to satisfy wall, floor, and ceiling system needs. If a prospective tenant desires to upgrade from the systems offered by the landlord, he may elect to receive an allowance in dollars toward the purchase of different materials or systems. Nevertheless, the manager or landlord determines a prescribed system for each surface in his building before the leasing process can begin. He must also coordinate all systems beforehand.

A facility manager must also determine standards and coordination guidelines for the systems in the space to be occupied. The ceiling and flooring systems present the best potential variation and therefore have the simplest solutions. For instance, large, open areas are normally capped with a suspended ceiling that universally covers the space. Housed within the suspension skeleton is a configu-

Exhibit 11-2. Design factors covered by policy or standards (percentage of respondents).

	Percentage Written	Percentage Unwritten	Percentage None
Office types	54	30	16
Space allotments	55	29	16
Artwork/plants	26	41	33
Furniture arrangement	46	33	21
Office locations	31	37	32

Source: *Facility Management Practices, 1996* (Houston: IFMA), p. 25.

ration of lighting fixtures that collectively produce adequate ambient light. (A review of fixture placement should be made later to determine a minimum amount of glare and general quality of the light.) The amount of light required varies according to work performed and whether light sources are also located at the task. Sprinkler systems (when required) utilize either the suspension skeleton or plenum produced by the suspension of the acoustical or reflective panels. Plenums also house air-handling systems (heating, ventilation, and air-conditioning—HVAC) and often serve as air return ducts for the HVAC system. The light reflectance quality of the ceiling is important in calculating the overall performance of the space and is usually presumed to be at least 80 percent reflective. The suspension skeleton is also used to support speakers when sound masking systems are deployed.

Materials placed on the floor offer the potential for sound absorption and aesthetics but do little to complement the acoustical or illuminated environment. Carpeting or soft floor covering may absorb the sounds of impact (walking) but not represent efficient noise reduction. Hard-surface flooring may contribute to sound reflectance, however. The color and texture of floor covering are often below the presumed 20 percent reflectance formula used to predict illumination levels in a space. Lower performance may require more illumination. The ceiling presents few physical hazards for occupants, while the floor must present adequate footing (nonslip) under all conditions. Several different materials must be used to ease the transition of walking from hostile outside environment into the workplace. Perhaps the most significant aspect of coordinating floor covering systems is understanding the required maintenance for each material or condition. Traffic patterns and intensity may also determine the floor covering.

Walls are often overlooked when considering both illumination and acoustical performance. The illumination predictability formula is 80/50/20: an 80 percent reflectance is expected from a ceiling system, 50 percent from the walls, and 20 percent from the flooring system. Most wall surfaces have assumed a decorative role in the interior design of a space. When dark colors or heavy textures are used, the 50 percent reflectance may be diminished. As with floor coverings, diminished reflectance requires additional illumination in the ceiling.

Footprints of space (potential variations) may be somewhat determined by accessibility standards. A barrier-free environment will have noticeably wider circulation space than is required by standard regulations and codes. Be aware of the philosophy of your organization in regard to accessibility when developing standards of space utilization. Insist on isometric drawings of each workstation to ensure performance needs. Also test on site at least one configuration of the various standards, using employees under conditions similar to those that will actually be encountered.

Furniture systems are usually limited to partitions and componentry of a workstation. In reality, seating must be considered part of the system. Most seating today has adjustable features touted by manufacturers as productivity enhancing and ergonomic. While it is true that the technology of office seating has improved greatly, no significant findings support increased productivity as a result of the new seating technology. You should ensure that testing of seating be completed under work conditions before making the final selection. Exercise care to analyze manufacturers' claims.

Effective and Efficient Space Allocation

After the decisions have been made regarding furniture systems, a facility manager begins the task of dividing up the space for employee use. Effectiveness and efficiency of space are not synonymous. Effective use of space implies that the space function is maximized—that is, each worker at a workstation is provided with maximum functional support for each task at hand. Space efficiency is the ability to achieve maximum density per square foot. The ultimate objective is to provide maximum support in as small a space as possible without constricting the workers.

A second efficiency may be achieved through design of multiple workstation modules. CADD programs use the principles of space planning to help you design a single workstation, then reproduce it as many times as necessary for a single drawing of a multiple workstation module, thus simplifying the planning process.

Office support furniture and equipment continues to change. The most futuristic innovation, developed to meet the need for quiet and privacy within a team environment, is the individual workstation that resembles an airplane cockpit. The cockpit is outfitted with the individual's computer, screen, and ergonomic seating. This workstation can be independently controlled for air quality, lighting, and temperature, and plug in/plug out of existing building systems.

Conventional Panel-Hung Systems

Conventional panel-hung systems require that panels of standard module width be used (most common are two-foot widths and four-foot widths). The most common workstation standards are then expressed in extensions of those modules.

Aesthetics are enhanced with partition strings on 45-degree angles with the horizontal walls in the space, and with radius panels at the termination of panel runs or as entrances to individual workstations. An efficient arrangement is small squares with replicated panel widths in the same side of each workstation. Aisles should be minimized (within code compliance) and circulation space kept to a minimum. To minimize design time on the project, use CADD to design multiple workstations.

Circular Radiating Clusters

The most efficient use is maximum-density clusters (six workstations) arranged as close together as possible. The visual arrangement is similar to "spots" when viewed in plan and will defy a truly aesthetic appearance. While these clustered workstations increase density significantly over conventional panel-hung systems, workstation function may be significantly reduced. It's a trade-off between density and functionality.

Clustered Panel Systems

Providing the modularity of conventional panel systems, clustered panels may even be reconfigured into or interfaced with conventional arrangements. These systems provide maximum function at minimal per-workstation costs with indicated flexibility.

When using CADD, select from a variety of footprints that range from two to eight workstations in a single grouping. Different from other systems, clustered panels can further group up to sixty-four or more workstations for the most efficient design. They maximize circulation space and the efficiency difference between a circle and a square (3.1416/4) to demonstrate the greatest possible functional density.

The aesthetic appeal of this system is unique. Linking patterns of groups form soft organic shapes in a space conducive to departmental communication and interaction. It also provides a significantly greater capability for lateral filing than does any other system.

In a recent survey, nearly 75 percent of senior business executives, government officials, facility executives, and building association leaders queried felt that the government should fund research and development studies of office productivity. Over 93 percent of that same group felt that high-quality work environments can increase worker productivity.[4]

Productivity Information

A number of furniture manufacturers have made claims that their specific product increases productivity. Some studies support the claim that appropriate furniture and other work-support tools also contribute to increase productivity, although those studies do not claim product specificity. Perhaps more important than furnishings in determining productivity are how people view their jobs. According to Robert Nolan, who writes on issues of office productivity, there are five basic expectations of people with respect to their workplace:[5]

1. Job security
2. Sense of community
3. Well-defined job expectations by employer
4. Feedback on performance
5. Opportunity

Sometimes a facility manager or space planner will project productivity increases under certain conditions or using a specific product or technology. Yet it appears that employee perceptions, not specific pieces of furniture, are most important to productivity. You are well advised to discount the productivity claims of manufacturers and establish productivity projections based on established figures.

Product Specifications and Contracts

Many products appear to be similar, but do not take advertised claims at face value. Test a product that appears to approximate the purpose and scope desired, and be sure such testing is done under controlled conditions and as close to actual working conditions as possible.

Guarantees for products should be for at least as long as their tax depreciation schedule. Manufacturers' suggested maintenance programs should be included in every purchase. Each specification package should contain provisions for warehousing the product if the space is not available for occupancy on the projected date. In addition, penalty clauses will be a deterrent for late delivery or faulty merchandise. Finally, all specifications should ensure product replacement availability at a specific future date, to ensure aesthetic and maintenance continuity.

All furniture manufacturers offer dealers standard discounts on their products. When a major company makes purchases over a period of years, the total may be much more than a dealer purchases in a year. Your contract with the manufacturer can be written to cover future furniture needs as well as current ones, thereby including a discount that may significantly exceed the normal wholesale price available to dealers.

Refining the Budget

An economic model is essential to the birth and life of any project. An economic model is a budget, a guide, or sometimes an educated guess. All models presume certain conditions and may achieve a high degree of accuracy if those conditions hold true. It is essential for a facility manager to minimize the variance from the presumed conditions. In other words, a successful project results from well-defined project parameters.

Assuming that attention was given to the data-gathering stage and that the data were thoroughly analyzed, budgetary parameters should be fully understood by this point. The workstation standards will be helpful in establishing the cost figures for purchasing furnishings, warehousing needs, maintenance programs, churn factors, and installation or construction costs. Assuming that the architectural and design fees are hard numbers (not open ended), those numbers may also be safely projected into the budget.

The most difficult numbers to project are costs of internal time to complete the project (estimates of supervision, employee downtime, survey involvement). Those numbers are estimates and come from a number of different sources. Ask for documentation supporting the estimates that come from outside sources.

As the design progresses, the budget should become more specific. Ordinarily, the project budget should be locked in by the time that design is 30 percent complete.

Notes

1. Vivian Loftness, "Research: Fundamentals for Design Professionals," *Construction Specifier* (May 1989): 112.

2. *Facility Management Practices* (Houston: IFMA, 1996), p. 15.

3. Carol Farren, *Planning and Managing Interior Projects* (Kingston, Mass.: R. S. Means Company, 1988).

4. *On-Site Research Findings; National Summit on Building Performance* (Washington, D.C.: Cramer-Krasselt, 1996), pp. 5, 15.

5. Robert E. Nolan, Richard T. Young, and Ben C. DiSylvester, *Improving Productivity Through Advanced Office Controls* (New York: AMACOM, 1980).

12

The Construction Phase

Pulse Points

- *Both design-build and fast-tracking offer opportunities for cost savings but place greater pressure on the design team.*
- *Costs can be minimized by selecting the correct method of contracting and construction process for major projects.*
- *Prequalify design firms and builders.*
- *Award good performers; drop nonperformers.*

One of the difficulties of trying to break an integrated subject like facility management into its component parts is that the reader loses the sense of concurrency and integration that is necessary to manage facilities well. For example, construction cannot be divorced from either planning and design (Chapters 10 and 11) or project management (Chapter 9). In fact, partnering and the trend toward design-build have blurred what distinctions existed between these functions. In most major projects, it is neither desirable nor financially wise to move consecutively from concept, through planning, to design, and then construction.

Particularly in the private sector, once a decision has been made to commit to a construction project, all parties try to compress the schedule as much as possible so that the business purpose of that project can begin as early as possible. I once heard a builder say, "All of our projects are now fast-track!" Since construction is often started before design is complete, there is great pressure on getting all of the "front-end things" right. Business issues drive construction also. For example, for some companies, a scenario where a developer builds a building to their specification and then leases it to them might best meet both of their technical and financing needs.

Construction of new facilities always brings particular attention to the facilities department. At times construction has been called the glory function of facility management, since the programming, planning, and design come to fruition.

Construction is often defined as the installation or assembly of a facility. For practical purposes, most large facility departments handle two kinds of construction, often using a dollar value ($100,000, for example) to differentiate between major and minor construction.

Major construction normally is funded with capital funds, as part of a multi-year capital construction program. Minor construction is similar to alterations, and although it can change the very nature of the facility, it often is funded out of the annual budget.

Minor Construction and Alterations

Almost all organizations fund some level of work that could be capitalized but comes from the annual operating budget. The most common reasons are that there must be funds available to meet reactive needs, and the size of the projects is below the company cutoff for capitalization. Thus, funds for minor construction often are mixed with maintenance and repair moneys, and they compete for priority. In fact, that can become such a problem that the U.S. military has put a ceiling on the total annual dollars that can be used for new work, minor construction, and alterations versus maintenance and repair.

For most companies, a typical minor construction project is related to moves or expansion to accommodate new space or equipment needs. It is typically $10,000 to $50,000 in scope, and can be designed and constructed with in-house resources. This type of job is best managed by a project manager focused on the user. An alternative is the interior designer or space planner who also coordinates design, construction, moving, communications, installation, furniture and furnishing installation, and project turnover.

In general, specialized construction management systems are not cost-effective on such small jobs, though Program Evaluation Review Technique (PERT) and GANTT charts may be used to report to management. Often, off-the-shelf project management systems such as Microsoft Project are used. In medium-size organizations, it is not uncommon to have 150 to 200 such projects going annually, mostly to implement churn. With so many small projects occurring in such a brief time frame, the facility manager is unable to oversee most individual projects and must devote most or all of his time to managing the program as a whole.

Minor construction is fairly easy to reduce to a routine that is highly efficient, providing there are standards and available design and construction capability. The management challenge is to keep this work from absorbing maintenance and repair funds.

Major Construction or Renovation

Some facility managers never manage a major construction or renovation project, while others construct new facilities on almost a routine basis. Most, however, have at least one experience with a major capital project. Because these projects have high visibility in the boardroom, every facility manager should be comfortable with this type project. In fact, because these projects have historically been given to a retiring vice president, seizing the initiative may be one of the biggest challenges for a facility manager.

Initially, the key to managing a major construction or renovation is organizing the design-build team; this is explained in Chapters 9 and 11. Early on, a decision needs to be made regarding the contractual arrangements needed to manage and build the facility. For example, if a structure already exists on the site, you may have to bid the asbestos removal and facility demolition separately from the construction services. The extent to which the in-house staff manages the construction depends on the form of contract employed. The choice is usually between construction management and general contracting.

Construction management (CM) is one popular method of contracting. It is the inevitable result of building more complex buildings and the need for better continuity, at least from design through turnover. In a recessionary period, CM also offers substantial reductions in project cost. CM is different from general contracting:

Construction Management

1. Places premium on the ability of the construction manager.
2. Requires significant participation by the facilities department.
3. Needs better coordination between design and construction.
4. Better for phrased construction.

General Contracting

1. May be the only option for a small facility department.
2. Commits the facility manager to lump-sum contracting.
3. One contractor performs most trade work.
4. The project is not so large that it requires phasing.
5. There is little need for close coordination between the architectural-engineering firm (A-E) and the contractor.

Hiring a construction manager should reduce the total project cost or the time to design and construct. Sometimes the company can fill the construction management function without hiring additional people.

Although the term *construction management* has been used for several years, actually there are three generally accepted CM practices. In one form, the construction manager is retained by the facility manager early in the design stage, then assists in managing the design process, offering his expertise to ensure that the facility manager's interests are represented.

In another form, the construction manager is hired following completion of the design. He then is responsible for the construction process, helping the owner obtain contractors for the various segments of the project, providing project coordination, and expediting the work.

In the third form, the construction manager may actually perform portions of the work with his own crews or contract for the work with other companies if that is less expensive. I have seldom seen this used, for obvious reasons. (See Exhibit 9-1.)

The Construction Process

The most common method for major construction is the conventional construction process. When the design work is completed, the bidding process leads to selection of one or more contractors to handle the construction. There are many alternatives to this process that may be useful under certain circumstances. In the public sector, law often requires that construction projects be awarded by competitive bid.

Following are explanations and definitions of some alternatives to the standard competitive-bid process, based on completed designs for large projects. These alternatives are intended to save time and money but usually increase owner involvement. Thus, the success of these alternative processes depends on the owner's knowledge, ability, and expertise in construction management. Those are only some of the alternatives. Variants seem to appear regularly.

Design-Build Alternative

Under this process, one firm usually has responsibility for both the design and the construction of the facility. The design-build format can be used in a competitive-bid process, but it requires extensive planning and a method of analyzing the proposals submitted by the candidate firms. This method gets the construction underway as the plans for each segment are completed, rather than waiting for the total project design. It saves time and therefore money. It also controls cost in that a price for the project is established early on in the design process. If executed properly, design-build promotes the team concept and encourages integrated problem solving, two other major advantages.

This alternative may, however, be limited by a strong desire for design compatibility among various buildings to be constructed at different times. Thus, heavy programming responsibility falls on the facility manager.

Fast-Track Alternative

Fast-tracking compresses the time between the start of design and completion of construction. This works well on relatively large projects and can be adapted to either competitive bid or negotiated contracts. Many facility managers feel that, given the cost of capital, all major projects should be fast-tracked to some degree.

As with design-build, fast-tracking saves time by starting construction on selected parts of the project prior to completion of designs. The designer must complete segments of the construction documents in a sequence that follows the proposed sequence of construction. Once the design for a phase is finished, work is contracted. Then other portions of the design are completed. This pressures the design team and tests the competency of the designers. The process requires careful cost-estimating allocation to ensure that funds are sufficient for the entire project. Fast-tracking also restricts the designer's ability to incorporate desired changes into the project after the initial construction contracts are awarded.

Turnkey Alternative

A turnkey process has great appeal to small facility departments facing a unique, one-time project. The contractor or developer arranges for and obtains all necessary construction financing and may, in fact, manage the project from concept through construction. Once the project is complete, the contractor exchanges the title of the building for either full payment or future payments.

Selecting a Builder

North America is blessed with many companies that can design and build large, complex facilities. In fact, excellent builders can mobilize at almost any site, some of them elsewhere in the world. Nevertheless, a builder must be chosen carefully, using these criteria:

1. Successful completion of multiple projects at the location selected
2. Successful completion of similar multiple projects
3. Financial stability
4. A qualified and compatible manager

I admit to a certain discomfort with some methods for analyzing the technical capabilities of a builder. The selection often takes on aspects of a beauty contest, compounded by the fact that the references given seldom provide either an "encouragin' or discouragin' word." Most selection processes encourage bureaucratic procedure rather than commonsense evaluation. I favor a two-step evaluation procedure, the second phase involving an interview with the manager of each company.

Construction Contracts

The traditional construction contract is a fixed sum, reached through competitive bidding or negotiation. In recent years, however, other types of contract have been used to meet both market and management needs. The advent of construction management, with fast-track and design-build alternatives, may help companies gain some of the benefits of these innovative construction contracts. Following is a brief explanation of some of the common contract alternatives.

Guaranteed Maximum Price

The guaranteed maximum price (G-max) establishes a maximum project cost. It then provides incentives to the contractor to reduce this cost. The maximum cost can be obtained through competitive bid or negotiation, and the contract provides the means of apportioning the financial savings that are established.

By its nature, this contract shifts considerable design responsibility to the contractor, so the designer and owner must review all cost-saving measures proposed by the contractor. The major difference between design-build and G-max is that in the latter the owner controls the proposed design deviations. In design-build, the contract is for the design, with owner review and approval.

Since the G-max form shifts most of the responsibility for design omissions to the contractor, it is necessary that the company have a strong, detailed design at the beginning of the process. If the design is poor or incomplete, the contractor is likely to inflate the G-max price to cover the ambiguity.

Cost Plus Percentage

In the cost plus percentage contract, the facility manager pays the actual cost of the project but allows a fixed percentage for overhead and profit. There is no incentive on the part of the contractor to control costs.

Cost Plus Fixed Fee

The cost plus a fixed fee contract is structured to remedy the problems associated with cost plus percentage by limiting the cost ceiling. It eliminates any incentive for the contractor to drive the cost upward, since the profit margin is set.

Cost Plus Fixed Fee With Upset Figure

The fixed fee with upset figure contract is a compromise. It establishes a fixed cost ceiling for the completed project, and the contractor realizes a profit as long as costs remain below the fixed ceiling.

Multiple Prime Contracts

Most facilities are constructed with a single prime contract that covers the entire project. An alternative is to award multiple prime contracts, preferred by some large facility management organizations. In these contracts, each of the prime contractors has a direct contractual relationship with the owner. The company must hire a construction manager or must have one of the multiple prime contractors provide project coordination.[1]

Construction Documentation

Many companies suboptimize their ability to execute construction projects—and later, alteration and renovation—because they fail to obtain complete documentation. Exhibit 12-1 presents documents that should be considered as deliverables for every project.

The items most often forgotten or issued too late are move lists, demolition plans (including cable removal), and communications plans. Because all trades

Exhibit 12-1. Construction documentation for experienced in-house renovators.

Item	Always Needed	Remarks
Demolition plan (includes art relocation)	No	Can be overlay or notes.
Architectural plan	Yes	
Signage schedule	Yes	
Finish plan	No	Can be notes.
Telephone plan	Yes	
Electrical plan	Yes	
Electrical schedule	Yes	
Wire plan	Yes	
Wire labels	Yes	If used.
Cable removal plan	Yes	If cable moving required.
Fire/life safety plan	Yes	
Fire/life safety schedule	Yes	
Cable labels	Yes	If cabling involved.
Furniture plan	Yes	Or reference to a standard.
Furniture schedule	No	Can be notes.
Reflected ceiling plan	No	Only if major ceiling alterations.
Mechanical plan	Yes	Only if major mechanical work.
Specifications	No	Notes normally suffice unless out or major construction.
Details	No	Normally needed for millwork only.
Move (from-to) lists	Yes	

must be coordinated, it is necessary for all plans to be issued and viewed by the construction manager in toto; piecemeal issuance can only cause delays or confusion.

For experienced alteration or renovation crews who regularly work with the same design team and buildings, the volume of construction documentation can be reduced substantially. This is also true when the company uses demountable partitions, standard furniture, standard office layout, and good office and space standards. Document everything that is needed—but *only* what is needed.

Facility Management Concerns During Construction

Besides that the project will be constructed on time and within budget, the facility manager must concern himself with these factors during construction:

1. Building systems
2. Maintainability
3. Operating costs, particularly energy management
4. Staffing and organizing
5. Turnover procedures and training
6. As-built drawings, warranties, and sample books

Paying attention to these issues during construction will help ensure that the company will assume an operable building at turnover and that initial operating problems will be minimized.

In an informal survey of facility managers, several of whom are heavily involved in construction, the following were found to be typical of cost savings or avoidances that could be expected from good facility management related to construction:

1. *Good programming (5 to 20 percent).* You will save money if you carefully define your requirements up front.
2. *Value engineering (10 to 30 percent).* Your design-construction experts can often recommend different products or methods that will reduce costs and improve quality.
3. *Fast-track construction (5 to 10 percent).* Savings here are in both the cost of capital and the earlier productive use of the site.
4. *Design-build construction (5 to 10 percent).* Design-build saves time and thus costs, and it allows for effective cost control.
5. *Innovative procurement (5 to 20 percent).* Savings here vary from the use of such things as national sales contracts and multiple prime contractors.

Cost Control

I want to stress again the need to do life-cycle costing for all major components of significant construction projects. One of the places where the facility manager should inject himself into the process is to ensure that he sells life-cycle costing to his management. Someone on his team will be able to crunch the numbers (although the facility manager should review and challenge them), but only he is in a position to sell the results of life-cycle costing to management. It is often a hard sell, but an incentive to do so is the fact that the facility manager and his budget will be living with the result for the life of the building.

Because of the high cost of major construction or renovation projects, cost control is always an issue. Unfortunately, it is often misunderstood. Too often, it is viewed simply as driving the initial capital cost down. Also, nonfacilities managers do not realize the cost of late operational decisions that affect design or construction. Exhibit 12-2 is a graphic representation of the effect that timely decision making can have on project costs.[2] Early in the project, the project manager should develop an expenditure profile and should track expenditures against it closely.

Exhibit 12-2. Relation between timing of decisions and cost savings.

Savings
Design
Materials
Methods

Cost of → Changes

The decisions made in the
conceptual and schematic phases
have the greatest impact
and the least cost commitment.

Programming and Planning
Conceptual Cost Management

Cost

| Design | Contract Documents | Construction | Use |

Time

Source: Larry Gleason, "Modeling Facility Construction Alternatives," *IFMA Conference, 1987 Proceedings* (Houston: IFMA, 1988), p. 317.

Efficient Management

In construction, there are great advantages to the proper use of computer-assisted facility management. Computers can be especially useful in three areas: payments, schedules, and change orders.

Payments. Computer-generated payments to A-E firms and to contractors are virtually required to administer construction contracts on large projects. This is especially true when using CM techniques or multiple prime contractors. You could have as many as twenty or thirty contracts for a single project. This way, payments are triggered by completion of schedule items.

Scheduling. Monitoring schedules is an area that benefits from automation. Most contractors prepare detailed schedules in order to mesh the work of subcontractors and the delivery of material. Commonly, both construction documents and schedules use the Construction Specification Institute classifications of work as a basis for the computer network, and that information is often shared with the design-build team. By comparing schedules to completion dates, you can spot bottlenecks in the process quickly enough to correct them.

Change orders. Change orders are of two types: *pending change orders* (suggested changes not yet approved by all parties) and *approved change orders* (changes that have been approved). Normally there are more pending change orders than approved change orders. The computerized network can ensure that all parties have a record of these changes and a method to resolve change issues quickly.

Quality Control

I recommend a qualified construction inspector for projects over $250,000. This is in addition to the inspection services normally performed by the A-E firm. Although I am unaware of any major policy change from the American Institute of Architects, my observation is that architects tend to shy away from providing inspection services for clients. I am sure that this is driven by the litigious nature of the construction business. At one time, architects used to be so actively involved that they often were project managers for small owners. Now they provide only the necessary on-site presence to ensure that their design is being generally followed. This is not intended as a criticism but as a situation to which the facility manager of a major project needs to respond by providing inspection and work validation services beyond those provided by the architect. Other services that should be provided on large projects, either with in-house or contracted personnel, are cost estimating and schedule review; construction accounting and auditing; and legal, code, and permit advice.

Control of construction is exercised through the review and change approval process. Major reviews should coincide with major events, but team reviews should be held at least weekly. I favor a two-tiered review approach, with a technical review always preceding a management review.

One quality-control item often ignored, but which can preclude many problems, is operational testing prior to acceptance. If a mechanical system is designed to perform in a certain way, the mechanical engineer should design a test to ensure compliance, and the system should be tested. No manufacturing facility would ever be acceptable without such tests, yet office building systems are frequently accepted without significant testing.

Involvement of In-House Personnel

It is extremely important to keep in-house personnel involved in the construction process. The builder should feel comfortable with them on the construction site, and they should be actively involved in reviews and testing. The facility being constructed is unique, a one-time effort, which in-house personnel will have to operate, maintain, and repair. The best time for these employees to become familiar with the building is as it is built. Some A-E firms, construction managers, and general contractors view involvement of in-house staff as threatening. You can dispel that attitude, making it clear that in-house personnel will be involved.

Turnover Procedures

Too often the turnover of a facility seems almost an afterthought. Here are some considerations for the end of a project:

1. Beneficial occupancy
2. Punch lists
3. Preparation: completion of work, sign-off
4. Operating tests: composition, scheduling
5. As-built drawings: shop drawings, cable management schema, medium (CADD, reproducibles, copies), distribution, completion date
6. Warranties
7. Finish and sample boards
8. Attic stock: inventory, storage method
9. Training

These considerations are frequently handled through a best practice called commissioning. *Commissioning* is the effective and efficient turnover of a major project or building from the builder to the owner and occupants. I strongly advocate the commissioning of major projects. Attention to these details will add inestimable value to a project. If the facility manager is prepared to handle it, the information contained in items 5 and 6 (as-built drawing and warranties) can be supplied in automated format along with pictures and schematics, maintenance schedules, and instruction books for all major equipment. A major project's completion, if properly managed, can provide major impetus toward a complete computer-assisted facility management system. Sometimes the cost of automating can be funded in the project cost.

For all major projects, I attempt to perform a postoccupancy evaluation (POE) six to eighteen months after occupancy. There are now consulting firms that specialize in POEs, but whether you use an outside consultant or your own staff, you should accomplish these objectives:

1. Determine whether there was a correct program for the project.
2. Measure whether the goals of that program were met.
3. Gather input from the staff on overall effect of the program.
4. Determine corrective action for the next similar project.

POEs raise expectations. If you are not willing to make corrections or adjustments, do not bother to conduct them.

Potential Problems With Construction Projects

In recent years, there has been concern about inefficiency and low productivity in the construction industry. While all of these problems may not be applicable to an individual project, being aware of them may help you avoid them:

1. Failure of both parties to understand the project's scope
2. Irrelevant contract requirements
3. Too generous decisions on contract appeals
4. Reliance on negative incentives
5. Excluding the builder from planning and design
6. Inadequate claims processes

There are some suggested fixes, most hinging on a new relationship among the user, A-E, and contractor, whereby teamwork rather than confrontation is emphasized and awarded:[3]

1. Invite the builder aboard early.
2. Use the design-construct approach more often.
3. Read the contract.
4. Seek realism in pricing; do not go blindly for a lump sum.
5. Use value engineering constructively and cooperatively with incentives for active participation.
6. Unless absolutely unavoidable, eliminate sequential procurement.
7. Eliminate cut-and-paste contracts.
8. Use incentives for really good work.

For facility managers who manage large, multiyear construction programs, there are other suggested remedies:

1. Use design standards and standard designs that can be site adapted.
2. Benchmark and document the performance of designers and builders. Award the good performers, and stop doing business with the nonperformers.
3. Prequalify design firms and builders whenever possible.
4. Whenever possible, build flexible facilities that are not unique to your organization. The future is unpredictable, so hedge your company's bets through flexibility. One of my better management decisions was to insist on access flooring and "overdesigned" electrical systems in new buildings in the early 1980s.
5. Keep the operations and maintenance staff on the project team from concept through turnover. Their inputs will often save the company from major errors and operational problems that will cost the company annually well into future.

Some of these measures are probably considered anticompetitive by the public sector, which is a shame. Public-sector facility managers have been given more flexibility to get away from firm, fixed-bid contracts, but there still is a long way to go to give public-sector facility and project managers the tools needed to optimize quality while minimizing resources. As I appealed for flexibility in design, I feel just as strongly that facility managers need flexibility in contracting and then need to be held rigorously to producing results that are acceptable to their customers.

Disputes

I have long been bothered by the litigious nature of construction in the United States. It often seems that everyone on a major project sues everyone else on the project. And ironically, opponents in a lawsuit on one job often are working together on the next. Is this really a system that serves anyone but the lawyers?

I recommend that anyone doing a large amount of construction contracting seriously consider alternative dispute resolution (ADR) both to settle protests and to resolve disputes. Partnering, arbitration, mediation, and minitrials are all examples of ADR methods.

Notes

1. Richard A. Eustis, "Construction Phase," in *Facilities Management* (Washington, D.C.: APPA, 1984), p. v–71.
2. Larry Gleason, "Modeling Facility Construction Alternatives," *IFMA Conference Proceedings* (Houston: IFMA, 1988), p. 317.
3. "Contract Construction Procurement," *The Military Engineer* (November–December 1988): 590–693. By permission of The Society of American Military Engineers (SAME).

Section V

Operations and Maintenance

Some facility managers look at existing space as merely something to be tolerated until the next alteration. Some even shun operations and maintenance, perhaps because they think those functions tie them too closely to the boiler room. The fact is that in active companies, all space is in play at all times; it is being maintained, repaired, altered, or renovated constantly. Furniture is moved, exchanged, or replaced. New signage replaces old. Light fixtures are relamped.

When I was an operations and maintenance manager, the facilities staff annually responded to over 50,000 service requests (30 to 35 daily just for moving) and corrected over 200,000 deficiencies under preventive maintenance.

This is a major effort that needs to be organized well and managed intensely. Operations and maintenance are big business and important business. There is no greater challenge than to provide quality services at minimal cost around the clock, which seems to be the standard against which operators and maintainers are judged.

Two issues have dominated operations and maintenance throughout my professional life. One is that maintenance and repair is consistently underfunded, often while companies are expanding their capital expenditures. A university facility manager supposedly said, "Everyone is anxious to endow a new building, but no one ever endowed a maintenance and repair contract." Studies that document the underfunding of maintenance and repair abound, particularly in the public sector, yet the situation seems just to worsen.

Second, because we have not consistently used life-cycle costing or solicited the advice of operators and maintainers during design and construction of facilities, we are faced with a bigger operations and maintenance challenge than need be.

As facility managers have downsized and outsourced in recent years, it appears to me that they have both outsourced and downsized operations and maintenance functions to a greater degree than the other functions of facility management.

13

Work Coordination

Pulse Points

- *The work reception center is the facility department's eyes and ears, receiving requests and prioritizing work.*
- *The work reception center can be the means to control and manage a charge-back system.*

As vice president of Facilities West, the late Art Hahn, one of my professional heroes, promoted good facility management through what he called pulse points, or critical operations. One of these pulse points is the *work reception and coordination center* (WRC), the eyes and ears of the facility department. It is the single point where all, or nearly all, facility services are received, prioritized, tasked, coordinated, and evaluated.

No matter the size of the organization, the WRC can provide a full complement of services. In the smallest organizations, the WRC is often the assistant to the facility manager. In large organizations, the WRC may be a separate work unit (see Exhibit 13-1). Managing the WRC is a high-stress job requiring frequent breaks and probably rotation after a period of time. One way to relieve battle

Exhibit 13-1. Work reception and coordination center.

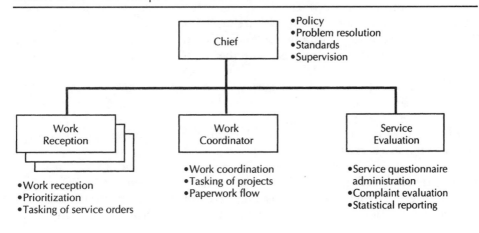

fatigue here is to hire service receptionists from a temporary agency and rotate them after about six months. Another approach is to rotate a mix of nonmanagerial technical staff through the WRC on three-to six-month details. The latter builds widespread mission appreciation within the entire organization.

Under one operating concept, employees trained in telephonic techniques operate within a rigid framework, normally a checklist. The stress here is on accurately gathering and passing on information to the appropriate service provider. The second approach is to employ service receptionists who understand completely the operations and nuances of the facility department. On the surface this would appear to be preferable, but it tends to reduce the volume of requests that can be handled and occasionally causes conflicts because the service receptionists start to make judgments beyond their knowledge.

Excellent WRCs can operate under both concepts; whichever is used, training and quality control are essential. If the work receptionists are not controlled, management decisions will be usurped, with the facility manager unaware.

Equipped with the proper automated system, the WRC can also be the center for the invoicing of all chargebacks. Some facility managers have made their WRC the chargeback enforcers. By its nature, it is at the core of the gathering of information for calculating unit costs and benchmarks. If the department is so equipped, the service orders for all preventive and cyclic maintenance can be both generated and closed at the WRC. Finally, it should be the hub of the department's service evaluation.

Work Prioritization and Flow

The premise of a WRC is that the receptionists have the authority to task the routine work of the department. Priorities vary from organization to organization and from time to time; however, most WRCs prioritize work by criticality, dollar value, and complexity.

Prioritization by criticality involves determining whether work requested is needed to protect life or property (priority 1), is detrimental to operations (priority 2), or is routine (priority 3). Typically, priority 1 requests are handled immediately by telephone. Priority 2 requests are tasked on a written service order and the work accomplished within one workday. Routine service orders (priority 3) are also tasked by a written request, with the work accomplished in three to five workdays.

Prioritization by dollar value is purely a policy matter, and recognizes that, above a certain level of funding (say, $1,500 to $2,000), management and/or the design team scrutinizes the assignment before it is tasked. Another somewhat more complicated alternative is to limit the effort (one to two workdays, typically) that can go into a service order.

Prioritization by complexity is also a matter of policy. Typically, any task that changes the form or function of the facilities is not immediately tasked for implementation, even though the dollar cost may be small. It is first sent to the planning and design division. For instance, frequently all electrical service orders are passed through planning and design regardless of implementation cost, since outlet installation can have far-reaching effects.

An effective method of screening requirements before they reach the WRC is to appoint a mayor for each building or a facilities point of contact (POC) for each major element; some large organizations use a combination. For instance, the POC in each department screens requirements and passes them on to the mayor of the building. There are advantages to this system, but it can add an unnecessary level of bureaucracy if the POCs and mayors are not empowered to reject frivolous requests and are required to prioritize the requirements.

It is also extremely important that work flow be properly established. Proper work flow ensures that 90 to 97 percent (by volume) of the work of the facilities department is handled routinely. That allows the facility manager to concentrate on the 3 to 10 percent of the work requiring managerial intervention. One of the signs of a facility department in trouble is that staff members call the facility manager directly to resolve routine work requests. Another sign is more than one point of entry for work coming into the facilities department.

Exhibit 13-2 shows the entry and distribution of work within a typical facility department. Exhibit 13-3 is a detailed work flowchart for routine service orders.

Procedures

The WRC is the driving force behind all routine work in the facilities department. Since this work constitutes such a high percentage of the department's mission, it is important that it be done well. While each organization has its own unique requirements, there are common procedures. For example, the WRC should have

Exhibit 13-2. Work flow within a typical facility department.

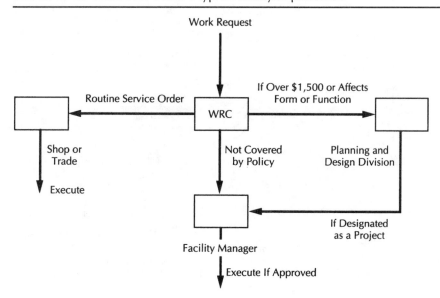

Exhibit 13-3. Simplified current work flow call to work reception center.

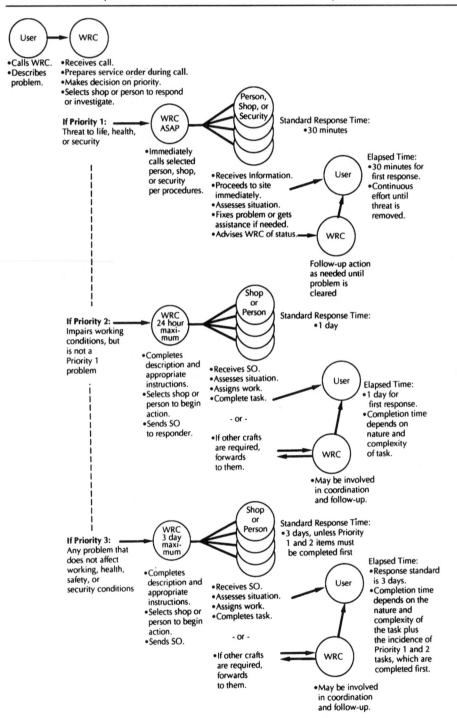

the capability of receiving work requests twenty-four hours daily and be staffed one half-hour before and after normal duty hours. Stagger the work hours of the receptionists or use other operational personnel in addition to the regular receptionists.

It is now very common for the WRC to receive facility requests through e-mail. A macro is provided on the company intranet to ensure that all information that is needed is collected systematically. One university is trying to use the Internet to network its widespread campuses to the WRC in the facility department.

Also, it is counterproductive to spend great effort confirming whether those requesting work are authorized to do so. At one time I required almost all requests be in writing and signed by an officer of the company; only a few services could be requested by phone. The service reception center had a book of authorized signatures against which to check. We were literally buried in paper. Faced with the prospect of either increasing WRC staffing or falling further behind in processing the requests, we eliminated the paperwork and converted to almost 100 percent phone requests. The only requests now requiring paperwork are signage, so that the name is spelled correctly, and furniture, because we cannot meet the requests for six to eight weeks and it is easier to file paper.

An answering machine is a must, because a good WRC frequently has a queue for service. The answering machine should be capable of tracking the following items:

- Total number of calls
- Number of calls answered within a specified number of rings
- Average waiting time
- Number of calls not completed (the caller hung up)

All incoming calls should be answered within two rings or get a recording informing the person that the call is on hold and offering an option to call back at a less busy time. If the WRC requires certain information, the caller should be so reminded at that time. Callers on hold should also be reminded every twenty to thirty seconds that the next available work receptionist will take the call. Some WRCs tape all incoming calls; check with the legal department before doing so to ensure compliance with company policy and local law.

Decisions concerning seemingly small matters can sometimes make a real difference in the quality of a WRC. For example, what is an appropriate background sound for callers on hold? Our preference is for easy listening music, but others have had success with all-news radio or company information bits. We have found it most efficient for work receptionists to use telephone headsets, freeing both hands. That becomes even more important with increasingly automated workstations.

Staffing the WRC is subject to many variables. Even if there is only one work receptionist, that person needs breaks—extended ones. Otherwise fatigue and stress make the job unappealing. The justification for additional staffing is often documented in the log of the telephone answering machine. If the average wait time, the number of calls dropped, or the response time exceeds management's standard, more staffing is probably justified.

Work Coordination

The WRC must coordinate all work: preventive maintenance, cyclical maintenance, maintenance and repair projects, service orders, alteration projects, and capital projects. It is a facility manager's nightmare, for example, for a wall to be painted under cyclic maintenance two days before it is demolished as part of an alteration project. Not only is this wasteful, but it destroys the department's credibility. Work should be coordinated with other service organizations. The WRC should be aware of all conferences, parties, facility projects, and after-hours activities so that proper support and no conflicting activities will be scheduled. In a large organization, a particular individual should coordinate work, control the flow of paperwork through the facilities department, and task all nonroutine work. In a medium-size organization, this individual can also handle service evaluation. In a small organization, the amount of work can be small enough so that the facility manager or work receptionist can also function as work coordinator. (For additional guidance on aspects of work control, see David R. Howard, *Critical Issues in Facilities Management; Work Control.*)[1]

Work reception and coordination is one of the facility management functions most often automated (56 percent) but its rate of automation seems to have slowed.[2] There are many excellent systems that allow the work receptionist to task the appropriate shop directly using an automated service order. Once the work is completed, the shop enters the time and materials expended, and the service order is closed. Preventive maintenance and project work can be similarly automated. The system can print out expenditures to date by shop, by service-order number, by budget code, by building, or by organization. In modern organizations, there is a separate printer and PC in each shop so that service orders can be processed there.

Service Evaluation

The WRC is in a unique position to evaluate service, both quantitatively and qualitatively. For service orders, I recommend the following quantitative evaluation each month:

1. By shop, evaluate
    - Service orders carried over
    - Service orders received
    - Service orders completed monthly and year-to-date
2. By shop, by priority category, evaluate
    - Number completed within time standard
    - Number not completed within time standard

To measure service-order performance qualitatively, send questionnaires to approximately 30 percent of the service recipients. Another approach is to target one to two buildings or organizations each month. The results of these questionnaires can be compiled and reviewed monthly, quarterly, and annually along with quantitative results.

Custodial services are measured qualitatively by questionnaire—similar to service orders.

Projects normally are evaluated using a postoccupancy evaluation or with a special questionnaire. Quantitatively, projects are evaluated on whether budget was met, schedule was adhered to, and the program was met. The WRC can administer project evaluation as a matter of administrative convenience, but it is probably best evaluated by the planning and design division or directly by the facility manager.

The importance of the WRC in customer relations cannot be overemphasized. Since 90 to 97 percent of the department's work flows through the WRC, its image is largely determined by how courteously, effectively, and efficiently work requests are treated. The work receptionists must be courteous and diplomatic, even when staff calling in work requests are not. They must be able both to give the status of requested work (automation helps immensely here) and understand the implications of even the most innocent request. Your local phone company (and some communications consultants) can provide in-house training to help work receptionists both maximize their use of time and improve their telephone etiquette. The training is well worth the cost.

Notes

1. David R. Howard, ed., *Critical Issues in Facilities Management*, vol. 2 (Alexandria, Va.: APPA, 1988).

2. "Facility Management Practices," *IFMA Report 16* (Houston: IFMA, 1996), p. 24.

14

Facility Operations

Pulse Points

- *Facilities operations is a multidimensional function, requiring solid management skills.*
- *Disaster recovery has major facility complications but should not be managed by the facility manager.*
- *Managing the company's environmental program can provide visibility to the facility manager.*
- *Indoor air quality may become a major environmental issue.*

Most facility management literature gives either of two impressions of facility operations: it does not exist, or it is a big machine that is turned on daily and operates smoothly with little or no funding, problems, or management attention. Neither could be further from the truth. Facility operations is a multidimensional function of facility management. It's often the forgotten function, but good management and organization ensure that 95 to 97 percent of problems are solved so that management can focus on the 3 to 5 percent of problems that truly need their attention. The truth is that facilities operations account for 50 to 75 percent of the facilities budget.

Facility operations includes these areas:

- Plant operations
- Energy management
- Hazardous waste management
- Recycling
- Inventory management
- Communications and wire management
- Alterations management
- Relocation and move management
- Furniture installation
- Disaster recovery
- Maintenance and repair

- Security
- Fire and life safety

Maintenance and repair are discussed in Chapter 15; fire and life safety are covered in Chapter 16.

Plant Operations

Of all facility operations, the one function most commonly relegated to the back burner is plant operations. That is unfortunate because there is nothing back burner about modern plant operations. A bright, highly proficient operating engineer bemoaned recently that plant equipment had evolved much more rapidly than had the education and licensing requirements for operating engineers. The skills he *really* needed were in electronics with some basic computer skills, whereas he had been trained in the traditional steam fitting, sheet metal, and plumbing skills.

There is no absolute definition of *plant*, but for the purpose of this book, consider the plant to be made up of the following systems:

1. Heating, ventilation, and air-conditioning (HVAC)
2. Mechanical and electrical vertical and horizontal transportation
3. Major electrical
4. Emergency power
5. Plumbing

In North America, the energy crisis of the early 1970s precipitated a revolution in building systems. Concurrently, computer-controlled building systems were just reaching the market. Together they made it possible, for a relatively modest capital cost, to provide individualized environments to a degree never before possible, at a substantial savings in both cost and size of the plant. Today it is not uncommon to see the HVAC system of large complexes controlled by a personal computer that also troubleshoots the system and provides a historical record of its operations. Such systems are commonly co-located with fully integrated fire and life-safety or security systems.

Historically, buildings have had their own engineer, be it a jack-of-all-trades. Some have even had a second maintenance mechanic. During the late 1970s and early 1980s, however, it became increasingly popular to gather all building operations staff under central control and dispatch them where and when needed. As a result, little preventive maintenance was done, the occupants felt deserted, maintenance was ignored to accomplish project work, and intimate knowledge of the building was lost.

Today, it is felt that some type of resident facility management technical staff is best for all occupied buildings over 250,000 square feet. For large complexes, there is controversy over how to organize the plant operations staff. Many departments have their own operating engineers, but increasingly this function is being contracted out. One possible way to organize a plant operations unit is shown in Exhibit 14-1. Note that elevators are part of the operating plant. It is a good match since elevators are electromechanical equipment.

The plant operations function has perhaps the most routine tasks, but that does not mean they are not important, even critical, to facility operation. Unsatisfactory heating and cooling is the most common building complaint in office buildings. If the chief executive officer (CEO) is trapped in an elevator or Legionnaire's disease breaks out among the staff, the critical nature of plant operations immediately becomes evident.

The key to cost-effective plant operations is a solid, continuing energy management program and centralized building management. The former is discussed in the next section of this chapter. As for the latter, it is possible to operate an automated building maintenance system (BMS) under two different philosophies. The most cost-effective system has one individual (not necessarily even a knowledgeable one) monitoring all building systems from a central location manned twenty-four hours a day. That individual recognizes problems as displayed on a computer screen and notifies the appropriate operations personnel for corrective action.

The second approach has building functions monitored separately. In the most common arrangement, there are both a security operation center (also covering fire and life safety) and a building operation center, with these functions monitored by technical experts. This latter allows a higher degree of initial technical input but also is more costly.

Most new building designs incorporate an automated building maintenance system. It is also possible to retrofit these systems into existing buildings. Control points, detectors, and computer capacity can be increased incrementally as funding and installation capability become available. Several companies make total building systems, and each year more features are added, especially with the move to individually controlled environments.

Exhibit 14-1. Organizing for plan operations.

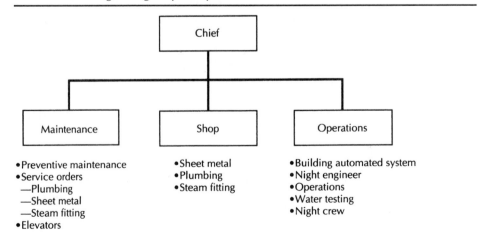

Energy Management

Energy management is not a separate function but rather an activity that spans every facility system. Modern energy management had its genesis in the oil crisis of the early 1970s. Two results came from that crisis: remarkably more efficient (and smaller) energy-consuming equipment and an understanding that energy is a major cost element and needs to be contained. The sudden appreciation for energy undoubtedly was a factor in the rise of facility management as a profession. The person who paid the light bill suddenly became an important corporate player.

Some of the impetus of the 1970s has been lost as oil prices dropped. Even some of the mandated public-sector measures are largely ignored. At most, traditional energy management now appears confined to measures that can be designed into new facilities, which have no effect on company employees, or are implemented by substituting energy-efficient equipment for older equipment. That is unfortunate because, from a baseline that represents no real effort at energy management, savings and cost avoidance of 30 to 33 percent are possible with a good energy management program. Some of the potential savings are displayed in Exhibit 14-2. One consultant I have heard speak feels savings and cost avoidances in excess of 90 percent over the status quo are possible.

There are many techniques and devices for energy management that have proved effective. The following are elements of a good energy management program:

1. The organization of the program is based on responsible committees to set policy and sell the program.
   - Appoint an energy manager responsible to the facility manager.
   - Have two levels of committees: a steering committee chaired by a senior manager with membership of the budget director, the facility manager, and two or three line managers, and a technical committee chaired by the facility manager.
   - Appoint the senior administrative person in each department responsible for user-dependent energy management matters (for example, turning off the lights) in that department.
2. All policy is developed by the technical committee, approved by the steering committee, and signed by the CEO. To be effective, energy management must be perceived as a management program, not a facilities program.
3. A detailed energy consumption baseline is established for each utility. Consumption against this baseline should be calculated at least annually to track progress. Utility companies will assist in these analyses.
4. A hierarchy of energy management measures is implemented:
   - Capital intensive (payback less than seven years suggested).
   - Moderate cost (can be budgeted in annual budgets with no significant effect).
   - Low cost or no cost.

Exhibit 14-2. Energy saving potential.

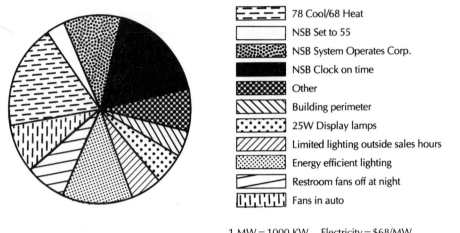

	78 Cool/68 Heat
	NSB Set to 55
	NSB System Operates Corp.
	NSB Clock on time
	Other
	Building perimeter
	25W Display lamps
	Limited lighting outside sales hours
	Energy efficient lighting
	Restroom fans off at night
	Fans in auto

Item	1 MW = 1000 KW MWH/Year	Electricity = $68/MW $/Year	% of Total
1. Night setback (NSB) system			
• Operates correctly	1,556	105,800	8.6
• Clocks on time	3,377	229,600	18.6
• NSB thermostats set to 55	211	14,300	1.2
2. Temperatures: 68° heating, 78° cooling	2,847	193,600	15.7
3. Fans in "auto" and operate correctly	1,972.2	134,100	10.9
4. Restroom fans off at night	1,235.2	84,000	6.8
5. Energy-efficient lighting	3,250	221,000	17.9
6. Minimum lighting on prior to opening	1,086.2	73,900	6.0
7. Outside lighting off when unnecessary	696.4	47,400	3.8
8. Display lamps all using 25 watts	768.7	52,300	4.2
9. W/H restroom, cage room lights off	121.8	8,300	0.7
10. Tight-fitting weather stripping	122.4	8,300	0.7
11. Truck doors kept closed	352.6	24,000	1.9
12. Dock seals installed	30.9	2,100	.2
13. Compactor doors kept closed	26.4	1,800	.1
14. Hot water heater set to lowest temperature	45.4	3,100	.3
15. Pneumatic tube system off when not needed	39	2,700	.2
16. Conveyor off when not in use	136.8	9,300	.8
17. Small orders received through driver door	293.8	20,000	1.6
	18,168.6	1,235,500	100%

Source: Lloyd J. Vye, "Best Products Reduces Utility Budget by Millions," *IFMA Journal* (April 1989): 14.

    5. Energy management is incorporated into all designs, and all new designs are reviewed from an energy management perspective.

    Nearly 60 percent of facility managers continue to practice traditional energy management measures such as thermostat regulation and investing in energy-efficient capital equipment.[1] However, the electric power industry is currently in the midst of deregulation. Although it is unclear how this will play out, deregulation could offer large facility departments a real opportunity. Most observers believe that direct access to the electrical generation market (commonly referred to as retail wheeling) will take place over a period of time, although it is well under way in some states.

Increasingly, companies will be developing an energy strategy with particular emphasis on leveraging whatever volume advantage a firm has to obtain more favorable terms from privatized suppliers. This development is not without drawbacks. Caveat emptor now becomes the cardinal rule when purchasing energy, just as it is with any other commodity in a free market. Although there may be a price advantage to large users, facility managers must now worry about the quality of electricity provided, guarantee of source, and price stability. There are other concerns that small users will get left behind and also that the price of inefficient plant will have to be absorbed by someone (hopefully not your company).

Depending on the sophistication of a company's current energy management and its ability to exercise some muscle in the market, facility managers and their companies stand to reap some real benefits. Already, utilities are downsizing and cutting costs so that they will be competitive in a deregulated market; industry consolidation, if controlled, should have the same effect.

Increased competition and marketing should work to facility managers' advantage. Cost savings may not be the only fallout of energy deregulation. In addition, value-added services (maybe the utility will actually own and maintain a company's chillers and boilers) may be intriguing to certain facility managers. Finally, a nearby co-generator may be willing to sell energy at below-market rates to absorb excess capacity. All of this can be confusing, if not outright scary. In order to manage this process, Wayne Robertson, director of energy consulting at Heery International, suggests the following actions.[2]

- Build a team; at first you may need to depend upon a consultant.
- Evaluate facility requirements using an energy audit.
- Actively seek out your utility to ensure that they notice you.
- Seek package discounts and rate incentives.
- Form or be involved in a users' group.
- Aggressively seek rate options.
- Perform a co-generation study and design.
- Evaluate peak shaving generation and gas cooling opportunities.
- Look for local co-generation projects.

By moving aggressively now, the facility manager may establish a structure to permanently reduce energy operating costs.

Energy services companies (ESCOs), most of which are former electric utilities repackaged to provide an array of energy services, offer the facility manager both new products and services. ESCOs now provide resource planning software, energy conservation products and services, on-site energy systems, and retail-wheeling advice. The extent to which ESCOs give truly independent advice is yet to be determined, but they certainly provide expertise to facility managers that was not generally available before deregulation.

Hazardous Waste Management

This topic includes a variety of management challenges, from abating asbestos to disposing of contaminated medical waste. The recommendations alone could fill a book.

Asbestos

By far the most common hazardous waste is asbestos. After much nervousness, even panic, facility departments have learned to cope with asbestos and approach its abatement in a commonsense manner. It is possible to abate asbestos and to continue operations in the same building. The following are trademarks of a good asbestos abatement program:

1. Appointment of an abatement operations and maintenance manager.
2. Training of an in-house abatement crew or hiring of a reputable contractor. (I strongly favor the latter.)
3. Securing the services of an environmental hygiene firm to do independent testing. This firm preferably does not work for the facility manager (suggest the health or human resources department), which ensures its independence.
4. Establishment of abatement files as follows:
   • Historical record of all abatement efforts
   • Air quality reports following each abatement effort provided by the hygienist hired by the contractor to do testing.
   • Record of procedures on each abatement site.
   • Disposal record from the disposal contractor.
5. Enactment of an internal relations program for staff that is both general and site specific. The independent environmental hygienist can be an excellent instructor.

The best arrangement has the contractor mobilize within a certain time to abate asbestos against previously approved rates. Some facility managers have one such contract (this ensures uniformity of abatement); others use two or three contractors so that one is always available when the need arises.

Some facility managers hire a contractor, often using the lowest bid, and then adopt a "see no evil, hear no evil" philosophy about the handling of asbestos waste. It is a managerially unsound approach and can place the company in legal jeopardy should improperly disposed asbestos be traced. Contrarily, there are both good contractors and good consultants. It is unnecessary to hire someone who tries to bully or frighten you with horror stories. Hire a contractor (or consultant) who will be responsive and will work both to protect the health of the staff and minimize disruption.

Do not fear asbestos; manage it!

Other Waste

Many facility managers are faced with handling either hazardous manufacturing or medical waste. Fortunately a company that handles medical waste normally also has the knowledge and experience for proper storage and disposal. Perhaps in no other area is the old saw, "If in doubt, do it right," so applicable. In the past some organizations have simply turned over their waste to a disposal contractor and washed their hands, without concern for proper disposal or interim storage. That is not only bad management but runs counter to public concerns and legal trends. Protestations that the contractor erred will not even be heard. To protect the company:

1. Have competent legal advice for dealing with hazardous waste issues.
2. Hire a waste management contractor with a proven track record.
3. Use an environmental hygienist, preferably hired by your medical department, to monitor your in-house and contractor's handling, storage, and disposal of hazardous materials.

For a discussion of the relatively new regulations facing so-called small (waste) quantity generators, see "Complying with Hazardous Waste Regulations," in the AIPE's *Guide to Better Facilities Management*.

Recycling

Recycling remains one of the functions most affecting facility management and is expected to have a high priority in the future.[3] Based on anecdotal information, there still seems to be too much instability in markets and imprecision in laws to manage recycling effectively. However, several facility managers have made a name for themselves within their company by actively pursuing, normally with employee input, an aggressive recycling program.

Initially, you may need a half- to full-time person to establish a proper recycling program and oversee implementation. (The recovery of valuable by-products from industrial processes is not what is being discussed here. Normally their capture and reuse is under the purview of the vice president for manufacturing.)

Most recycling consists of segregation and either resale or disposal of the segregated products. Commonly, waste is segregated as follows:

1. Paper (newspaper, white paper, all other)
2. Aluminum cans
3. Glass bottles and jars (clear, green, brown)
4. Scrap metal
5. Styrofoam
6. All other

Most current programs segregate only three to five of these products at the facility level, with all other waste going in the "all other" category for disposal.

Recycling is not cheap ($5 to $20 per employee for initial containers). Often in urban areas, interim storage space or extra segregated dumpster space simply is not available. Personnel to segregate waste is an additional expense. But some companies have worked with local agencies to employ the disabled for this chore.

Unfortunately, many facility managers who have tried to be out front on recycling have experienced frustration. For example, some who funded the additional costs of recycling from the sale of paper have seen the bottom drop out of the paper market as more and more companies turned to recycling. Large organizations should consider cogeneration of waste materials if it can be cost justified and if the facility is in an area where the stack effluent will meet Environmental Protection Agency (EPA) standards.

Some degree of segregation is needed at the workbench, production line, and desk level. Generally the facility manager is expected to provide the three Ps: policy, the proper container, and pickup. However, the program will be suboptimized if viewed as solely a facility department's program and responsibility. Company management must support the recycling effort for it to be successful.

Despite the cost, the often confusing nature of the legislation, the lack of markets for many recycled products, and the additional space requirements, most companies realize the need for recycling and are making an honest attempt to implement a program.

Indoor Air Quality

Indoor air quality could be the Achilles' heel of facility managers. Many buildings have been constructed so that air quality cannot be adequately controlled. In the traditional office building, for example, temperature can often be controlled only by zone. In order to reduce operating costs, the amount of fresh air (and humidity) brought into the building with each change of air has been severely limited. Often ducts are filled with fungi, dirt, and dust (which is stirred up each time the ductwork is modified), and filters are often ineffective for the type of dust and pollen to which employees are allergic.

A new announcement of federal indoor air quality standards has seemed imminent for the past several years but appears to be hung up politically at the EPA. Nevertheless, indoor air quality problems will only increase, regardless of more stringent regulation. Facility managers need to adopt a program that emphasizes good operational practices (better space layout, for example), improved maintenance practices (better custodial cleaning, for example), as well as capital investment to correct past problems.

Employees will continue to insist on more control over their indoor environment and better air quality. In the long run, providing better air quality can lead to better employee efficiency. This is an area where facility management can contribute to the bottom line.

Inventory Management

An accurate inventory of facility property has two purposes. First, managers like to have an accurate count of what they manage. Second, for tax purposes it is necessary to know what furnishings and equipment of what vintage are on the books so that they can be depreciated properly.

In general, the rules for inventory management are not made in the facility department. Inventory management is much like purchasing or procurement—vitally important but dependent on policies and procedures most often set by others. By far the facility manager's greatest involvement is with furniture inventory (74 percent), with 62 percent responsible for furniture disposal and 35 percent responsible for the disposal of other property.[4] The inventories to manage these functions can be maintained through a number of methods, the most promising of which is bar coding.

Bar coding is a technique to affix a number to a piece of property in order to track its physical location and create a file on that piece of property. A handheld scanner can download information into a computer and track individual pieces of furniture, certain types or components of furniture, furniture from a certain manufacturer, or even standard furniture sets. Bar coding the locations also makes it possible to maintain inventories easily; some manufacturers even offer their products bar coded.

While bar coding is moderately expensive, it is efficient and effective for inventory management in mid- and large-size organizations. Implementing a bar code system requires a well-thought-out inventory schema and a good bar coding system.

The principal considerations for implementing a bar coded inventory system are as follows:

1. What is the degree of detailing desired in tracking? Units? Assemblies? Parts? Once the numbering system is set, stick to it.
2. Will color, fabric, or condition be described ? That may dictate the system.
3. How will locations be defined? Are those locations understandable to designers? To users? Others may want to tap in to the inventory for their needs.
4. Will the inventory be differentiated regarding depreciated value, owned versus leased, and other factors? If so, a smart code may be needed in the bar code.
5. How will the initial tagging objectives and strategy be done? Some staff object to having their furniture tagged unless they are present, yet waiting for their presence slows the process. Placement of the bar code on any single piece of furniture must be consistent and accessible yet aesthetically acceptable.
6. How will the information be updated? Establish an update procedure.

Properly managed bar coding can allow management of property from acquisition through disposal.

Of course technology may be changing this. The high costs of manual inventory procedures will eventually make way for laser bar-code reading and direct input into a computer database. This will allow an up-to-date inventory of furniture in use and available for distribution. Then reliable inventory printouts will be more important. Also, fallout from unfriendly takeovers will force company financial officers to change the way furniture is accounted and inventoried (from a depreciation schedule inventory to an assets listing inventory). In this way, a current, accurate valuation of total assets is possible.

Communications and Wire Management

Slightly more than half of most facility managers manage telecommunications.[5] That may present a problem because no other function in this information age has such a profound influence on facilities as data and telecommunications work.

For years the communications function consisted of paying the telephone bill to the local phone company. Suddenly this function has become one of the most dynamic, largely owing to deregulation of the phone system, increasing computerization of business functions, and interconnections of computers through hard-wiring or the telephone system.

Communications is where the information systems department and the facility department come together. The communications function is as likely managed in the information systems department or as a separate division than in the facility department. This is because, to the information services department, the communications system is the electronic highway over which information flows. To the facility department, the communications system is a major user of space (antennas, risers, file servers, modems, closets, and wire trays), requiring additional trades on projects, and a set of wires and outlets that must be accommodated and that restricts layout flexibility. But no matter where the communications function is placed, there must be close and continuous coordination, starting with planning and design. Generally communications engineers, particularly those with a voice communications background, have not been trained to design and document their wire installations to the degree other building elements are planned and designed.

There is a legitimate debate within facility management concerning the degree to which communications should be documented. Should communications wiring and devices be drawn, or should they be documented by alphanumeric schedules? Should all communication runs be depicted, or should only termini be shown? Or is the best system some combination or permutation of the above?

My preference is for documentation in the form of drawings of the following:

1. All communications risers
2. The type and location of outlets unless standardized
3. The location of all equipment (muxes, net commanders, file servers, etc.)
4. The location of any communications element for which space planning is necessary

5. The location of all frame rooms, closets, and cabinets
6. All fiber-optic runs
7. The entry point of outside services
8. All antennas
9. All communication ducts
10. All cable trays

This is the minimum for effective wire management. Room-type information should be recorded on a communications overlay; information on the cable plant and risers should have separate sheets, just as mechanical and electrical systems do. Although it is not specifically a part of wire management, I like to record on key plans the basic power requirements and heat output data for each piece of office technology equipment in place. This information can be maintained on the overlay of room information, as an equipment schedule, or in a separate alphanumeric database. It should be capable of being manipulated so as to assess the effect of moving office technology on the HVAC and electrical systems.

It is my experience that the average (even the better-than-average) architectural-engineering (A-E) firm does an inadequate job of planning and designing telecommunications and data communication systems. Perhaps the reason is that they did not have to do so when Ma Bell existed. Consequently, design services must often be obtained from a specialized communications consultant. When the facility is large enough to justify such a firm, a design-build company can design, build, and maintain all low-voltage systems, not just data and telecommunications.

Communications management is a function of the nature of the company or business. It is quite a different task to rely on the local telephone company than to run one's own telephone switch. Exhibit 14-3 is one possible organization for a communications division in a facility department of a large corporation with a broad range of communications needs. Note especially the need for the electronic communications specialist. Using this model, applicable organizations can be scoped up or down. One rule of thumb for communications organizations is that there be one professional for each $750,000 in annual communications expense.[6]

With the arrival of data communications, premises-based switching, private satellite communications, local area networks, and facsimile transmission, the communications function suddenly is a full plate. Several principles are in order:

1. Various technologies must be understood because functionability increasingly is user driven.
2. A wide variety of solutions from multiple vendors exists for every communications problem. Don't be the first to buy in; try to protect against obsolescence.
3. Communications is a business function. Conduct an economic analysis before choosing among options.
4. Look for opportunities to maximize technology by expanding existing systems. For example, voice, data, mail, fax, e-mail, and messenger service probably would benefit from single management.

Exhibit 14-3. Possible organization for communications division of a facility department.

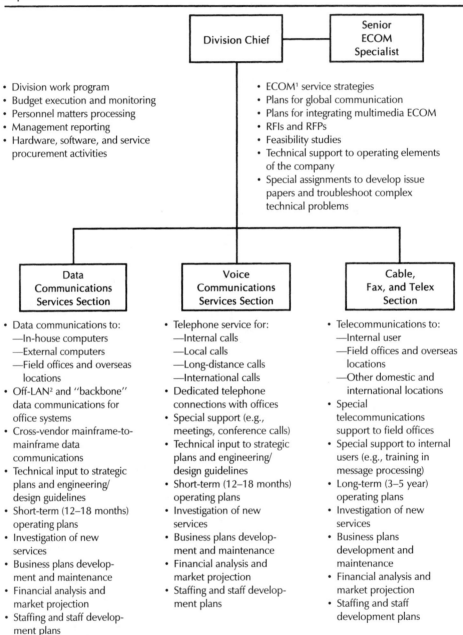

| Division Chief | Senior ECOM Specialist |

- Division work program
- Budget execution and monitoring
- Personnel matters processing
- Management reporting
- Hardware, software, and service procurement activities

- ECOM[1] service strategies
- Plans for global communication
- Plans for integrating multimedia ECOM
- RFIs and RFPs
- Feasibility studies
- Technical support to operating elements of the company
- Special assignments to develop issue papers and troubleshoot complex technical problems

Data Communications Services Section

- Data communications to:
  —In-house computers
  —External computers
  —Field offices and overseas locations
- Off-LAN[2] and "backbone" data communications for office systems
- Cross-vendor mainframe-to-mainframe data communications
- Technical input to strategic plans and engineering/design guidelines
- Short-term (12–18 months) operating plans
- Investigation of new services
- Business plans development and maintenance
- Financial analysis and market projection
- Staffing and staff development plans

Voice Communications Services Section

- Telephone service for:
  —Internal calls
  —Local calls
  —Long-distance calls
  —International calls
- Dedicated telephone connections with offices
- Special support (e.g., meetings, conference calls)
- Technical input to strategic plans and engineering/design guidelines
- Short-term (12–18 months) operating plans
- Investigation of new services
- Business plans development and maintenance
- Financial analysis and market projection
- Staffing and staff development plans

Cable, Fax, and Telex Section

- Telecommunications to:
  —Internal user
  —Field offices and overseas locations
  —Other domestic and international locations
- Special telecommunications support to field offices
- Special support to internal users (e.g., training in message processing)
- Long-term (3–5 year) operating plans
- Investigation of new services
- Business plans development and maintenance
- Financial analysis and market projection
- Staffing and staff development plans

1. ECOM = electronic communications.
2. LAN = local area network.

5. Multiple options and vendors should increase the leverage of the facility manager.

John Richardson describes the communications revolution this way:

> Some day when you leave your office for the day, a sensor in your building will note your departure. Automatically the lights will be turned off and the heat turned down. You will ride home content in the knowledge that your organization has put new ideas to work to control spiraling communications cost and improve worker efficiency. You will, in effect, have taken advantage of the revolution in semiconductor technology.[7]

As Richardson's description shows, communications is becoming more entwined with facilities. Even now the telephone can be used to control both individual HVAC and lighting. Therefore, companies and facility managers need to reexamine who should manage communications. Companies continue to put the two disciplines under separate management, at their ever increasing risk. Whether communications is managed independently or in the information services department, the facility manager must ensure that planning, design, installation, and even maintenance are coordinated, since no single other function has such a pervasive and encompassing effect on facilities.

Alterations Management

There is probably no other function so popular as altering space; 55 percent of facility managers say that they do it continually.[8] Everyone enjoys a renovated cafeteria, or an upgraded workplace, or a facelift on the assembly line. Since alterations are so popular, they must be carefully controlled or they will hemorrhage the facility budget. This is a particular problem where funds for alterations are mingled with funds for maintenance. Unless alterations are well managed, maintenance funds will be diverted into alterations, to the detriment of the department. This has grown to such a problem that the U.S. Army, for example, restricts the amount of maintenance and repair funding that could be diverted to alterations.

In corporate North America, where churn rates of 20 to 30 percent are the norm, alterations are a way of life. In fact, downsizing often accelerated the necessity to alter space. Alterations can become the preponderant function of the facilities department—the yardstick by which the facility manager is measured. This creates a project mentality in the department, whereas the proper approach views alterations as one function, albeit an important one, in a facility's life cycle.

There are a number of standards that allow alterations to be managed well and to the advantage of the organization:

1. Space, so you don't move walls six inches to suit someone's ego.

2. Materials, so you don't use mahogany paneling where drywall will do.

3. Construction practice, so that you don't build in bookshelves where a free-standing bookshelf will suffice.

4. Layout, so you're not reconfiguring an office because someone wants his back to the door.

5. Engineering, so that you are not providing eight electrical outlets in a room but are providing proper access to electrical and data outlets.

If adhered to, these standards allow minimal guidelines for construction, particularly if the workforce is stable. That leads to a 30 to 40 percent savings in design costs.

A second major means of control is proper document flow between the design division and the alterations division, within the alterations division, and through the work reception center to ensure that alterations work is coordinated with maintenance work.

Someone should be tracking the flow of a project from inception through closeout. In large organizations (those handling more than one hundred projects annually), both the design division and the alterations division need to establish single points of contact through which all projects enter and leave the division, and formalized routing documents and an automated system for tracking project progress through the system. In large organizations, this tracking is often done for the department by a work coordinator in the work reception center. The issuance and pass-off between divisions should be formally noted, probably as critical events in the project management system.

Computer-assisted design and drawing systems make the upkeep of accurate drawings relatively simple, provided later alteration drawings use official construction drawings as a base and later changes in the field are incorporated. Too often, partial drawings or schematics (cut sheets) are used to do small alterations or renovations. That practically guarantees that the information will not be updated in the database. Given that 30 percent of all space is renovated annually in the average corporation, costly as-builts will be completely out of date within four years. Actually, drawings that are 10 to 20 percent out of date tend to be viewed as obsolete, so less than a year's failure to update can ruin a good set of facility drawings. The facility drawings listed in Exhibit 14-4 should be on hand for alterations.

As important as they are, few alteration programs have good estimating support. Proper estimates of alteration costs require specialized skills. The estimator must be familiar with construction costs in general and, more important, with the costs of altering space at that site. He must be capable of both gross (for working and conceptual estimates) and detailed estimating and must work on many small estimates but have a database unique to the site. Above all, the estimator must work rapidly and accurately. (There is an excellent discussion of a PC-based support system in Sanford Gerstel's *Critical Issues in Facilities Management; Computer Applications.*) Since the estimator needs site-specific knowledge to work properly,

Exhibit 14-4. Facility drawings required for alterations.

Essential	Optional Layers²	Schedules	Others
Base building	Reflected ceiling	Electrical panels	Typical
Key plans¹	Electrical	Floor design loads	perspectives
Site survey	Mechanical	Security devices	Renderings
	Fire	Communications	
	Life and safety	conductivity	
	Plumbing	Historical	
	Mechanical room	information (e.g.,	
	layout	architect, when	
	Parking	constructed)	
	Communications	Finishes	
	Data	Masonry	
	Communications	Space by floor (e.g.,	
	Security	gross, core,	
		circulation,	
		occupiable)	
		Ceiling heights	

1. Key plans are base building drawings with single-line room drawings. For each room and room occupant, some information is provided (e.g., phone number, name, organization, grade, and applicable standards).
2. Some of these layers may have sublayers. For example, the plumbing overlay could be divided into water supply and sewage.

an outside estimator is of little value. Therefore, the facility manager should employ a staff estimator or use someone hired as part of the A-E package. There is no effective cost control without proper estimating.

I have found it helpful to categorize work by size. Except for projects that require design, I allow the work reception center to assign work under $2,000 (best estimate) directly. For larger projects, I feel specific authority is needed. Here are some helpful rules for assigning large projects:

1. Placement in the work plan is authority for the design division to begin conceptual design and obtain a working cost estimate.
2. Projects under $100,000 can proceed for design and execution if the working estimate is within allocated funds (unless the facility manager desires to allocate funds quarterly or semiannually).
3. Projects over $100,000 can proceed beyond concept only after specific approval by the facility manager.
4. Projects whose conceptual estimates exceed the funds allotted may proceed only if authorized by the facility manager.

This system is workable, and though seemingly bureaucratic, dampens the tendency to overspend on the alterations budget or to expend all alterations funds in the first quarter of the fiscal year.

If too many projects are chasing too few funds, there should possibly be an alterations prioritization committee. This committee is most effective if it is a user group, with the facility manager as secretary. The committee establishes priorities for the alterations budget and reviews progress and reprioritizes at midyear. If the committee members are chosen properly, consensus is not difficult; however, it must be certain that committee policy allows some deviation to meet health, safety, and operational emergencies.

The manager of alterations must insist that workers are doers, not thinkers or designers. All changes other than small field changes need to be referred back to the design division for redesign, approval, and additional funding. If this rule is not strictly enforced, expect leakage of 15 to 25 percent of the alterations budget.

The alterations program is implemented in many ways. Increasingly, the work is contracted out, often to a term service contractor responsible for operations, maintenance, and alterations or minor construction. Some large companies even provide design services to ensure that all aspects of the facilities mission are integrated at the contractor level (i.e., they see the big picture). A very successful variant is to have a body-shop contract whereby skills are ordered by number of tradespeople to meet the peaks and valleys in a work program. Often in such a program tradespeople stay in the facilities even though the contractor changes upon rebidding; they are de facto in-house crew.

I prefer to use the designer as project manager during alterations. That fixes responsibility, allows for rapid decisions on changes, and means a single contact from concept through project completion. Some large design firms have separate project managers oriented toward client organizations who coordinate both the design and execution phase of all alterations.

Most project management systems are too sophisticated for alterations. For the vast majority of such projects, data entry efforts exceed the benefits since projects are simple, relatively low cost, and of short duration. A weekly report is often of more value. There are successful automated systems that track annual alterations work rather than individual projects.

Relocation and Move Management

With 20 to 30 percent churn rates, corporate America must accept relocation as a fact of life. Even manufacturing facilities are subject to relocation.

Actually there are two levels of relocating. The first is strategic and involves a major acquisition or disposal of space; this is increasingly cost-driven.[9] That is not the type of relocation I discuss here.

Relocation management in facility operations is management of departmental staff relocations caused by adding or losing staff, loss or gain of leases, or movement to a more suitable space. In many organizations, these moves are funded from the same budget as building maintenance.

I prefer to separate alterations from relocations for two reasons:

1. Management frequently likes to focus on the annual or unit costs of relocations. Alteration projects tend to have higher unit costs than relocations, which distorts record keeping when the functions are combined.
2. Often relocations are mandatory; there is some degree of choice in whether alteration projects will be done.

The controls and procedures for alteration management equally apply to relocation management. Two interesting phenomena have arisen:

1. Relocations have become so prevalent that large international developers and real estate companies have developed relocation networks. Those networks promise to handle all aspects of personal and corporate relocations.
2. Moving companies in major metropolitan areas now often have specialty units to relocate libraries, computing facilities, medical facilities, etc.

Organization

Almost all companies employ a moving company (some have staff movers) to move furniture, equipment, and supplies within their facilities. Often this function is managed by the facility manager; if not, it still has a major impact upon the facilities and their operation.

Move management entails the following:

1. Major inter- and intrabuilding moves
2. Moves to support the alterations program
3. Moves to relocate facilities stock
4. Service-order moves
5. Delivery of supplies within the institution
6. Fixed moving commitments (e.g., two movers to the loading dock, one mover delivering copy paper)

The first four of these functions are directly controlled by the facilities staff; the last two tend to be managed by others, and they work relatively unsupervised. Consequently it is often necessary to send the most dependable movers on fixed commitments and supply delivery. Though these movers are not always working for the facilities department, they are viewed by staff as facilities people, so they must be at their best.

Service-order moves are handled through the work reception center. There also should be close coordination with the food service staff, the conference services staff, and the security staff to ensure that setups and takedowns for major events are systematically provided. Keeping lobbies, cafeterias, and conference rooms set up properly at all times is a major challenge.

For construction or alteration projects, movers are just another trade that needs to be scheduled—this time to clear for construction, install or reinstall furniture, and deliver personal goods. The project manager is responsible for seeing that moving crews are scheduled.

Often, when a division's staff evacuates an area prior to construction, they leave behind files, office supplies, even obsolete office technology. The custodial staff normally is trained not to touch such items, yet they must be cleared out before construction can begin. The move manager or a responsible mover can go through the space, then contact the office supply room, the administrative officer of the evacuating staff department, and the appropriate file room to set a suspense date for removal. All items left after that date are treated as trash.

All move coordinators need both short- and long-term storage. Long-term storage can be at a location off-site. As a rule of thumb, the long-term storage site should be able to service the facility within two workdays. The short-term facility requires immediate access to the loading dock, should be sized to meet all demands with lead times less than two workdays, and should contain items that experience has shown need to be available on a short response time. A portion of short-term storage facility should be secure storage.

Once construction is complete, the offices need to be set up and the staff's personal belongings moved in. That is the normal sequence of events, but be alert for special conditions. It is embarrassing to have to remove a newly installed and stained mahogany door frame because a senior executive's sofa will not go through the door. Move supervisors and lead movers should be expert in the organization's entitlement and layout standards. Once the staff occupies an office, and it is discovered that it was laid out incorrectly, it is difficult to change. To avoid this, have the move coordinator review the final punch list from the staff's perspective. They are on-site at the appropriate time and all other crafts should be essentially complete, so it should be crystal clear to them exactly what needs to be done to complete the project and turn it over to the users in A-1 condition. One creative facility manager photographs each desk prior to a move and tries to recreate that setup after the move.

Procedures

My preference for providing moving support is a term contract with a local firm for movers and equipment. I normally include provision for local storage. If possible, a core crew with at least one supervisor stays in the facility, supplemented by additional movers as needs demand. For large evening or weekend moves, the moving contractor can hire off-duty military personnel complete with first-line supervision (a sergeant or petty officer), if possible, to work with the company's crew.

Moving requests are handled just like other facility work requests: through the work reception center. However, provide a separate dispatcher for all move-related work, because the number of inquiries and amount of required handholding is very high.

Prior to a move, distribute packing boxes. It should be department policy (1) what is user packed, (2) what is mover packed, and (3) what is not to be moved. Everyone should be in agreement, and items should be clearly labeled, normally with a color code. Also, company policy should clearly state to what degree items are to be designated on a manifest. There is a trade-off between the cost of documentation and the chance of an item's being lost. (For example, I do not manifest interoffice moves.) I have found it helpful to provide premove instructions. Even with such instructions there is a certain amount of customer interface to ease the trauma and increase the efficiency of the move. Give special thought to items requiring special moving (e.g., a safe or artwork).

The movers must control the freight or service elevators, either through dedication or an elevator key system. Also, there should be staging areas for temporary storage of goods. Access to loading docks at both origin and destination must be arranged. If traffic will be disrupted, make special arrangements with local police. Ordinarily, the moving company makes these arrangements.

Some degree of tender loving care is required for customers in the two or three days after a move. Assign a crew of movers, working with the move coordinator, to make post-move adjustments. On day 2, the handymen, again coordinated by the move coordinator, can assist in hanging pictures, replacing doors, and the like. On day 3, the handymen can go systematically through the area, correcting nicks and dings and spot painting. On all three days, day porters make a midday trash pickup, and movers remove packing boxes and excess furniture. Each of the first three nights after a move, there should be heavy cleaning, with carpet spot cleaning on the third night.

Move management must always be mindful of three principles:

1. Security is at its weakest during the chaos of a move. Take extra security precautions.
2. People are under stress during a move. Try to plan and execute the move calmly and efficiently.
3. Always have an alternative plan for critical parts of the move, like another freight elevator, or a single moving truck, or a security system requiring special access.

Experienced movers, a well-informed staff, and plenty of supervision can ensure a smooth move.

Furniture Installation

My experience has been that furniture attic, or back-up, stock should be 4 to 10 percent of total inventory, with a minimum of at least one backup item for each component or set and two for all common components. Bookcases and lateral files seem to disappear because they are easily defended as exceptions or special cases, so additional attic stock may be required.

With gradual conversion from case goods to systems furniture, the skills necessary to install furniture are not necessarily best provided by movers. In fact, in some areas union work rules preclude this. I prefer initial installation by the company providing the furniture, but the best installation crew is a matter of economics and personal preference. Some in-house capability is desirable to satisfy any urgent needs to reconfigure, install, or remove furniture. In large organizations frequently there are specialized installation needs—specialized shelving comes to mind. It is best to have these special items installed initially by the manufacturer but reconfigured or reinstalled by the department's alterations crews or maintenance personnel.

Once furniture is installed, treat it like all other building elements. Inspect and repair it under a preventive maintenance program. Respond to service orders and conduct cyclic maintenance, particularly refinishing and upholstery cleaning. Finally, plan for replacement. It is best to have a minimal repair capability for jobs like spot cleaning and caster replacement during work hours, with heavy repair (reupholstery, refinishing, major cleaning) done on a scheduled or off-hours basis.

Disaster Recovery

Catastrophe can strike even the most prepared organization. Flooding, fire, earthquake, or other natural disasters occur at any time, as can sabotage or serious vandalism. Certain companies are particularly vulnerable to strikes. Proper planning, however, can ensure that the company's business is disrupted as little as possible and that loyal employees will not have to wait long before resuming their work.

Disaster recovery planning and implementation certainly have a large facilities component. To be most effective, they should be managed by a company business manager because the recovery planning must support the business plan of the company. I participated in a disaster recovery planning effort that originated within the administrative structure of an institution. It was never accepted because it was never viewed as relevant by line managers, and administrative managers were not knowledgeable enough of business functions to make proper disaster recovery decisions. Because the outward manifestation of disaster planning is often framed in terms of facilities, there is a tendency to view disaster recovery as strictly a facilities function. That is fallacious and should be resisted.

A substantial part of disaster recovery planning should be already in place to meet the common problems of an effective facilities department. For example, there should be:

1. Adequate routine physical coverage of the premises to ensure that 99 percent of all problems can be solved when they occur and that help can arrive quickly to solve the other 1 percent.
2. Good engineering drawings of all buildings and an up-to-date assessment of major equipment and structures.
3. A notification chain (and an estimate of travel time) for staff and contractor personnel.
4. A twenty-four-hour contact point at all major utilities, the police department, and the fire department.
5. The provision of an alternative site for critical functions.

There is no commonly accepted format for a disaster recovery plan, but a possible format is shown in Exhibit 14-5. In addition, the following steps should be taken to prepare the facility department for a disaster:

Exhibit 14-5. Disaster recovery plan format.

I. Introduction
  A. Assumptions
  B. Considerations
  C. Definitions
  D. Objectives

II. Requirements (normally by organization)

III. Strategies and Discussion (includes selected strategy)

IV. Detailed Procedures

V. Appendixes
  • Notification and assembly plan
  • Command center plan and manning
  • Staffing and team composition
  • Administration and logistics
  • Communications
  • Facilities
  • Data processing
  • Vendor/contractor
  • Legal
  • Labor (if applicable)
  • Public relations
  • Budget and finance

---

1. Designate an alternate facility command center and rendezvous point. The center should be capable of twenty-four-hour-a-day operation.
2. Designate an emergency response team.
3. Prestock a complete facility database of drawings, schedules, and instruction books, as well as equipment for the emergency response team.

The goal of disaster planning is to restore the operations of the company. That goal must be kept in mind or effort might be diverted into counterproductive activities. For example, it may be best to emphasize an alternative site rather than reconstruct the principal site. Larger organizations should perform a vulnerability assessment.

Disaster recovery always needs to focus on both the short and long term. The short-term plan stresses continuity of operations, quick reaction, and quick damage assessment (e.g., retain, salvage but clean, or throw away), with a horizon of less than six months. The long-term plan stresses a return to predisaster conditions with code and operational improvements implemented. The long-term plan may have a three- to five-year horizon and should be fed by the short-term plan.

Since most facility managers never experience a disaster, and almost none experiences more than one, it is easy to overlook the more costly and difficult problems:

- Heat damage to structural steel not readily inspectable
- Soot damage
- Dampness and corrosion, particularly in communications equipment, office technology and building systems
- Art restoration
- Hazardous materials cleanup
- Mold formation
- Condensation in drains and lines during cold weather
- Too much or too little water in high-pressure boilers

Each of these problems should be assessed and planned for in addition to the usual fire, water, and structural damage expected.

Because not even the largest organization can have all the necessary skills in-house, disaster recovery planning is perhaps most effectively done by a disaster recovery consultant. Additionally, disaster recovery planning requires input from both operations and planning and design. Often the senior planning and design person leads the planning effort; then, if the plan has to be executed, the facility manager or senior facilities operations person is in charge.

While not principally responsible for disaster recovery planning, the facility manager in most companies is a major player. Recent floods, the California earthquake, and the Oklahoma City bombing have magnified the importance of good disaster recovery planning. The IFMA periodical, *Facility Management Journal*, provides helpful information in an annual issue devoted to disaster recovery. See also the Disaster and Recovery Planning subsection listed under Books in Appendix A.

Notes

1. *1996 Corporate Facilities Monitor* (Houston: IFMA, 1996).
2. "Power Buying." *Facilities Manager* (January–February 1997): 24–25.
3. "Facility Management Practices," *IFMA Report 16* (Houston: IFMA, 1996), p. 28.
4. "Demographics and Trends," *IFMA Report 2* (Houston: IFMA, 1986), p. 34.
5. "Facility Management Practices," *IFMA Report 2* p. 14.
6. John R. Richardson, "Telecommunications; Changes in Management, Regulation and Technology," in *Facility Planning Technology*, McKinley Conway and Linday L. Liston, eds. (Norcross, Ga.: Conway Data, 1987), p. 919.
7. Ibid.
8. "1989 Modernization Survey," *Buildings* (June 1989): 120.
9. Eileen Carstairs, "The Corporate Relocation Game," *Corporate Design and Realty* (January–February 1987): 35.

15

Maintenance and Repair

Pulse Points

- *The facility manager needs to educate management in the cost of ownership.*
- *A company should budget 2 to 4 percent of the replacement value of its facilities for annual maintenance and repair.*

In 1989–1990, I participated in a National Research Council study of the maintenance of public buildings in North America. The resulting report, which emphasized our failure to maintain and repair properly our inventory of public buildings, made these recommendations:

1. Agencies should make qualified staff and managers specifically responsible for maintenance and repair (M&R) and should ensure that they are trained and recognized. M&R funds should not be diverted to minor alterations and improvements.

2. M&R programs should be built on formal condition assessments.

3. The annual M&R budget should be 2 to 4 percent of the current replacement value of the facilities, excluding land. This amount is over and above the amount to overcome a backlog of maintenance and repair.[1]

Although the explanation does not appear anywhere in the published study, the brevity of those recommendations was driven by our desire to recommend some simple rules that could be understood and sold to the legislators who appropriate the money for maintenance and repair of public buildings.

This report was enthusiastically accepted and is often quoted, but, I must admit, it was a failure. A new report by the Association of Higher Education Facilities Officers and the National Association of College and University Business Officers indicates that for institutions of higher learning, deferred maintenance levels have risen $5.5 billion since 1988, and the gap between institutional capacity to fund capital needs and the funds available continues to increase.[2] Observation and anecdotal information from other parts of the public sector confirm that the situation continues to deteriorate.

In 1997 the National Research Council reconvened a new committee to go back over the same ground because some agencies that tried to use the yardstick of 2 to 4 percent were told by their legislative overseers that it was "too simplistic." The fact of the matter is that our companies historically do not want to provide adequate funds to maintain and repair public buildings. We continue to add to our inventory but don't maintain what we have. We have probably built more than we can afford, but most assuredly we have built more than we are willing to maintain.

M&R in the private sector has been equally ignored. The reasons range from a concentration on short-term goals, to a lack of penalty for underfunding M&R in any specific year, to the tenuous and ill-perceived connection between building maintenance and the corporate bottom line. During this period of emphasis on cost cutting, facility managers were lucky to maintain level funding of M&R, to say nothing of reducing backlog.

Public authorities face the dilemma of shrinking budgets and control tax rates, while responding to increased calls for services. Decisions to underfund the M&R of public buildings are often made because the officials do not understand the implications of underfunding, nor, in many cases, do they even have the criteria to alert them that they are underfunding.

It is often difficult to discern the consequences of a reduction in M&R. The physical evidence is usually not immediately visible; several years may pass before the effects can be observed. And facility managers do not themselves usually have evidence that they can use to defend their requests, nor can they describe in specific terms the consequences of underfunding. Yet the costs to correct the effects of long-term underfunding often exceed the cost of the M&R that would have precluded those deficiencies. No single M&R program model can fill every need at every corporate level, yet there are principles and concepts that ensure a cohesive approach to M&R. Before discussing the elements of such an M&R model, let's agree on some basic terms.

Key Terms

• *Maintenance*—the work necessary to maintain the original anticipated useful life of a fixed asset. It is the upkeep of property and equipment. Maintenance includes periodic or occasional inspection, adjustment, lubrication, cleaning (nonjanitorial), painting, replacement of parts, minor repairs, and other actions to prolong service and prevent unscheduled breakdown, but it does not prolong the life of the property or equipment or add to its value.

• *Repair*—work to restore damaged or worn-out property to a normal operating condition. As a basic distinction, repairs are curative, and maintenance is preventive. Repair can be classified as minor or major. Minor repairs are those associated with maintenance activities that do not exceed one to two workdays per task. Minor repairs do not appreciably prolong the life of the property or equipment or add to its value. Major repairs are those that exceed two workdays per tasks, or are beyond the capability of existing maintenance personnel. Major repairs often are defined as those that can prolong the life of property or equipment, but should not increase its value. They usually require contracting for repair service.

• *Replacement* of building-related components or systems—the act of replacing an item of permanent investment or plant equipment. It is the exchange or substitution of one fixed asset for another having the capacity to perform the same function. The replacement may arise from obsolescence, wear and tear, or destruction. In general, as distinguished from repair, replacement involves a complete identifiable item.

The Cost of Ownership

When a corporation or public authority decides to acquire a new building, it commits itself to a stream of costs that will be realized throughout the life of the building. (See Exhibit 15-1.) The total cost may be identified as the cost of ownership of the building. This cost of ownership concept is useful in developing budgets for M&R. If authorities recognize that the costs of M&R are informally committed at the time of acquisition, then understanding the annual M&R budget is easier.

The stream of costs includes the cost of the acquisition itself—that is, the cost of acquiring the site, the costs of design and construction, or the cost of purchasing an existing building. These costs are visible and, unfortunately, are frequently considered to be the only costs worthy of immediate attention during acquisition. But several other costs accompany the acquisition decision. Operations costs must be accounted for throughout the useful life of the building. The building's functional costs, such as the cost of personnel to maintain, repair, and replace major building elements, are also part. Included are the costs of utilities and of cleaning

Exhibit 15-1. Typical costs of ownership.

Acquisition
  • Site costs
  • Design
  • Construction or purchase

Operations
  • Utilities
  • Custodial

Maintenance and repair

Replacement of components

Alterations and improvements

Rehabilitation and replacement

Disposal

the building. In addition, routine and recurring maintenance of the building is realized as a stream of costs, as are costs of repair and replacement of major building components such as boilers and air-conditioning systems.

The stream of costs also includes the ultimate replacement of the building or its rehabilitation, assuming the function continues longer than the economic life of the structure. Ultimately, the stream of costs includes the cost of disposal. This may be demolition or the cost of sale to another party. The authority planning to acquire a new building should acknowledge these costs and view them as inherent in the ownership of the building.

Another cost component should also be recognized: alterations and improvements. If alterations and improvements permit a change in the use of the facility, then the accompanying costs are associated with the cost of ownership relative to the new function. If alterations and improvements are incurred without a change in function, then they must be justified in terms of increased efficiency or effectiveness. Too often alterations and improvements are funded from the operations and maintenance (O&M) budget, where they often eat up the funds that should go to M&R.

Organizations typically fund maintenance using procedures that inhibit effective M&R. Budgets are prepared and funds for building operations and maintenance are combined, usually resulting in a relatively large outlay. Inevitably, the operations component of O&M is significantly larger than the maintenance component. When management must reduce a budget, they then look at O&M as a whole. However, those responsible for managing the buildings can exercise very little control over the operations component. As a result, operations is typically fully funded and maintenance is reduced. There are specific effects associated with underfunding M&R (see Exhibit 15-2). Unfortunately it is possible to under-

Exhibit 15-2. Effects of underfunding.

Code failures	Service failures
	• Power
Structural failures	• Heating, ventilation, and air-
	conditioning (HVAC)
Safety failures	• Leakage and intrusion
Health failures	Premature loss
Excessive costs	Loss of contents
• Excessive replacement	
• Minor failures lead to major	Social costs
failures	• Poor aesthetics
• Treating symptoms, not the	• Poor morale
cause	• Inability to attract best employees
• Increased consumption of	• Increased pollution
utilities	• Loss of readiness
Lower productivity	Absenteeism and turnover

fund routine and recurring M&R for a period of time without immediately visible results.

Corporations should recognize the cost-of-ownership concept. All elements in the stream of costs should be funded at an appropriate level. Although the M&R component varies from building to building, it is possible to develop a relationship between this and an inventory of buildings. For instance, different relationships have been developed to express average levels of M&R. Cost per square foot is frequently the yardstick for determining an appropriate level of M&R budgeting.

A simple method of stating M&R needs is in the annual percentage of replacement value of the building. In order to understand this relationship, consider the elements of an M&R budget: routine and recurring maintenance plus the cost of annual repairs (including the costs of the replacement of major components, such as boilers and air-conditioning units). The long-term, average relationship between the replacement value of an inventory of buildings and annual M&R requirements is in the range of 2 to 4 percent. The specific percentage for any inventory depends on several factors, including the age of the buildings, the type of construction (permanent vs. temporary), the loading of the buildings, and the climate. My observations and discussions with facility management experts indicate that M&R funding at 2 percent of replacement value is minimum; any lesser amount results in a degradation of inventory over time. Of course, this recommended range may not be as relevant to a small inventory of buildings in a local community as it is to a large inventory at a state or federal agency level. However, even with small inventories, the 2 to 4 percent range of M&R funding is valid over time.

Repair or replacement of major deficiencies in building components that have evolved as a result of long-term M&R underfunding is an implicit part of the stream of costs. When funding is not available for all repair projects in a given year, a backlog of repair projects is created, and the condition of the property and the significance of that condition must be assessed in order to reduce this repair backlog. Cost of ownership implicitly recognizes the need to correct high-priority deficiencies with a structured program to reduce repair backlog, but such corrections are outside the 2 to 4 percent funding range for any one year.

On the other hand, fully funded M&R results in an equilibrium point of funding that maintains the inventory and backlog of repairs. At this point, routine maintenance is fully funded, as are routine repairs. In an era of fluctuating budgets, good management dictates that maintenance be funded first, with repairs variable. Alas, repairs continually postponed also escalate into disasters. At the minimum, authorities should strive to reach this funding equilibrium; otherwise, the buildings are consumed through lack of maintenance and repair.

An organization can determine replacement value in several ways. The controller, in fact, will probably dictate how it is to be done. The simplest approach estimates what it would cost in any given year to replace a building to perform the same function as the original. Another approach applies escalation factors to the acquisition cost of the building. Some companies have developed computer programs to perform this calculation and to provide a replacement value or current plan value for the total inventory each year. A number of indexes are available, including those published by the U.S. Office of Management and Budget for the U.S. federal government and those published by *Engineering News Record*. There is the potential for inaccuracy in any of these estimates, particularly since some public buildings are over a hundred years old. It is necessary for each company to evaluate its inventory and develop the best approach for determining its replacement value.

The company is bound by the procedures established by its reviewing authorities for the formulation and presentation of its budgets. I am not recommending a single approach appropriate for all levels of detail and budget formats. The cost-of-ownership concept, however, does provide a framework for indicating the funding level for M&R. Management can then take a long-term look at funding levels and develop a strategic plan for appropriate M&R funding.

Maintenance and Repair Management System

To be effective, an M&R program must operate in the context of a complete facility management system. Maintenance, like all other functions, needs to be goal oriented. Exhibit 15-3 shows one approach to establishing goals and objectives for an M&R program.

It is difficult to present one M&R management system equally applicable to all organizations; no two building maintenance organizations are organized identically. However, the model in Appendix F-5 is as comprehensive and applicable as possible. It starts as a classic management model: planning, organizing, staffing, directing, controlling, and evaluating. However, the next level of detail is a checklist for good M&R management. Automated facility management (such as computer-assisted facility management, or CAFM) is often a possibility. While priority should be on systematizing maintenance management, whether automated or manual, the database for facility holdings in excess of 100,000 square feet should be automated for efficient management.

The elements in the M&R model are closely interrelated. There are, however, a number of feedback loops:

- Planning-programming-budget-execution-evaluation
- Budget-accounting-work plan-management information system (MIS)
- Capital budget-maintenance and repair budget
- Condition assessment-level of annual funding
- Work management-staffing-work standards-output

Managers should establish policies and procedures to monitor each of these periodically and regularly.

The following are the elements of an effective M&R management program, roughly corresponding to the model; where an item is contained under several management functions, it appears where first noted.

Exhibit 15-3. Universal maintenance objectives.

Overall maintenance goal: Provide economical maintenance and housekeeping services to allow the facility to be used for its intended purpose.

Specific maintenance objectives:

- Perform daily housekeeping and cleaning to maintain a properly presentable facility.
- Promptly respond and repair minor discrepancies in the facility.
- Develop and execute a system of regularly scheduled maintenance actions to prevent premature failure of the facility and its systems and components.
- Complete major repairs based upon lowest life-cycle cost.
- Identify design and complete improvement projects to reduce and minimize total operating and maintenance costs.
- Operate the facility utilities in the most economical manner while providing necessary reliability.
- Provide for easy and complete reporting and identification of necessary repair and maintenance work.
- Perform accurate cost estimating to ensure lowest-cost solutions to maintenance problems.
- Maintain a proper level of material and spare parts to support timely repairs.
- Accurately track the costs of all maintenance work.
- Schedule all planned work in advance, and allocate and anticipate staff requirements to meet planned and unplanned events.
- Monitor the progress of all maintenance work.
- Maintain complete historical data concerning the facility in general and equipment and components in particular.
- Continually seek workable engineering solutions to maintenance problems.

Source: Gregory H. Magee, *Facilities Maintenance Management* (Kingston, Mass.: R. S. Means Co., 1988), p. 14.

Planning and Programming

A good M&R management system starts with the basic data, plans, policies, procedures, and standards to set proper priorities, describe the facilities and their condition, define the work, establish standards, and organize the work into a plan that is both responsive and doable. (In many cases, however, because of years of underfunding, the database has deteriorated.) The inventory of facilities describes the category of facility, states its condition (whether by ongoing inspection or a condition assessment), then assesses the critical nature of any deficiency. New elements, whether capital additions or correction of errors, are entered at least annually.

Exact categories, priorities, and definitions of work are developed. Preventive maintenance, for example, is differentiated from repair. Facility managers select definitions and categories of work that fit their needs and then stay within those definitions to determine the elements of their work plan. Other common ways to categorize work are by priority for accomplishment (e.g., emergency vs. routine) or by approval level required to implement (e.g., $1,500 or less, $1,500–$20,000, $20,000–$100,000, or over $100,000).

The annual departmental M&R work plan contains major M&R projects in priority order, a lump sum to fund preventive maintenance, and a lump sum to fund routine service-order M&R work. A prioritized list of underfunded requirements, in priority order, is also attached.

Generally M&R is planned and funded annually; however, it should operate with a midterm plan that sets priorities on major and cyclical M&R and that provides three- to five-year guidance on the thrust of the M&R program.

Budgeting

Of all the functions of a good M&R program, budgeting usually requires the most management attention; it is, after all, the lifeblood of M&R, an annually controlled function with multiple review points. Each company identifies its requirements in its own unique way (e.g., bubble up or top down), but often all sources of requirements are not considered (What impact will more carry-out fast food in the cafeteria have on carpet maintenance?). There needs to be a comprehensive scheme to collect requirements.

In the model, requirements are examined and prioritized before being submitted in the budget. If funds are likely to be available beyond the critical requirements, they are rank-ordered by priorities established in the midyear plan. Alteration and minor construction funds are not mingled with M&R funds. There are strict rules governing the leakage of M&R dollars into alterations funds.

When the budget is assembled, the manager conducts several analyses, including historical comparisons, unit cost comparisons, comparison to a target percentage of current replacement value, comparisons to the current year's budget, and trend analyses. Variances then become a principal part of the narrative of the budget along with new issues. If the funding guidance is lower than the accumulated requirements, statements of the impact of the funding constraint, by category, are submitted.

The cost accounting and MIS are responsive to proper M&R management requirements. A proper system is able to produce current cost data to assess requirements for preventive maintenance, minor maintenance and repair (service orders), cyclic maintenance projects (by project), and repair projects (by project). It is capable of doing so by time period and by facility. If cost comparators are used, the MIS is able to calculate them.

Each large company decides whether to track expense or commitment data, or a hybrid of both, during budget execution; smaller companies, particularly those with an inventory principally of buildings, track the unit cost (recommended dollar per square foot) of preventive maintenance and service orders. (Some larger organizations prefer to track total M&R dollars by activity code, with special emphasis on critical trends.)

The effect of the capital budget on the M&R budget is worth mentioning for at least three reasons: (1) additions to the capital inventory add to the base for

M&R, (2) decisions based on life-cycle costing, rather than more capital costs, have positive, major downstream effects on future M&R budgets, and (3) designing to maintain is a principal concept in all design policies.

Organizing

Organizing an M&R management program at the national or international level (usually a staff function) or at the local level (usually both a staff and a line management function) can be very different. However, certain common features should be in place.

1. A manager is clearly in charge of M&R, from policy through evaluation.
2. The M&R program is placed where it is not subjected to competition for new construction funds.
3. A clearly defined channel for gathering, categorizing, and executing M&R is in place to ensure coordination with operations, alterations, and capital construction.

The M&R manager has an analysis capability and a good information system. In medium and small companies, buildings are metered (data collection systems put in place) to collect comparative data by individual building or within a facility category. Finally, well-developed material management and purchasing functions—knowledgeable of and responsive to the M&R manager—are essential for a well-run program.

Staffing

Staffing for good M&R management varies significantly according to the size of the company, yet a number of principles are common:

1. The M&R program staff is as technically competent as the capital program staff. The M&R staff is involved in reviewing all capital projects.
2. Only when necessary (because of the small size of the building inventory, for example) is M&R a part-time staff function.
3. The M&R program is staffed to inspect for deficiencies, as well as to inspect the M&R work done.
4. Training is available to improve management and technical skills.
5. Leadership qualities in a manager are emphasized, so the M&R program is proactive.

The correct mix of contract and in-house staff is an important item for consideration, particularly during the program execution phase. I do not have specific guidance, but the best situation is what the manager is comfortable with and can afford in terms of salaries and staff positions. Tasks related to policy, standards, budgeting, work plan development, and quality control and evaluation should be retained in-house.

Directing

The function of directing is almost synonymous with implementing. The common threads at any level are:

1. An appropriate level of design and documentation
2. The ability to respond rapidly to a crisis
3. A recognition that a substantial portion of the workload is reactive

Over time, experienced managers can predict the last two items reasonably accurately despite their apparent unpredictable nature.

The quality of direction in an M&R program normally reflects the information available to the manager. For example, how can limited funds be properly prioritized unless the manager has determined the most critical needs? Proper direction is based on a number of factors, including established priorities, condition assessment, criticality of need, and the work plan.

In many large companies, a major function is allocating M&R funds among executing activities. This allocation often dictates how the activities will execute their work plan. Factors to be considered include the following:

1. Budget guidance
2. Priorities
3. The ability to execute the work plan
4. Criticality of facilities
5. Quality of the submitted requirements
6. Past performance history
7. Condition assessment

Particularly at medium to small facilities, a strong work management and coordination center, automated diagnostics, and commissioning procedures for new buildings can be directed and have strong influences on a good M&R program.

Controlling

The principles of M&R control are consistent for all types and sizes of companies. Control devices include policy, procedures, standards, work plan, budget, approval levels, management information systems, and documentation. The manager, given whatever level of resources, balances and manipulates the following:

1. Control of the budget
2. Control of expenditures
3. New crises
4. New priorities
5. Possible windfalls

To do so, it is absolutely essential that a real-time management information system be available. Above all, someone should be accountable for all aspects of the M&R program.

Evaluating

With the emphasis on benchmarking, M&R evaluation has taken on an entirely different character from early in the 1990s. Traditionally, facility managers evaluated their M&R program according to factors such as these:

- Comparison of the year completed with the prior year or an average year
- Whether priorities were met
- What critical facilities were accommodated
- Trends such as total backlog or against a target percentage of the replacement value
- Leakage of M&R dollars
- Comparison by activities; category or building, leakage, and percentage of work plan executed
- Whether the right skills were employed

Benchmarking of M&R has become prevalent. That has been driven by the quality management movement and is largely concerned with matters of efficiency. The benchmarking process involves identifying specific areas for study, measuring performance in these areas, identifying other companies against which to benchmark, comparing the department's performance against its benchmarking partners, and then figuring out who has the best practices and how to implement those best practices into the department. The professional associations have assisted in this regard. The Building Owners and Managers Association (BOMA) publishes the *Experience Report* annually. The International Facility Management Association (IFMA) publishes *Benchmark Report* triannually. APPA has developed and published a benchmarking model called the Strategic Assessment Model, which, among other things, assesses M&R. The model includes fifteen benchmarks by which colleges and universities can assess their maintenance program against others and a recommended standard. Some possible M&R benchmarks are contained in Exhibit 15-4.

If the benchmarks generated by the professional associations are inadequate, the facility manager can hire a benchmarking consultant to help gather the data and find data against which to compare. Once the benchmarks have been established and implementation procedures are in place and functioning (my experience is that it takes two to three cycles to get the bugs out), then the manager should set goals and objectives to improve M&R. This process involves allocating resources. However, once the facility manager has decided to emphasize a certain area—improved customer satisfaction, for example—and has implemented procedures to do so, the benchmarking process should be able to track progress so that responsibility can be fixed, success can be reinforced, and failure can be recognized early.

Exhibit 15-4. Typical benchmarks for maintenance and repair.

Efficiency Benchmarks	*Effectiveness Benchmarks*
Total and work time per work order	Percentage of customer services for which customer satisfaction is measured
Cost per work order—total and by category	
Total maintenance and repair costs—total and by category	Percentage of positive comments received—total and by category
Costs as a percentage of replacement costs	Backlog of deferred maintenance
	Hours available vs. hours worked
Number of work orders completed on time for preventive and routine work	Ratio of preventive maintenance hours to routine maintenance hours
Funding of maintenance and repair as a percentage of the total facilities and capital budget by time period	Equipment failures
	Number of work orders by time period by category
	Number of positive comments received per time period

Putting Maintenance and Repair in Context

I have already mentioned the serious problems of underfunding of M&R in North America. Since this condition has existed throughout my professional life, I doubt that top management and legislative bodies will suddenly change and adequately fund M&R. Therefore, it is essential for facility managers to ensure that they are using allocated funds wisely. Often they are simply spending money without making any rational decision as to where they get the biggest payoff from our limited funds. Central to good decision making in this area is *condition assessment* (CA).

In its simplest terms, CA is a total audit of the facilities with a detailed list of discrepancies, including code violations. Most contain a funding profile for the next five to ten years for M&R and a projected replacement date for building elements and equipment. A benefit that I discovered during a CA is that I learned which design firms truly designed for maintainability and durability and which manufacturers produce equipment with the longest service lives. Another spin-off is to observe outside experts and their technology and techniques to assess the condition of the company's facilities. Some of those same technologies are applicable to the department's M&R program.

Almost all large architectural-engineering (A-E) firms have CA capability. In most cases, they can do their work with minimal destructive testing. I strongly advise against trying to do CA with in-house staff. They can guide and oversee the operation, but they don't have the amount of time available for the in-depth analysis required by a good CA, and they may unconsciously bias the results. Although the cost is admittedly high, the CA can be the heart of a reasonable M&R plan and program. Another benefit of using an outside consultant is that management will listen (where they may not listen to their internal experts). Although it was costly, the CA I did at the World Bank formed the basis of strategic facility decisions for at least ten years, the absolute maximum time that large facility departments should allow between CAs. Another approach for very large organizations is to conduct a CA of a sampling of facilities—10 to 20 percent—each year so that all facilities are audited within a time frame of five to ten years.

The Maintenance Plan

I have found that public-sector agencies are far ahead of their private brethren in organizing comprehensive maintenance programs. However, in implementation there is less variation because everyone invariably underfunds M&R. Every building element should be covered by an appropriate level of maintenance, determined by management and considering (1) the cost-effectiveness of maintenance through increased serviceability and extension of service life and (2) the desired appearance of the facility elements.

There are almost an infinite number of approaches to maintenance and repair, but they tend to fall into one of six categories:

1. Inspect and repair only as necessary (IROAN).
2. Cyclical repair—repair performed on a specific cycle (e.g., replace roofs every seventeen years).
3. Preventive maintenance—maintain equipment according to a preestablished checklist and cycle (e.g., change generator oil every 100 hours or semiannually, whichever occurs first).
4. Predictive maintenance (the use of sophisticated nondestructive testing to avert the breakdown of critical equipment).
5. Breakdown maintenance most of which can be repaired on a service order (e.g., a burned-out light bulb)
6. Repair projects (e.g., replace all window assemblies in a factory).

A comprehensive maintenance program uses each of these techniques to ensure that every facility component is maintained and repaired in a cost-effective manner consistent with facility standards.

From my observation, plant systems have the most thorough and sophisticated maintenance plans, particularly for preventive maintenance.

Historically, custodial service (janitorial service, carpet and floor cleaning, window washing, and insect and rodent control) has not been considered part of maintenance, but that is incorrect thinking. These services are an integral part of comprehensive maintenance. For example, carpet repairs are minimized if carpet cleaning is done effectively. The guru of custodial services is Edwin B. Feldman of Atlanta, Georgia. He has written a number of books on custodial service, the best of which deals with designing for maintainability, which should be top priority for every architect, engineer, interior designer, and facility manager.[3]

The maintenance plan should include user input. Users can play both active and passive roles. For example, they can:

- Use trash receptacles.
- Report spills quickly.
- Use equipment, particularly elevators, properly.
- Report deficiencies.
- Place signs only on authorized bulletin boards.
- Refrain from using water fountains as slop sinks.
- Turn off lights when not in use.
- Turn off water faucets.
- Use walkoff mats to clean feet.
- Report unsafe conditions.

It is estimated that this level of staff involvement can reduce building maintenance costs by 10 percent. The actions can occur through a number of stimuli, such as managerial emphasis, pride in the organization and its facilities, and an education or internal relations program.

Preventive Maintenance

I have been most successful operating a preventive maintenance (PM) program with three teams:

1. Plant
2. Exteriors, interiors, furniture, security, fire and life safety systems and furnishings
3. Electrical switchboards, floor panels, and devices

Preventive maintenance of specialty items (elevators, building controls) is best contracted through the manufacturer. All told, these teams report all items beyond their capability to the work reception center so that a service order can be processed.

All three PM teams, particularly the second, need to understand the limits of their maintenance work and when a service order must be written. Painting is always an issue. The PM team should paint, but only spot painting; the PM foreman must be sensitive to when excessive spot painting will produce a leopard look and when the painters should be called in.

The PM team cycle is largely determined by each manufacturer's recommended maintenance frequencies. I try to have all public and executive areas inspected weekly. I inspect thoroughly the building exteriors annually and examine the garages and back hallways at least semiannually. The second PM team effort is concerned primarily with occupied areas of the building. It should try to visit these areas quarterly. Each building occupant, particularly the administrative staff, should know the particular handyman on the PM team. For this reason, the team members must be capable of interaction with the staff. If this program is managed well, it is the best public relations program for the facilities department as well as its eyes and ears.

Increasingly facility departments, but particularly their vendors, are using sophisticated, nondestructive methods to predict equipment failure before it happens, among them, thermography, wear-particle analysis, ultrasound, oil analysis, and vibrations analysis. Often these technologies are used in tandem or as a second opinion before a critical piece of equipment is pulled off-line. These technologies can also often be used to identify sources of energy inefficiencies. Some of these technologies require expensive equipment and extensive training; others can be brought in-house at a reasonable cost if the demand for predictive maintenance exists. Predictive maintenance, not surprisingly, is most often used in maintaining industrial facilities because the technology and expertise already exist to maintain the production equipment.

Cyclical Maintenance

This topic does not appear in most books on maintenance management because it is not a pure category of work. Rather, it is a concept—a convenient way of thinking about maintenance. Experience shows that certain items need to be maintained on a certain basis. For instance, battery-powered clocks need new batteries semiannually. The team can use the weekends to set the clocks forward and back for daylight savings time and also change the batteries. If not done sooner, all interiors should be repainted every three years. Though carpeting will often last ten to twelve years, for a number of reasons, I replace it every six years. Cyclical maintenance is actually replacement, but of a nature that expedites planning and budgeting. Ensure that cyclical maintenance practices are in agreement with the life expectancy of the products. For instance, you may have convinced your boss to switch from broadloom to carpet tile because the latter's greater life expectancy justified the higher initial cost.

The Work Reception Center

I have already discussed the role and operation of the work reception center (WRC) in Chapter 13. The WRC is key to a successful M&R program. It is the one place where anyone can report a facilities problem and get action, without fuss or long bureaucratic review. A typical history of problem solving in the M&R program is as follows.

	By Number of Problems	By Cost
Preventive maintenance	75%	50%
Service orders	24	30
Projects	1	20

Several conclusions can be drawn from these data, but one that is inescapable is that M&R projects can often be solved through a good PM program and a work reception center. If the WRC functions properly, the facility manager and the maintenance manager (if there is one) can spend their time managing major repair projects.

For the WRC to function properly, the staff must:

1. Be given authority to task shops directly to accomplish all but exceptional work.
2. Have clear guidance on what work is an exception.
3. Be equipped with a maintenance management system that allows them to develop, track, and close work orders and to develop work and cost history by shop, user, and facility.*

Realistically, all but exceptional service orders should be completed within seventy-two hours. Whenever this cannot be achieved, the WRC should notify the individual with a brief explanation and a probable completion date.

Repair Projects

Despite all best efforts, some repair projects will arise each year. In addition, the value and complexity of some work may make it necessary to develop and control it as a project (a major roof repair is a good example). Some companies allow certain major repairs to be capitalized, but normally that is not possible. Because these projects tend to be large and often require design, they need to be planned and programmed. They also need to be spread over a number of years so that they do not have too severe an impact on any one single annual budget.

Migration of Funds

Most organizations fund all their alteration and renovation projects from the same account as maintenance and repair. That is an invitation to long-term neglect of the latter. There are nearly always alteration and renovation requirements far in excess of the funds available. Unless controls are established, it is almost inevitable that alterations will consume a greater and greater portion of the annual O&M budget. Two controls have been used effectively.

1. Setting a dollar amount or percentage ceiling on the annual amount of alterations work
2. Allocating the funds, using a user's priority board chaired by the facility manager

I predicted in 1995 that there would be a greater appreciation for the need for better maintenance and repair. That has not happened, and facilities continue

---

*For an excellent discussion of the benefits of a computerized maintenance management system, see Kalman Feinberg's presentation, "Computerized Maintenance Management Systems as a Financial Tool for the Facility Professional," in *Proceedings of World Workplace '95*, pp. 91–100. Proceedings are available from the International Facility Management Association.

to degrade. The emphasis on downsizing and cost reduction and the need for relatively fewer facilities have masked the coming crisis. As we all know, you can "pay me now or pay me later." For facility managers who want to be on the cutting edge, I offer the following techniques:

- Wider use of building diagnostics and condition assessment, particularly technology-based, continuous-read systems.
- Increased application of preventive maintenance to all aspects of facilities and their furnishings, not just the plant.
- Formulaic funding for normal maintenance and repair—for example, 2 to 4 percent of replacement value.
- Better use of M&R funds through CA and the use of computerized maintenance management.

There are two outstanding books on maintenance management that should be part of every facility department library: John E. Heintzelman's *The Complete Handbook of Maintenance Management* and Gregory Magee's *Facilities Maintenance Management*. These books provide both solid maintenance philosophy and cost-effective techniques for implementing and maintaining a quality maintenance program.

Notes

1. *Committing to the Cost of Ownership* (Washington, D.C.: Building Research Board, 1990), pp. xi–xii.
2. Harvey Kaiser and Jeremy S. Davis, *A Foundation to Uphold* (Washington, D.C.: APPA, NACUBO, Sallie Mae, 1997), p. 2.
3. Edwin B. Feldman, *Building Design for Maintainability* (Atlanta: Service Engineering Associates, 1982).

16

Facility Services

Pulse Points

- *Most administrative services should be considered for contracting out. They require expertise that is not likely to be on staff.*
- *Facility managers should anticipate the expanded or new services that their customers will demand.*
- *When faced with managing a new administrative service, benchmark with and learn from the best-in-class.*

In this chapter we discuss the general administrative services that facility managers have traditionally managed, as well as some emerging services. As middle management has been reduced in companies and agencies, facility managers have taken on a broader spectrum of managed services, to the point that many are questioning again whether *facility manager* is really a descriptive term for the position.

According to a recent survey, the general administrative services managed by facility managers were as follows:[1]

Service	Percentage	Change in Past Eight Years
Security	71	+13%
Mail services	54	+10%
Communications	53	+10%
Copying services	44	+ 2%
Records management	50	+10%
Moving and shipping	50	+11%

Clearly there has been an increase in the role of facility managers as organizations have flattened.

Certain facility managers, of course, manage functions not even surveyed. Each service mentioned here is a major management function. However, I discuss only some managerial considerations plus how each of these services affects and is influenced by traditional facility services. I refer to the manager of each specific service by that job title (for example, security manager). Large organizations may have a technical manager to handle these specialties for the facility manager, but often that individual is the facility manager in smaller organizations.

Traditional Services

Food Service

Food and facility services are inextricably intertwined. Capital costs for food service facilities are high. Food products soil carpets and furniture. Food preparation areas have high maintenance costs. Because of the fear of spoilage, food service equipment must be kept functioning continually.

Food service is often performed at five levels:

1. Coffee service
2. Carry-out and fast food
3. Full-service cafeteria
4. Private dining rooms with table service
5. Banquet and party service

Increasingly, companies are placing coffee services in the workplace. First, it reduces the time away from the desk. Second, it provides a meeting place for employees to mingle informally. It is interesting to observe these coffee bars. Some are austere and communicate the message, "Get your coffee and don't dawdle." Others are more elaborate, with tables and chairs encouraging communication. Neither approach is right or wrong; each simply reflects the company's approach to work.

These coffee bars require day-porter service to keep them operating and clean. Some companies hire the replenishment of the coffee bars; some use in-house personnel; in others, volunteers make the coffee. Cleanup of the equipment and the immediate area, however, is best done by a day porter. Also, decentralized coffee bars cause an increase in carpet staining, probably because staff often get their coffee in open cups rather than in the covered cups normally sold in a cafeteria. Recycling is changing the face of coffee service (ceramic cups are making a comeback), but it is not making it less complicated.

Whether the company should subsidize food service is an often-debated issue. The consensus is that there is an advantage to have staff eat on the premises so a subsidy is justified. This subsidy most likely consists of paying the rent, utility costs, and repair and maintenance costs rather than defraying the actual costs of food and service.

When food service is provided, the issue is whether to contract out or provide in-house service. During this era of staff reductions, most companies are using food service contractors. There are numerous competent contractors available, with some specializing in cafeteria, fast food, or coffee. Others provide the full spectrum (table service dining and banquets as well), but at a higher cost owing to increased overhead.

Another concern is whether to hire a national contractor or a local one. A national company centers on the resources available, allowing the client a wide range of talent to support the food service operation. But local companies involve their management or ownership in the operation. The parameters of profit for a regional company are less than for a national contractor.[2]

The company needs to set the tone for the quality of its food service. It is difficult to make the banquet and private dining rooms profitable at a price competitive with local restaurants unless some of that overhead is borne by a high-volume cafeteria. That is particularly true if the food service operation is required to "eat" a large amount of official entertainment costs. The company needs to decide whether food service is to be a profit center, a break-even operation, or a subsidized service. The contractor can then recommend options to meet the company's objectives.

Maintenance of the food service equipment is always somewhat vexing. One approach is to hire a maintenance package from the food service contractor; another treats food service equipment the same as other installed equipment. The amount of equipment often is the determinant. When justifiable, my preference is to have the maintenance mechanics assigned to the facility department but under the operational control of the food service manager, who also determines their working hours. The security force, all engineers, and all electricians must be extremely sensitive to the specialized needs of the food service facilities, particularly for uninterrupted gas, electricity, and refrigeration. Many facility managers tell sad tales of failing to reactivate power to a food service walk-in refrigerator following weekend maintenance and finding spoiled food on Monday morning. Remember that food storage and preparation occurs at other than "normal" hours.

Reprographics

One of the catch terms of the early 1980s was the "paperless office." Anyone who has ever managed the reproduction function for a large organization knows the term is a myth. Paper enters a facility and has images imprinted in volumes unthought of even ten years ago. It is not unusual for a large company to produce hundreds of thousands of copies annually.

It used to be necessary to hire outside art and design people and a commercial printer, or to establish an internal print plant, if the company needed high-volume, high-quality printing. But with the advent of high-speed copiers, volume no longer was an issue. Then desktop publishing began providing sophisticated graphics and layout. With PC-based desktop publishing and color laser printing, highly sophisticated color reprographics will be almost completely decentralized to the work units. My department can now produce documents at desks that only five years ago we would have sent to art and design and then to a printer.

Because the technology (and also the philosophy) of reprographics is changing so rapidly, it is difficult to assess the impact of reprographics on facilities. Generally, the cost and ease of installation and maintenance of desktop copiers permit wide dissemination of equipment down to the lowest work units. It is reasonable to require users to "eat" the space to support a desktop copier, but most companies place high-speed, high-volume copiers at designated central locations. Quite often they are stacked vertically so that an employee always knows what location to go to on a floor to find the copy machine.

The location of these copy machines should be chosen carefully. They require large volumes of paper. That paper needs to be moved to the copier in bulk and replenished often. Moving paper in bulk can be extremely damaging. Storage and movement of completed products can be a similar problem. In some exceptional cases, the storage of paper or documents actually can exceed normal floor-load criteria. Also, these machines require a dedicated electrical circuit, substantial space, and special ventilation, particularly if they are used full-time.

Most companies prefer to lease their equipment, although various options are available for buy-lease, maintenance, and copy paper supply. Another decision is whether to have permanent attendants man the high-volume copy centers or to allow staff to operate them. The choice depends on the complexity of the equipment and the expected volume of use. In addition, there is a trend toward decentralizing the support and leasing of desktop copiers directly to work units.

Digital technology is playing an increasing role as the technology is simplified and as consumers become more familiar with applications. Digitization allows different pieces of office equipment to communicate with one another, thus enabling workers to accomplish many tasks while seated at their desks. For example, a letter can be scanned into a computer, printed, copied, and faxed with just a few keystrokes. In addition, the full-color copier is coming into its own. PC-based color copies are now available to everyone at a relatively low cost.

In some cases, the volume and complexity of printed material still require a printing facility. The first option, particularly in urban areas where pricing is competitive, is to contract out. Normally at least two rates are established: one for normal printing and one for immediate turnaround. Ensure that requirements for expedited printing are spelled out in all contracts with printers.

The second option, housing a print plant in the facility, presents unique challenges. Newsprint comes into a facility on large rolls, which are difficult to handle without damaging the facility. Both newsprint and the completed product require some degree of humidity control and storage space. Also, a print plant places a major demand on freight elevators.

Mail and Messenger Services

One of the legends of the corporate world is the chief executive officer (CEO) who began his career in the mailroom. Surprisingly, there are many examples of people who have risen through the ranks from the mailroom. One theory is that if you understand how mail is distributed, you understand how the organization works.

Managing the mailroom requires concentrating on essentials and details. Since mail is one means of communication, there is merit in common management for all communications means in the company. The five factors critical for success are personnel, facilities and equipment, technology, adherence to postal regulations, and emphasis on users.

Staffing is the most challenging area for the mailroom manager. There is a diversity of personnel and of products, particularly when the staff is a mix of in-house and contractors or vendors. Products may include first-, second-, third-, and fourth-class mail; parcels; overnight express mail; registered and certified mail; facsimile and telex; and messenger services. During a recent consulting contract, I was observing the mailroom in the late morning. At the same time, the company's mail clerk was trying to service a U.S. Postal Service mailman, three parcel service delivery men, and two messengers.

Good human resources management in the mailroom does not differ from management in other areas of the company. People must be challenged. Everyone must understand the mission of the mailroom and must realize that they contribute to that mission. Motivation is essential, as is participation in establishing goals and decentralization of responsibility.

Many mailrooms resemble a sweatshop. To avoid this, the facility manager should seize every opportunity to (1) use industrial design to make working conditions more efficient and more pleasant and (2) improve production and reduce boredom. The location of the mailroom (access to the loading dock, controlled access of outside vendors, central location) is critical for effective operation and security. The following points should be considered in design:

1. Work flow should be from left to right, owing to traditional mail equipment design.
2. The layout should be flexible.
3. L- or V-shaped mail-sorting areas are best.
4. Since many tasks are repetitive, study the ergonomics of all workstations.
5. Minimize interruptions through proper layout.
6. In midsize and large companies, use a mail conveyor system.
7. Involve security in determining the mailroom's location.

The availability of entry-level personnel, a traditional source for the mailroom, is becoming tenuous. This means the mailroom manager may have to resort to nontraditional approaches or replace people or functions with technology. Part-time employees such as retired employees or high school students may be hired to supplement the full-time staff. Mailroom jobs can also be enhanced through cross-training.

Ultimately, users will determine the success or failure of the mailroom. Constantly evaluate and seek user feedback.

- How do users feel about the mailroom's performance in general?
- How do users measure the mailroom's operation?
- What can the mailroom do to serve users better?

Never underestimate the value of public relations. Consider an open house in the mailroom. Participate in the company briefing for new secretaries. Consider promoting a mailroom user group.

A real challenge is staying current with postal service and other vendor rules and incentive programs. To do so, keep a library, obtain vendor briefings, and join the local Postal Customer Council.

Smooth work flow, minimum interruptions, and intelligent selection of carriers cut mailroom costs.

Lee Yeaton, vice president of Pitney Bowes Management Services, recognizes the challenges of managing a cost-effective mail center. Mailrooms traditionally are low on the priority list of corporate concerns even though, according to a Pitney Bowes study, mail accounts for over 9 percent of operating costs at Fortune 500 companies. He recommends examining the entire process, not just the mail center:

- Focus on the areas that will affect the business the most.
- Ensure that you are communicating by the most economical method. It often costs less to send a fax than a first-class piece of mail. And 17 percent of third-class mail is never opened, much less read.
- Are duplicates eliminated from the mail stream?
- Is all mail properly classed?
- Does mail conform to postal automation standards?
- Is your business mail reaching the right customers? Should the recipient be paying postage instead of you?
- Do you stay in touch with postal and technology changes that can reduce costs while increasing customer service?[3]

The proper application of technology is yet one more area for cost-cutting—for example:

- An integrated system connecting scales, meters, a security system, and a PC
- An electronic scale with a memory capable of accounting against a budget, of calculating chargebacks, and that is adjustable for postal rate changes
- Postal meters

The mail must go through, so ensure all equipment has responsive maintenance and repair backup.

More than $10 billion was spent in 1989 on overnight delivery service.[4] The accounts payable manager can determine how much the company spent on this service. The reality is that 30 percent of these costs probably can be cut. Express mail and overnight delivery have become almost routine in modern business. To manage express mail costs, focus on three major areas: use, rates, and bills. Consider the following as mailroom procedure:

1. Select the proper mode such as same-day service via air, ground or fax; overnight service via air or ground; two-day service and three- to five-day service. Many services do "best way" calculations if asked.

2. Express delivery is a highly competitive industry. Vendors readily offer discounts to their large customers, but discounts are inconsistently applied.
3. Specify when the material is needed. Sometimes express has become a habit, not a necessity. Log and publish the use of express if there is an appearance of abuse.
4. Get the U.S. Postal Service booklet, *Priority vs. Price.* Certified mail-return receipt can be a less costly alternative to express when urgency is not an issue.
5. Check for errors. Billing errors and overcharges are frequent. Often discounts are not given.
6. Consolidate packages going to the same destination, which is less expensive than sending multiple packages.
7. Obtain a one-time external audit targeted on cost-effectiveness.

Finally, if priority or express mail has become a major expense, which it has in most companies, appoint an express mail manager to lower the costs.

Increasingly, companies are seeking more rapid ways than mail to communicate. However, I believe that the mail and mailroom will be with us for the foreseeable future. Trends in mail are as follows:

- More user-oriented postal services and interconnection of public and private technologies or systems for the advantage of each and discounts for participants
- More work-share programs between the postal service and private companies
- More electronic postage transfer
- Bar-coded addressing and sorting
- PC-based addressing systems
- Robotics in high-volume user mailrooms

Just how rapidly this field is changing is exemplified by the facsimile machine. The fax greatly reduces the workload on central mail services. Companies that grew to operate worldwide providing priority mail service suddenly found their existence threatened. The use of e-mail should have a great effect on both "snail mail" and fax, but most companies find that the expected trade-off does not occur. The volume of all three seems to increase. Conventional mail and priority mail are likely to remain necessary for heavy freight and printed matter like books and brochures. But the mail service manager will have an even greater array of price and technological options in the future. The department's success will depend on how quickly new cost-effective methods are instituted for receiving, processing, distributing, collecting, and disseminating information (not mail).

Transportation and Fleet Management

Normally the facility manager is not the fleet manager in a company with a primary role in transportation (e.g., a newspaper, retail, or wholesale marketing company). Often, however, the facility manager finds himself the manager of a small fleet of executive sedans, service vehicles for facilities staff, and shuttle buses.

Executive sedans present special problems not only because they have high visibility and sensitivity but because of security concerns. Often the drivers perform a security function also. Chauffeur service, of course, can be maintained in-house, but it can also be contracted as part of a security contract or with a chauffeur service. The provision of sedan service for the company is similar to that of chauffeur service. Sedans can be owned, provided as an unique package, or be part of a fleet package.

Whether to own or lease vehicles is very much a function of the facility manager's willingness and resources to operate and maintain a fleet. The primary reason for maintaining in-house fleet management is control. Leasing arrangements now largely negate that reason. A leased fleet can be responsive and well controlled, so the trend is to lease; I suspect that is prompted by resource, legal, and liability considerations as much as anything else.

Regardless of how the fleet is managed, certain principles should be observed:

1. Vehicles should be centrally dispatched and controlled.
2. Parking, whether on-site or off-site, should be provided for all vehicles. I hold that vehicles should not be garaged at an individual's home or be allowed to be taken home except as an infrequent exception. It becomes viewed as a perk and can create unnecessary morale problems, as well as serious liability exposure.
3. Maintenance can normally be provided best through outside sources (the lessor or the dealer). Extended warranties available on most vehicles actually make maintenance relatively economic. Fleet rates for maintenance services can be negotiated.
4. If you provide gas and oil (or use a credit card), someone should check consumption per vehicle monthly. Another easy-to-implement control is to insist that the normal provider of gas and oil dispense only into an authorized vehicle (license number clearly indicated on the credit card invoice), not a separate container, without a separate approval document.
5. Assign licensed drivers or operators to each vehicle and allow operation by someone other than the driver or operator only as a management exception.

In medium to large facilities, other vehicles can often improve the efficiency of the facilities department:

- A self-propelled or towed extendable personnel lift
- Golf carts
- Small pickups
- A self-propelled material lift

• Street or sidewalk sweepers
• A four-wheel drive vehicle (with a bull-blade for snow, where appropriate)

Many large companies find that a shuttle bus system is necessary in large urban areas. The shuttle can improve normal distribution of mail as well as move people, but it must run on a consistent schedule. Early or late operating hours are some of the most important times for shuttle service; whether employees can use the shuttle as a primary commuting means is a policy issue.

It is important that shuttle pickup points be easily accessible (sometimes special security arrangements must be established). Drop-off locations should be out of traffic so that riders can be discharged or taken on in safety. Pickup points should also be selected and illuminated so that persons waiting for the shuttle feel safe and are not exposed to accumulated exhaust. If possible, panic phones should be available at all pickup points.

Shuttle drivers can be one of the most valuable tools for internal public relations for the department (or one of its most serious PR problems). The drivers should know not only their routes but the location of common facilities (cafeterias, lobbies, etc.), the schedule of daily and special events, and the identity of principal company officers and their office locations.

Records Management

Unless a company's core business is closely tied to records management (an insurance company, a library), properly managing records has been underemphasized. This is likely to change in the near future as companies are increasingly dependent on accessing more information faster yet buried by the increased volume of information. Typically records were maintained at two or three locations (office, central file, historical file) with no uniform policy on records retention or archiving. But the inability to share information, shrinking facilities, and increased computer-generated paper have brought records management to the forefront. It is now estimated that 95 percent of business records are still stored on paper.[5]

Records management at the work-unit level is important to both the records manager and the facility manager, but it is difficult to control. Companies try to control pack rats by limiting the number of files issued, but there are so many exceptions granted that the approach is ineffective. The most effective controls are well-developed records management policies and standards for review, retention, disposal, retention, and archiving. If the pack rats are ever to turn in their files to a central location, they must be assured that their information needs will be met responsively (most seem to require twenty-four-hour response) and without effort. Central files and archives must be located, equipped, and managed to provide that level of service.

Some of the more common media to store files are tape, disk, microfiche, optical disks, and CD-ROM. These new media, while they store information in much smaller volume, still offer substantial file management challenges. Some of the popular file management techniques are:

- Numbering systems
- Color coding
- Automated indexes to paper-based filing systems for active records
- Automated file change-out and control system
- Automated records center for inactive records
- Computer-assisted microfilm retrieval systems
- Automated vital records or disaster recovery plans on databases
- Development and application of networking or communication technology to provide multiuser configurations

One of my mentors told me long ago that when faced with a problem for the first time, I should go to the expert in that area and adopt that person's solution to the problem (little did I know that he was stating the essence of benchmarking). Applying that philosophy to records management, look to the companies for which records are their lifeblood and have either major government oversight or fiduciary responsibility (insurance and mortgage companies come to mind) for best practices in record management. USAA, for example, is recognized for its records management procedures.

Security

In the wake of the bombing of the Murrah Federal Building in Oklahoma City, the Justice Department reviewed security at federal facilities around the country. The review resulted in 8,500 recommended countermeasures. Threat analysis is a vital first step to physical security, and federal efforts in this area can be helpful to all security managers. Federal buildings are rated in five security levels, from minimum security (level 1) to facilities that are densely occupied and critical to national security (level 5). A similar rating could be applied to commercial buildings.

The General Services Administration (GSA) has established fifty-two security standards for federal buildings with occupants. These address traffic patterns, parking, lighting, physical barriers, closed circuit TV, entrance and exit controls, employee and visitor identification, intrusion-detection systems and other aspects. These standards can be used directly or be modified for commercial use.

Improved security is not cheap. The GSA, for example, estimates the minimum security features for a level 4 building to add about 3.3 percent to construction costs.[6]

Today security often is managed by a separate department in large organizations, but whether or not the facility manager has direct responsibility for security, the service has tremendous impact on physical facilities—their design, their operation, and their policies.

It is the administrative service most often outsourced, according to a recent study. Of facility managers having security responsibility (71 percent), 61 percent outsource the function.[7]

Basically, there are three parts to a good security system:

1. *Personnel* who enforce rules and procedures, respond to alarms, assist tenants or visitors, locate and report possible problems, investigate and report incidents and accidents, and provide information to staff concerning security in their areas

2. *Physical devices* that extend the ability of the security officer by providing a delay to an intrusion, alerting the security officer to a problem, and allowing response time

3. *Policy and procedures* that control access to the facility, regulate movement within the facility, monitor for problems, provide a response to hazardous conditions and a method of reporting such conditions, and teach the staff good security and safety

If one has not been done, a security and safety assessment should be conducted by competent in-house staff, a security contractor, or a consultant. The local fire and police department might assist. This assessment should examine the following as a minimum:

External Factors

1. Neighborhood
2. Outside emergency services

Own Facilities

1. Perimeter
2. Interior of the building
3. Lobby control
4. Elevator control
5. Fire stairways

Security and safety systems should be designed to meet the specific needs documented in the assessment. Systems available range from simple to highly sophisticated—and expensive. The system that is chosen should (1) meet necessary codes, (2) fit long-term growth plans, (3) be supportable for at least five years, (4) can be supported seven days a week, twenty-four hours daily, and (5) is compatible with existing systems and power supplies.

The best systems, however, are only as good as the company's security and safety policies and procedures. For example, deliveries should be restricted to loading docks, service entries, and service elevators. Similarly, all employees should be encouraged to report unsafe conditions and suspicious persons and to safeguard both personal and company property. Those steps alone greatly reduce security and safety problems.

Key control can be a major irritant because good security procedures run counter to operational effectiveness. Key control, except in rare cases, must be implemented at the building level and varies with the resources and skill levels available. A master key system should be used only where absolutely necessary. Possession of a master key should be determined by need or status. If keys must be issued to tenants, it is good practice to change locks and issue new keys periodically. Never issue keys on a long-term basis; require that they be turned in periodically and revalidate the need.

Cleaning personnel should be admitted to secured areas by security officers, not given keys. Keys should be under the control of security personnel during nonworking hours, and they should check them at the beginning of each shift.

Each key should be stamped "Do not duplicate" and numbered. There should be a record of the names of the persons and date when keys are issued. When a key is lost or stolen, conduct an investigation. If it is a sensitive area, change the key cylinders. When a person leaves the company, make every effort to obtain all keys by withholding final compensation.

Lighting is perhaps the most important security and safety aid while also being functional and decorative. Effective lighting depends on a reliable power source. Generally, the source is primary power, usually supplied by either a local power company or an on-premises generator; an auxiliary generator, with an automatic switchover; or battery-operated lights with automatic switches and trickle chargers. Only the most critical lights function off the batteries. Lighting can be controlled by a number of devices. Control is normally a compromise among operational efficiency, energy management, and security or safety. Common light control devices are switches, monitors or light level sensors, or timed light sweeps.

Alarms permit the most economical use of security forces. Basically, an alarm is a method of alerting either a specific response group or the community at large that there is a danger, intrusion, or malfunction. Exhibit 16-1 lists some common types of alarms. Generally the alarms do not initiate any action.

Basic components of an alarm system are a triggering device (contact points, metallic tape, ultrasonic, laser), a means of transmitting a signal, a monitoring device or station, and a power source. The same considerations mentioned for selecting a security system in general also apply to alarm systems. In addition, insist that they are UL-approved.

Among the most sophisticated security devices are access control systems. These systems control entrances and special security areas. They are also used for monitoring parking areas and elevators and for controlling lighting and other energy-dependent equipment. But besides monitoring people and electronic equipment, access control systems can track the location of parts, critical files, or other objects.

Some common access control systems are retinal scanners, fingerprint or handprint scanners, access control cards, magnetic strip cards, magnetic dot cards, embedded wire cards, and proximity cards. Combined with a photograph, these cards become identification cards. Some companies incorporate a watermark or stamp to make counterfeiting difficult. When interfaced with a computer, these access control systems can identify who enters a specific location and when. The system can also be set to sound an alarm if someone uses the card after hours or uses an unauthorized card.

Visitor control is another area where efficiency, security, and politics clash. To avoid problems, visitors should be greeted by a receptionist or guard who confirms the appointment and asks the individual to sign in and out. In some instances, guests should be escorted to the person they are visiting, and in secure areas, even escorted to and from the lavatory. Messengers too should be confined to outside the security perimeter. Some companies have created bullpens for them. Service personnel are often allowed to enter areas where even trusted employees can't go. Organizations shouldn't allow someone to service a machine

Exhibit 16-1. Types of alarms.

Alarms by Type

A. Fire alarm
    1. Detect heat, smoke, etc.
    2. Transmit a signal and/or activate a sprinkler.
B. Intrusion alarms
    1. Detect an intruder.
    2. Transmit a signal.
C. Warning/special-purpose alarms
    1. Detect a problem in a machine, etc.

Alarms by Control Type

A. Local alarms system
    1. Detects and transmits a signal to an alarm on or near your premises.
    2. A bell, horn, etc.
    3. Depends on scaring the intruder or someone calling for help.
    4. The least effective.
B. Proprietary system
    1. Owned and operated by the company or individual.
    2. Detects and sends a single to a monitor to the premises where action can be taken (to a guard on a console).
    3. Good if there is a procedure for response and employees to perform the function.
C. Central station
    1. Detects and transmits a signal to a central location where some action is taken (police or fire department notified or a contract security officer sent or both).
D. Automatic dialer
    1. A detecting device connected to a telephone which, when activated, will automatically dial the police and play a recorded message.
    2. Some communities have outlawed dialers, due to high false alarm rate.

Circuits

A. Independent circuit. The best is a direct line from the company to the central station, using protected telephone lines.
B. Loop circuit. Several companies are on the same circuit to the central station. It is cheaper, but less secure.

until they confirm that a repair has been requested, and the service person should be escorted at all times. Finally, vendors must also be watched. They should not have unlimited freedom.

The average commercial or industrial business has ten to fifteen visitors per year per employee, and up to 40 percent never return their temporary badges.[8] To deter unauthorized use, some badges now automatically turn a different color when a visitor goes outdoors. For guests who should be in a building for only a limited time, there is a badge that voids itself after several hours, with the word *expired*. Also available are badges that automatically expire after one day, a week, or a month.

Security procedures are highly site specific. However, all security personnel should be trained to handle openings and closings, visitors, confrontations with staff, unauthorized personnel, and after-hours emergencies. In large organizations, contracting out security services is often considered. The perceived advantages of in-house guards are as follows:

- Known personnel
- Lower turnover
- Loyalty
- Sense of ownership
- Better control
- More familiar with the facility
- Training and performance can be judged more readily
- Security force is to company's own specifications.

For an excellent discussion of creating a security program in two widely different sites, see "How GSA Is Strengthening Security After Oklahoma City" and "Behind the Scenes of a Safe Urban Campus" in the July–August 1997 edition of *Facility Management Journal*. A facility manager should be able to design an excellent security management program using the information in these two articles.

The perceived advantages of a contract force are as follows:

- Lower expense
  —In-house guards generally earn more than contract guards
  —Few fringe benefits are paid
  —Liability insurance, payroll taxes, uniforms, and equipment are paid by agency
- Disinterest
  —Personnel are not part of the company
  —Personnel hold loyalty to the company, not to other employees

In a large, stable workforce, a proprietary system may be better; where flexibility is required, a good contractor may be better. A survey conducted by the American Society for Industrial Security (ASIS) showed that approximately 40 percent of those companies responding used contract services for 50 percent or more of their guard needs. Over 50 percent said they did so for economy or to avoid administrative problems of labor and personnel, and their experiences were rated from fair to good.[9]

Security managers increasingly are being asked to provide services such as identification document issuance and control, parking control and security, loss prevention, crime prevention, criminal investigation, safety program, executive security, and physical aspects of computer security. Whether to hire a national company or a local company for any of these services is a question along the same lines as for other services. With a national corporation come all the resources like training, emergency manpower, new services, new equipment, and liability exposure. But a local company may be a known quantity, and it may know its employees better.

Security has become a more important function primarily because of potential terrorism, revenge cases, and increased crime, particularly drug-related crime. Its importance through the next decade is unlikely to diminish, as increasingly companies look to ensure a safe working environment.

Communications

Automation of the workplace has placed unprecedented demands on a company's communications network. In the 1980s, there was no bigger headache for facility managers than cable management. At the same time, deregulation of the telephone industry meant that a company could own its own telephone system, and unparalleled options of equipment and services were suddenly available. Not surprisingly, many communications managers found themselves ill prepared to handle the technical, policy, and operational issues that surfaced. The facility impacts alone were monumental and, in buildings thirty to fifty years old, at times seemed overwhelming—thus, the rise of the communications manager and the consultant for smaller companies.

Communications needs are truly unique to each company, often to departments within the company. Nevertheless, some extremely sophisticated assessment techniques are available. When assessing communication needs, look for the following as a minimum:

- Number of incoming and outgoing calls
- How many people use the lines
- Growth: location, personnel, businesses, profit

For a number of years following telephone deregulation, many companies chose to own their own, premises-based phone system. Some of that ardor seems to have subsided. Leasing again seems to be the financing option of choice. Still, there is increased sensitivity to communications and greater expectations for these in-house systems. I recently observed a FM supervisor at a retreat. He was equipped with a mobile phone, a beeper, and a radio. For service providing instant communications has become a necessity. So, don't forget the following:

- Customers want choices.
- Poor systems give a poor impression of the company.
- Systems are expected to save time, energy, and money.
- Systems are often used as input and switching devices for other building systems.

Common features of modern systems include automatic call-back, message waiting, speed dialing, call waiting, call forwarding, teleconferencing, "Do Not Disturb" memos, intercom, toll restrictions, least-cost routing, station message detail recording, voice and data switching, and interface with voice mail. When buying a communications system, consider the following:

- What is included in the contract price
- Costs avoided by using new features
- Operating costs
- Maintenance costs
- Flexibility, particularly the ability and cost to expand
- Ability to switch equipment among company locations

It is increasingly evident that the telephone and telephone infrastructure will be used for a broad range of fax, videotext, and data transfer or retrieval services. These capabilities will be enhanced as fiber optics becomes more prevalent. A study of telecommunications, based on telephone interviews and mail surveys of 167 companies, found the following:

- *Corporate telecom networks.* The typical company surveyed had 808 domestic and 27 international network nodes. Typically, more than 20 large computers and 5,000 terminals and PCs were linked into these corporate networks on either a dedicated or dial-up basis, users noted.
- *Key issues facing telecom management.* Almost all of the communications executives interviewed named two or three "key" issues that they planned to address during the next twenty-four to thirty-six months. Named in order of importance, the issues included central site network management; LAN/WAN connectivity and LAN integration; consolidation/network integration; and integrated services (ISDN).
- *Telecom operations.* More than $20 million was the typical budget for voice and data communications among the respondents. Nearly $6 million was being allocated for data communications equipment and service alone. These executives reported an average of 38 people assigned to their telecom groups.
- *Other key issues.* Also mentioned as central issues were cost-effectiveness, network availability, international expansion, and network capacity/band width.[10]

Electronic and Information Security

Electronic and information security is a corollary to records management, communications, and security. It applies to information security for electronic tools, particularly software, and for the company's informational data bank. Partly, information security is a victim of the information explosion. Administrative personnel, archivists, and librarians are overwhelmed by the volume of information to be managed and sometimes fail to protect it to the degree they should.

The mobility of employees among companies, some of whom are competitors, makes information security even more difficult. Also, systems themselves tend to aggregate data. They are designed to meet operational needs, and security is often an afterthought. In addition, security of reports is threatened by each new wave of equipment, such as color copiers and printers, that makes counterfeiting easier, along with unauthorized copies. To counteract this, distribute updated reports only if prior ones are handed back for shredding.

Shredders too are taking on additional importance. Some machines are so advanced that they can shred entire cartons of data, still in the carton. As another tactic, security specialists are using encryption to transmit reports. Encryption, however, has operational problems, and its lack of acceptance limits its use. In sum, our best hope for better information security may be better employee training and a campaign that emphasizes the importance of information and intellectual property.

Emerging Services

In this chapter we have discussed general administrative services commonly managed by facility managers. There are also some emerging services that will have an impact on the traditional functions when introduced.

Art Program

It has become fairly common for some capital costs to be set aside for purchase and installation of works of art; 0.5 percent of a major project is a common figure. Quite often those funds are used to buy a few major pieces for the entrance or lobby plus a large number of relatively inexpensive pieces to adorn corridors and office walls.

I prefer to consider all but major pieces of art as furnishings and include them in the planning and design of space. Limited funds are best used for prints rather than originals because it allows a broader distribution of art with limited funds, and it decreases inventory and security concerns. One successful program has been to box-frame 15-by-18-inch photographs of company operations and hang them in appropriate areas. This can be a valuable supplement to the art program and improve the quality of the workplace.

The degree to which art should be appraised, curated, accounted for, and secured can be a problem. Major pieces obviously should be secured. Large sculpture requires few security precautions beyond protection from weather and graffiti. Smaller pieces may require a pedestal, enclosure, and alarms. How extensive the inventory is must be carefully assessed for cost-effectiveness. I suggest any inventory be kept at two levels:

1. A PC-based management-level list that allows callup of a piece by property number, title, artist, location, assigned unit, value range, and place of purchase.
2. A card-based list that contains the following: photograph, property number, title, artist, gallery, and initial purchase price, medium, appraised value, and date of appraisal. (With a CADCAM, this file, too, can be PC-based.)

What degree of inventory to maintain is also extremely complex. For example, it probably costs up to $50 per entry to prepare either of the inventories. Obviously it is not cost-effective to inventory $25 to $75 prints. However, if ten of those prints are lost in a year, which is a good possibility, documentation is necessary to make an insurance claim. If the insurance deductible is relatively low ($500 per incident, for example), an inventory helps recovery of part of the loss. The collection should be reappraised every three to five years.

Large organizations should consider having an in-house frame shop, preferably contractor operated. Besides supporting the art program, a frame shop can be a superior service provider by:

- Supporting in-house exhibitions and photo or art displays
- Framing items like official maps, photos, and certificates
- Maintaining and relocating the company's art, when necessary, for alterations or painting
- Updating the location portion of the art inventory
- Maintaining the art locker—the storage room for all pieces not currently exhibited

Art selection, when there is a capital expenditure, is best handled by a volunteer employee committee, possibly chaired by the design manager. The committee should understand its budget, how much space it is expected to furnish, whether it be permitted to select a major piece and where it will be sited, any procurement rules, and the time schedule. While volunteer committees are sometimes difficult to deal with, art affects employee morale, so employee input is desired from the beginning.

Even with a professional design staff and a dedicated art advisory committee, it is probable that at least a part-time art consultant will be necessary. That consultant will probably be hired on a hourly basis and can assist with appraisal, maintenance, security, and purchasing advice. However, the consultant should not be allowed to sell art to the company. Whether the consultant is allowed to sell art to individuals in the organization is a policy decision.

Shared Services

Shared services are not really a "service," but a way of delivering services; it is ordinarily associated with property management rather than facility management. The landlord of a building with multiple tenants establishes service centers for services such as fax, high-speed copying, parcel mailing, cables, conferences, and exercise facilities, and charges the tenants for usage. This relieves any one tenant of high initial costs to establish the service. Much of the early publicity for smart buildings promoted this concept.

However, these shared services generally were not well accepted. Perhaps tenants wanted more flexibility than the service centers could provide. Perhaps billing was a problem. Perhaps developers had difficulty recovering their capital costs in a reasonable time while charging a bearable rate. Perhaps demand for services was too erratic and fluctuated too widely to permit effective and efficient management.

Increasingly, however, corporations are using one type of shared service: temporary workstations. Because of the ability now to plug in and plug out telephones and data communications, workstations are being set aside for use by transients, consultants, and excess staff. A variant is to use small conference facilities with easily relocatable partitions as hot-body offices, although the viability of this latter concept is not yet established. While local area networks and flexible telecommunications permit adequate communication among geographically separate members of the same work unit, employees still want turf with recognizable boundaries and social interaction with fellow workers.

Child Care

Of all benefits possible in the workplace, none has captured management's support so quickly as child care. While the human resources chief ordinarily has staff responsibility for child care, the facility manager has major responsibility for space, construction, maintenance, and repair of in-house day care facilities. The importance of a safe, clean facility cannot be overemphasized. Just let any trace of asbestos be found or the water in the drinking fountain be out of tolerance for lead, and concerns will be loudly voiced.

Child care developed from a single-parent, low-income issue into a major domestic policy issue. Corporate decision makers raise child care as a boardroom agenda as they face recruitment competition for a shrinking labor pool. Real estate developers view child care as a valuable marketing tool in an age of empty office buildings. A brief glance at corporate demographics reveals a 45 percent increase in the number of working mothers since 1950. By 1990, 60 percent of new entrants into the workforce were women. Eighty percent of women in the workplace will have a child at some point during their careers.[11] Child care is rapidly being recognized as a means to broaden recruitment, reduce absenteeism, lower turnover rates, improve public image, and increase morale. Some employers are even using the availability of day care as a determinant between relocation sites.

Some employers are exploring on-site child care options, but many find the realities daunting. Operating a child care center can incur significant risk—and just opening one can easily cost $250,000. Although the corporate staff can help with zoning and permits, offering a child care center requires hiring people with necessary skills. Consequently, the company must make sure that the apparent need is both broad-based and continuing before consent is given.

The most common form of day care management is contracted out, with policy set by a board of employee-parents. If the facility manager supports a day care center, he must ensure that service is nearly instantaneous and extensive. Any problem in the day care center must be given a high priority.

Health and Fitness Facilities

Many facility managers who offer health and fitness centers exhibit frustration over their inability to control costs, particularly capital costs. Often that signifies that the facilities are driving the health and fitness program. The facility manager never gets ahead; this year the employees need an aerobics room, and next year there'll be a demand for a track. When the weight room is still in construction, someone will lobby for a swimming pool.

The health and fitness facilities offered to employees should reflect the program the company has established. Once management decides on a program, the facilities for that program can be planned and constructed.

I feel that the best fitness programs are designed by a professional, guided by an in-house board of directors. Whether the consultant simply helps establish the program, policies, and procedures, or also operates the facility with his own attendants, instructors, and safety personnel, is a corporate decision based largely on the risk manager's willingness to allow employees to use facilities without supervision. I have seen extremely successful programs run without supervision and without legal or insurance problems, while other companies insist on a full-time, CPR-rated professional staff.

Some of the facilities in common use are:

- Urban walking and running courses
- Par cours (suburban areas)
- Aerobics rooms
- Weight rooms
- Exercise equipment rooms
- Saunas
- Handball, squash, and/or racquetball courts
- Multipurpose courts
- Massage rooms
- Tennis facilities
- Running tracks
- Swimming pool

The last three require large space and considerable capital outlay. In general, they are prohibitively costly in an urban environment. A swimming pool brings with it a whole set of engineering, construction, operations, and safety problems beyond what most companies want to tackle.

Whether the company has an institutional health and fitness program or not, changing lifestyles almost dictate that employees have access to showers and locker space. There is a particular demand for lockers and showers at the end or beginning of the workday, as well as at noon.

Company fitness programs tend to draw the most competitive employees. In turn, employees become advocates for their personal preference in equipment and operating hours. For this reason, an employee board of directors should develop and promulgate policy for the fitness center; the facility manager alone cannot and should not try to sort through each proposed addition or change.

Fitness centers have a major impact on facility management. They tend to have high capital costs, particularly if retrofitted into existing space. Athletic facilities are not by their nature more costly to operate and maintain, but because they often reuse existing space, their design may be suboptimized and therefore more costly to operate than a new facility designed specifically for fitness. Finally, fitness buffs are often zealots; as such, they expect superior services, and their expectations can bring pressures that result in increased operating costs.

Concierge Services

Another emerging service is a concierge in buildings to handle a variety of tasks like obtaining gifts for a spouse, giving out and receiving dry cleaning, and the like—tasks best done during normal working hours.

This concept has worked well in fine hotels for years. With married couples both employed, the need for a concierge at work to handle the mundane but necessary, and sometimes extraordinary, chores becomes more and more viable.

The concierge service is run by an independent contractor who normally offers a menu of services. Some offer to take on almost any task. Most concierges perform for cost plus tips by getting a fee from the vendors to whom they take their business. Others charge a fixed, advertised fee per service. They are normally provided a lobby location, and often are provided heat, light, and electricity gratis. Frequently, there is no need for special provisions, since those services already exist in the lobby.

To the extent that it can be provided with little cost or disruption, concierge service can be of real value to employees. It represents the type of employee-oriented services that companies will use to attract and hold quality employees.

Some Final Words on Outsourcing

I am a strong proponent of outsourcing these administrative services because the result is a more technically competent level of service. The facility manager retains control and ensures customer service. There may be some temporary initial savings if the company has substandard personnel or high company benefits, but the long-term savings are in operational efficiency, ease of human resources management, and the ability to stay up-to-date technologically.

Outsourcing is with us ($23 billion in services will be outsourced by the year 2001).[12] Facility managers need to develop their skills as outsourcing managers as much as they need to develop any technical skill. As my favorite consultant, Stormy Friday says, "We need to view outsourcing as a tool, not a weapon."[13]

Notes

1. *Facility Management Practices* (Houston, IFMA, 1996), p. 14.
2. John Soat, "The Ins and Outs of Contract Services," *Administrative Management* (February 1986): 59.
3. Lee Yeaton, "It's Past Time," *Today's Facility Manager* (March 1995).
4. Philip Binkow, "Control Delivery Service Charges and You'll Save," *Office* (December 1989): 56.

5. David O. Stephens, "What's Ahead for Records Management in the 90's?" *Office* (January 1990): 135–136.

6. Robert Hager, "Building Security: Are You Overlooking Something?" *The Military Engineer* (December 1996): 25–27. By permission of The Society of American Military Engineers (SAME).

7. *Facility Management Practices,* p. 14.

8. Robert Linn, unpublished class notes for a course on facility management, New York University.

9. Soat, "The Ins and Outs," pp. 59–60.

10. "Telecom Management: The Key Issues," *Office* (February 1990): 17.

11. Cheri L. Sheridan, "Child Care: The Issue of the 80's," *Business Properties Magazine* (November 1988): 39.

12. Paul Tarricone, "Outsourcing Turns to Smart Sourcing," *Facilities Design & Management* (February 1997): 40–43.

13. Ibid.

Section VI

Facility Management Practice

In this section I discuss a variety of topics under the umbrella of facility management practice. Emphasis here is on management rather than the technical aspects of the facility manager's mission. I begin with some administrative tasks such as procurement and personnel management, then discuss outsourcing, partnering, and benchmarking. I close Chapter 17 with a discussion of work process loops, which each facility manager should ensure are working correctly within the department. Chapter 18 discusses the premier role of quality in providing facility management services.

Chapter 19 explores the management aspects of the department's budget, recognizing that facility managers will be measured in the same manner as other managers in the corporation. Chapter 20 delves into the matter of computer support for facility management, including what new features the future will bring. And Chapter 21 concludes with a consideration of several issues of special relevance to facility managers.

17

Administering the Department

Pulse Points

- *The facility manager must build solid, trusting relationships with the procurement staff.*
- *Contractor evaluation criteria should reflect what is truly important to the facility staff and their customers.*
- *Outsourcing is a staffing, not an organizational, issue.*
- *Partnering requires a well-developed system and procedures to be successful. Above all, it takes a commitment to make it work.*
- *In benchmarking, get beyond the metrics.*
- *The facility department normally faces a broader range of issues than most human resources departments are used to handling.*

A number of overall administrative functions are essential to the proper functioning of the department. We have discussed the various kinds of planning in Section II. In addition, as part of the design-build cycle we covered the managerial duties of developing programs.

In this chapter, we discuss procurement, a major responsibility of facility managers, yet one where responsibility is often shared outside the department. We examine outsourcing, partnering, benchmarking, and evaluation. We close with a systems approach—a look at a number of management loops that the facility manager should ensure are alive and well within his department.

Procurement

A centralized procurement system can present challenges for the facility manager. The operational elements (of which the facility manager is one) generally function from one set of priorities, while procurement officers* frequently operate from another. Thus, an effective procurement operation depends largely on the successful integration of these two sets of priorities.

For the most part, the user is chiefly concerned with quality of goods and services, response time, and reduced paperwork. Users may not always give primary consideration to price. Depending on the urgency of a request and the trade-offs among speed, quality of service, and cost, facility department users may sometimes wish to forgo competitive bidding and specify a preferred vendor.

The procurement officer, on the other hand, must follow procurement procedures, particularly in the public sector. These procedures include open competition, fair and equal treatment of all bidders, and cost-effectiveness. The procurement officer must be concerned principally with the cost-effectiveness of the procurement function, since he is judged primarily on his success in controlling costs. Fortunately, most procurement departments have become more service oriented than they were a decade ago. However, a natural tension will always exist.

If you understand these different priorities and are willing to negotiate, explore alternatives, and compromise, you'll ensure a procurement system that meets both your and company objectives.

Reduced to its basics, the procurement process is a response to the need for goods or services. Goods are normally obtained through agreements called *purchase orders,* either for a one-time purchase (PO) or for a period of time (blanket purchase order, or BPO). During the term of a BPO, orders can be placed against the BPO and are limited only by a cumulative dollar figure.

Services are normally obtained through agreements whose contents vary widely but at a minimum spell out the scope of services to be provided, the term of the agreement, and the basis for compensation. The term may be fixed or may set a certain total dollar value. The price may be stated as a fixed amount or may be an estimate that cannot be exceeded without a formal change to the agreement.

All such contractual documents should contain a time frame for performance, a basis for costing, specifications describing the goods or services being acquired, and the general and special conditions. *General conditions* set the legal framework for the relationship between the company and the vendor. The agreements are prepared by the purchasing department and reviewed by the legal department, as necessary. The terms and conditions of a purchase order are preestablished and incorporated into the PO. For the most part, these conditions do not change; that is what makes them general. *Special conditions* are those that relate to a specific procurement and contain specially written paragraphs that define such items as working hours, security requirements, and special access. These provisions are prepared by the purchasing department staff, based on specific requirements the facility manager identifies. For simple contracts, the general and special conditions are often encapsulated in the agreement part of the con-

---

*I use the terms *purchasing department* and *procurement department* and *procurement officer* and *purchasing officer* interchangeably, since these terms vary widely from company to company.

tract; for complex procurements, the special conditions may be incorporated in the performance work statement.

Successful procurements do not just happen. They require technical input, managerial supervision, and cooperation between the facility and procurement staffs. The facility manager has a responsibility to manage the technical part of the procurement process as carefully as the procurement officer manages the form and process. While the purchasing and legal staffs may offer assistance, the facility manager is responsible for accurately defining the requirements.

In some cases, primarily in service contracts, the facility manager may be designated as the contracting officer's representative (COR) during contract execution. The COR represents the contracting officer in day-to-day relations with the contractor. The COR is usually empowered to enforce the contract but is not permitted to change the scope or terms of it. Changes can be made only by the contracts office and must be in writing.

The Procurement Process

Purchasing departments normally are organized according to functional responsibility. It is extremely important that the facility manager become familiar with the procurement officers who handle each type of request. Units having direct impact on procurement are the purchasing and contract sections, although organizations may vary in what they call them. The *purchasing section* is responsible for acquiring goods or services via standard purchase orders or preestablished terms and conditions, such as the federal General Services Administration Schedule. The *contracts management section* is responsible for acquiring goods and services that, because of their nature, performance period, or other criteria, require specific terms and conditions. Construction, consulting services, and multiyear buying arrangements generally fall into this category.

Despite what has developed historically in some organizations, budgetary control is not a function of procurement. Facility managers certify that funds are available for a requested procurement, since they control their budgets.

Exhibit 17-1 is a flowchart depicting the various stages of procurement. Listed below are three variations on these procedures and several cautions:

1. When a procurement request is received by the purchasing department, it is entered into the system and assigned to a procurement officer according to the nature of the request. Even on contract renewals, the procurement clock does not start until the properly completed request is received.
2. Any directed (sole-source) procurement must be justified even if there is only one local source of the goods or service. It is the facility manager's responsibility to justify a directed procurement.
   - For utilities, for example, a sole-source procurement is commonly agreed on between the facility manager and the purchasing department.
   - For a unique item (replacement part for an existing system) for which only one local vendor exists, a brief memo of justification should suffice.
3. An item ordered by phone directly to a vendor without a PO or before a

Exhibit 17-1. Procurement process flowchart.

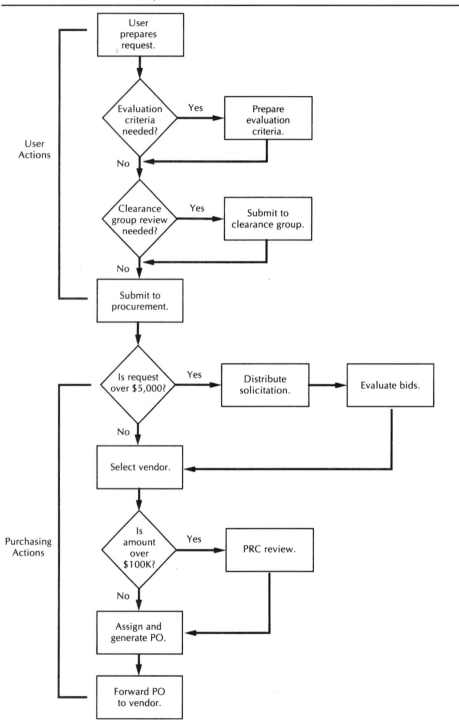

PO is cut makes a contract with that vendor. The person placing the order could be held liable for payment to the vendor.

Evaluation criteria must be established in order to differentiate among bidders. This should be done jointly by the facility and procurement staffs. Selection criteria can include:

• *Lowest responsive bid.* Procurement staff are solely responsible for this type of evaluation, which is used only for the most straightforward bids. These procurements typically involve reorders, routine and well-defined user requirements, or name-brand purchases. When this evaluation criterion is selected, the award is made to the bidder submitting the lowest prices.

• *Lowest evaluated bid.* The facility and procurement staffs agree on the technical criteria for evaluation. The internal procedures of the unit determine who should approve the selections criteria developed by the facility manager in consultation with staff. All vendors are rated, and a floor (minimum passing technical score) is set. The vendor with the lowest bid that passes the technical floor is selected.

• *Highest evaluated bid.* The facility manager and the procurement officer agree on the technical criteria for evaluation. All vendors are rated, and those falling below the floor are eliminated. Those above the floor are reevaluated, perhaps by interview, with price being one evaluation criterion (25 to 40 percent). This is an elaborate process but has proved an excellent way to select the best all-around contractor.

• *Unique service.* For the procurement of unique consulting services, including architectural-engineering (A-E), the contractor is usually selected on the basis of technical merit rather than price. Final price is usually negotiated with the most technically qualified firm.

Procurement takes time. Further, larger procurements tend to take more time; that is, the larger the bid, the more formal the process and thus the more time it takes. The following time periods indicate average number of business days from receipt of request until the order is placed or an agreement is transmitted to the vendor:

Procurements valued at less than $5,000:	5 days
Procurements valued at $5,000–$10,000:	10 days
Procurements valued at $10,000 to $50,000 involving a short list of vendors with a subsequent technical evaluation:	20–30 days
Procurements valued above $50,000:	30–45 days
Procurements subject to public bidding:	50–75 days

There is a tendency to underestimate the complexity, requirements, and time needed for procurements. Also, the purchasing department is probably not staffed to handle every procurement on an exceptional basis. For sure success, start early. Remember that on top of this processing time, there may be a two-week to six-month delivery period.

By and large, a company that ends up with an unacceptable contractor probably did not do the procurement process well. Here are some helpful points:

1. Develop, with the procurement department, a vendor questionnaire for use in evaluating bidders. Do not hesitate to request modifications if needed.
2. Provide a chairperson for any evaluation committee. He, in turn, recruits members for the committee. The committee should be composed of three to five members, in addition to the contracts officer, each of whom possesses expertise, interest, and commitment. Consider using in-house consultants as advisers, but be aware of their client base in order to avoid conflict of interest.
3. Keep on track during committee deliberations and interviews. Be democratic, but keep questions and comments focused on the needs of the procurement. Set the ground rules in the opening remarks and stick to them.
4. Finalize the evaluation criteria. The procurement staff will not open vendor submissions until the criteria have been finalized. Get agreement on the type of evaluation (one-step, two-step) and evaluation criteria before starting. Decide how scoring totals will be determined (for example, throw out high and low and average the rest).
5. Make sure the committee has had an opportunity to do its homework and has read the technical proposals before the first meeting.
6. Ensure that each committee member performs an independent rating of each vendor submission.
7. Have the procurement officer schedule formal interviews with bidders following their team members' area of interest.
8. Make sure the facility manager concurs with how the contracts officer converts bids to scores.

A procurement review committee (PRC) often reviews awards of $100,000 or more, although management may review a proposed procurement regardless of the dollar value. The PRC might be composed of representatives from the legal department, the planning and budget department, and two operational managers. Following the evaluation and prior to the award, the facility manager should expect to appear before the PRC with the supporting procurement officer, who will present the proposed procurement in a prescribed manner. The facility manager may then be asked to supplement this presentation with additional technical information. In most cases, the results of the PRC is announced the day following. A PRC usually meets monthly; supplemental meetings or informal reviews may be scheduled to consider time-sensitive procurements by discussing the matter with the appointed procurement officer. The procurement officer will most likely arrange for the special PRC review.

Disposal

Every piece of equipment and furniture, every major assembly, and many building components become obsolete, or they are replaced by a newer item or a standardized one. For these reasons, every organization should have the capability of disposing of equipment or furniture.

Before an item can be offered for disposal, two determinations need to be made: (1) that the item is in excess of the organization's needs, and (2) that it has a residual value. Those determinations are the province of the facility manager, often with the help of the controller for determining residual value. The actual disposal is normally done by a disposal officer. The best system is one in which the disposal officer for a commodity (furniture, for example) is the purchasing officer for that same commodity; some procurement departments have individuals who handle only disposals.

A critical issue always is whether to trash an item or to put it up for disposal. Often that decision is best made by a knowledgeable individual using an on-site assessment. However, if an economic analysis is made, the costs of transporting, storing, and conducting walk-through inspections by potential purchasers must also be considered. Again, this is an issue that defies exact analysis. A spare executive chair, though it may have no depreciated value, could be more valuable than when it was purchased. Also, if it is the only spare for the set of boardroom chairs, its value is inestimable.

A good disposal program, if properly executed, can return funds to be used for facility programs. Often funds recovered through disposal go into a general fund, and this is a disincentive to prompt disposal. Other options are sale to company employees or transfers to local schools or charities.

Some Tips

Listed below are some additional tips and suggestions to help ensure success in procurement:

1. Do not expect a requirement to be treated as an exception. Handle 99 percent of business by the book, so that when an exception is really needed, it will generate a sympathetic response from the purchasing officer.
2. Include the purchasing and contracts managers in your major project planning.
3. Identify procurement policy exceptions early in the process so they can be addressed by the purchasing staff before the last minute.
4. Submit BPO and service contract renewals three months before the end of the fiscal year. This enables the procurement staff to program this workload for completion, on a routine basis, prior to the start of the new fiscal year.
5. Track procurement actions the same way operational projects are tracked. Include procurement actions as key project milestones in facility projects.

6. Process payments quickly. This fosters faster vendor response time and can result in prompt payment discounts.

7. Report outstanding or unsatisfactory vendor performance, in writing, to the purchasing department.

8. Be prepared to answer all technical questions in any prebid conference and, if appropriate, conduct a site tour. Bidders should not contact you directly prior to submitting a bid. After the procurement staff has released a solicitation and prior to the contract award, all communications with a potential vendor must be conducted through the appointed procurement officer.

Human Resources Management

I often observe that facility managers find themselves managing a mixed blue-collar–white-collar workforce in a company environment that is strictly oriented toward white-collar staff. The problem that this can create was driven home vividly to me when a young HR specialist called me and expressed regret that our advertisement for a building engineer had not been answered by a single college graduate. Where I valued practical expertise in grading jobs, the culture of our organization emphasized academic degrees. Therefore my employees were always undergraded. One of the real challenges of many facility managers is in getting the human resources department to understand the department's employee needs and the management environment in which a facility manager works.

I am convinced that facility departments must have some mix of staff and contractors to operate effectively. (We discuss outsourcing in the section following.) My point is that because of the diversity of the workforce, the facility manager often finds himself being his own human resources manager because the company is unable to support him adequately in this area.

Unfortunately, employment law has become so complex that its managerial manifestations can seem overwhelming. At times it is so intimidating that some managers shrink from actions that they should take for good morale and discipline. Managers who have a unionized workforce have an additional level of complexity to deal with. Interestingly, the professional associations have not presented the level of training in human resources management that I think would be helpful. One of the problems in training mirrors the problem in the workplace. There are few experts in the broad range of human resources problems facing facility managers. Managers nevertheless need training, and I strongly recommend that each facility manager take a professional development course in human resources management.

Contracting Out

One of the hottest topics of the past ten years within facility management has been outsourcing. When companies are willing to contract out their accounting department, for example, it is not surprising that the facility department is a candidate for outsourcing. If you are not core business, you had better perform your own analysis of the costs and benefits of contracting out, because, if you don't, someone else will do it for you.

I am an unabashed advocate of outsourcing to the maximum and have done so in my own practice. The reasons most often given for outsourcing are as follows:

- Outsourcing saves money, particularly if in-house staff have high benefits.
- A contracted workforce can better adjust to fluctuations in work.
- Contractor personnel provide better access to higher-quality skills.
- Large contractors can use their size to get price breaks on supplies and services.
- Outsourcing allows the company to concentrate on its core business.
- The number of employees is greatly reduced.
- Particularly in the public sector, you save authorized personnel spaces.
- With outsourcing, the company can provide services or a level of service that in-house personnel cannot.

Having said that, I should add that there are good reasons *not* to outsource some functions. For instance, no contractor can do strategic facility business planning. Also, many companies have facilities whose operations are so sensitive that facility staff serving them need to be company employees (although that type of facility does not occur as often as you might think). You must not, as one of the top facility management consultants, Martha Whitaker of Callison Architects, Seattle, says, "outsource your soul." Most of the objections to outsourcing are concerned with loss of control or that the workforce will be less loyal to management if contracted. Certainly, a judgment needs to be made by every organization when considering outsourcing, but my observation is that facility managers tend to be too conservative when outsourcing. Pressed to cut costs and personnel spaces, I would use my limited resources for top-flight contract managers and planners while outsourcing the technical work and supervision.

In almost all of the services offered by the facility department (discussed in Chapter 16) contracting to a third party is a viable option. The trend, in fact, is to contract out more. Outsourcing of facility management in the United States is expected to increase over 500 percent between 1996 and 2001.[1] Most companies end up doing what they feel comfortable with, and that's fine. The company must decide three issues: (1) what level of control is desired, (2) what level of service is required, and (3) what response level is required. If these can be met by a contract, the company is probably better off contracting out as long as specifications ensure the services. In most cases, three- to five-year service contracts are best. Contracting annually to exclusively low bidders tends, over several rebids, to rachet quality down to an unacceptable point.

Cost savings from contracting out can be illusory. Make sure the contracts maximize use of limited management time, allow for more flexibility in matching resources and workload, and produce the efficiencies and economies of scale on large contracts.

According to the Outsourcing Institute, the following are the most important factors in contracting out:

- Understanding company goals and objectives
- A strategic vision and plan
- Selecting the right vendor
- Ongoing management of relationships
- A properly structured contract
- Open communications with affected individuals and groups
- Senior executive support and involvement
- Careful attention to personnel issues
- Near-term financial justification
- Use of outside experts[2]

Each of those factors has its own applicability to a particular situation, but I would like to mention several key aspects. Traditional low-bid, adversarial contracting will not work. Perhaps formal partnering is not necessary, but when you are widely outsourced, your contractor is now your staff. I am convinced that a facility manager can get as much loyalty from a contract staff as from in-house staff.

Facility managers should go slow in outsourcing, and use fact-based decision making. They must know their costs of doing business, including distributed overheads, before making the cost comparisons necessary for good decision making on outsourcing. That sounds elemental, but too many outsourcing decisions have not been made when they should have or have failed to produce promised savings solely because the cost figures for current operations were fallacious.

Once the decision is made to outsource, the facility manager should work with the procurement staff to outsource one function at a time rather than the whole department at once. One of the most important things to do, and one of the most difficult, is to be honest with staff and to keep them informed as the outsourcing analysis proceeds. No facility manager should ever get in the position of promising staff continued employment, but he should be sensitive to their concerns.

Just as you wouldn't send your child to a school without first checking its credentials and talking with the teachers, don't pick a service provider out of the phone book. Do some research, talk to management, and get a list of previous customers from the potential contractors. And check out their employees, who may be working for you soon.

Methods of Contracting Services

If the facility manager decides to contract for services, there are multiple ways to do it. One is to contract for a specific project based on a given set of specifications. As an alternative, the contractor could be selected to provide a general service (electrical, for example) based on a listing of unit costs for those services. During contract execution, individual tasks are then approved for execution based on an expedited approval process. As an alternative, two to five contractors for each service can be prequalified for capability. For a specific task, the work can be assigned on a rotation basis or to the low bidder in an expedited bidding process.

My personal preference is to gather functions into broad groups like custodial services or building maintenance. These services are then bid on an hourly basis by skill. The contractor provides an on-site superintendent and all first-line supervision, but the facility management staff assumes responsibility for work assignments, quality control, and, therefore, cost control.

One note of caution for those who employ contractors. The Internal Revenue Service is increasingly investigating cases in which companies convert staff into contract positions or hire new staff as private contractors to avoid paying social security taxes. Be careful to observe the "duck rule": "If it looks like a duck and quacks like a duck, then it's probably a duck." Contract employees normally (1) work for a contractor's supervisor, and (2) are subject to be moved to other job sites. If the only reason to convert a staff position is to avoid taxation and the personnel continue to function like staff, the company could be liable.

It is worthwhile to discuss the need for the facility manager to define both his requirements and the quality of the contractor needed to meet those requirements. Often when there is unhappiness with the procurement process or with a contractor's performance, the root problem is in inadequate specification or selection criteria.

The evaluation criteria and their comparative weights must reflect what is truly important to the facility manager (references, bonding capability, financial stability, stability of the workforce, ability to perform a specialized task), particularly if prequalification is used. Then the facility manager must set the cutoff score low enough so he will retain competition high enough to eliminate those with whom he cannot live. This sensitive process, of which the facility manager is only one participant, explains why procurement is an art, not a science. Time spent on properly defining a requirement and on properly stating and weighting selection criteria will not only lead to a much smoother bidder evaluation process, but will probably secure a better contractor.

Some purchasing departments and facility managers burden themselves with one-year term service contracts. My experience is that a three-year term contract with two one-year options and pricing tied to a local pricing index is almost ideal because it provides continuity of service, yet ensures the continuation of competitive pricing.

Too many facility managers abrogate their responsibilities and rights in service contracting. Like all other functions, service contracting needs to be managed, and the facility manager must understand clearly and exercise his responsibilities.

Contractor and Consultant Evaluation

Service contractors and consultants should be competitively evaluated as part of the procurement process. When negotiation or directed procurement (sole sourcing) is not allowed, use a two-step procedure when the dollar cost of the procurement (say, $250,000) justifies it. The first step is an evaluation of technical ability, references, insurability, and financial capability. The second step is to evaluate four to six short-list contractors using the results of an interview, previously submitted material, and costing information.

How are these evaluations to be scored? Many public agencies unfortunately are tied to selecting the contractor or consultant submitting the lowest bid. Except for the most simple tasks, it is preferable to use the "most qualified" method and allocate 30 to 45 percent of the total score to price. In this way, the number of points allocated to the pricing of each contractor is calculated as follows:

Score of contractor (points)

$$= \text{Max score (points)} - \text{max score} \times \frac{(.5)(TS\text{-}LC)}{LC}$$

where:

TS = Price of contractor being evaluated
LC = Price of lowest contractor

Partnering

A facility manager who tries to manage a fully contracted department through a low-bid contract that emphasizes the adversarial relationship with the contractor is doomed to fail. I encourage facility managers in this situation to think of contract personnel, at least from an operational point of view, as being their employees. The facility manager works with the management of the contractor to provide customers seamless, customer-oriented service. Anything in the contract or his relationship with the contractor that gets in the way of serving customers has to be changed. Mutual focus on customers is the essence of partnering.

That philosophy deemphasizes the importance of the form of the contract and emphasizes results. Initially, this will be difficult. First, if the company has a centralized procurement function, the contact there may be reluctant to deviate from the exact wording of the contract. Second, no contract is perfect the first time. The facility manager needs to understand that and act accordingly, working with the contractor to create win-win situations. Regularly scheduled operational reviews with the contractor are very helpful in this regard. In some cases, the facility manager must be willing to give, expecting the contractor to do so in the future. If that doesn't occur, this may be the wrong contractor.

For every major contract I have, I specify that the contractor have a manager or senior supervisor on site (I pay). That individual must have the ability to speak for the contractor on all operational matters. After about six months, the contractor's front office becomes not much more than a pay and personnel office for my contract. I meet with the contractor's front office personnel only when we have a problem, or quarterly, to ensure they understand where we are going as a department and how it affects their contract.

The facility manager must be confident in his ability to administer contracts so that he can manage the fine line between cooperation with the contractor and keeping that contractor at arms length. When faced with a conflict (and they will come up), he can resolve it by determining what is best for his customers.

This concept works as well for supplies as it does for services. One very large facility management organization turned all of its supply activities over to a local supply house. After a few initial problems, they were amazed to find that they got their materials faster, with less paperwork, and at a cheaper price because of the contractor's muscle in the local marketplace and expertise.

Some organizations like to have formal partnering agreements with their contractors. Often these agreements address open and effective communications, how problems and disagreements will be resolved, use of the team approach, trust in both the experience and commitment of all team members, and the goal to which all are committed.

Successful partnering is dependent on a team approach to common goals, with both partners able to talk frankly and as equals. I have always been the most successful by motivating the contractor toward exceptional behavior and performance. To most contractors, the greatest incentive is a contract extension with a suitable price adjustment. For a contractor who is performing exceptionally, that is a slight cost to pay. Department stability is a major payoff.

On the other side of the ledger, not all contractors are capable of being good partners. In my experience, one very fine company had to be dropped because its president would not let go and let his on-site supervisor meet my customers' needs. There are as many challenges for the contractor as there are for the facility manager.

Outsourcing and partnering are inextricably tied to one another. The modern facility manager needs to be a contract manager extraordinaire; in all but the exceptional case, his success will depend on how well he orchestrates a primarily outsourced workforce to meet organizational goals. It is a different management model, but one that can work exceptionally well as long as the transition to it is slow, thoughtful, and uses facts, not opinion.

Benchmarking

Every facility manager should have a working knowledge of benchmarking as part of his managerial tool bag. Benchmarking has become a part of the language of our profession, if not the practice.

Key to good benchmarking is having accurate data, particularly cost data. Consistent programmatic budgeting makes that so much easier. Second, we need to know what the true costs of each service is, including overheads. Whether we benchmark externally or not, we need to know our *true cost of doing business.* Unfortunately, budget formats and accounting systems often are so convoluted that true costs are difficult to calculate without excessive manipulation. Producing accurate unit costs should be a priority of the financial management system.

Do not confine benchmarking to costs. For instance, it can be important to you as a manager that 96 percent of service orders in one geographic area are closed out within three days, while only 67 percent of them are closed in a similar facility in another area. That discrepancy should cause you to question why. Neither number is "right"; they are different. Operational improvements will be possible as we examine why they are different.

Beware of numbers that represent a broad universe when you are benchmarking. Experienced benchmarkers realize that there are so many reasons that the measurement of benchmarks is not consistent that you would like the two organizations or functions being benchmarked to be as similar as possible. For example, comparing my cost of carpet cleaning to a national average is of very limited value. However, there are several national companies that maintain large databases of facility management cost data. Some of the International Facility Management Association (IFMA) councils have active ongoing benchmarking groups for certain industry groups. Often, however, a facility manager can do benchmarking locally just by making some phone calls to similar other organizations.

Benchmarking partners may vary. I like to benchmark against an organization that is as close to my own business organization, even that of a competitor, as possible. Then I like to benchmark against a facility department that is as similar to mine as possible. Finally, I like to benchmark against the organization that is considered best in class in the function being benchmarked. For instance, if I was benchmarking the response time of my services reception desk, I might use the local electric or telephone company as my benchmarking partner.

Remember to get beyond the metrics in benchmarking. The reason there is a difference is the important factor. You might find out that the electric company gets 10 percent better response time than you do in services reception, but they have two additional staff in this area. You then have the information necessary to make a decision on staffing.

Benchmarking is a concept from total quality management (TQM). Applying good TQM principles, we measure (benchmark), then make necessary changes, implement, and measure again. This internal benchmarking is a valuable tool for plotting the success of management changes over time.

Evaluation of Routine Work

The first line of effective qualitative control in the FM realm is effective supervision. When dealing with contractors, for instance, effective supervision has two components: (1) by the contractor or consultant, and (2) by the owner or user. When hiring contractors or consultants, ask about their quality assurance policy and procedures, and emphasize the importance you place on quality work.

The facility manager has three responsibilities that help ensure quality control:

1. Setting the standards
2. Determining what testing is desired
3. Inspection! Inspection! Inspection!

For small organizations, effective supervision of ongoing work can be handled by the architect or design firm, or by companies that specialize in inspection and testing services. In larger organizations, in-house staff may perform some quality control functions, but outsiders are likely to be hired.

For preventive maintenance, service orders, small projects, and ongoing services like custodial, sample customers monthly, using questionnaires. The work reception center can send, receive, and analyze these questionnaires. (My experience is that to get a 10 percent sample returned, 30 percent of each service should be sampled, with questionnaires equally distributed for buildings and organizations.) For services like janitorial, concentrate questionnaires on one to two buildings each month but ensure that all facilities are surveyed twice annually.

Once the questionnaires are returned, the facility manager can evaluate small projects on a quarterly basis as to the following:

1. Number scheduled vs. number completed
2. Number completed within or over budget
3. Number completed on or over schedule

For preventive maintenance, analyze adherence to schedule and qualitative results of the questionnaires. For ongoing services such as custodial, look monthly for trends of satisfaction or dissatisfaction by building or by area, since that is how such services are normally delivered. Analyze service orders monthly, by trade, in the following ways:

1. Number outstanding
2. Cost per service order vs. historical average
3. Numbers completed within established time criteria
4. Satisfaction or dissatisfaction of customers with the service

Departmental Evaluations

The idea of evaluation often makes a facility manager nervous. The truth is that all organizations need to undergo self-examination from time to time to maintain their own health.[3] Unfortunately, evaluation is often linked to punishment. If that is the ultimate purpose of evaluation, subordinate managers will resist being evaluated, and the staff will sabotage the effort, making the validity of results doubtful.

Approximately every ten years, conduct a departmental evaluation. For unsophisticated facility departments, this may be no more than a hard look at functional responsibilities.

Most large organizations have internal organizational review methods. If not, you can either compare your department with others (i.e., benchmark), rate the department in its company context, or—most likely—use a combination of those two methods.

Comparators

One of the most frustrating situations for a facility manager is the almost inevitable desire by management to match certain facility costs and outputs against outside comparators. In fact, the Building Owners and Managers Association (BOMA) annually produces the *BOMA Experience Exchange Report*, an inch-thick document of facility costs for the United States and Canada, considering the following variables:

- Geographic location
- Size of facility
- Age of facility
- Type of occupancy
- Public or private sector
- Program costs (lease costs, operating costs)

These comparators are the best of their kind within the industry, but are inadequate for following reasons:

1. They are based predominantly on a property management rather than a facility management philosophy of management.
2. Though BOMA attempts to collect data in a uniform manner, it is extremely doubtful that reported operating costs, particularly unit costs, are calculated consistently by everyone who contributed to the database. Unfortunately it is impossible to capture costs in the BOMA format from many facility budgets.
3. Despite a heroic effort by BOMA, its excellent system to classify and measure space is not used by a high percentage of facility managers. This has a major effect on unit costs and lease costs calculated on a square-footage basis.
4. BOMA cannot account for the quality expectations of various organizations. What is an acceptable level of facility operations to Acme, Inc., would get the facility manager at the Gotrox Corp. relieved.

Other common comparators are those from similar organizations (bank vs. bank), sector (state government vs. state government), or facility type (laboratory vs. laboratory). However, it is extremely difficult for an individual organization to gather comparative data from other organizations, particularly if the organization is a competitor. And once comparator data are gathered, the same problems exist as with BOMA data.

If comparators are to be used to measure departmental efficiency and cost-

Exhibit 17-2. Annual facilities report.

I. Executive Summary ("bullet" style)

II. Introduction
   A. Environment
   B. Objectives
   C. Major challenges going into the year

III. Resources
   A. Financial display by program
   B. Human resources display by program

IV. Accomplishments
   A. Narrative by program
   B. Statistical data
      1. Energy consumption and savings
      2. Space trends
      3. Lease trends
      4. Projects
      5. Service orders
      6. Preventive maintenance

V. Problems and Recommended Solutions

effectiveness, the best comparison is against historical data within the organization. Then the facility manager can use other means (inspections, questionnaires) to evaluate the effectiveness and quality of the service.

If you insist on comparing yourself to others, then benchmarking is the choice. Benchmarking is at the heart of total quality programs.

Annual Facilities Report

It is my experience and observation that facility managers are not good at relations within the organization. There are several theories why, but it is undeniable that all of us could do better in this area. One of the routes to a better image is to tell your story, and one of the very best vehicles for this is the annual facilities (or state of the facilities) report.

There is no set format for such a report, but Exhibit 17-2 is an example. Another approach is to prepare a facilities annex to the company's annual report. Either way, the annual report can serve as both an evaluation tool and a public relations device.

Two excellent annual reports emphasizing how given resources were applied to accomplish the FM mission and support the corporation are those prepared by the facility managers at BellSouth and the World Bank.

The Facility Management Loops

There is always a tendency to present an instant solution—a panacea—to every management problem. Facility management does not lend itself to simplistic approaches or simple solutions. The function is highly integrative, and facility managers must have their fingers on the pulse of each subfunction, while also tending to the external relations of the department.

One model that I have found successful to ensure integrated problem solving pays particular attention to groupings of related activities that feed one another in loops. While it would be simplistic to say that managing these loops will solve all problems, I do believe that every facility manager should understand completely these work processes and ensure that they are managed well. If this is done, many of the integration problems that plague so many facility managers will be eliminated.

Planning, Programming, Budgeting, Execution, Evaluation

Particularly in large organizations, the staff inevitably gets divided between those who are planners, programmers, and budgeters, and those who are operators and responsible for execution. This separation can lead to damaging discontinuities and major misalignments between available resources and operational requirements.

In a format that is organized by a facility program, the long-range plan should feed the midterm plan. The annual work plan then flows from the midterm plan. Once approved, that annual work plan is bumped against reality and is presented as a budget for execution.

Evaluation, however, is often the missing link. The execution of the budget must be evaluated for quality and quantity, effectiveness, and efficiency. This evaluation will uncover shortfalls that must be fed back into the system as work plan corrections. Budgetary weaknesses and factors requiring adjustments in both the current midrange and long-range plans will appear during execution of the annual work plan. The plans should be adjusted accordingly, at least annually. This process, though it is described here as consecutive, is actually both concurrent and ongoing. It constantly carries today's success and the corrective actions of yesterday's failures into the future and determines the ability of the facility department to:

1. Learn from its mistakes.
2. Capitalize on its successes.
3. Change with the changing environment of its company.
4. Survive.

The competent facility manager must control the planning, budgeting, execution, and evaluation loop for each program.

Budgeting, Accounting, Work Planning, Management Information Systems

Rather than a loop, these functions are a series of tasks that, despite having a high degree of overlap, are too often treated separately within facility management departments. The successful facility manager recognizes the commonality in these functions, particularly as they are being automated, and can reduce automating costs greatly while increasing the department's reporting accuracy.

At the core of these processes is a definition of facility programs—those building blocks of facility management. If a facility manager is on the right track, he will plan by program, budget by program, account by program, and report by program. Programs are the crosswalk from what he does to what he pays for.

All too frequently, the budgeting and accounting are automated under a set of accounts established outside the facility department. The work of the department typically is tracked by a work management system, which is heavily weighted toward project management. The management information system (MIS) typically is administratively oriented or can utilize the accounting system only to the extent that interfaces can be designed or material extracted by hand and fed into the MIS. This duplication of data tracking causes significant problems of cost accounting and inconsistent reporting.

The major problem with such a mode of operation is that any typical question (for example: "How much facility support have we given to the marketing department at 625 High Street, floors 4 and 5, this fiscal year?") is likely to have three answers rather than one. That ensures organizational bickering and chaos. The facility manager's contribution in these areas should be to force programmatic planning, budgeting, and reporting.

The facility manager should be able to track a request for supplies or services from inception to delivery. He should know what part purchasing, receiving, accounts payable, and the cashier play in this process, how transactions flow through these staff elements, as well as understanding what type of procurement document (purchase order, blanket purchase order, or contract) the department has with each vendor. Having this knowledge not only makes the facility manager less vulnerable to bureaucratic excuses for why something does not get done, why the order hasn't arrived, or why the vendor hasn't been paid, but also makes him more sensitive to the complexities of ordering and receiving goods and services—one of the keys to his success.

The facility manager who properly manages budgeting, accounting, work planning, and reporting not only minimizes the effort expended on these functions, but will find the management information available will be more correct and more consistent.

Capital and Annual Budgeting

Too few facility managers examine and act on the relationship between the capital and annual budgets. There appear to be several reasons for this:

1. The organization's unwillingness to provide adequate capital funding to design maintainability, life-cycle savings, energy management, and value engineering into major projects
2. The facility department's inability to analyze and quantify life-cycle costs
3. The lack of understanding of new facility technologies that truly can reduce operating and maintenance costs

If your organization is actively engaged in a capital improvement program, this relationship should be examined carefully. Start by examining the new materials, service delivery systems, and technologies that offer a possibility of personnel, operational, or maintenance savings. In general, the facility manager probably needs the assistance of vendors and consultants to do this. I prefer not to do it under the pressure of a specific project, but sometimes that is the best time to get the necessary focus. A five-year horizon for technology improvements is probably appropriate.

There are several areas that might be questioned at this point in history—for example:

- Should fiberoptics be pulled to individual workstations?
- Should large manual mailrooms be installed in organizations even while fax and e-mail become more widespread?
- What new cleaning technologies should we install in buildings?
- Should we sponsor cogeneration? Should we install thermal storage?

Capital expenditures now, in some of these areas, could substantially reduce operating costs in the future.

Once the facility manager has decided what technological features are affordable in new capital improvements, the entire design should be scrubbed for maintenance and operational savings that can be realized. This process can be started by ensuring that the architect assigns personnel who understand operational efficiency and maintainability, but it is best ensured by having operators and maintainers review the design at concept, at 30 percent, and at 80 percent completion.

All of this will be for naught if company management views these capital improvements to achieve technological, operational, and maintenance reductions in life-cycle costs as either goldplating or other suspect requirements. The facility manager must be capable of computing the life-cycle cost reductions from these measures and defending them through project reviews.

The capital costs of a new building are small compared to the life-cycle costs. Well-spent capital funds and a good understanding and management of the interdependence between the capital and annual budget can aid significantly in good facility management.

Condition Assessment, Maintenance, and Annual Level of Funding for Maintenance and Repair

Properly maintained facilities normally are well-documented facilities. Too often the facilities inventory has been inadequately maintained for so long that no one in the department knows the exact state of the facilities or the cost to bring those facilities to the desired state of repair. At this juncture, it is often necessary to conduct a condition assessment. Another scenario for a condition assessment (particularly by outside experts) is when the board of directors or legislative body has indicated that the facility department's estimate of the maintenance backlog is not credible. This seems to happen frequently in public-sector situations.

Condition assessments can be bought into many levels. At any level, however, they are costly.[4] Also, money spent on assessing the facilities, though necessary, normally is money diverted from maintaining facilities. If 2 to 4 percent of the replacement value of facilities is invested annually in normal maintenance and repair (not backlog reduction), condition assessment should be required infrequently and only for highly specialized needs.[5]

The interrelationship of documentation, adequate resources for maintenance and repair, and a properly managed maintenance program cannot be overemphasized. Good maintenance and repair need to be managed just as competently as any capital project. Whenever one of those factors is absent, the program will be suboptimal, and eventually a condition assessment will be required to fill the void. If that occurs, the information in the condition assessment should be acted on and the facilities returned to their normal state of repair as soon as possible.

Work Management

Another important loop is work management: work standards, staffing, work reporting, and outputs. It is a loop that has been emphasized too much. Too often the approach to improving efficiency in the facility department has been to increase the work standards or to reduce the staffing. Both of those measures may be laudatory and necessary, but they often result in reduced quality of work or cheating in time reporting.

Personally I am not committed to work standards because they are too easily corrupted. (The ultimate example is paying for standard tasks in auto repair facilities, none of which requires the effort for which the customer pays. Both the dealer and the customer know that, yet the charade continues.) Work standards complicate union relations. Unions and management can cast positions etched in stone based on work standards, even if they are outmoded, based on old technology, or incorrectly measured. However, in certain situations the facility manager is forced to use work standards.

If used, work standards should be simple, clearly stated, and agreed to by both management and the applicable trades. The standard should be in enough detail so that if technology later changes (switching from incandescent bulbs to fluorescent tubes, for instance), it is evident that the standard should be adjusted.

Time accounting becomes a critical component of this loop. Is each employee required to account for eight hours each shift? If so, to which job is travel time charged? Is it realistic to require all technicians to account for 100 percent of their hours on the job? What are the rules for allocating overhead hours? Unless the facility manager carefully manages the time accounting system, he will find these rules driving operations. Time allocation rules, like work standards, can become locked in concrete despite the fact that conditions and technology have changed. In fact, time accounting rules established merely for administrative convenience can become work standards if not used carefully.

The facility manager who wants to manage the work output of the department needs to put particular emphasis on work management. Too often a push for new levels of productivity falls solely upon the workforce. The facility manager must avoid that situation because it invariably leads solely to confrontation, and improvement is seldom primarily within the power of the workforce. Both work standards and time allocation rules must be necessary, but they should be managed well and capable of being changed.

Notes

1. "Major Industry Players Convene at First World Summit," *Outsource Report* (April 1998): 3.

2. Paul Tarricone, "Outsourcing Turns to Smart Sourcing," *Facilities Design and Management* (February 1997): 42.

3. L. Terry Suber, "Evaluating Plant Management," in *Facilities Management* (Washington, DC: APPA, 1984), pp. vi–5.

4. Building Research Board, *Committing to the Cost of Ownership* (Washington, D.C.: National Academy Press, 1990), p. 21.

5. Ibid., pp. 18–19.

18

Managing Quality Facilities

Pulse Points

- *The customer, and the customer alone, defines the quality of the product or service provided.*
- *The facility manager must use every means available to measure his customers' perception of services.*
- *Do it right the first time!*
- *The facility manager must set quality goals and track them over time.*
- *Measure efficiency, effectiveness, and response.*
- *Empower employees, but empowerment without training is chaos. Make everyone in the department feel responsible for the total facilities mission.*
- *Use every means available to publicize services and successes. The facility manager needs to be the chief publicist for the department.*
- *Develop a profile on each customer.*

One of the oft-repeated complaints of facility managers is that they are the victims of the management "flavor of the month." Total quality management (TQM) has been mentioned as one of those management themes whose time has come—and passed. I recently asked a group of international facility managers how relevant they felt TQM was to their practice of facility management. Not surprisingly, most agreed that in its totality, TQM is passé. However, when I started to quiz them on details, even they were surprised at the extent to which they (and, most important, their customers) had adopted the elements of TQM into their business lives.

TQM made an irrevocable imprint on businesses in the early 1990s. While they may no longer call it TQM, facility managers now manage in ways that are a result of the emphasis on quality. This chapter is organized around the characteristics of TQM that a successful facility manager must understand and incorporate into his business practices.

Some facility managers both recognize TQM and integrate it into their practice. In *Quality Facility Management*, Stormy Friday and I address in detail very practical examples of integrating facility and quality management for the betterment of both the facility department and the supported business. Essential to that process are what we call the Five Pillars of Quality.[1]

The Five Pillars of Quality

1. Quality services start with customer service. Only the customer will define whether you are performing the right service and how well you are doing it.
2. You must be committed to continuous improvement.
3. You must be willing and able to measure and be measured.
4. Employees must be empowered, must be held responsible, and must view themselves and their jobs within the broader context.
5. Quality service should be both recognized and marketed inside and outside the company.

In addition, Stormy and I observed three conditions within outstanding service organizations. My experiences since then have reinforced that observation. First, employees in quality service organizations view themselves as totally responsible for the entire facility and feel that "it's *my* job!" Second, in great organizations, employees do things right the first time. Finally, outstanding organizations are totally focused on meeting the service needs of their customers.[2]

Customer Service

Basic to the practice of TQM is customer service, and the bedrock of customer service is the fact that the customer, and the customer alone, defines the quality of the service or product provided. As APPA's former executive director Wayne LeRoy has put it so well, we must respect *customer sovereignty*, we must provide *customer service*, and we must ensure *customer satisfaction*. Many facility managers have difficulty understanding this customer-centered principle. Even more refuse to let it guide their practice. At its most basic level, this principle holds that it really does not matter what our education or experience tells us; we have to do what the customer says. That is difficult for a facility manager, particularly a strong and experienced one. Facility managers tend to feel that as facilities experts, they know what is best for facilities—and that normally is true. What they sometimes fail to understand is what is best for the business (as expressed by their customer, the business unit).

One of the easiest ways to understand this concept is when a full, well-administered chargeback system is in place. The business manager is going to insist on preeminence even in facility decisions as long as he is paying for them. As long as what he desires is not illegal, unsafe, insecure, or harmful, the facility manager's job is to use his facility expertise to help that business manager carry out the facilities aspects of his business decisions as efficiently and effectively as possible.

For this reason, managing customer service is really managing expectations. In order to do that, facility managers need to measure those expectations in a uniform and impartial way. In this regard, they and their employees must be willing to be measured. If that concept is not understood and supported by employees—down to the last tradesman—they will sabotage the system. The facility

Customer Service Truths

1. Poor service is the number-one reason companies lose business. A full 68 percent of customers stop doing business with a company because of poor service.
2. Ninety percent of the customers that stopped doing business with a company made no attempt to tell the firm why.
3. Seventy percent of dissatisfied customers never complain because it is not worth their time; they think company personnel won't listen if the customer does complain, or they think the customer won't do anything about their complaint.
4. The average dissatisfied customer tells nine or ten others of their dissatisfaction.
5. Conversely, the average satisfied customer tells only five people.
6. It takes ten dollars in new business to replace one dollar of lost business.
7. It costs between five and ten times as much to attract a new customer as it does to keep an old one.
8. Quality service is the main thing that differentiates one business from another.
9. The first sixty seconds establishes the tone and first impression of a meeting.
10. Each time a customer comes in contact with a company employee for the first time, it is a new first impression.
11. The same attitudes that lead to increased customer satisfaction can lead to increased employee performance.
12. Customers pay more for better service.
13. Ninety-five percent of dissatisfied customers would do business again with that same company if their problem were solved quickly and satisfactorily.
14. The company person, no matter what rung on the ladder, should always ask himself or herself, "What can I do to satisfy the customer?"
15. Every company employee is involved in sales.
16. Excellent service leads to increased sales.
17. Companies should pay attention to how they spend money. It's unwise to overspend in some areas and underspend in others.
18. Customers will tell a company where it needs improvement. We need to ask customers how we can make our business more pleasurable, convenient, and suitable for them.

Source: Richard Tyler of Richard Tyler International, as quoted in *Modern Office Technology*, February 1993.

manager needs to do the internal sales job to convince employees that the long-term success of the organization depends on having accurate customer service data. But he must avoid telling them that their performance will not be tied to their ability to serve customers properly. Exactly what he is trying to do is constantly improve the organization through goal setting, measurement, and adjustments. Ultimately, he may even tie compensation, at least in part, to employees' ability to meet customer needs and to work as members of participatory teams.[3]

Two of the first questions to ask in customer sampling are, "How often am I going to sample?" and "What do we measure?" Appropriate statistical sampling is the topic of entire books. Let me give some basic guidelines. Sample customer opinion of every major event, such as the relocation of a department or the construction of a new facility. For normal work orders, I prefer to sample every one for a set period—say, one month each quarter—rather than a percentage throughout the entire year. There are advantages and disadvantages to that approach, but when sampling customer response to every single service order during a fixed time period, I pay particular attention to the geographic distribution (building/location) and organizational distribution of my sample.

Surveying in depth is increasingly difficult to do. Fifteen years ago, I used an extensive mail customer survey, which provided me a great deal of information about my customers' perceptions of our services. I was among the first to sample customer opinion within my organization. As more and more service providers in our organization turned to surveying for customer service, customers got "surveyed out," and my response rate fell to almost to zero. While maintaining the survey format for major projects, we switched to a response card for service orders. The response card asked the customer to rate only five things:

1. Did we do what you wanted us to do?
2. Did we do it well?
3. Did we do it in a timely manner that was acceptable to you?
4. Did we look good and clean up after ourselves?
5. Did we check with you to ensure that you were happy?

Each question had a place for comment, and there were three lines at the bottom for general comments.

Many companies are using their intranets to automate customer service sampling. All of the techniques that I already noted can be fed over the company network to the appropriate customer, who, with a few keystrokes and an emphatic touch of the Enter key, can send a service response reply to the facility manager's database, to be screened and compiled for statistical analysis. One enterprising facility manager conducts a random drawing for prizes such as a bottle of good wine or a floral bouquet to encourage customers to respond to service inquiries.[4]

Eventually, though, the customers rebelled against *any* written surveys, so we turned to running focus groups of a diverse profile of customers on each of our services. Initially we had service providers in each focus group. That was a mistake because they immediately became defensive, and that attitude stifled our

Assessing Customer Expectations of Service Quality

1. Excellent facility departments will have modern-looking equipment.
2. The physical facilities of excellent facility departments will be visually appealing.
3. Employees at excellent facility departments will be neat.
4. Materials issued such as pamphlets or statement will be visually appealing in an excellent facility department.
5. When excellent facility departments promise to do something by a certain time, they do it.
6. When a customer has a problem, excellent facility departments will show a sincere interest in solving it.
7. Excellent facility departments will perform their service right the first time.
8. Excellent facility departments will provide their services at the time they promise to do so.
9. Excellent facility departments will insist on error-free records.
10. Employees in excellent facility departments will tell customers exactly when services will be performed.
11. Employees in excellent facility departments will give prompt service to customers.
12. Employees in excellent facility departments will always be willing to help customers.
13. Employees in excellent facility departments will never be too busy to respond to customers' requests.
14. The behavior of employees in excellent facility departments will instill confidence in customers.
15. Customers of excellent facility departments will feel safe in their transactions.
16. Employees in excellent facility departments will be consistently courteous to customers.
17. Employees in excellent facility departments will have the knowledge to answer customer questions.
18. Excellent facility departments will give customers individual attention.
19. Excellent facility departments will have operating hours that are convenient to their customers.
20. Excellent facility departments will have employees who give customers personal attention.
21. Excellent facility departments will have the customers' best interests at heart.
22. The employees of excellent facility departments will understand the specific needs of their customers.

Source: Adapted by *Facilities Manager* from Zeithaml, Parasuraman and Berry, *Delivering Quality Service* (The Free Press, 1990).

customers' saying what they really thought. After that, our focus groups were customers only. If you have never done this, I suggest that you do so as a best practice. Repeat using focus groups about every three years or examine one-third of your services every year.

Despite the difficulties, it is important to track customer response over time. For an item that needs improvement—timeliness for instance—the facility manager must set goals, improve staffing or procedures, and then measure again. He will not always succeed, but often the analyses with employees will (1) uncover problems that he did not even know existed, (2) give employees buy-in to the process, and (3) confirm to all the seriousness with which he treats customer service.

Let me make one last point on sampling customer service: Facility managers must make every effort, by every means, to talk to customers and obtain their ratings in a meaningful way. The greatest problem is to keep the medium fresh and to gather data consistently over time so that meaningful analysis is possible.

Closely aligned with talking to customers is the need to ensure that services are readily accessible to customers. I am amazed by the bureaucracy that still exists, particularly in government, to request services ("Submit Form 211-7-8 in four copies"). Modern facility departments are geared to accept customer requests by multiple modes and, through the use of automated forms or checklists, format the needed information in a way that is usable. One university is considering using the World Wide Web as the medium for its facility work requests. Assisting customers to request facility services easily is one of the roles of the work reception center (WRC), discussed in Chapter 13, which should be not only the control point for work reception and coordinating but also the point for management of customer service sampling and statistical compilation. The WRC is ideally situated for this function.

Finally, to satisfy customers, the facility department must produce. Services need to be delivered within an acceptable time (agreed to with the customer) by service providers who are neat, clean, well uniformed, and technically competent. They should be able to verify the customers' needs, get the work done, and ensure customer satisfaction before leaving the site. That takes intensive customer service training of all workers, even contractors, an area that most facility managers neglect.

Continuous Improvement

At the heart of quality facility management is the concept of continuous improvement. Unfortunately, in practice, continuous improvement is the antithesis of the way many of us manage. By our nature and training, I find that we are interested in creating the big, perfect organizational machine and then stepping back and watching it run. Unfortunately, in the changing governmental and business climates in which we manage, the external environment is changing rapidly. Similarly, both our use of and response to technology demands change. In that type of environment, if we aren't continuously improving, we are going backward.

That is why continuous improvement is so important. In fact, it must be a major business objective of every facility department: Goals need to be set, results measured (see Measure! Measure! Measure! below), improvements assimilated into the service delivery system, and incentives and disincentives tied to constant improvement right to the worker/technician level.

Perhaps the easiest way to understand constant improvement is to discuss the Shewhart cycle: Plan, do, check, act, try again with new information, and then repeat the process. One way to look at this is as shown in Exhibit 18-1. This process is simple to draw and comprehend but difficult to implement over a long period of time. Two human reactions enter the equation. First, people get bored, and instead of seeking meaningful improvement, they bureaucratize the process. Also, unless service workers and supervisors have truly bought in to continuous improvement, they will manipulate the system and the data so that improvement appears to be happening but really isn't. Those kinds of attitudes and actions will disappear only if there are total buy-in throughout the workforce, in-depth quality service training, and adequate incentives and disincentives tied to superior quality management. The challenge is to keep the process fresh after the first year.

The WRC should be the center of sampling and collecting data regarding continuous improvement. Because it receives, tasks, coordinates, and accounts for work already, it is the ideal vehicle to manage continuous improvement for the facility manager. He should use this vehicle to provide the metrics on quality management for the facility management information system.

Measure! Measure! Measure!

No one aspect of TQM can be separated from the others. I always am concerned whenever, for some reason, we break quality management into its components. For instance, constant improvement requires that we measure ourselves consistently and constantly and set goals that we try to achieve and against which we are measured.

The measurement aspect of quality management is the toughest part for which to get buy-in at all levels. We intellectualize the need for measurement, but none of us likes to be measured, because our experience shows that there is always some sort of punishment for failing to measure up. But how will we ever know if we are meeting objectives and customers' expectations unless there is a dispassionate, consistent way to measure progress—or failure? How do we know that we are achieving constant improvement if we are not measuring against some

Exhibit 18-1. Shewhart cycle.

Plan	Plan
Do	Do
Check	Check
Act	Act
Repeat with new information	Repeat with new information

baseline? How do we know after the Plan and Do phases of the Shewhart cycle that we are proceeding in a way that justifies the resources committed to improving a process? Measurement—consistent measurement over time—is fundamental to good-quality facility management.

As a practitioner and as I observe others, it is apparent to me that we have part of the measurement equation well in hand: efficiency. Due, perhaps to the emphasis on benchmarking, more and more departments have developed metrics to measure their costs (e.g., total facility costs per square foot, utility costs per square foot, total costs per occupant). (I remain highly critical of the quality of the data used; however, that is the subject of another book.) Overall, facility managers are moving rapidly to measure how efficiently they manage.

Some facility managers are doing a good job of measuring response. How long does it take the WRC to answer trouble calls? How long does it take the engineering force to answer a hot-cold call once tasked? By category of project, what is the cycle time? Response is a major factor in customer service and quality management (one of the factors where customers are most dissatisfied with their facility department). The facility manager should install systems and procedures to monitor response by type of work and track it over time.

Measuring effectiveness seems to be the Achilles' heel of most facility quality management efforts. It is ironic because it does not matter how efficient or responsive the facility department thinks it is. Effectiveness is solely determined by customers, and the biggest challenge is to figure out how to measure their opinions. No one way will work. In fact, every vehicle for measuring customer perception of facility department effectiveness seems to have a declining life, which makes it very difficult to compare results over time. That is one of the biggest challenges of managing quality facilities. I know of no perfect solution, but the facility manager must use every avenue available—written, electronic, focus groups, and others—to stay in touch with the perceptions of customers.

Finally, facility managers need to become familiar with the techniques of sampling and the practical applications of statistics. Terms such as *median, mean, standard deviation,* and *normal distribution* should be as familiar as *HVAC, leasing,* and *churn rate.* Once statistics are gathered, facility managers should be able to display and analyze data using such methods as histograms, scatter diagrams, Pareto charts, and trend charts. I suggest a basic college statistics course to any facility manager who has not had one.

Reengineering

Often I see facility managers tinkering with their organizations, policies, and procedures to try to achieve major improvements. In fact, what is actually needed is an entirely new approach. I once worked with an organization that was committed to major improvement through a well-led participatory management process, an excellent reengineering initiative. As I observed the process and results, it was evident to me that results of the organizational shakedown were basically "rearranging the deck chairs on the *Titanic.*" The organization suffered mostly from

outdated skills, unusually restrictive union conditions, and a less than fully productive work environment. Managers were spending an inordinate amount of
their time solving human resources problems. The situation was a prime example
of one where outsourcing would help, yet the manager bristled when I suggested
it because his management had arbitrarily said that no outsourcing would be
considered. My point is that for true improvement, management needs to remove
preconditions and let facility managers be limited only by the resources available
and their imaginations.

For a formalized approach to reengineering, read Champy and Hammer's
Reengineering the Corporation. Innovation in processes (reengineering) is as applicable to the public sector as to the private, though sometimes more difficult to
implement. *Banishing Bureaucracy* by David Osborne and Peter Plastrik specifically addresses reengineering the public sector.

The top four reasons that reengineering efforts fail are as follows:

1. Resistance to change (60 percent)
2. Limitations of the existing systems (40 percent)
3. Lack of executive consensus (40 percent)
4. Lack of a senior executive champion (40 percent)

Three of them reflect on management.[5] Don't enter into a reengineering effort just
because it is the "flavor of the day." It is hard, foot-slogging work, and requires
high energy and great tenacity. Implementation of reengineering is fully as important as design. The most common errors that contribute to the failure of reengineering are trying to fix a process instead of changing it, not focusing on the
business process, ignoring everything except the process design, neglecting people's values and beliefs, being willing to settle for minor results, and quitting too
early.[6]

The facility manager's attitude is critical. He must indicate full support for
reengineering (even if some of his pet oxen get gored), see that needed training
is provided to all who need it, and be unmerciful in ensuring that things like
compensation are tied to full implementation of reengineering.

Empowerment

Frontline workers need to have the flexibility to handle almost any situation they
are sent to correct. Anyone who does not believe that as a management philosophy should conduct a detailed analysis of callbacks for one month and find out
the reason why workers had to return to correct a situation that they had previously been sent to solve. In an informal survey that I have conducted over the
years, and in my own practice, callback ranged from 10 to 30 percent of total
service calls—a terrible waste of human resources, particularly considering the
attendant travel time and customer dissatisfaction. Fully half of all callbacks could
have been solved during the initial visit had workers been trained and permitted

to do multitrade work or had they been allowed to task the correct colleague in the organization to perform the work. I decided that my workers acted like automatons ("I'm sorry, ma'am, but I can't do this job because it is not part of my job, but someone will be here to fix it sometime") because we managers had not given them the authority to solve problems ("Ma'am, this problem is beyond my ability, but I have called the master electrician, and she will be here at 2:00 this afternoon to fix this problem for you. If she does not show up by 2:15, please call me at this beeper number."). If everyone tries to do the right thing the first time and all technicians view themselves as customer problem solvers, efficiency and effectiveness will rise substantially. Here are three rules in this area:

1. If a worker can fix something, he should do it right the first time.
2. If health, safety, or operations is involved, make sure that the worker is empowered to take responsibility for seeing that it is reported immediately to the right person and that he follows up until the problem is solved.
3. A worker should fix anything that he can. If he can't fix it, he should take responsibility for reporting it properly and by following up to see that it does get fixed.[7]

Nothing facilitates empowerment in an organization as much as staff reductions. Most facility departments cannot afford to have checkers checking checkers and the organizational sclerosis that vertical decision making causes. Everyone needs to share in decision making and accountability to a greater extent than ever before—daunting to some and even job threatening to others. It is my experience, for example, that some of the very best supervisors have the biggest problem with the concept of empowered teams.

One quick word about empowered teams: I strongly believe in them to solve individual problems and for a limited duration. It makes good sense that those closest to the problem probably have the best solutions to it. Choose leaders carefully; my personal bias is to appoint the leader rather than to have him elected. Ensure that there is representation on the team from all interested and affected parties. Then once the team arrives at a solution and the facility manager blesses it and provides the resources, there is more likely to be complete acceptance.

Empowerment without training is chaos. Front-line mechanics and workers must not only be multiskilled, but also must be able to talk to customers. They must be customer oriented, and they must understand how the entire department works so that they can tap the right resource if the problem is beyond their ability to solve. That approach is very different from the way craftspeople have traditionally been taught to act and react. The facility manager will obtain excellent results only after solid commitment to empowerment and reasonably intensive training. If both are not present, forget empowering teams. Empowerment without training will only complicate the problems.

Public Relations

My generation of facility managers tends to view our mission as creating a big, efficient, service-providing machine that we want to turn on and watch hum. We don't really want to deal with customers (they always complain or want something that we can't give them) because *we* know what is better for them and for the facilities. Because we hold these attitudes, one of our greatest failings is that we do not sell our departments and services well. Often we don't market our services and department because we think that it is self-evident that everyone appreciates the wonderful services that we provide. Unfortunately, quite the opposite is true. Facility managers are almost universally viewed as naysayers, non-team players, and noncontributors to overall corporate goals.

For all of those reasons, facility managers need to be much more conscious of public relations in general and marketing their services and department in particular. I feel so strongly about this that I teamed with Stormy Friday, whom I consider the foremost expert on marketing facility management services, to write a book on the topic. (The remainder of this section is heavily influenced by Stormy's ideas, which frankly have become so intertwined with my own that I no longer can separate them.)

Particularly in this era of downsizing, there will not be a position on an FM organization chart marked "Public Relations." In fact, the main public relations person for the facility manager needs to be the facility manager himself. Much of the public relations and marketing work is external to the department. Only the facility manager has the prestige and the access to the target groups who need to be reached.

If there is still doubt that marketing and public relations is needed, perform the Three 5's Test in Exhibit 18-2. From my considerable experience, I believe that most facility managers will fail the Three 5's Test, and that underscores the need for better marketing of facility departments and services. The key to marketing is setting realistic objectives:

1. Increase the awareness of facility services.
2. Decrease the resistance to a particular service or set of policies and procedures.
3. Improve the image of the facility organization as a service provider.
4. Enhance customers' knowledge about facility services.
5. Disclose specific qualifications about facility services.

The purpose of marketing is to increase service awareness, knowledge, and qualifications while decreasing resistance to the facility department's policies and procedures.[8]

The development of a marketing strategy is an excellent area for participative management. Use the five objectives as a format to elicit suggestions for specific strategies to implement each.

Some tools can make public relations and marketing efforts more effective. I strongly suggest that facility managers develop an annual public relations plan. Keep it simple. Initially, it should define the target groups to reach in priority order (top management, visitors, specific employee departments—whatever fits the company) and then design one or two simple actions to be implemented to achieve the marketing objectives. For instance, there might be a major effort to

Exhibit 18-2. Three 5's Test.

1. Select five individuals at random while walking through the facility, and ask them the following questions:
   - Do you know who I am?
   - Describe five services provided by the facility department.
   - Describe the last five services provided to your department by the facility department.

This can be humbling. If four out of five individuals don't know you or the services you provide, you need to be concerned about how your value to the company is perceived.

2. Maintain a log of phone calls over a five-week period that you personally answer. Track the following:
   - Who the calls come from
   - The nature of the call

If more than half of the calls are not from senior managers or if more than half are complaints, you are in trouble because you have failed to gauge properly your customers' perceptions of your services and do not have sufficient visibility with top management.

3. Review the agendas for executive staff meetings that you have attended over a five-month period. If you have not made a major presentation or contribution in 80 percent of the meetings, you have failed to project the value-added worth of your department and are not being heard adequately by top management.

Source: Stormy Friday and David G. Cotts, *Quality Facility Management* (New York: Wiley, 1995), p. 135.

improve the department's image with visitors through better custodial maintenance of lobbies and better visitor reception training for the security staff.

Second, develop a customer profile for each of the department's client groups and its leader. Again, this is information that should be gathered over a period of time (and it will change). The WRC can be particularly helpful in providing information regarding problem areas in departments and buildings. A suggested format for a customer profile is contained in Friday and Cotts, *Quality Facility Management*, but the format is really not important. The facility manager should review the pertinent customer profile before every meeting with a department head or upper management. The review might also indicate a need to provide service of a different quality or response time to individual customers.

Finally, determine the actual costs of doing business and whether the department is cost competitive in the market. One of my clients was openly challenged by customers who said that FM services could be obtained outside the organization at a cost savings and more responsively. Eventually all facility managers will face that same challenge. Ordinarily there is a bias toward using in-house services, but that bias disappears when the cost is more than 10 to 15 percent over market or when the service cannot be obtained responsively.

Facility managers who cannot speak and write well do their department a great disservice. Most of our education and training has not stressed effective communication, the downfall of many technically competent facility managers. I keep a dictionary, a college-style manual, and a freshman English book near my desk at all times. For those who do not speak well publicly, I strongly urge joining a local Toastmasters group or taking an individualized course in business communications (which encompasses the way that participants look, act and speak). In addition, many facility managers would benefit by enrolling in a course on expository writing at a local college or taking a business writing program. A facility manager who does not write and speak well will not have the confidence to be the type of leader that the department deserves.

Notes

1. Stormy Friday and David G. Cotts, *Quality Facility Management* (New York: Wiley, 1994), pp. 3–4. Copyright 1994 John Wiley & Sons, Inc. Reprinted by permission of John Wiley & Sons, Inc.

2. Ibid., p. 3.

3. For an excellent discussion of tying compensation to quality service, read Laura J. Davis and Michael L. Hagler, "Quality Service Through Employee-Defined Performance Management," *Facilities Manager* (Summer 1994): 48–59.

4. For an excellent discussion of what can be done with e-mail, see Donna Schliewe, "The Role of Electronic Mail in Customer Communication," *Facilities Manager* (Summer 1994): 44–47.

5. Compiled by Organizational Universe Systems, P.O. Box 38, Valley Center, Calif. 92082, http://www.improve.org/reengfl.html.

6. Ibid.

7. Friday and Cotts, *Quality Facility Management*, pp. 92–94.

8. Ibid., pp. 96–98.

19

Managing the Budget

Pulse Points

- *Facility managers should view themselves as businesspeople.*
- *The facility manager should structure the budget to be his principal management information system tool.*
- *Capital projects have annual cost implications (depreciation and operational costs).*
- *The facility manager should plan for 5 to 15 percent more discretionary work than budgeted.*
- *The facility manager should understand and manage his annual expenditure profile.*
- *If chargebacks are used, expend the effort to make them meaningful. The concept of a fixed package of services for a realistic internal rent (with services outside the package provided on a fee-for-service basis) is a best practice.*
- *Programmatic budgeting is a best practice.*
- *For a major project, the facility manager should invest early in a good project accounting system and accountant.*
- *The facility manager should know the true cost of providing major services and should benchmark those cost metrics with competitors, similar organizations, and best in class.*
- *Better facility business planning and the reduction in churn offer the two best opportunities for facility cost reduction.*

Financial management remains one of the weak links of facility management. Since facilities are second only to human resources among corporate expenditures, financial management is an area with great potential for improvement. Facility managers, viewing themselves as businesspeople, are key to this improvement.

When I ask facility managers to think of themselves as businesspeople, I mean six things.

Business Issues for Facility Managers

1. Know your business.
2. Know the language of business.
3. Understand, in detail, how you affect your company's business.
4. Be able to use capital budget evaluation tools.
5. Institute good financial controls.
6. Implement cost reduction and containment.

Most facility managers are knowledgeable about the technical aspects of their business but less skilled in understanding how they affect their company's bottom line. For instance, a facility manager must understand that, as a major cost center, the facility department will be constantly scrutinized. Also, facility managers tend to talk to upper management and business colleagues in "FMspeak" rather than in the language of business. (Chapter 5 gives some of the tools to do this.) They need to understand concepts like the net present value of money, life-cycle costing, and the cost of capital and then make their business arguments in those terms. Similarly, they need to build partnerships within the company based on their ability to help colleagues achieve their business goals (which are often defined as a financial ratio, the numerator or denominator of which they influence).

But although they need to think and speak like businesspeople, only in the rarest of cases should they advertise themselves as a profit center. Several facility managers have spun off the in-house department in their companies as an FM service firm serving other companies as well, but that is the exceptional case. In general, facility management is, and is viewed as, a cost center. Nevertheless, the successful facility manager will be as good a businessperson as the owner of a private FM service company because, in the current environment, the in-house department will have to be cost competitive or it will be outsourced.

Good financial management is based on good facility business planning, a subject covered in Chapter 4. The best practice here is programmatic planning and budgeting, which allows tracking the operations and maintenance (O&M) program, for example, from the long-range plan, through the annual work plan, and into the current annual budget. Unless the facility manager is a player in company business planning, he will always be short of resources and at a distinct disadvantage in financial management.

Key to good management is knowing the actual costs of doing business, yet too few facility managers have ever calculated the costs of each of their services. It is not uncommon for large facility departments to be offering sixty to seventy services, each with a direct labor cost, a cost of material, a direct overhead cost, and some allocated overhead cost. Facility managers need to know what those costs are and how they change over time for three reasons. First, there is so much emphasis now on cost control that managers who do not know their actual costs will fail. Second, many departments use chargebacks or allocations to charge customers for services. Facility managers who don't know their true costs will be in a constant battle with customers over the appropriateness of chargebacks. Third, once costs for all services are correctly calculated and tracked over time, the facility manager will note that five or six of those costs are the real drivers. These then become the cost categories that the facility manager will concentrate on and are the categories that will be used to benchmark with others.

Key to being able to track costs accurately and over time is a good budget format, which allows costs to be identified easily. (My recommended planning and budget format is in Exhibit 4-2.) The budget should be the main facility management information tool, and programmatic budgeting allows this. That is why it is a best practice.

To be successful, the facility manager should have the ability to:

- Develop and execute facility business plans.
- Develop, execute, and evaluate budgets.
- Administrate chargeback and allocations.
- Understand depreciation.
- Develop appropriate benchmarks and cost comparators.
- Calculate life-cycle costs.
- Calculate cost justification and project prioritization values.
- Understand pertinent ratio analysis.

At the center of these financial management skills is the ability to format, develop, and manage an annual budget. The remainder of this chapter focuses on those skills.

Before beginning a discussion of those skills, it is worth noting again the perceptions that exist regarding facility budgets. FMLink, the preeminent FM Internet information service, asked three resource questions of its customers. In March 1996, it asked if facility managers expected staff reductions greater than 10 percent in the next year.

> *Yes:*   36 percent
> *No:*   64 percent

In July it asked if facility managers thought their annual budgets would be lower in the upcoming year:

> *Yes:*   45 percent
> *No:*   55 percent

In September 1996, facility managers were asked if, compared to two years earlier, there were at the time more short-term cost-cutting decisions that would cost more in the long run:

> *Yes:*   81 percent
> *No:*   19 percent

Almost concurrently 252 business managers were asked by the International Facility Management Association (IFMA) about their perception of facilities. Cost information was the information that they most wanted from their facility department, and they perceived facilities as follows:

A liability or cash drain:	3 percent
A cost of doing business:	60 percent
A resource that can provide a competitive edge:	37 percent

Ninety-six percent of those same executives said that for the profession to thrive in the future, facility management must demonstrate positive financial impacts.[1] The message here is that facility managers are not meeting the business expectations of upper management (or don't understand those expectations). Facility managers who are likely to succeed are those who are meeting their company's business expectations; those who don't will continue to fight the cycle of constantly diminishing resources until they are doomed to failure and outsourced. One way to success in facility financial management is through proper budget management. In the remainder of this chapter, we will concentrate on the annual budget.

Budgets are the *lingua franca* of an organization, particularly in the public sector. In any organization they show who's in and who's out, and they directly reflect the organization's priorities. Budgets need to be structured, should reflect the information needs of management, and should parallel the planning format so that work can be tracked from one year to the next. Finally, budgets should flow from the planning process of the company.

Programs, Planning, and Budgeting

In the current management environment, form does not have a high priority. However, I cannot emphasize too strongly how important it is to organize a budget by program so that the programs can be tracked, from plan to budget and over time within the budget. Second, the budget should be formatted so that the key indicators used for financial management, particularly benchmarks, can be easily calculated. Finally, the budget format should facilitate financial accountability so that department managers are held accountable for funds assigned to them. Unfortunately, the statements of accounts in most companies meet none of those criteria, and not enough facility managers fight to get their budget formatted in such a way that it is truly the chief financial information management tool.

Proposed or ongoing programs are the building blocks of the department's budget. A program—leasing or maintenance and repair, for instance—is what facility managers plan and budget for. Thus planning new programs is crucial to effective budgeting. A facility manager who is not actively engaged in planning is doomed to a reactive mode (back to the boiler room!). There is no major company initiative that does not require major facility planning, and the facility manager must be positioned to ensure that that happens.

The budget is important in all facility departments; in the public sector it is absolutely essential. In a government agency, the budget is the essence of the organization. It is the benchmark against which the facility manager will be judged, since there is no profit or loss statement for an agency. The importance of formulating, executing, and evaluating the budget, particularly to the public-sector facility manager, cannot be overstated.

For the budgeting process to work, it is essential that: all costs are planned and budgeted as part of some program, and programs are stabilized year to year so that the budget can be a management information system and costs can be compared.

Some facility managers don't know how to budget and account properly for the funds entrusted to them. Although the facility manager is not an accountant, it is difficult to see how he can be a good manager without understanding the details of money flow: how goods and services are procured, how vendor accounts are set up in the controller's department, and how invoices flow from submittal through issuance of payment.

A facility manager should be capable of setting up a management information system to monitor the department's budget for the fiscal year. He should be able to determine whether funds can be shifted between accounts and to what extent individual accounts and the total budget can be exceeded or underspent without drawing corporate sanction. Likewise, the facility manager should be able to determine who can or should commit funds and at what level. He should set up approval procedures so as to monitor spending. Without this knowledge, he cannot hope to control the administrative processes both internal and external to the department. In this chapter I discuss these various elements of budget management, beginning with the types of budgets a facility manager will deal with.

Types of Budgets

There are three basic types of budgets: administrative, operational, and capital.

Administrative Budget

In many organizations, the facility department budget is part of the company's administrative budget. As I use the term, however, the administrative budget refers to those items of overhead that the facility department shares with other departments in the company. Exhibit 19-1 is an example of an administrative budget.

Often the administrative budget controls not only the funds for human resources but also the number of positions. That makes hiring a greater number of less expensive (and therefore less qualified) employees difficult. Also, normally the entire administrative budget is not *fungible*—that is, the manager may not transfer funds from this budget to another, or vice versa. Often within this budget, personnel costs are *fenced*, meaning they are not fungible even within the budget.

I also have included the amortization of capital projects in the administrative

Exhibit 19-1. Administrative budget.

I. Personnel
    A. Salaries
        1. Full time
        2. Temporary
        3. Overtime
    B. Staff supplements
        1. Consultants
        2. Contract
    C. Benefits
        1. Regular leave
        2. Sick leave
        3. Group life insurance
        4. Health insurance
        5. Retirement
    D. Training and conferences (travel and fees)
        1. Internal
        2. External

II. Office Expenses
    A. Supplies
    B. Rental
    C. Utilities and fuel
    D. Clothing and uniforms
    E. Office automation
    F. Telecommunications
    G. Automotive
        1. Fuel and oil
        2. Maintenance and repair
        3. Rental
    H. Reproduction
    I. Advertising

III. Depreciation of Capital Accounts

budget. If that figure reaches 8 percent of the annual budget in any one year while the total budget remains relatively fixed, the facility manager must control future capital expenditures better because payback is having a deleterious effect on the annual budget.

Operational Budget

The operational budget covers funds that the company gives to the facility manager to perform his mission. Exhibit 19-2 represents an operational budget.

The level of detail in the budget is a matter of choice, negotiated with the

Exhibit 19-2. Operational budget.

I. Utilities
   A. Electric
   B. Water
   C. Heating
      1. Gas
      2. Fuel Oil
   D. Energy savings

II. Rentals
   A. Land
   B. Operational facilities
   C. Other
   D. Lease income

III. Planning and Design
   A. CADD development and maintenance
   B. Consultant fees
      1. Planning
      2. Design
      3. Furniture
      4. Audiovisual
      5. Kitchen
      6. Art
      7. Signage
      8. Life safety
      9. Energy management
     10. Other
   C. Photography and renderings
   D. Reproduction and printing
   E. To plan and design capital programs
   F. To support capital projects

IV. Maintenance and repair
   A. Preventive maintenance
      1. Grounds
      2. Exteriors and roofs
      3. Interiors
      4. Electrical
      5. Plant and HVAC systems
      6. Security and life-safety systems
      7. Furniture
      8. Kitchen equipment
      9. Other
   B. Custodial
      1. Janitorial

      2. Trash removal
      3. Window cleaning
      4. Carpet cleaning
      5. Insect/rodent control
      6. Blinds and drapes
  C. Maintenance and repair
      1. Grounds
      2. Exteriors and roofs
      3. Interiors
      4. Plant and HVAC system
      5. Telecommunications
      6. Office technology
      7. Elevators
      8. Security and life-safety systems
      9. Furniture
     10. Electrical systems
     11. Kitchen equipment
     12. Signage
     13. Other

V. New Work
  A. Alterations
  B. Construction
  C. Noncapital equipment
      1. Direct operational support
      2. Other
  D. Grounds improvement

VI. Moving
  A. Direct support
  B. Other

Note: All budget categories in programs III through VI could have both material and labor subcategories.

boss and the chief budget officer. Since I favor bubble-up budgeting (aggregating budget figuring from the responsible work units that will execute the work plan), I also favor detailed budgets, since each item must be estimated anyway. The only question is how many subelements must be rolled up and how many can be displayed. In most cases, each line in the operational budget can also be divided into labor and materials, if desired. An item like preventive maintenance of interiors is likely to be a single line and a single cost, extrapolated from historical data. Conversely, alterations will have a separate listing of all recommended projects.

    Many facility managers cringe at the detail shown in these example budgets; however, some facility managers consistently fail to provide comparative data. The degree of detail is determined by management information needs. If you are frequently asked how much it costs on a square-footage basis to remove trash (or the annual reproduction and printing costs for building drawings), then show that item clearly.

From this point forward, when I say "annual budget," I mean one containing both the administrative and operational aspects.

Capital Budget

The capital budget is a multiyear presentation. It provides information on the major buildings, furniture, furnishings, and equipment that the company needs to perform its mission. What may be capitalized is determined by both tax law and company policy. Often that policy sets a floor (for example, $50,000) under which certain purchases (furniture, for instance) cannot be capitalized for any one purchase. Each line in the capital budget is a separately justified project. The justification and costing sheets become a part of the capital budget.

Many organizations repay themselves by charging against the annual facilities budget the amortization cost of the outstanding capital account. When that depreciation approaches 8 percent of the annual budget, it starts seriously to affect annual operations, and future capital expenditures should be rigorously controlled.

Major capital projects have annual budget implications. For example, the construction of a new building could reduce lease costs and perhaps reduce alteration costs temporarily. However, there will be corresponding increases in administrative costs, utilities, and maintenance. During a major capital project, the annual budget normally increases, at least to the extent of funding the project team, unless its expenses are capitalized.

The facility manager should use the capital budget to solve the major long-term construction and replacement requirements uncovered in the strategic planning. In capital budgeting, it is very important to play by the rules for two reasons:

1. Most companies make the facility department pay back or depreciate its capital investments. Depreciation should be kept in the 6 to 8 percent range of the annual budget. When it exceeds that limit, it becomes a burden.

2. The facility manager loses credibility with the controller if he breaks the rules.

For more on the capital budget, particularly tools to prioritize or make decisions between projects, see Chapter 5.

Chargebacks

A device for controlling facility costs that has gained currency is the chargeback, a means by which the company's divisions are charged for facility services according to their use. The theory is that business managers will be more cost conscious if they have to pay for facility services.

Chargebacks have become predominant in facility management as both business and government have moved to business unit accountability. Chargebacks depend on the facility manager, as a monopoly provider, setting his own rates. The advantages of chargebacks are that they promote cost consciousness, facility costs become more apparent to line managers, and costs can be more readily tied to a product.

Opposition to allocated facility costs comes in primarily two forms. First, allocation rules tend to be arbitrary, difficult to calculate and justify, and therefore there is a significant administrative burden and an opportunity for conflict with line management. Second, some items are best funded by the company, and upper management must realize that the facility manager needs some discretionary budget not available under pure chargeback.

To administer chargebacks accurately, the facility manager must first accurately account for his cost. Most facility budget formats make accurate cost accounting difficult, a problem compounded by other factors. Consider the difficulty of fixing rates between two sets of space. The first is a loft converted to office space that has inadequate HVAC in the hottest and coldest months. The second space is a leased manufacturing facility where electrical distribution is a constant problem and part of the manufacturing floor has been converted to administrative space. Should each manager be charged the same amount for space? How should the qualitative differences be handled?

Chargebacks are most successful where the service or product cost can be directly and easily measured. Also, it is relatively easy to charge back for services or products that are above a norm or standard. Finally, chargebacks are effective when costs must be allocated to a company product. For that reason, my observation is that manufacturing companies often have the best handle on their facility costs.

Over the past two years, I have informally polled my students on chargebacks, and the results are disturbing. As the process of allocating facility costs has become more widespread (it is now the norm, not the exception), facility managers have lost faith in this technique or largely ignore it. They view allocating facility costs as an administrative burden or a source of constant friction with line managers. In my informal survey, about a quarter of the facility managers say they have had to devote a person to administering chargebacks because of the complexity of setting rules and the constant complaints from line managers about allocations. Facility managers seem about evenly split on whether chargebacks really do cause line managers to alter their behavior.

Few advocates of allocating facility costs implement total chargeback, recognizing that some facility costs are best managed centrally and that facility managers need discretionary funds to meet the reactive part of their mission.

Managing an effective chargeback system emphasizes the need for facility managers to be able to calculate the true cost of each product and service, including overheads. The most effective chargebacks charge a "rent" for space based on gross square foot occupied and for which the line unit gets a bundle of services spelled out in an internal "lease." Services over and above the standard are also charged back. Automation allows us to calculate allocations properly and to administer a flexible chargeback system. If your company determines that chargebacks should be used, it is worth the effort to put a business-like system in place and to make it truly effective as a management technique. For a best practice in this area, see Alan D. Wilson's "Distribution and Measurement of Laboratory and Office Space Costs in *1995 Winter Best Practices Forum on Facility Management* (Houston: International Facility Management Association, 1995), pp. 193–211.

Budget Formulation

One of the problems that facility managers have traditionally had with finance departments is that the facility budget has some unique characteristics. That often complicates budget preparation, makes it difficult to explain and defend, and ensures it will be viewed as a source of cuts when funds are needed elsewhere in the company.

First, the FM department budget is large—normally the second largest expense budget in the company. That means it will draw attention.

Second, it is diverse, covering accounts such as space planning, reprographics, rent, security, utilities, mail distribution, and waste management. Each of those categories requires a different method of budget projection and justification, which complicates budget preparation.

A large part of the facility budget is driven by government regulation. Often these regulations have been written in such a way that the cost for compliance is difficult to determine (the Americans with Disabilities Act, for example). Trying to project regulatory compliance costs is often like trying to hit a moving target while blindfolded.

Facility managers need funds to react because theirs is a business where reaction is a fact of life. The facility budget must allow the facility manager to react to disasters. Even a new boiler can break down, and, when it does, there must be funds to fix it. We make our best guesses about the need for heating in the winter and cooling in the summer, but if our estimates were too low, the utility companies are still going to send a bill that has to be paid.

Utilities represent the best example of yet another characteristic of facility budgets. A large portion of a facility budget is not discretionary. If we have an active lease, we are going to pay the rent whether we have people or activities in the leased space or not.

That leads me to the final unique feature of facility budgets: they have both long and short-term aspects to them. For example, it is easy to slight the maintenance accounts in the near term, but you then compound the major repair and capital improvement accounts in subsequent years.

In the ideal system, the annual budget derives about 70 percent from the midrange work plan if the company has a sophisticated planning system. If it does not, formulating the budget is an exercise in gathering requirements, extrapolating historical data, and guesstimating. (See Section II on planning.) Either way, the question often is what the proper base should be for projections. Exhibit 19-3 is a suggested matrix for extrapolating budget data into the future. All data are ordinarily displayed in constant-year dollars. Normally the budget year is

Exhibit 19-3. Projecting budget data.

Category	How Projected	Source
Capital	Gather discrete projects annually	Call for projects; estimate concepts
Utilities	Estimate discrete new requirements	In-house records
	Project annual growth from 3- to 5-year curve	Utility companies
Operations	Arithmetic projection	Unit cost indicators
Nondiscretionary maintenance and repair	Arithmetic projection (projects can be gathered discretely)	Unit cost indicators (estimate projects from concept design)
Custodial	Arithmetic projection	Unit cost indicators
Nonproject moving	Arithmetic projection	Unit cost indicators
Discretionary projects	Gather discrete projects annually	Call for projects; estimate concept
Lease costs and income	Review leases	Leases
Personnel costs	Arithmetic projections	Use actual salaries and benefits or standard salaries and benefits
Training and travel costs	Gather requirements	Actual costs for training and standard costs for travel
Office equipment and vehicles	Gather requirements for purchases; arithmetic calculation of operational costs	Call for requirements; cost data on vehicles/ equipment
Nonprojects design and engineering	Guesstimate	Historical data

the base year, although some companies prefer to use the previous year so that comparisons can be drawn.

In large organizations, the facility department budget is often assigned to a budget analyst because it is so large. In smaller organizations, an analyst from the budget department or the controller may have the responsibility, along with responsibility for several other budgets. In very small organizations, the facility manager's supervisor may be the only analyst. The job of the budget analyst is (1) to ensure the budget is in compliance with budget guidelines, (2) to see that the budget interfaces with other department budgets and that there is no duplication, and (3) to be a liaison between senior management and the department.

There are several ways to approach the budget analyst. The best is to be cooperative, using the analyst as a sounding board for each new budget and obtaining information on new initiatives. The two of you will never agree on all issues, but you can ensure that there are no surprises in the relationship.

Traditional Problem Areas in Annual Budgeting

My observation of many annual facility budgets in both the public and private sectors indicates that the greatest problem is the lack of a useful budget format. Most facility department budget formats are poorly done and need to be put into a program format. That point cannot be overemphasized. Programmatic budgeting and a consistent budget format are key to budget estimating, formulation, tracking, analysis, evaluation, accountability, and benchmarking.

Hand in hand with the necessity for an appropriate format is the need to have valid budget data. Because budget formats are poor, costs are not transparent and cannot be tracked over time, so at budget time, good, valid data are available for future projection.

Another issue that has been magnified in the past several years is the underfunding of facilities and the reduction of facility staff. Some of this is caused by facility managers' failure to justify budgets and human resources needs in business terms, failure to communicate well with upper management, and failure to document well the actual costs of doing business. Having said that, the fact remains that facility departments are traditionally underfunded and understaffed. How many companies, for example, reinvest 2 to 4 percent of the replacement value of their building stock in annual maintenance and repair? Securing adequate resources remains perhaps the greatest challenge to the facility manager. The answer to this problem lies more in the business and communications skills of the facility manager than in just better data, but better data are essential also. Facility managers need to look to outsourcing creatively to solve their staffing problems.

Closely aligned with the fact of underfunding is that companies have traditionally taken a short-term view of their facilities. There is intense pressure on private-sector managers to increase shareholder value, and that translates to cost cutting and a short-term perspective on their facilities. In some cases, that may even be the correct economic decision if the facilities are leased or likely to be sold or abandoned. However, in owned government facilities, the old adage, "You can pay me now or pay me later," is true. Maintenance deferred means costly breakdowns, possible loss of productivity, and higher repair bills down the road.

Others With an Interest

The budget is not formulated in a vacuum. Others in the company have a legitimate interest in the budget. The controller obviously has an interest in faulty accounts; his automation system may limit the number of accounts displayed, for example. Also, he needs to maintain some semblance of order and format among all budget units to make the whole budget understandable. This insistence on uniformity can be a problem when the work of the company is vastly different from the work of the facility manager.

As you develop the budget, keep others informed; bring them along as budget decisions are made and priorities shift. For example, the human resources department chief or budget analyst will exhibit interest in the human resources section of the budget. Line managers with major annual or capital projects have an interest in seeing at least that portion of the budget approved. Since they probably assisted in justifying the project, they should be informed if the project is reprioritized, reduced in scope, or downgraded.

Last but not least, your manager will want to review the budget even if he does not have to approve it. Keep the boss informed of the general level of requests by program, obtaining guidance on all new initiatives and any major problems before actually formulating the budget. As the budget takes shape, inform your boss of major changes or problems. He can help with the problems, and needs to know the changes so that they do not get blindsided in the board room. "No surprises" is the best policy.

Budgeting Details and Characteristics

There are two kinds of budget increases. The first recognizes program growth; the second acknowledges inflation, rate increases (utilities, for example), or increases beyond the influence of the facility manager (personnel raises, for instance). Normally it is the responsibility of the facility manager to quantify and justify all growth in a program. Increases in rates or inflation ordinarily are granted automatically by the budget department or controller, to the extent that they can be quantified. Often this latter type of increase is awarded after all budget deliberations are completed, so that the proposed budget can be compared to the previous year's in constant-year uninflated dollars.

Many programs lend themselves to accurate budgeting—utilities, for example. On the other hand, discretionary annual projects should be planned at a level to 15 percent over budget guidance. Some projects drop out during the year, so there should be well-developed projects ready to substitute rather than go for something momentarily convenient or easy.

Often, in the final stages of budget formulation, the facility manager will receive instructions to submit more prioritized requirement or to group existing requirements in a band in case a last-minute decrement occurs or a cut is necessary. Grouping is done only for discretionary programs. Common bands are 3, 5, or 10 percent of the program, starting from the bottom of the priority list. Building and decrementing a budget by bands is far superior to a random or across-the-board method, but it works better for project-related work than for something like utilities.

A good budget has the following characteristics:

1. It contains categories the manager and others feel need to be managed.
2. It is work-plan driven and reflects programs being managed.
3. It is structured the way the facility manager operates and ties together resource management and responsibility.
4. It provides management information on total costs, comparative costs, and easy-to-compute unit costs.
5. It identifies subunit manager responsibilities.

Communications and Security

A facility manager should expect the same level of savings from proper planning, design, and operation of the communications, security, and safety systems that he achieves from facilities. Exhibit 19-4 assumes that the planning and design savings and avoidance have already been credited. Good management and new technology can actually save both capital and annual costs. Cost avoidances occur because proper security, safety, and communication systems avoid insurance costs. They also avoid human resources costs by increasing productivity.

Areas for Cost Savings

An emerging theme among facility managers is that the facility department should be viewed as a profit center. I share their enthusiasm for good facility management, but I am concerned about overselling ourselves and the profession. It is my experience that profitability comes from extensive leasing and/or real estate development, which are more closely aligned with property management than with facility management as I define it.

There are, however, many areas for cost savings, particularly of life-cycle costs. Often facility departments have the reputation of devouring too large a share of the administrative budget without tangible results for the company. The facility manager should publicize the economic contributions of this department.

In this chapter I review, by major department functions, where cost savings opportunities exist. I have not included generalities like "manage better here" and instead confine myself to traditional management functions. A summary matrix of cost savings and cost avoidances is shown in Exhibit 19-4. The magnitude of these savings is purely experiential; I have done no research in this area.

Facility Planning and Forecasting

Good planning can conservatively save 5 to 10 percent of the typical costs on a capital project by permitting the design-construct cycle to proceed on a schedule that precludes costly crashing. This does not rule out fast-tracking, which in some industries is the most economical way to manage a capital project. But good long-term planning has payoffs in all facilities programs, even annual ones. For example, accurately predicting when a facility will open or close can avoid penalties to service contractors.

A good annual work plan can favorably affect the quality, quantity, and cost of work accomplished with an annual budget. Most obvious, however, the plan better uses existing funds and achieves higher-quality work because the work will have been designed, planned, and executed at a normal pace.

It is difficult to isolate the savings achieved with good capital planning apart from long- and midrange planning. For sure, rational capital planning that borrows and pays back on most favorable terms will offer welcomed savings.

Exhibit 19-4. Opportunities for cost savings and avoidances.

Function	Cost Savings (%)[1] Capital	Annual	Avoidances[2]	Areas Affected
Facility planning and forecasting strategic and mid-term planning	5–15	10–20	15–25	Construction costs, O&M cost, leasing costs, financing costs
Lease administration	–	5–10	5–10	Utility costs, build-out costs, shared costs, property management costs
Space planning, allocation, and management	–	3–5	–	Rents and space-related costs
Architectural-engineering planning and design	8–12	10–30	20–30	Maintenance costs, energy costs, operating costs, construction costs
Workplace planning, design, and specification	–	–	3–7	Employee efficiency
Budgeting, accounting, and economic justification	1–2	2–3	–	Accuracy of accounts, better budget utilization
Real estate acquisition and disposal	2–5	2–5	5–7	Operational costs, acquisition costs, disposal price
Construction project management	7–10	7–10	10–15	Construction and alteration costs
Alterations, renovations, and workplace installation	–	2–3	7–10	Project costs, staff disruption costs
Operations, maintenance, and repair	–	7–10	15–20	Energy costs, maintenance costs, capital costs, insurance costs, and major repairs
Communications and security	2–3	2–3	7–10	Avoid insurance costs and increase productivity, save communications costs

1. Percentage of funds in current-year program.
2. Average mutual percentage over lifetime—capital and annual.

Lease Administration

For a landlord, good lease administration can be critical to the margin of profitability. Proper metering of facilities, a good tenant workletter, a well-developed lease, and proper allocation of shared costs alone can save 5 to 10 percent of costs without diminishing the facility manager's reputation as a quality lessor. As the lessee, proper lease negotiation, particularly in a soft market, can help avoid at least 5 to 10 percent of the costs of a medium-term lease.

Space Planning, Allocation, and Management

In this area, I have a belief that is probably counter to the majority of line and facility managers. Having moved thousands of employees annually within a company, I know that there is great potential to reduce the churn—the near-constant moves within our organizations. Among IFMA members, the mean number of annual moves in 1996 was 694, at a mean cost with construction of almost $4,200 per move.[2] There is a potential savings of billions of dollars by reducing this churn by one-third. Why, in this era of advanced tele- and datacommunications, the intranet, and e-mail, must every worker in an organization be located contiguously? We do that at a tremendous cost, yet are in the most cost-conscious era in history.

Microlevel forecasting, planning, and design are major items of interest in every organization; however, sometimes management emphasis is not in the right place. For example, one organization estimated that it was losing 6 percent of its net usable space each year to the increased storage of paper, two-thirds of which was duplicative. Analyses of space utilization trends by category and user assisted the facility manager in maximizing use of space. Since most facility costs are directly related to space, every square foot saved or better utilized produces savings. If space is not managed well at the microlevel, eventually there are capital or lease costs to produce more space.

Architectural-Engineering Planning and Design

Value engineering, life-cycle costing of new building technologies and equipment, designing for energy efficiency, and designing to maintain are interrelated, highly effective ways to reduce and avoid costs. On large projects, value engineering alone can probably save 5 percent of capital costs and avoid 10 percent of operating expenses. In many organizations, life-cycle improvements must save approximately 10 percent to be adopted. The basis for any solid energy management program is good design. Good design for energy management should be expected to reduce annual energy costs by at least 10 percent and to avoid at least that much in the future.

Workplace Planning, Design, and Specification

Although no one has calculated the increase in office productivity that effective workplace planning can produce, it seems very obvious that 5 percent is a realistic goal for office workers. That much increase can perhaps even be achieved for manufacturing, engineering, and other functions. The increase in productivity should be directly translatable into cost avoidance. In fact, when we achieve improvement in employee productivity, we are leveraging expenses well. Employee costs are the largest administrative expense in a company.

Budgeting, Accounting, and Economic Justification

In many ways, this category is the key to cost savings and avoidances. Unless funds can be accounted for properly, savings or cost avoidances cannot be documented. Unless you can utilize the economic justification tools, you do not truly know what the savings or avoidances mean.

When project accounting, budget accounting, and financial accounting are conducted under separate systems, as they often are, facility managers sometimes misspend their budget. Often they actually have more funds available than their budget accounts say. This excess is either lost or misspent on projects requiring little design or management in the final days of a fiscal year. My experience is that loss can amount to 1 to 3 percent of the annual or capital budget. Programmatic budgeting tracked on one system can reduce that loss to zero.

Real Estate Acquisition and Disposal

It is difficult to separate the benefits of long-range planning of space, real estate planning, and real estate operations. In fact, they work together and are highly interdependent; but because I truly believe in the benefits of planning, I have weighted the savings from planning more heavily in my matrix.

Proper site selection can produce significant cost avoidances. One convincing example is moving all possible industrial activities and storage of an organization out of costly urban space and serving the downtown facility remotely. Transportation-related facilities are particularly sensitive to proper site selection.

The marketing and timing of property for disposal can produce significant savings. A discreet broker who knows the local market well can be a substantial help in disposing of excess real estate.

Construction Project Management

The savings shown in construction project management for savings and cost avoidance are those that can be achieved by a superior project manager over one who is merely good and those that recognize the planning and design savings discussed previously. A major factor in selecting a project management firm and/ or builder is their track record on cost savings and how such savings will be shared.

Construction management has become extremely sophisticated, and there are many competent construction managers. Can, however, the construction manager harness the decision-making apparatus of the company so that timely decisions are made? When that occurs, the initial costs and the cost of changes for both major and minor construction can be reduced 7 to 10 percent. Constructing to maintain good turnover procedures and the preparation of good as-built documentation should conservatively avoid 10 to 15 percent in future alteration, renovation, and operational expenses.

Alterations, Renovation, and Workplace Installation

Perhaps the numbers show for this category give a false impression because they assume that the savings/avoidance from good planning, designing, and specifying have already been taken. So, in percentage terms, these numbers may seem small. However, these percentages are applied to a base that is often 30 to 40 percent of the facilities budget, so the actual savings are great.

Also, in this area, good on-site management will minimize the disruption to company employees before, during, and after the project starts. For organizations that churn at 30 percent, this cost avoidance is significant. Also, proper installation for the more sophisticated communication, fire, and life-safety systems probably generates 2 to 3 percent cost avoidance.

Operations, Maintenance, and Repair

This is the category where costs are principally avoided by good prior planning, design, project management, and operation. Good management in this area reaps real savings and avoids substantial costs because this category can account for 40 to 50 percent of the facilities annual budget.

The principal savings in the annual budget are through energy management and good inventory control. However, the major impacts here are in cost avoidance. Good maintenance will ensure the availability of key facility systems and reduce the lost time caused by system failure. Good cyclical and preventive maintenance programs can substantially reduce the need for major repair. Correction of hazards and a well-maintained facility reduce both insurance premiums and the funds paid out for liability and personal injury. A good O&M response is the basis for a disaster recovery program, the ultimate in avoiding costs.

All of us need to reenergize our energy management efforts, which we have let slide from the last North American energy crunch in the early 1970s. More efficient equipment alone can reduce energy consumption by 10 to 30 percent and therefore has an acceptable internal rate of return (IRR) for capital replacement.

Software available from the Environmental Protection Agency's Energy Star Building Real Estate Management Program allows users to analyze the cost of building upgrades to include tenant recovery options, future occupancy impacts of the upgrade, financing alternatives and produces savings, net present value, IRR, payback, net operating increases, and asset value changes.[3]

The deregulation of utilities promises great savings for large users. Agents will help companies find the lowest-priced electricity and often work on a contingency basis. Facility managers should be exploring how deregulation will affect their companies so that they will be ready to act when it occurs.

Finally, in the area of O&M, many facility managers have outsourced extensively. One top area for additional cost savings is to explore shared savings with the contractors. Rewarding the contractor for being cost conscious can create a win-win situation while ensuring that the savings are documented and good for the long-term viability of the department and facilities.

Budget Completion

When the budget is assembled, the facility manager should conduct several analyses, including historical comparisons, unit-cost comparisons, detailed comparisons to the current year's budget, and trend analyses. Variances then become a principal part of the narrative, along with discussion of new issues. If the funding guidance is lower than the stated requirements, describe the impact that funding constraints, by category, will have on the department. It is important to view the annual budget as a tool to help manage and monitor the department's work while also meeting the reporting requirements of the accounting department and the boss.

Budget Execution

In many organizations, so much effort goes into formulating and defending the budget that executing it is almost an afterthought. In actuality, executing the budget largely determines how successful the budget is. Because organizations are dynamic, budgets must be also. Some projects suddenly drop by the wayside and completely new projects come along necessitating new, unplanned actions. Executing the budget means accommodating these changes.

Expenditure Levels

A variety of fiscal years are possible:

- Coincident with the calendar year
- July through June
- October through September

Ordinarily, annual budgets do not allow funds to be carried over from one fiscal year to the next. This means that the fourth quarter is a hectic one. Everyone is scrambling to execute the remaining portion of the annual work plan, and at the same time end-of-year funds become available from other programs. Particularly in the public sector, there is a reluctance to commit funds in an orderly flow. After an almost inevitable peak of expenditure at the start of each fiscal year, everyone wants to save for a rainy day. There is, however, a risk in doing that. If the mid-year review shows that the commitment rate is not at or near target, the department could have its funds withdrawn and given to some other department.

Exhibit 19-5 depicts the traditional and desirable expenditure profiles for an annual budget. Traditionally, at the start of a fiscal year there is pent-up demand for services. Concerned that he will not have funds for an emergency, the facility manager puts on the fiscal brakes until past midyear review, when he begins an end-of-the-year buying binge. Thus, the peaks and valleys make workload management in the facility and purchasing departments difficult. Also, because so much of the work plan is executed in the final quarter, the projects that are done tend to be those that can be pushed out the door easily, rather than those of greatest benefit to the company.

The more desirable expenditure profile also shows an early hump caused by the inevitable buildup of demand from the last fiscal year. But that hump is flatter, and the spending soon levels out until midyear. After the midyear review, expenditure activity increases slightly but not dramatically. The small hump at year's end reflects a minor increase in year-end funding for well-developed projects. This profile greatly reduces the demands on design, project management, and procurement resources, and at the end of a budget year, the facility manager should be able to close out his budget within ±0.5 percent.

With a normal work backlog, it is best to exceed the budget by 0.3 to 0.5 percent. There are no medals given for being closer than that, and your department can use that bonus to reduce its backlog.

Exhibit 19-5. Typical annual expense profile.

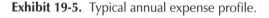

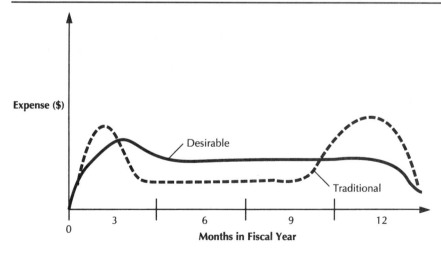

Control of Spending

Much managerial effort goes into establishing and maintaining control of the budget. In many organizations, funds are allocated on a periodic basis for one purpose. For example, from a facilities annual alteration budget of $1 million, a company might allocate $300,000 for first-quarter projects. That ensures that the entire alterations budget will not be spent in the first quarter; allocated funds cannot be committed or expensed without an additional transaction.

Funds are committed through legal documents like contracts. Once the funds are committed, to decrease the obligation the facility manager has to resort to negotiation, arbitration, or the legal system. For instance, when five chairs are ordered at $1,535, those funds are committed and are not available for another use. Once the funds are spent, an expense is incurred—for example, paying $1,507 plus $26 shipping for the five chairs once received. When the check for $1,533 is sent out, the department incurs that expense. The $2 that was overcommitted, for whatever reason, is lost. It is very important to understand whether your budget report reflects funds allocated, funds committed, or actual expenses, since each category leads to much different conclusions. I strongly recommend tracking expenses.

Periodic reviews are a major control mechanism, so hold budget execution reviews with subordinate managers. For capital projects, conduct formal reviews monthly. For the annual budget, conduct informal reviews at midyear and three-quarters of the way through the year. If funds can be reprogrammed and effectively used, also conduct reviews monthly in the last quarter, weekly in the last month, and daily in the last week.

As another control method, use a double-signature authorization system for requirements and payment. It is helpful to require a technical manager to sell you the need for a new requirement before you approve it. Similarly, it is responsible to have two managers validate all expenses before they are sent for payment.

Because of human nature, people are uncomfortable with change. However, most of us realize that we work in a management function that is highly reactive. Change is almost inevitable, and we need to develop skills and procedures that permit us to manage change effectively. This is particularly true in executing the budget.

Budget changes have many sources: management decisions, shifts in priorities, new initiatives or opportunities, unforeseen cost increases, or an inability to execute planned work. Regardless of the source of a change, a facility manager needs to have procedures that minimize its impact. Failure to do so can have a serious impact on funding personnel, and work effort, particularly design.

Budget reports during the year should provide essential information quickly and easily. With no more than one simple division, the facility manager should be able to answer such questions as these:

- What are our unit custodial costs at 1325 Neptune Street vs. 1603 Mars Avenue?

- What percentage of our new work (alterations, minor construction) budget has been expensed as of July 31?
- What are our lease costs at the end of the fiscal year? Compared to last month? Last year?
- What percentage of our total facilities budget is spend on maintenance and repair?
- How does our unit cost for maintenance and repair compare to the General Services Administration standard for this city? To the Building Owners and Managers Association Experience Report for our category? To the International Facility Management Association benchmark?

Since the budget should reflect priorities, if preventive maintenance is a priority, do the expenditures reflect that? Also, how does the department's actual expenditure profile fit the intended profile? Budget reports should be structured in a way to provide such information almost instantaneously.

A facility manager will never truly control his budget unless he understands how transactions flow through the organization. Exhibit 19-6 is a depiction of such flow. The stations may vary, but the principle remains the same; for example, some companies may have a receiving section that verifies receipt of goods and validates the invoice for payment. Note that this system is reasonably complex, involves a substantial paper flow, and is operated by low-paid personnel. Therefore, if the budget is to be properly debited, it is necessary to monitor the transaction flow reasonably closely. Knowledge of this system also makes it possible to pinpoint anomalies that appear in budget reports.

Exhibit 19-6. Transaction flow through the organization.

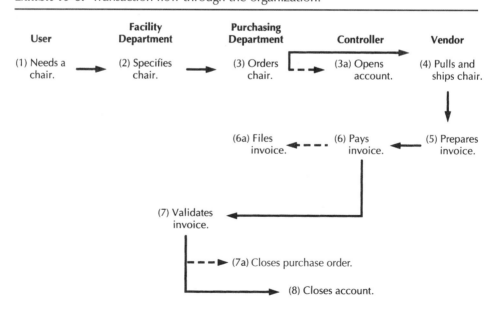

Budget Closeout and Evaluation

The end of the annual budget year can be hectic. Often there are funds available, but they are lost if they cannot be committed by the end of the fiscal year and expensed by the end of the accrual period. In many companies, managers are required to make their best guess of the funds they will commit in that final sixty days before the end of the fiscal year. Those funds are then accrued (saved), but they must be expensed before another arbitrary date, often sixty to ninety days after the end of the fiscal year, when that year's budget is put to bed. Accruals not expensed then must be charged against the following year's budget, a double hit to be avoided at all costs.

Budget closeout can be both much smoother and much more effective if there is a backlog of projects on the shelf for year-end funding or for execution immediately in the new fiscal year. Work out the expedited procedures in advance with the purchasing department.

Since the final quarter of a fiscal year and the start of a new fiscal year are periods of such intense activity, there is little time for a rational evaluation of annual budget performance. That is counterproductive, since budget management needs as much scrutiny as the management of technical functions.

The budget postmortem need not be formal, but it should involve the departmental accountant and all department managers. In this review, focus on four issues:

1. Did we do what we said we were going to do?
2. Did we do it effectively, given the resources we were given?
3. What lessons were learned, and how can we apply them to the current budget?
4. Are our budgets in balance and supportive?

These reviews should look at the budget format and process as well as the execution. It is a good time to ask such questions as these:

- Do we have more capital assets than we are willing to maintain?
- Do our standards need adjustment? Can we meet those standards with our current budget?
- Is the amortization of previous capital projects having a serious effect on our annual budget?
- What did our expenditure profile look like? Was it what we wanted it to be?
- What percentage of our total budget is administrative? New work? Maintenance and repair? Is that good or bad? What are the trends?
- Was the fact that we were on or off target good or bad? Could we have influenced it more?
- Is our budget structure conducive to good management? If not, how should we change?

Project Accounting

Project accounting is a topic that should be covered in an entire chapter in a book devoted only to project management. I touch only the highlights here. If the facility manager is asked to manage a major (multimillion dollar) project, he needs to be supported by a separate project accounting system and project accountant. Company accountants and most facility management accountants do not understand project accounting, which has its own set of accounts based on project work items. There certainly can be a feeder from the project accounting system into the company accounting system, but the importance of the project manager's having separate project accounting cannot be overemphasized.

A common practice is to organize project accounts to coincide with the sections of the specifications dealing with different work items (with perhaps several lines for "soft costs," which are outside the scope of the project contract). In most cases, these accounts are numbered in accordance with either the Construction Specification Institute's MasterFormat or Hanscomb Associate's UNIFORMAT. Both can be easily adapted for use with the common project management software so that project management and accounting go hand in hand and are mutually supportive.

Desired budget and accounting reports are as numerous as project managers, but the following are what I consider the minimum for good project management and accounting:

- *Estimate of probable cost.* Breaks out the latest construction estimate by work item and provides a cost, a percentage of the total work, and a unit cost for work item in the project (actually subitems in most cases). The recap should break out the work by estimated site work, building cost, soft costs, and total cost.

- *Master project budget.* Breaks out the original budget among all work items and subitems that the project manager wants to track.

- *Lists approved changes with their effect on the budget and expected changes with their anticipated effect on the budget.* As backup, each item has a listing by vendor of invoices, changes approved, and the remaining budget for that item.

- *Budget/cost comparison,* organized by item and subitem. Lists the current budget, the current contract amount, the budget variance, the amount billed to date, and the amount yet to be billed for each line item and subitem.

Most good project software permits one entry of any figure, and all affected project accounts will be adjusted accordingly.

Proper accounting for project funds supports the essence of good project management. The facility manager must not only account for current change and overruns, but must be able to project the cost of changes that have not yet been approved. No company accounting system can provide the response that the project manager needs on a major project. Invest effort early on in a good accounting system and project accountant.

Cost Comparators and Benchmarks

At the start of this chapter, I mentioned the need for facility managers to know the costs of their services and then to select those costs that are drivers of the department, to attempt to influence them positively, and to monitor them closely. In addition, those key unit costs should be the basis for benchmarking.

Costs, a measure of efficiency, should not be the only category that a facility manager benchmarks. He should benchmark effectiveness (as perceived by customers) and response as well.

The bible for benchmarking is Robert Camp's 1989 classic, *Benchmarking*, which should be in every facility manager's tool kit. After using Camp's methodology and ensuring that he understands the components of our costs, the facility manager should benchmark with competitors, with similar companies, and with best in class. In its initial stages, benchmarking will concentrate on the metrics. However, the real value, once the metrics of both partners is understood, is in exchanging information as to how the "better" value was achieved.

Remember two things when benchmarking. First, the law of diminishing returns applies. It requires much more effort and funding to squeeze out the last five percent of improvement. Is it worth it? Second, your management does not necessarily want you to be best in class in every category of your service since there is a cost in doing so. The lobby of a manufacturing facility need not have the visitor appeal of a top hotel, for example.

Benchmarking, if properly used, is a valuable tool for implementing and monitoring continuous improvement. Good cost accounting is the basis for good benchmarking, and a good budget format makes the computation of unit costs both accurate and easy.

Notes

1. *Views from the Top . . . Executives Evaluate the Facility Management Function* (Houston: IFMA, 1997), pp. 1–3.
2. *Benchmarks III* (Houston: IFMA, 1997), pp. 34–35.
3. "EPA Software Rates Upgrade Cost Viability," *Facilities Design and Management* (November 1997): 13.

20

Information Systems and Other Technology

Pulse Points

- *Do not try to develop and automate data and procedures simultaneously.*
- *When estimating automation needs, do not underestimate the effort needed for data entry or overestimate what building data are truly needed for good management.*
- *FM automation can increase departmental efficiency and effectiveness; it should be justified within the company as a tool necessary for good business practice.*
- *Don't automate bad policies and procedures.*
- *An omnibus facility management information system (FMIS) is now available to integrate the major FM functions. Facility managers of large companies should consider a system linking computer-aided design and drawing (CADD) and a geographic information system through a relational database.*
- *Research indicates that it is as important to be able to communicate data from FM technology tools as to possess the tools themselves.*
- *Facility managers should be using the Internet and intranet to communicate better, for training, to gather information and advice, and to review products and services.*
- *New communications technologies should be exploited to increase departmental efficiency.*
- *When purchasing an FMIS, develop an implementation plan consisting of a needs analysis, a budget, and an implementation schedule.*
- *Don't tie FMIS procurement to another big project.*
- *Ensure that the FMIS will mesh with company business systems.*
- *Training on the Internet represents a paradigm shift: Training is no longer a one-time event; with the Internet we can train when and where we want. In addition, access to training materials via the Internet allows us to integrate training into problem solving at work.*

The widespread use of the term *facility management* occurred simultaneously with the proliferation of business office automation. Some of my greatest challenges as a facility manager have been accommodating one personal computer per employee into buildings that were under construction and those over fifty years old when neither we nor our architect-engineering team knew much about accommodating office technology. The situation has improved with time, but office technology accommodation still provides a major challenge to the facility manager. The facility impact of office automation is discussed in detail in the excellent book, *Office Automation, Best F.M. Practice,* by Jon Ryburg, of the Facility Performance Group.

It is not too much of a stretch to say that business automation has increased the visibility of the facility manager. Now FM automation technology offers the facility manager the opportunity for better management of the buildings and services than could be imagined twenty years ago. Effective fielding of facilities automation has a spotty history. It is widely accepted that more than half of the software bought to make facility management more effective ends up as "shelfware,"[1] a disturbing fact given the current state of facility management, which sorely needs analytical and communication tools.

E-mail, groupware, and the use of the Internet and intranet are so widespread in most businesses that I will refer to them only as they affect a specific FM automation application. This is not to say they do not contribute to an effective, efficient department. In an admittedly unscientific survey in May 1997, FMLink reported that 84 percent of respondees used Internet or intranet in their corporate FM work. E-mail alone gives the facility manager a way to communicate effectively with customers that was virtually unavailable fifteen years ago.

The search for an acceptable FMIS has not been an easy one, nor have the solutions been neat. For example, in 1981–1982, the company I worked for wrote a specification for an omnibus FMIS that would allow us to manage each FM function well and provide the department the ability to share information within and without. We were unable to acquire such a system at that time—the technology was not there—so we automated each function independently but had no ability to share the information outside the department or feed information from one functional system or another. Finally, just after I left that company in 1996, departmental management made the decision to junk the "stovepiped" functional systems and buy a single, omnibus system.

The most common building-related FM functions that have been automated are as follows:

1. Drafting and design, commonly designated as CADD
2. Space planning and management, normally inherent in CADD systems
3. Project, construction, and move management
4. Work order and maintenance management
5. Building operations and energy management
6. Lease management
7. Asset (inventory and allocation) management
8. Telecommunications and data communications management

  9. Regulatory compliance management
 10. FM financial and procurement management to include chargeback administration

A recent survey of facility professionals from Fortune 500 companies shows that 92 percent of those responding expressed a desire to retain or implement some type of FMIS in the near future—either automating individual functions or obtaining an omnibus system. Of those surveyed, 82 percent used their FMIS for space management (the principal use noted), but the most frequently cited future use (71 percent) was for managing departmental chargebacks.[2]

Every one of the functions mentioned above has been automated by multiple vendors and can be installed normally on a desktop computer, which leads us to ask how best to automate and what automation system is best for a particular company. We really have gone beyond deciding whether to automate FM functions. The issue is how best to do so.

The facility manager has two options when seeking an FMIS or automating his department. The first is to automate each of the listed functions individually. That was my experience, because when my company automated, that was the only option. Often this approach also ensures that you obtain an excellent solution to your problem—lease management, for example. Some facility managers of primarily leased facilities need only a few functions automated. In addition, the facility manager can often do a better job of automating by focusing intently on one function and ensuring that it works well before moving on to the next.

If the FMIS is built function by function, it may be possible to find a system integrator who can connect all of the functional subsystems into an integrated system. Normally, however, that is prohibitively costly or technically infeasible.

The second option is to buy an omnibus system, with separate modules for all (or most) of the functions and the capability for data to be exchanged and used between the modules. There are at least four North American companies offering such omnibus systems.

Need is one of the factors that determines the way to automate. If the department's work is 90 percent project management, then the chosen system must do that function very, very well. Besides need, size and complexity of facilities are the major determinants of what type of FMIS is most appropriate. Those relationships are depicted in Exhibit 20-1.

Research

Probably due to the expense of FM automation, a lot of research is being done on the subject. Data suggest that FM computer usage is related to computer usage in the business as a whole. The facility managers who use FM technology the most are managers of research and data facilities. Within industry groups, manufacturing and government show the highest overall usage. Across all types of facilities, design and drafting is the function most often automated (59 percent), with facility managers often using automation to control inventory (58 percent) and main-

Exhibit 20-1. Facility management information system.

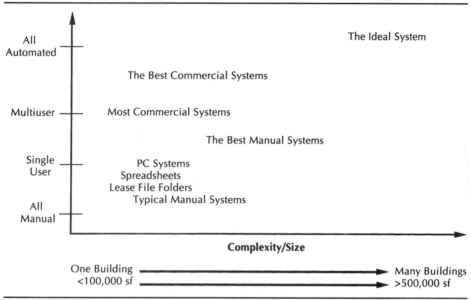

Source: Jeffrey M. Hamer, *Facility Management Systems* (New York: Van Nostrand Reinhold, 1988), p. 17.

tenance (56 percent). No other function was automated by more than half of the respondees. Only 29 percent of them sought an omnibus FMIS solution.[3]

In January 1997, Professor Robert E. Johnson and his staff at the Texas A&M CRS Center for Leadership and Management in the Design and Construction Industry completed an excellent study of FMIS among Fortune 500 companies. It provides good information about the current status of FMIS, how FMIS is perceived, and the future of applications. According to the study, the most helpful application of information technology is to improve inventory management. Sharing information with partner firms, improving collaboration among dispersed team members, improving real estate management, and improving both team and overall productivity also had high perceived value.[4] E-mail was perceived to be the technology with the most value. Also rated highly were CADD, the ability to share files, and shared databases.[5]

Interestingly facility managers felt that over the next five years, it was likely that a broad range of information technologies will become more useful in helping them manage their facilities. E-mail retained its primacy in the five-year projection. Facility managers also had high hopes for omnibus FMIS systems, project management and scheduling software, CADD, shared databases, wireless communications, intelligent building technologies, electronic data interchange, and sharing e-mail files.[6]

One of the conclusions that I draw from this research is that while it is important to facility managers to have the tools to manage the functions mentioned at the beginning of the chapter, they are most concerned with being able to communicate the data from those tools to their constituencies in a way that makes it possible for their customers, teams, management, and the department all to use the information.

A February 1997 Facilities Design and Management survey had some interesting revelations about FMIS systems. In this Internet-conducted survey, facility managers strongly felt that they could not do without an FMIS, and both cost and technology issues were less important than in earlier surveys. Interestingly, technology expenditures were expected almost to double this year (at a time of generally flat or decreasing budgets).

Technical support for software is still an issue. Only 28 percent rated their software dealer as extremely good. Space forecasting, inventory and management systems were not only the most popular systems, they had the highest rating for customers' being extremely satisfied (55–62 percent). Interestingly, space forecasting also had the highest number of facility managers who were extremely dissatisfied with their software (9 percent), followed by financial management, document management, and telecom/datacom management systems (5–7 percent).[7]

Trends

I have already discussed the direction that practitioners felt their companies would go in using FM technologies in the next five years although it is my opinion that either we are not asking the right questions or facility managers are just not very good predictors of the future.

Two individuals have been my mentors in the area of FM technology, particularly trends in the industry. Jeff Hamer of Asset Direction, Inc. in Agoura, California, is a true pioneer in the development of FMIS. He has always viewed an FMIS as a tool to help the facility manager better support the company's business. Eric Teicholz of Graphic Systems, in Cambridge, Massachusetts, is perhaps the best known of all FM technology experts. A prolific writer, he is the expert in developing user requirements for an FMIS and in managing the process to field the technology. I am indebted to both and often cannot separate their views from my own. Their thinking has greatly influenced me in the area of trends.

The most pervasive trend in FM is undoubtedly the opportunities available through the Internet. Facility managers have only scratched the surface of using the Internet to become more effective managers, but everywhere I go, and all facility managers with whom I talk, are experimenting with the Internet as a source of information and better communication. I am working with an entrepreneurial group to provide FM training through distance learning. No longer is it necessary to bring a facility manager to, say, Orlando for a two-day seminar on disaster planning. We can make the same seminar available on a self-paced basis at his workstation. The facility manager can attend any seminar, at home or at work, at a pace and time that is convenient to him. Further, before he starts into a practical application of, for instance, disaster planning in his workplace, we can provide him an update of the material he studied when he took the seminar on-line, pertinent regulations, and other relevant material. The facility manager, using the Internet, totally controls his own training. Later, if he wants information on a particular mechanical system, he can go to that company's web site for product and technical information not formerly available to him directly. Similarly he can visit an information site, such as FMLink, or a chatroom to question his fellow FMs about a particular problem. Through the Internet (or an intranet) the facility manager can share information among dispersed sites, strengthen partnering arrangements through shared information, and set up a work order system. We are just beginning to use the Internet successfully in facility management, but the trend will be to greater and greater use.

A second important trend is the flexibility contained in new FMIS systems that link CADD systems with a geographic information system (GIS) through a relational database. Particularly for managers of large, geographically dispersed facilities, the ability to link graphics to data and then to ask the questions that are pertinent to facility management rather than what has been preprogrammed into the computer is exciting.

Communications technologies and handheld computers combined with software assessment tools offer outstanding opportunities to revolutionize the way facility managers collect information about the status of buildings, conduct building assessments, and manage work in facilities. Imagine a maintenance technician conducting an off-hours inspection of a manufacturing facility. During his inspection, he discovers a major operational problem. He calls it in on his cellular phone so that correction can immediately commence. He enters routine problems into his computer using deficiency and location codes. If there is a problem with a particular piece of equipment, the technician can go to a central location and log on to access automated maintenance instructions, maintenance history, and warranty information (including pictures and operational diagrams) about that piece of equipment. At the end of his shift, he can download his handheld computer into the work management system, which issues work orders for all deficiencies noted. Once those deficiencies are corrected, the workers (who might be contractors) enter time and materials into their handheld computers under the work order code and number. Then they download the data into the work management system at the end of their shift. The work orders are not only closed out, but the time and material are transferred to payroll or to vendor accounts for payment at month's end. At the same time, the assessment data gathered, combined with other assessment data, will provide management with funding profiles for maintenance, repair, and capital replacement.

The obvious difficulty in discussing trends is that there are many opportunities to be wrong. Technologies change; some even fail. New technologies will provide opportunities that I have not even thought about. However, I am reasonably sure that in the short term, the Internet, the linking of CADD with GIS, and the development of new assessment tools will be among the technologies offering facility managers the opportunity to work smarter and be more responsive to the business needs of their companies.

Year 2000 Problem

Facility managers are in a unique situation regarding the Year 2000 problem: They can expect little help in identifying and correcting the problem on their unique systems because their IT departments know little about them. Most experts expect that facility managers will receive major support from their vendors. There appear to be two major areas of concern: obsolescent systems no longer actively supported by a vendor, and embedded systems like HVAC controls, lighting systems, and building access systems. I recommend that facility managers appoint someone to a new position, that of Year 2000 project manager, and charge that manager with coordinating vendor efforts. In addition, your IT and legal departments should help you in writing contracts that require your vendors to meet their Year 2000 responsibilities. For helpful suggestions, see the book *Meeting the Year 2000 Challenge*, from BOMA.

Choosing a System

From this point on, I will discuss only an omnibus FMIS, one that manages the functions set out in the first section of this chapter. The considerations discussed can be applied to choosing an individual work management system or asset management system. I will discuss how to select a system, justify it, and manage a successful installation. Successful management of this process is essential if we are substantially to decrease the amount of "shelfware" that represents both wasted funds and lost opportunities.

Three issues are present in every FMIS procurement; success will depend on the ability to manage them.

First, vendors are infamous for overstating their systems' capabilities—but facility managers are equally infamous for failing to understand what their automation needs really are. For instance, there will be a tendency on the facility manager's part to want to manage far more data than are necessary. At least initially, automate only those subfunctions that need to be managed intensely.

Second, there is a chicken-or-egg dilemma here. Prior to automating any single function, the facility manager will not know how best to do it. There is a synergy in automation that will not be recognized until the project is well under way. The vendor's experience can be helpful here, as is focusing clearly on the automation task at hand, but the facility manager needs to realize that as he automates, he will see opportunities for change and need to be prepared to capitalize on them.

Finally, always balance the urgency of need for an integrated system with slow, methodical implementation steps. Never throw out a critical manual system until the automated system has been installed and a successful test of the system has been made. Keep the long-range goal of complete integration in view, but do not expect it to happen overnight.

In order best to manage those three issues, Jeff Hamer has developed the following list of do's and don'ts:[8]

Do

- Postpone automation until processes are redesigned.
- Ask stupid questions about how things are done.
- Try out rough prototypes for early feedback from the people who will use them.
- Agree on goals, after first hashing out a model of how the problem works.
- Start by fixing a small but annoying problem to win friends.
- Structure big projects so that there are payoffs along the way.
- Select your best employees for the teams even if it means disrupting day-to-day operations.
- Settle for the 80 percent solutions.

Don't

- Try to use a big job to cover the costs.
- Set vague objectives such as "improving productivity."
- Design your project to minimize conflict within the organization.
- Assign project implementation to a technically proficient person unskilled in negotiation.
- Assume that interviewing users reveals exactly what they need.
- Start by looking for places to apply the hottest new technologies.
- Leave technology for last, or you'll overlook opportunities for using it.
- Emphasize incremental improvement if what you really need is fundamental change.

Another important issue is to bring management along throughout the automation process. When there is a good business case, this is much easier to do than ten years ago when management tended to view technology, particularly in a noncore function, as a "nice-to-have" rather than a necessity. The pervasiveness of technology throughout the company has helped here also. Management is likely to ask the following kinds of questions:

- What was the current system meant to accomplish?
- What new tasks need to be accomplished that the current system cannot handle?
- What tasks are currently performed that are no longer necessary?
- What alternatives are available to handle both the old and new requirements?
- What characteristics of each alternative fit well or badly with what needs to be accomplished?
- Last, and perhaps most important, what is best for and what will be accepted by the users?[9]

An additional question that will be asked is, How much does it cost? Facility managers should be able to answer by calculating an internal rate of return, a net present value, or a return on investment. At least one of those figures should already be available since they were used to choose among competing technologies. Costs include hardware and software, conversion of existing systems, training, maintenance and operations, and one-time costs for data input. On the other hand, savings result from any reduced operational costs and from reductions in relocation costs, direct labor, and any savings in space.

One of the simplest but most complete approaches to selecting and implementing an FMIS system has been developed by the Logistics Management Institute, a federally funded, nonprofit research organization that excels in FM consulting (see Exhibit 20-2). This approach may be more elaborate than necessary in every case, but the point is to get a plan. To quote Jeff Hamer again, "No action steps equals no action"[10] and "Even a bad plan is much better than no plan."[11] Another statement that is relevant to purchasing an FMIS is by David Weisberg of Technology Automation Services in the December 1997 *A/E/C Systems:* "In general, I strongly believe that architecture and engineering firms should buy the best hardware and software products that they can afford at any given point in time."

Two substantive documents are critical to the chances of a successful FMIS procurement and implementation once management has bought in. First, there must be a detailed needs analysis for each function that is a candidate for automation. It should consider not only specific problems to be solved by automation, but the need to integrate functions and share information between organizational units and possibly contractors. During the needs analysis, a manager needs to be particularly mindful of company initiatives that might affect his FMIS during or shortly after implementation. For example, designing a system to operate independently, only to have the company become completely networked shortly after FMIS implementation, could render the entire system obsolescent, if not obsolete.

The needs analysis provides the framework for the installation plan. Actually the plan cannot be completed until basic decisions are made on what system will be procured. Do not forget the plan for postinstallation activities, such as system and data update, controls, access procedures, and training.

Once the facility manager has completed the needs analysis and installation plan, he can start to form a detailed budget, the implementation team, and a project schedule. Managing this process is much like managing any other complex project. One word of advice: Assign a budget to each line item of the implementation plan, and make conscious budget reallocation decisions each time a change is necessary (and there will be changes). Ensure that perhaps up to 10 percent of the implementation cost is retained for contingencies. Even if the process is managed well, costs appear during implementation that could not be anticipated in the planning phase. Be cautious, however, because automation projects have a history of cost overruns. The battlefield is littered with the bodies of FM warriors who allowed their implementation budget to grow unchecked until management stepped in, stopping the project and firing the responsible manager.

Here are some guidelines that have proved successful in evaluating and selecting software and will lead to better integration of the total system. The system should:

- Be an enterprise system that contains all the software functionality supporting facility and real estate management functions.

Exhibit 20-2. Approach to FMIS selection and implementation.

Facilities Capabilities Overview

- Provide an overview of FMIS software products on the market.
- Describe FMIS applications.
- Discuss typical training requirements.
- Discuss the general price range of FMIS packages.

Functional Requirement Determination/Needs Analysis

- Review existing LAN/WAN, server, and hardware configurations.
- Develop inventory legacy systems.
- Interview functional/divisional offices; help desk staff and customers; determine needs and expectations.
- Determine business processes for work orders and preventive maintenance, major capital project planning and tracking, space analysis, lease administration, materials management, budgeting, and asset management.
- If requested, recommend business process improvements that could be made prior to implementing an FMIS.
- Develop functional requirements.
- Develop functional requirement priorities on organizational needs and management objectives.
- Brief the staff on prioritized functional requirements for an FMIS.

FMIS Product Analysis and Recommendations

- Survey market literature and associations.
- Develop a Request for Information tailored to the organization's functional requirements.
- Review updated product demonstrations.
- Interview FMIS vendors.
- Document product features.
- Develop a matrix comparing selection criteria to product and vendor features using weighted values.
- Perform a customer satisfaction survey and site visits to organizations that have bought the top-rated product.
- Brief the staff on the results of the matrix.
- For the leading products, coordinate on-site FMIS demonstrations.
- Recommend the FMIS.

Conceptual Design and Implementation Plan

- Develop a conceptual design to include:
    1. Hardware requirements for the selected FMIS
    2. Planned interfaces with legacy systems
    3. System administration issues such as database administration, server operations, backup and storage procedures, training, and contingency planning

(continues)

Exhibit 20-2. (continued)

- Develop a generalized implementation plan and schedule for the FMIS applications the organization will purchase and use.
- Produce a report on the selection process, conceptual design, and implementation plan.

Implementation Support

- Purchase FMIS software and supporting hardware.
- Ensure proper installation of client server hardware.
- Conduct vendor training.
- Develop a detailed implementation plan.
- Conduct regular implementation team meetings.
- Supervise data entry and drawing development/updating.
- Conduct initial and full product rollout.
- Conduct training of all users and customers, if needed.
- Supervise integration with legacy systems.
- Develop and publish instructions and procedures.

Source: Modified from a copyrighted (1977) procedure of the Logistics Management Institute.

- Be modular by allowing use of one or more applications through multiple business units and have the ability to add applications as required.
- Be an off-the-shelf solution, since it offers quicker implementation and better technical support so time and effort can be spent on data standards and input.
- Tie functional and business areas into a singular database and graphics environment.
- Integrate with the organization's standard database, operating system, and networking environments.
- Be able to integrate with the corporate financial and human resources systems.
- Integrate with the CADD system.
- Be easy to use and therefore increase productivity due to shorter ramp-up time with decreased training and support costs.[12]

Many FM systems tend to be unique, and this can be a problem. Many of these systems—project management and financial management, for example—need to mesh with the company's information system. For that reason, an automation system needs to be particularly sensitive to the compatibility issue. For example, you might prefer to adopt Microsoft Project as your project management system rather than to buy a unique construction project management system. Do not be so self-centered in the automation effort that you forget that you must support the business systems of the company.

Selecting a specific system to meet the department's needs is the bottom line of the FM automation process. Actually, good general procurement procedures should ensure the acquisition of the appropriate system, but certain aspects need emphasis. First, I strongly suggest that unless your company has specialized internal expertise (most information systems departments do not have a clue about FM systems), a specialized consultant should be hired to help write specifications and select a vendor. Most major metropolitan areas have consultants who specialize in advising on procuring FM systems.

Second, reduce the list of possible vendors to a short list of two to three, and if at all possible, visit not fewer than two organizations that have each system being considered. Take a small but representative group to visit, but maximize the visit by deciding, with the help of a consultant, what to look for and what questions to ask. A predetermined scorecard of weighted criteria is often helpful to ensure that all systems are analyzed uniformly. Do not forget to inquire about technical support, data upgrade issues, training, and both successes and problems encountered during installation and operation. Compose the team, and visit so that technicians talk to technicians, finance people talk to their counterparts, and the facilities manager speaks to his counterpart. Two questions that I always ask are where the system has exceeded or failed expectations and if he would buy the system again knowing what he now knows.

Third, after reducing the potential vendors to a short list, ask the vendor to prepare a demonstration in the company's facility, using its data and hardware, if possible. Try to demonstrate an activity that is representative of the facility department and important to its success.

Finally, in your contract, give the vendor incentives to make suggestions during the implementation phase that will save money or make the system and the department more effective. Suggestions considered for incentives need to offer truly unexpected opportunities for savings. For an incentive program to be successful, allow the vendor to share in the savings.

Just one note to dampen undue enthusiasm: In a study of the impact of CADD on architectural-engineering firms, automation was found not to be the effective multiplier that it was predicted to be. Productivity gains of 50 to 70 percent were achieved, but it often took a decade to do so. How CADD was used appeared to be a bigger factor than what system was purchased and used. The most productive firms were those that automated most broadly, emphasized training, had the best internal electronic communication to share data, had specific automation managers, and whose basic administrative procedures were better defined prior to automation.[13] While CADD cannot be exactly equated to FMIS, there is a message here for us, and we ignore it at our own peril. Managing the implementation of an FMIS will probably be the single most important event in the tenure of a facility manager. Do it right![14]

Other Technologies

It is difficult to provide a comprehensive overview of technologies that are being used to manage facilities better. The field is very broad, and new technologies enter the market weekly. Following is a listing of technologies that I have seen used with a few brief comments where appropriate. I have emphasized those that help to operate and manage better:

- *Bar coding*—to code-fix assets so that they can be uniquely identified and/ or their location fixed. Although it can be very effective, it is relatively costly to implement and difficult to sustain.
- *Cellular communications*—the principal communications means for work crews.
- *Rugged laptop computers and specialized input-output devices*—to record building deficiencies or assessments and download into the work management system to generate work orders.
- *Regulatory compliance software*—to analyze and document compliance with federal regulations.
- *Analytical software*—to analyze the effects of changes prior to actual installation. One example is an EPA-developed tool to analyze lighting upgrades. ProjectKalc can be downloaded from http://www.epa.gov/docs/gdcoar/ download.html. Other EPA tools are available for analyzing the cost-effectiveness of upgrading variable air volume systems, energy efficiency, and indoor air quality.
- *Environmental and energy management assessment software*—to provide technical and financial assessments of energy management efforts and environmental improvements.
- *Engineered management systems*—decision support tools that permit managers to decide when, where, and how best to maintain facilities.
- *Groupware*—for sharing information within the department or company, or among geographically dispersed groups.
- *Predictive maintenance technology and procedures*—to predict failure of critical equipment prior to failure.

In addition, there is a vast array of automation tools available to managers within the company to help them operate more effectively and efficiently.

Accessing the Internet

The Internet allows almost unlimited access to training and education for the facility manager, at his pace and on his schedule. Every significant vendor and contractor has a web site, where product and service information are available. FMLink and the web sites of the trade journals provide industry news and features—for example, recent regulatory changes that affect facility managers. Appendix C provides a listing of web pages and Internet addresses that offer facility managers more and higher-quality information than ever before available.

Although not all training is suited for it, the Internet will have a profound influence on how facility managers are trained and educated. As of the fall semester of 1998, prospective facility managers were able to take Michigan State University's first Internet course, an introduction to facility management. And, at the time this book was being written, the University of Manitoba was seriously considering offering a curriculum leading to a master's degree in facility management to those interested in graduate-level studies via the Internet.

At the same time, Meridian Knowledge Solutions, Inc. of Chantilly, Virginia, was offering Internet training via two sites. Known as the Facility Management Knowledge Center and the Environmental Safety Occupational Health Knowledge Center, the sites were designed to permit facility managers to obtain high-quality training where and when they want it. The advantage for the trainee is that training is converted from a one-time event to a renewable experience that is integrated with and supportive of work. In addition, because through the Internet a facility manager can obtain FM and real estate training tailored to his needs without leaving home, he not only saves time but also eliminates the need for high-cost travel. Moreover, his training materials, once mastered, will be just a few keystrokes away when he needs them for use on the job.

The Meridian Knowledge Centers were designed to provide services analogous to those offered by a college campus: a broad range of training, information, and networking opportunities. In addition to both self-paced and instructor-led courses, the facility management student, whether in New York, London, or Hong Kong, is able to access lectures by world-class speakers and a broad library of FM-related materials. He can also observe the latest FM products and services, network with colleagues worldwide, and review the latest job postings.

These Knowledge Centers also can provide training to those seeking professional designations, can administer the designation examinations, and can handle the necessary electronic commerce for those designations. And the Knowledge Centers provide potential benefits not only to individual students but also to professional associations, which can use the Centers as a means of projecting their training programs worldwide.

Notes

1. Eric Teicholz, "Technologies for Effective Facility Management," in *Federal Facilities Beyond the 1990's* (Washington, D.C.: National Academy Press, 1997), p. 55.

2. Philip L. Martin, "Improving the Bottom Line Through Computer-Aided Facility Management," *Metropolitan Views* (Summer 1996): 12.

3. *Facility Management Practices* (Houston: International Facility Management Association, 1996), p. 24.

4. *The Impact of Information Technology on Facility Management Practice* (College Station, Tex.: Texas A&M, 1997), p. 7.

5. Ibid., p. 9.

6. Ibid., p. 12.

7. Eric Teicholz, ed., "Space Functions Lead in '96 CAFM Survey," *Facilities Design and Management* (February 1997): 44–49.

8. Jeffrey Hamer, "Best Practices in Technology Management," in *Conference Proceedings of World Workplace '95* (Houston: International Facility Management Association, 1995), p. 969.

9. George Laszlo, quoted in *Managing Facility Technology* (Arnold, Md.: BOMI Institute, 1989), pp. 12–17. Reprinted by permission of the BOMI Institute.

10. Hamer, "Best Practices," p. 968.

11. Ibid., p. 966.

12. Robb Dods and Rein Vares, "Strategic Asset Management Systems for Facility and Real Estate Management," *Facility Management Journal* (November–December 1997): 16.

13. George B. Korte, "CADD and A/E Firms: 10 Years Later," *The Military Engineer* (April–May 1996): 27–28. By permission of The Society of American Military Engineers (SAME).

14. Five excellent references on implementing an FMIS follow. Jeffrey Hamer, "Best Practices in Technology Management," in *Conference Proceedings, World Workplace '95,* (Houston: International Facility Management Association, 1995), pp. 961–972; Peter S. Kimmel, "Critical Ingredients for a Successful CAFM Installation," in *Conference Proceedings, World Workplace '95* (Houston, International Facility Management Association, 1995), pp. 913–925; Eric Teicholz, "The Business Side of Technology," in *Conference Proceedings, World Workplace '94* (Houston: International Facility Management Association, 1994), pp. 99–108; Eric Teicholz, "Cost/Benefit Analysis Justifies CAFM Investment," *Facilities Design and Management* (August 1990); and Eric Teicholz, *Computer-Aided Facility Management* (New York: McGraw-Hill, 1992), which is out of print but available through amazon.com. This classic of the field is worth hunting for.

21

A Problem Solver Looks at the Future of Facility Management

I recently pulled a *Building Operating Management* article off Facilities Net, on the Internet—a summary of a survey of 323 facility managers. It appears that the sample may have been biased toward those with heavy operations and maintenance responsibility. What caught my attention was the fact that for the first time in close to a decade, facility managers were optimistic. Despite human resources cutbacks, for example, most facility managers think that their departments are more effective than they were three years ago.

Another interesting aspect of that survey involves the relationship of the facility manager with his manager. Sixty-eight percent of those responding felt that their departments were understood and appreciated. At the same time, those who did not feel appreciated felt that that was a major source of stress. Surprisingly, top management support did not seem really to help protect the facility manager's job, but 65 percent of the respondees viewed loss of their job as unlikely.

Several other perception issues are interesting. Facility managers and top management concur that providing quality FM services and cost control are key goals for the facilities department. Predictably, top management sees the importance of these goals as co-equal, while the facility managers considered providing quality services far more important. Only 27 percent of top managers view facilities as valuable in improving productivity, while 44 percent of facility managers rank better productivity as a top goal.

Some of the results of this survey are counterintuitive but interesting. Facility managers who have implemented broad-based management practices like strategic business planning and total quality management have improved the perception of the facility department within the company. However, benchmarking and reengineering are more common in companies where the value of facilities is less appreciated. (Perhaps they are being implemented for the express purpose of improving the department's image.)

One in five facility managers surveyed had lost a job from downsizing, but at the same time facility departments were being downsized by 40 percent. Facility managers have frustrations, particularly regarding inadequate budgets and lack of management interest, but most facility managers are optimistic about the future. Eighty-one percent would recommend the profession to a college student. The top recommendation that they would give to that student to prepare for the future is to be able to respond to change.[1]

One way to look at this survey is that it matters little whether it is representative of the profession or even valid. Nonetheless, it is an excellent vehicle for a hard look at facility management—where it still needs to improve in practice and as a profession and where it is going in the future.

Needed Improvements in Facility Management as a Profession

A good case can be made that facility management is gaining in recognition and appreciation within companies, and that seems to be the feeling of the facility managers surveyed. Although progress has been made in developing truly professional facility managers, I recognize some basic weaknesses in the profession that need to be addressed.

• *Lack of unity.* First, and perhaps most important, the profession is suboptimized because the professional associations are so fractionated. For example, if I were an editor at *Forbes* or *Business Week,* what organization would I go to to speak for this profession? AFE? APPA? APWA? BOMA? IREM? IDRC? IFMA? ISFE? NACORE? Where does the dean of a forward-thinking business school go when he wants information regarding educational requirements for a course or module in corporate real estate and facility management? Where does the federal buildings bureaucracy go for participants in studies, policy input, and research guidance? The proliferation of associations actually makes each organization less powerful than it would be by itself (the reverse of synergy). There have been recent meetings among some of the parties and signs of partnership, and it cannot come too quickly. For example, APPA has some superior publications and research that are scarcely known outside its membership. The BOMI Institute has an excellent publication bureaucracy that could serve all property and facility management organizations. The professional organizations that serve facility managers would do well to establish partnership goals, consider some consolidation, and have at least an annual summit.

• *Research.* Research needs to be of a higher quality. With the exception of APPA, research efforts are not well known outside each individual organization. Too much research time is spent defining facility managers and facility management rather than producing research helpful to practitioners. Some of the research that is being pursued is applicable to only a minute sector of facility managers. Too much of it concerns itself with the office building. The professional organizations try to do too much of the research in-house, while some of the universities that have FM programs struggle for research funds. The excellent work on FM technology by Texas A&M shows what can be done using university research. A multiorganizational summit, with NIST invited, to develop research goals would be desirable. Each organization could then fund whichever proportion of those goals is most sought by their membership, with universities doing the actual research. Three research topics need to be addressed:

1. How can it be proved that better facility management increases employee productivity and how much improvement occurs from which action?
2. How much should an organization invest annually in the maintenance and repair of its building inventory?
3. How should facility departments be organized?

• *Certification/designations.* Employers seem to be slowly recognizing professional certification and designations; I now see them being specified as a qualification or desirable trait in job advertisements. However, since different professional associations and university programs award different designations, facility managers are confusing the public and their management (as well as members who do not understand the difference between a certificate and certification). The professional associations and the universities need to come up with common designations and criteria. The BOMI Institute may be willing to relinquish its franchise to award certain designations if given a larger share of the publication market. Professional associations in North America need to get their collective act together so that they are ready to deal with the issue of international certification and designations.

• *Public relations.* There needs to be a broad-based improvement in the public understanding of facility management. Several target constituencies are vital. Since business schools at best offer one real estate class to their M.B.A. students, it is no wonder there is a lack of understanding of facility management among top managers of companies. Another target should be the business press. There are enough exciting and controversial FM topics to have one covered in each of the major business journals, the major metropolitan business newspapers, and *The Wall Street Journal* once a quarter. Everyone agrees that this is needed, yet there is no organized effort by the professional associations to see that it happens. Finally, we should be targeting the management gurus with information on trends and issues in facility management. Why doesn't the Center for Creative Leadership, for example, have a case study that emphasizes successful facility management?

• *Technology transfer.* A tremendous amount of knowledge and many tools for good facility management have been developed by the federal government but are unknown to the private sector. Professional associations certainly need to reach out to federal government members, but they also need to tap into some of the resources developed with tax dollars. Some of the web sites listed in Appendix C will help facility managers see what types of tools are available and will give them an initial contact.

Needed Improvements in the Practice of Facility Management

• *FM as a business function.* Facility managers need to view themselves as business managers and justify their departments and their initiatives in business terms. They need to use life-cycle costing and make go/no-go decisions and prioritize using net present value analyses or internal rate of return. There should be a facility business plan for every company business plan, and the facility manager must view himself as a businessperson, not as a technician. He must be able to speak the language of business.

• *New work methods.* Facility managers need to press for the support needed for telecommuting, hoteling, the virtual office, and all of the other new work forms that companies are using. If the preliminary evidence is any indication, the facility manager will find himself at the center of support, legal, and risk management issues raised by these new work forms and styles.

• *Organizational structures.* No one seriously questions that there are unique aspects of each of our departments. However, for too long, we have used these rather minor differences to justify failure to come to grips with how best to organize departments. APPA has been a refreshing exception to that statement. It realized that there is in fact a better way to organize the physical plant department on college campuses. Chapter 2 represents my contribution to the body of knowledge on this topic, but serious research needs to be done and practitioners need to start using best practices for best results. Finally, don't confuse outsourcing, which is a staffing issue, with organization. The best organization does not depend on whether staffing is in-house or outsourced.

• *Outsourcing.* I confess a bias toward outsourcing. It is time to outsource more intelligently. Specifically, facility managers should write performance-based contracts and partner with their outsourcing contractor. My personal bias is toward body-shop contracting by trade or function, with management being retained in-house except for large project work. Successful outsourcing occurs when the right contract documents and attitudes are in place so that the contracted employees feel they are the facility department's employees, and the facility manager feels they are his employees.

• *Customer orientation.* Successful facility managers realize that their customers expect to be part of all decisions that affect them, are used to just-in-time delivery of services, and want to share all pertinent information. Never before in my experience have expectations been so high. The customers want choices. If they are paying for facility services through chargeback, why shouldn't they have choices? Customer service demands will only increase. One of the greatest challenges facing facility managers will be to gather customer expectations for and perceptions of the department and how to communicate with customers through multimedia.

• *Response.* Another major cultural shift occurring in companies, and which will be applied to facility managers, is the need for improved response time. It will no longer be acceptable to tell customers that the department will change a light bulb in two days. The facility manager had better reengineer work methods and processes so that a technician can change that bulb routinely in two hours . . . or in twenty minutes.

• *Better tools and benchmarks.* Doing more and being more responsive with fewer resources means that facility managers need to be able to measure work realistically and have better evaluative tools. Some of these tools are coming online, but too many facility managers in the United States still tend to manage by intuition instead of bringing real rigor, particularly financial rigor, to their departments. Canadian and European facility managers have much more rigorous fiscal goals for each of their functions and use evaluative tools to ensure they are making progress toward those goals. Facility managers should be seeking tools that can better assess the condition of their buildings and help predict the funds and effort to maintain them in a state of high productivity.

• *Reinstitute energy management.* Facility managers in the United States need to reinvigorate the energy management measures that they instituted during the last oil crisis. New heating and cooling equipment is much more efficient than that installed twenty years ago. Not all of the measures that were implemented in the 1970s are saleable to management and customers in the current period of cheap energy, but some of the measures simply need to be restored. A company that is energy conscious will likely benefit from the deregulation of the energy industry currently under way in the United States.

• *Seek a differentiator.* In order to be recognized and to have credibility within the company, the facility manager needs to stand out. He has unique skills and is positioned to do just that. For instance, he might offer to lead the company's business planning effort if no business planning procedures are in place. That offer probably won't be accepted, but it might move the company to action, and the facility manager can then be a major contributor to company business planning. Similarly, the facility manager could be the company's environmentalist, could lead its emergency planning effort, or could be a major contributor to developing a risk management plan. Volunteering for additional responsibilities offers little risk because the facility manager would be a major contributor in such planning anyway. The upside is that the facility manager will be noted as both a business manager and a team player, both valued roles.

• *Public relations.* No one can represent his department better than the facility manager. He owes it to his department to promote it and to represent it well. Unfortunately, most of us, by education and personality type, would rather retreat to our offices and ensure that our departments run well. If you can't write, go to a community college and take an English course. If you can't speak publicly well, join Toastmasters. Because the facility function is not a core competency, the facility department starts out at a disadvantage within the company. The facility manager must work hard to level the playing field. I recommend a simple annual public relations plan for the department that outlines one or two specific actions to promote the department to each of its constituencies: company employees, management, visitors, department employees, and any others.

The Future

I certainly have no ability to predict the future, but I do get to observe over a hundred facility departments annually. My travels to China and Russia have also helped to coalesce my observations and opinions regarding the future. For those who desire other views on the future of facility management, I recommend the magazine roundtable of facility management experts gathered by *Facilities Design and Management* to celebrate its fifteenth anniversary as recorded in the 1997 special advertising section.

For my first observation, I return to my comments concerning the Internet. Using the Internet successfully, the facility manager will be able to transform his job. He will be able to access nearly any fact, refresh himself on any procedure before performing it, train himself at his workstation (or at home), get advice from experts in a chatroom, sample customer perceptions, and reply to customer inquiries. He will be able to do this from a location and at a time that are convenient to him. Effective use of the Internet can transform the role of the facility manager.

The profession will become increasingly international. One of the most pleasurable parts of my life has been to spread the gospel internationally and to help professional associations take root outside North America. As the economies of developing countries improve, businesspeople will start to be concerned about managing their facilities properly. Entrepreneurs are already taking FM services into some of these nations. As some of the great command economies privatize, the management of the huge inventory of state-owned facilities will be critical. The record to date is that managing those facilities has not had a high priority during privatization, perhaps because it is too closely associated with the old central planning model. This situation is fertile ground for some effective salesmanship by the FM profession.

Better tools are becoming available, and they will get even better. Facility managers soon will have an FMIS that is truly responsive to management needs. Facility managers, with little effort or training, can now choose the best fit among several buildings based on a profile of their company's operational needs. Predictive maintenance tools can allow them to repair critical equipment before it breaks down. New assessment methods and models will allow them to develop funding and maintenance profiles for facilities with minimal testing. The U.S. Department of the Army has already fielded some of these tools.

One of my colleagues and co-authors, Stormy Friday, feels that facility managers, or at least that title, will disappear. Downsizing started that process. Many middle managers were eliminated, and facility managers found themselves with broader administrative duties. Some have actually become vice presidents or directors of administration or general services, though they may not have those titles. I anticipate no diminuition of the concern for costs or expansion of the bureaucracy in the future. Facility managers over time are likely to take on more and more responsibilities. Those who are the best businesspeople, speak the language of business, and are perceived to support the company's business best will be successful.

Energy deregulation will be a major near-term challenge because it will affect every company differently. Some companies may become energy providers if that fits their business profile. Some major users will undoubtedly be able to negotiate better rates than they have now. Others may want to pool their energy needs to take advantage of their clout in the marketplace in that way. Others will see their energy rates rise.

I close this section, chapter, and the book by listing the skill set for the facility manager of the future as spelled out by Tony Zulkeski, one of the truly original thinkers in our profession. Here are Tony's "hot skills" for future FMs, with my slight modification for clarity.[2]

- Be a change agent.
- Be a decision maker.
- Be a people leader.
- Be an entrepreneur.
- Set and follow through on priorities.
- Develop and maintain a network.
- Get knocked around (be visible, be open to criticism, and manage by walking around).
- Don't confuse truth with conventional wisdom.
- Be the type of person whom other people trust.
- Be flexible.

Notes

1. The Facilities Net (Internet) version of "Coping in Turbulent Times," *Building Operating Management* (January 1997): 1–6.
2. Anthony G. Zulkeski, "The FM as Change Agent," *Facilities Design and Management*, 15th Anniversary Special Advertising Section, 1997, p. 64.

Appendix A

The Facility Manager's Tool Kit of References

During thirty-five years as a practitioner and fifteen years as a writer, educator and speaker, I have assembled what I consider my tool kit of references that I turn to time and again and periodicals that keep me abreast of not only topics of the day, but of new products and services available and of those individuals whose expertise I might need to solve a practical, educational, or research problem.

My tool kit is highly personalized. In general, I have used all of these references or have reason to believe that they are unique or the best in the field. (Many of my favorites are technical, which tend to go out of print in two or three years, an unfortunate fact of life.)

Books

General References

A college or publication house style manual
A college English text
A college basic statistics text
A college text on management theory and behavior
A college text on human relations management
Facilities Management, by Edmond P. Rondeau, Robert Kevin Brown, and Paul Lapides
Facilities Management: A Manual for Plant Administration, (4 volumes) by APPA
Facilities Management Casebook, 1996, edited by Keith Alexander

Building Commissioning

The Building Commissioning Handbook, by John A. Heinz and Rick Casault

Business Planning

Planning for Nonplanners, by Darryl J. Ellis and Peter J. Pekar

Communications

Communicating at Work, by Adler and Elmhorst
Managing the Interview, by John F. Olsen
Send Me a Memo, by Diana Boocher
We've Got to Start Meeting Like This, by Roger K. Nelson and Robert T. Nelson
Winning Numbers, by Michael C. Thomsett

Computer-Aided Facility Management

Computer Aided Facility Management, by Eric Teicholz
Facility Management Technology, by Eric Teicholz and Takehiko Ikeda

Datacommunications and Telecommunications Management

Handbook of Communications Systems Management, by James W. Coward

Disaster and Recovery Planning

Before Disaster Strikes, by Institute of Real Estate Management
Business Resumption Planning, by Emergency Preparedness Canada
Planning and Recovery—A Guide for Facilities Professionals, by Alan M. Levitt

Financial Management

Benchmarking, by Robert C. Camp
Successful Funding Strategies for Facility Renewal, by Matthew C. Adams

Human Resources Management

Tapping Potential: Issues in Human Resource Management, by APPA

Management and Leadership

Basic Tools for Facility Supervisors, by APPA
Leaders, by Warren Bennis and Burt Nanus
The Leadership Challenge, by James M. Kouzes and Barry Posner

Managing in the 90's, by Peter Drucker

Perspectives on Leadership in Facilities Management, edited by Charles W. Jenkins

Operations and Maintenance

Building Control Systems, by Vaughn Bradshaw

Building Technology, by Benjamin Stein

The Complete Manual of Corporate and Industrial Security, by Russell L. Bintliff

Electrical Distribution and Maintenance, by Mohammad H. Qayoumi

Energy Management Workbook, by APPA

Environmental Management, by Regina Clarke

The Facilities Audit, by Harvey Kaiser

Facilities Maintenance Management, by Gregory H. Magee

The Facilities Manager's Reference, by Harvey H. Kaiser

Facility Maintenance, by Donn Brown

Fire Protection, by David Wagner

Hazardous Materials and Solid Waste Management, by APPA

Managing Housekeeping and Custodial Operations, by Edwin B. Feldman

Safety Management, by Joseph Gustin

Water Quality and Systems, by Robert Reid

Organizational Behavior

Corporate Cultures, by Terrence E. Deal and Allen Kennedy

Groups That Work (and Groups That Don't), edited by J. Richard Hackman

Life in Organizations, edited by Rosabeth Moss Kanter and Barry Stein

Planning and Design

The ADA in Practice, by Deborah Kearney

Designing the Office of the Future, by Volker Hartkopf, Vivian Loftness, Pleasantine Drake, Peter A. D. Mill, and George R. Ziga

Facilities Planning, by Roger Brauer

Facilities Planning Handbook, edited by Lee Ingalls, Barbara Bruxvoort, and Jason Mihos

Managing the Reinvented Workplace, by William Sims, Michael Joroff, and Franklin Becker

Office Design, by Peter B. Brandt

The Office Interior Design Guide, by Julie K. Rayfield

Planning and Managing Interior Projects, by Carol E. Farren

Successful Interior Projects Through Effective Contract Documents, by Joel Downey and Patricia K. Gilbert

Total Workplace Performance, by Stan Aronoff and Audrey Kaplan

Workplace by Design, by Franklin Becker and Fritz Steele

Project Management

AMA Handbook of Project Management
Value Engineering, by Alphonse Dell 'Isola

Real Estate and Lease Management

Dictionary of Real Estate, by Jae K. Shim, Joel G. Siegel and Stephen W. Hartman
Managing Corporate Real Estate, by Kevin Brown, Alvin Arnold, Paul Lapides, and Edmond
    P. Rondeau

Security

The Complete Manual of Corporate and Industrial Security, by Russell L. Bintliff
Preventing Violence in the Workplace, by Charles E. Labig

Total Quality Management

At America's Service, by Karl Albrecht
Benchmarks, by Robert Camp
ISO 9000 Book, by John Rabbit and Peter Bergh
Managing Quality Facilities, by Stormy Friday and David G. Cotts
Quality Is Free, by Philip B. Crosby
Re-engineering the Corporation, by Michael Hammer and James Champy
Reinventing Government, by David Osborne and Ted Gaebler
Service America, by Karl Albrecht and Ron Zemke

Proceedings

Annual Proceedings of the Annual Meeting, APPA
Annual Proceedings of World Workplace, IFMA
Semiannual Proceedings of the IFMA Best Practices Forum

Magazines

Professional Journals

Facilities Engineering Journal, AFE
Facilities Manager, APPA
Facility Management Journal, IFMA
Journal of Property Management, IREM

Trade Publications

Building Operating Management
Buildings
Canadian Facility Management & Design
Construction Business Review
Contract Design
Engineering News-Record
Facilities Design and Management
Maintenance Solutions
Managing Office Technology
Today's Facility Manager

Newsletters

Facility Manager's Alert, by Progressive Business Publications
The Outsource Report, by Miller-Freeman
Pride, by Tompkins Associates

Appendix B

Best Practices in Facility Management

One of my greatest frustrations has been the failure of facility managers to practice, educators to teach, and the professional associations to adequately promote best practices. We do not each need to reinvent the wheel. Often the minor adaptation of a best practice can be highly successful. For too long, facility managers have ignored best practices, using the excuse that their department was unique, and thus ignoring the 70 to 80 percent of good facility management to be gained by adopting best practices.

The International Facility Management Association (IFMA) should be commended for its semiannual best practices forums where attendees are required to present a best practice as a prerequisite to attendance. The proceedings of these forums are an excellent source of implementable best practices for facility managers.

Following are examples of what I consider best practices in facility management. The list represents my personal experience or enough knowledge of the implementation of the best practice to recommend it. Where I have the name of a practitioner, I have provided that so that the individual can be contacted.

Annual report. Facility departments should publish an annual report for both internal and customer use. It should stress scope of services and accomplishments against goals and be eye-catching and easy to read. BellSouth Telecommunications Property & Service Management publishes an outstanding annual report.

Benchmarking. Using the book by Robert Camp as a guide, facility managers should initially identify at least one unit cost and one measurement of customer service, response, or effectiveness for every service provided. Once these measures have been identified, select the five or six that are critical and benchmark those measures with three groups: similar organizations, competitors, and best in class.

Building permits. After being pilloried by their management for failure to provide projects on a timely schedule, the Silicon Valley Chapter of the IFMA decided to partner with the permitting authorities in the various jurisdictions to expedite the issuing of permits while maintaining the public safety and interest. Using business process engineering techniques, permit processes were simplified and application processing times reduced substantially.

Capital budget decision making. All capital projects, and all annually funded projects over a certain value (perhaps $100,000), should be analyzed using either a five-year net present value analysis or by calculating an internal rate of return. Depending on the cost of capital and any internal guidance, projects can then be dispassionately accepted or rejected and prioritized if capital funding is limited.

Chargebacks and allocations. Facility departments should clearly define, perhaps in the form of an informal "lease," those services provided by the facility department for a base "rent." Services over and above this "work letter standard" are charged back to the applicable business unit. (See Space Allocation and Chargeback System below)

Cleaning and custodial quality management. By involving the end users in the setting of custodial targets, priorities and standards, the Boeing Defense and Space Group in Huntsville, Alabama, has eliminated the task-frequency-type custodial contract that so many facility managers find inadequate. Inherent in this partnering effort are other quality efforts; making custodians take ownership for their area of cleaning, quality inspections, and establishing targets in the contract document.

Computer-assisted facility management (CAFM). A large facility department should have a CAFM system capable of integrating work management, computer-assisted design and drawing, financial management, project management, space management and assignments, chargebacks, lease management, and inventory management. Systems now exist that can be operated by in-house employees and do not rely on a fixed menu of queries. Using a geographic information system application and a relational database, the facility manager should be able to obtain management information from his CAFM system as long as the raw data have been loaded.

Contingency consultants. Consultants will do their work for a share of the savings that they can gain for the client. Long-distance phone bill and energy bill analysis are common examples. If the facility manager checks out their references, such consultants can give the department value at no cost.

Coordination at the workplace installation level. The facility department that has a large volume of renovation and relocation projects should establish integrated work crews with all crafts necessary to accomplish the most common type of project. Even in contracted workforces, one craft should be the lead, responsible to coordinate each craft on-site at the appropriate time. By working together regularly, these teams will be much more efficient than when working as individual crafts. When possible, each team should serve the same customers.

Credit card use. Many facility managers use credit cards to increase response and reduce the administrative burden of their department. Some view credit cards as a way to reduce nonoperational staffing and the unnecessary "administrivia" associated with centralized purchasing. Contact Debbie Perrelli, Sikorsky Aircraft Corp.

Customer response. The facility manager cannot operate a successful customer service program without customer response. No one method will be universally successful. The facility manager must develop a program that includes surveys, response cards, e-mail, focus groups, and individual conversations with supported managers. The customer response program must change over time because any one method of measurement has a limited effectiveness cycle. It is important to track customer satisfaction over time. The IFMA Standardized FM Customer Satisfaction Questionnaire is outstanding, but after about two years of completing a single questionnaire, customers will stop filling it out. Remember the cardinal rule: The effectiveness of the facility department is as perceived by the customer only. The Friday Group of Annapolis, Maryland, is expert in facility management customer service, marketing, and public relations.

Empowered teams. The Facility Department of the Johns Hopkins University's Applied Physics Laboratory has a track record of using empowered teams in facility management to include tying compensation to performance as a team member. Contact is Jim Loesch, chief facilities engineer.

Energy deregulation and efficiency. Many of us should reactivate the energy management plans that over the years we have moved away from as the costs of energy and the emphasis on conservation have declined. Simply returning to the standards by which we operated in the early 1970s could produce major savings for our departments. Also, large energy users should have assessed, internally or through the use of a consultant, how deregulation of the energy companies will affect them. A knowledgeable consumer will be an economical consumer.

Facilities audit. A technical evaluation of facilities normally conducted by an architectural-engineering firm, which results not only in an evaluation of your building but an operations and maintenance funding profile and a capital renewal plan.

Facilities Day. Annually sponsor a Facilities Day, a combination of fun and facilities-oriented work by the company staff at large. This type of event has been successful at many companies and might contain a day to purge files and turn them in for permanent filing, trash clean-up, turn-in and redistribution of furniture excess to departments, the sale of used furniture and equipment through a silent or regular auction, a recycling demonstration, and a display advertising all FM services and how to obtain them. Attendance can be increased by offering prizes throughout the day.

Facility business planning. The single greatest way to save money is to do a more effective job of facility business planning. There should be a facility business plan for every company business plan. The plan should be structured in the same way that the facility manager budgets (programmatic budgeting) so that any program can be tracked from the strategic facility business plan through the annual work plan, to and through the budget. Once budgeted, the expenses in any one program can be compared to similar expenses in any time period (e.g., yesterday, last week, last month, last quarter, last year, two years ago). Similarly a program (such as the capital program) can be checked for its impact on any other program (such as operations and maintenance or leasing).

Improving response rates on customer surveys. Many facility managers have found that the response rate for customer service surveys has dropped off to rates that threaten the value of the input. By packaging their survey better, targeting it to a midrange reading level, overcommunicating, and institutionalizing customer feedback, facility managers can improve the value of data received. Contact is Geoffrey L. Smith, Arbitron Company, Columbia, Maryland.

ISO 9000 certification. The ISO 9000 standard for quality management creates the foundation for total quality management. If a facility manager seeks ISO 9000 certification, not only will the department improve, but it will likely become more understandable to business unit managers who deal with international standards in their products or services.

Maintenance and repair funding. Companies should annually fund the maintenance and repair program at 2 to 4 percent of the replacement value of the buildings supported. Custodial costs are not included, but a small amount of renovation, traditionally done with maintenance and funds, is included. This approach is recommended by the National Science Foundation.

Managing with metrics. Business units and their managers are judged based on a variety of ratios and numerical goals. Facility managers need to think like business managers and develop metrics by which they can be measured. The metrics need to evolve from the strategic business plan of the company. Contact is Ed Pagliassotti, TRW Space and Electronics Group.

Orientation of new employees. The facility manager or his representative should brief all new employees on services offered (a brochure is helpful), how to obtain them, and what type of response can be expected. Special programs like energy management and recycling should be stressed.

Philosophy of the department. Facility departments need to change from a production and process orientation to a business orientation, where the customer's perception of customer service is supreme. Facility managers need to view themselves as customer-oriented business managers, not technical managers.

Preventive maintenance in interior space. Apply the same principles to the building systems that are in interior space that you do to major equipment systems. Send two-person teams each quarter through all interior space. Their mission is fourfold: (1) to be the eyes and ears of the facility department to the administrative personnel of the organization; (2) to repair or replace any small items reported to them by their clients or that they observe; (3) to report any items beyond their ability to repair; and (4) to sweep through all public areas prior to business hours daily and sweep all executive areas weekly. Put them in distinctive uniforms so that customers see them whenever they are in the area. A goal of this program should be to form a bond between these teams and the customers they serve. These teams are an excellent source of manpower for light construction and renovation at peak times.

Programmatic budgeting. The budget is formatted and accounting is done by using facility programs, logical groupings of work. This permits the manager to measure the impact of programs on each other and track the growth or decline of programs from the facility business plan to the annual work plan to the budget. Once budgeted, programs can be monitored from month to month, quarter to quarter, and year to year.

Public relations. Facility managers at all levels should have an annual public relations plan. The plan should have two or three public relations objectives each year for each target group (e.g., customers, visitors, management) to publicize the work of the facility department.

Quality management metrics. Using the same type of total quality management (TQM) tools and methods that they apply to their business processes, the Facilities Department at Hewlett-Packard has installed a Quality Maturity System to integrate the principles of TQM into the very fabric of its facility management processes. Contact is Frank Yockey, Quality/Productivity Manager, Fort Collins, Colorado.

Serviceability. By using profiles of his organization and by developing profiles for buildings, the facility manager can make objective buy, build, or lease decisions by comparing the profiles. Contacts are Gerald Davis and Francoise Szigeti at the International Centre for Facilities.

Space allocation and chargeback system. The Laboratory Operations Directorate of IBM's Watson Research Center has created a space allocation and tracking system and chargeback mechanism that takes into account varying space types, demand on facility services, occupancy rates, and the quantity of space occupied. Rather than charge the same rate for all departments, this system recognizes the different demands on facility resources and adjusts "rents" accordingly. Contact is Alan D. Wilson, Fellow, IEEE.

Strategic space forecasting. Bottom-up space forecasting is often limited by the lack of strategic vision and misleading estimates by lower-level line managers. Companies have developed predictive tools for modeling space needs based on nontraditional indicators such as productivity targets, business outputs, and policies. Contact is William Adams, Project Management, Dallas, Texas.

Supplier Consolidation. Over the years, many facility departments have accumulated a large number of suppliers of goods and services. By consolidating those suppliers, the facility manager can often reduce administrative costs and get volume discounts. Often during the process, partnership arrangements can replace traditional contracting.

Work reception. All work should be received, prioritized, and coordinated by a single entity, the work reception center. This center can also be used to coordinate the sampling and gathering of customer service response.

Appendix C

Web Sites and Internet Addresses

Access to the Internet is the single greatest management tool that has appeared during my career. The Internet can change the way that we work. Training, regulatory information, networking, opinion, product and service information, information on the professional associations, and access to industry leaders are available to us on our desktops (or in our homes) when we want it. Some of these services traditionally have not been available because they were geographically remote or cost too much. Internet access changes that. Every facility manager should develop a working knowledge of the Internet as part of his managerial kit bag.

Peter Kimmel of FMLink has led the effort to provide needed information and networking opportunities to the profession. The profession owes him a debt of gratitude.

There is no major product or service that is not on a provider web site. Even if you don't know the exact address, it is easy to find almost any company just by going to the address http://www._____.com or org or gov. I have never failed to find a company that I was seeking in fewer than three tries. Because these sites are so easily found, I have not included them in the list that follows. Education sites are listed in Appendix D. I have included only those sites or addresses where some information is available at no cost. Unless noted, all addresses listed need to be preceded by http://www.

The web is increasing so fast that I no doubt have missed some sites and overlooked others. I hope you can find the sites here that will fit your needs. If not, experiment a bit using one of the search engines, and you will almost certainly find what you need on the web. In most cases, I have provided a URL (address for a web site). Where none exists I have included an e-mail address.

Good web surfing.

Cost Data

R.S. Means—rsmeans.com
Whitestone Reserach—whitestoneresearch.com

Energy Conservation and Efficiency

U.S. Department of Energy, Office of Energy Efficiency and Renewable Energy—eren.doe.gov
Environmental Protection Agency's Greenlights Program—epa.gov/green lights.html
World Energy Efficiency Association—weea.org
International District Energy Association—energy.rochester.edu/idea
Center for Renewable Energy and Sustainable Technology—solstice.crest.org

Events Information

American Institute of Architects—aia.org
Facility Management Knowledge Center—fmkc.com
FMLink—fmlink.com
International Facility Management Association—ifma.org

Job Mart

Facility Management Knowledge Center—fmkc.com
FMLink—fmlink.com
Friday Group—fridaygroup@erols.com
International Facility Management Association—ifma.org

Newsgroups and Forums

Facility Management Knowledge Center—fmkc.com
FMLink—FMLink.com

Outsourcing

Outsourcing Institute—outsourcing.com
Corbett Associates—corbettassociates.com

Professional Associations

American Institute of Architects—aia.org
American Planning Association—planning.org
American Public Works Association—pubworks.org
American Society of Civil Engineers—asce.org
American Society of Heating, Refrigerating and Air-Conditioning Engineers—ashrae.org
American Society of Interior Designers—asid.org
American Society of Mechanical Engineers—asme.org
American Society for Quality—asqc.org
APPA, the Association of Higher Education Facilities Officers—appa.org
Association of Energy Engineers—aeecenter.org
Association for Facilities Engineering—afe.org
Building Owners and Managers Association—boma.org
Euro FM—dis.strath.ac.uk/guests/eurofm

Institute of Electrical and Electronic Engineers, Inc.—ieee.org
Institute of Real Estate Management—irem.org
International Association of Professional Security Consultants, Inc.—iapsc.org
International Development Research Council—idrc.org
International Facility Management Association—ifma.org
International Society of Facilities Executives—isfe.org
NACORE–International Association of Corporate Real Estate Executives,
   Project Management Institute—pmi.org
Society of American Military Engineers—same.org

Professional Journals

Note: Professional journals can normally be accessed at their professional or-
   ganization's web site.
Facilities Journal—steve@appa.org
Disaster Recovery Journal—drj.com/special/srl.html
FMJ (Facility Management Journal)—communications@ifma.org
Journal for Alternative Office Environments—altoffice.com
Journal of Property Management—irem.org
The Military Engineer—same.org

Regulatory Information

Air Quality Standards for Smog and Particulate Matter—http://ttnwww.
   rtpnc.epa.gov/naaqsfin/index.htm
Americans with Disabilities Act—usa.net/ada_infonet
EPA—epa.gov/epahome/rules.html
FEMA emergency planning—fema.gov/fema/biz2.htm
OSHA—osha.gov

Reliability Information for Engineering and Maintenance

Machinery Information Management Opens Systems Alliance—mimosa.org
Maintenance and Reliability Center—engr.utk.edu/mrc
National Information Center for Reliability Engineering—enre.umd.edu/
   mainjs.html
Reliability Analysis Center—http://rome.iitri.com/rac

Research

American Productivity and Quality Center—apqc.org
American Public Works Association—pubworks.org
American Society for Testing and Materials—astm.org
American Society of Heating, Refrigeration and Air-Conditioning Engi-
   neers—ashrae.org
American Society for Quality—asqc.org
Army Center for Public Works—usacpw.belvoir.army.mil
Army Environmental Center—APGEA.army.mil:8080

Center for Building Performance and Diagnostics—arc.cmu.edu/cbpd
Center for Job Order Contracting Excellence—eas.asu.edu/joc
Center for Leadership and Management in the Design and Construction Industry—http://archone.tamu.edu/~crscenter
Construction Engineering Research Laboratory—cecer.army.mil
Facility Performance Group, Inc.—jonfpg@aol.com
Incoming Calls Management Institute—incoming.com
Interagency Benchmarking and Best Practices Council—va.gov/fedsbest/index.htm
International Centre for Facilities—info@icf-cebe.com
International Council for Building Research Studies and Documentation—decco.nl/obi
International Facility Management Association—research@ifma.org
Land Use Planning—planning.org/plnginfo
Lifecycle Management—navy.mil/homepages/navfac/pe/15home.htm#ilm
National Academy Press—nap.edu
National Fire Protection Association—nfpa.org
National Institute of Standards and Technology, Building and Fire Research Laboratory—bfrl.nist.gov
National Research Council, Federal Facilities Council—nas.edu/ffc
Naval Facilities Engineering Service Center—nfesc.navy.mil
Statistics—stats.gov

Standardization Associations

American National Standards Institute—ansi.org
American Society for Testing and Materials—astm.org
American Society of Heating, Refrigerating, and Air-Conditioning Engineers—ashrae.org
Construction Specifications Institute—csinet.org
Institute of Electrical and Electronic Engineers, Inc.—ieee.org
National Fire Protection Association—nfpa.org

Trade Associations

Association of Energy Services Professionals—dnai.com/aesp
BIFMA International—bifma.com
Business Products Industry Association—bpia.org
Carpet and Rug Institute—carpet-rug.com
International Foundation for Protection Officers—ifpo.com
Mechanical Contractors Association of America—mcaa.org

Trade Journals

Note: Professional journals can normally be accessed at their professional organization's web site.
Buildings—buildings.com

Construction Business Review—constructionsite.net
Facilities Design and Management—emcmorrow@mfi.com
Maintenance Solutions—maintsol@execpc.com
Today's Facility Manager—tfmgr.com

Training

American Public Works Association—pubworks.org
American Society of Civil Engineers—asce.org
APPA: Association of Higher Education Facilities Officers—appa.org
BOMI Institute—bomi-edu.org
Construction Specification Institute—csinet.org
Environmental Safety/Occupational Health Knowledge Center—esohkc.com
Facility Management Knowledge Center—fmkc.com
International Facility Management Association—education@ifma.org
Program Management Institute—pmi.org

Appendix D

Facility Management Education Programs

In Appendix C, I list many organizations that provide facility management training. Here I emphasize programs that provide in-depth education for facility managers. Many of these programs are degree granting.

In 1980, there was one educational program in facility management—the B.S. and M.S. program at Cornell University. Professor Bill Sims, Ph.D., CFM, IFMA Fellow, deserves special recognition not only for helping found this program but for nurturing it for almost twenty years. Many programs have come (and some have gone) during this period, but Cornell has continued to produce graduates who are highly sought within the profession.

Now colleges around the world are offering a variety of educational programs. (At this writing, Michigan State University has put its first course on the Internet—an introduction to facilities management—and the University of Manitoba was considering offering a master's-level facilities management curriculum on the Internet.) So many colleges and universities are offering such a variety of courses that it is hard to track them—or to even find them. I thank IFMA for its assistance in compiling the following list. The first five colleges are IFMA Recognized Programs; they have first-professional degree programs specifically in facility management and have submitted a self-study application that was reviewed and approved by a committee of peers.

IFMA has developed a recognized curriculum for a first-degree program. The contact is the Education Department at ifma.org.

Unless otherwise noted, the programs are located in the United States. Each entry lists a contact person at the institution. All phone numbers listed are those used when calling from the United States.

IFMA Recognized Programs

Cornell University, Ithaca, New York, offers a B.S. and M.S. in facility management. William Sims, Ph.D., CFM, (607) 255-1954.

Eastern Michigan University, Ypsilanti, Michigan offers a B.S. in facility management. Larry Darling, (313) 487-2040.

Ferris State University, Big Rapids, Michigan, offers a B.S. in facility management. Mel Kantor, (616) 592-2625.

University of Strathclyde—Centre for Facilities Management, Glasgow, Scotland, offers a master's program in facility management. Angie Houston, 011-41-553-4165.

University of Southern Colorado, Pueblo, Colorado, offers a B.S. in facility management. Mike Hoots, CFM, PE, (719) 549-2838.

Other Degree Programs

Arizona State University, Tempe, Arizona, offers an M.S. in design with a facility management concentration. Bob Wolf or Lorri Cutler, (602) 965-8685.

Brigham Young University, Provo, Utah, offers a B.S. in facility management. Loren Martin, (801) 378-6493.

Canadian School of Management, Toronto, Ontario, Canada, offers a certificate program, diploma, and fellow in facility management. Yvonne Bogorya, (416) 327-0309.

College of Dupage, Glen Ellyn, Illinois, offers an associate's degree in facility management. Steve Mansfield, (630) 942-3046.

Delaware County Community College, Media, Pennsylvania, offers an associate's degree in facility management technology. Larry Woodward, (610) 359-5027.

DePaul University, Chicago, Illinois, offers a B.A. and M.A. with individually designed areas related to facility management. Douglas Murphy, (312) 362-8001, ext. 5756.

Health Services Management Unit, University of Manchester, Runcorn, Cheshire, United Kingdom, offers an M.A. in health facilities management. Cliff Price, 011-44-061-275-2908.

Heriot-Watt University, Edinburgh, Scotland, offers a postgraduate diploma and an M.S.C. in facilities management and asset maintenance. William Wallace, 011-44-131-444-9511, ext. 4647.

Indiana State University, Terre Haute, Indiana, offers a B.S. and a specialized M.S. in interior design and facility management. James Landa, (812) 237-3303.

Michigan State University, East Lansing, Michigan, offers an M.A. and a Ph.D. in human environment, with a concentration on facility design and management. Dana Stewart, (517) 355-7712.

Mount Ida College, Newton Centre, Massachusetts, offers an associate's degree in facility management. John E. Williams, (617) 928-4565.

Mount Saint Vincent University, Halifax, Nova Scotia, Canada, offers a bachelor of home economics with a major in housing and facility management. Margaret Ellison, (902) 443-4450.

North Carolina Agricultural and Technical University, Greensboro, North Carolina, offers an M.S. in facility management. Ronald L. Helms, (910) 334-7575.

North Dakota State University, Fargo, North Dakota, offers a B.S. in facility management. Shauna Corry, (710) 231-8604.

Polytechnic of North London, London, England, offers an M.A. in health and facility planning. Polytechnic of North London, 011-44-607-2798.

Pratt Institute, New York, New York, offers an M.S. in facility management. Mary Mathews, (212) 219-0925.

Texas A&M University, College Station, Texas, offers an M.S. in facility management. David Bilbo, (409) 845-7003.

University College, London, England, offers an M.S. in facility and environment management. Anne Pink, 011-44-071-380-5911.

University of Florida, Gainesville, Florida, offers a B.S. and M.S. in facility management. Felix Uhlick, (352) 392-7288.

University of Manchester, Manchester, England, offers an M.A. in health facilities management. Cliff Price, 011-44-061-275-2908.

University of Manitoba, Winnipeg, Manitoba, Canada, offers an M.S. in facility management through distance learning on the Internet. Christine Adams, (204) 474-7488.

University of Reading, Berkshire, England, offers an M.S. in facilities management. Admissions assistant, 011-44-073-487-5123.

University of Tennessee, Knoxville, Tennessee, offers a Ph.D. in facility management. Nancy Canestaro, (615) 974-6295.

University of the West of England, Bristol, England, offers an M.S. in facility management. A. H. Spedding, 011-44-117-965-6261.

Wentworth Institute of Technology, Boston, Massachusetts, offers a B.S. in facility management. James Jeas, (617) 442-9010, ext. 327.

Woodbury University, Burbank, California, offers a B.S. in facility planning and management. Subodh A. Kumar (818) 767-0888.

Programs With Facility-Management-Related Courses

Anglia Polytechnic University, Chelsmsord, Essex, United Kingdom. David Lawrence, 011-44-0245-493-131.

Deakin University, Geelong, Victoria, Australia. Helen Tippett, Deakin.edu.au.

George Mason University, Fairfax, Virginia. Terrance Ryan, (703) 993-1657.

Kansas State University, Manhattan, Kansas. Carolyn Thompson, (913) 532-5992.

Montclair State College, Upper Montclair, New Jersey. Department of Technology, (201) 893-4161.

Oxford Polytechnic, Oxford, England. Department of Architecture, 011-44-607-2798.

Rochester Institute of Technology, Rochester, New York. Lynda Rummel, (716) 475-5027.

Royal Institute of Technology, Stockholm, Sweden. J. Brochner, 011-46-8-20-3541 (fax).

State Academy of Management, Moscow, Russia. A Porshnev, 011-095-371-13-22.

University of New South Wales, Australian Defense Force Academy, Canberra, ACT, Australia. Alan While, 011-61-6-286-1227.

York University, Downsview, Ontario, Canada. Peter Homenuck, (416) 736-5287.

Certificate Programs in Facility Management

George Mason University, Fairfax, Virginia. Kitty Hoover, (703) 993-8312.

New York University, New York, New York. Arlynne Lesser, (212) 790-1639.

Northeastern University, Dedham, Massachusetts. Roy Nielsen, (617) 320-8026.

Ryerson Polytechnic University, Toronto, Ontario, Canada. Ken Thompson, (416) 979-5000, ext. 6929.

University of California, Berkeley Extension, Berkeley, California. (510) 642-4231.

University of California, Irvine, Irvine, California. Dan Stokols, (714) 856-6904.

University of California, San Diego Extension, La Jolla, California. (619) 534-0406.

University of Melbourne, Parkville, Victoria, Australia. Graham Brawn, 011-61-3-344-6299.

Appendix E

Life-Cycle Cost Example

Life-cycle costing is a best practice that is not yet widely used in facility manage-ment. The reasons usually given are that management is only interested in first cost (a dubious excuse, if you really think about it) and that facility managers are either ill prepared or too busy to do the calculations.

Actually the calculations are relatively simple, especially when using auto-mated spreadsheets. The more difficult task is to obtain adequate projections of the savings and costs. A facility manager with a sophisticated department is likely to be able to project into the future fairly accurately. However, often facility man-agers have to depend on vendors or contractors to predict costs and savings in the future for new initiatives. Even that can work well provided that the facility manager views those predictions skeptically through the prism of experience.

The example that follows was developed by Professor John Preston when he was teaching facility management at Eastern Michigan University (and for which I thank him and IFMA).[1] It is an excellent example because it develops the concept of life-cycle costing and in a facility management environment. This is an example of a fairly simple application of life-cycle costing but, in its simplicity, it should give anyone confidence that they can perform life-cycle costing. For a discussion of using automated spreadsheets for life-cycle costing, see Professor Mike Hoots's excellent article, "Dr. Spreadsheet or How I Learned to Stop Worrying and Love Financial Analysis," in the January–February 1998 issue of *FMJ, the Facility Man-agement Journal.*

In this problem, we are faced with a decision of whether to buy more expen-sive but longer-lasting carpet. (Ignore the fact that in most organizations carpet is replaced after about six years because it has been cut, penetrated, and pieced during moves or has "uglied out.") We will do the same analysis twice to show the advantages and disadvantages of each. In most cases, the simple life-cycle and net present value analyses will be merely steps toward computing the average annual cost of whatever we are analyzing.

The simple life-cycle analysis table in Exhibit E-1 shows that high-quality carpet for our project costs $8,000 to purchase and $2,000 to install. Based on our records, our staff have told us that the life of that carpet is ten years, and it will cost us $1,000 ($800 labor and $200 materials) annually to maintain it to our high standards. Therefore, the total simple life-cycle cost of the high-quality carpet is

Exhibit E-1. Simple life-cycle cost for high-quality carpet (in dollars).

| | Initial costs | Annual costs | Year | | | | | | | | | |
			1	2	3	4	5	6	7	8	9	10
Purchase	8,000	Labor	800	800	800	800	800	800	800	800	800	800
Installation	2,000	Materials	200	200	200	200	200	200	200	200	200	200
Other	—	None	—	—	—	—	—	—	—	—	—	—
Subtotal	10,000		1,000	1,000	1,000	1,000	1,000	1,000	1,000	1,000	1,000	1,000
Total cost:	$20,000											

$20,000 ($8,000 installation labor plus $2,000 initial carpet cost plus ten years of maintenance cost at $1,000 per year).

The same simple life-cycle analysis for regular carpet is shown in Exhibit E-2. Not unexpectedly, initial costs for regular carpet are lower, but the annual maintenance costs are higher. Intuitively, as shown here, we note that the useful life of the regular carpet is seven vice ten years for the high-quality carpet.

Based on this simple analysis, it would appear that we would recommend to management the purchase of the regular carpet. However, this simple life-cycle analysis has two major deficiencies. First, it doesn't take into account the time value of money. Second, it is not valid for comparisons of projects, or options of the same project, that have different lifetimes. These analytical deficiencies lead us to take the comparison two steps further—the first of these is to do a net present value analysis based on the simple life-cycle cost figures.

The basis for conducting a net present value analysis is the old question, "Would you prefer to have $100 now or a year from now?" Although there are several practical reasons for answering, "Today!," the economic reason is that cash in hand today can earn income for us in that interim period. Therefore, we lay out the cash flows (savings or costs) from our options under consideration and then compute their present value using an appropriate discount (interest) rate (for example, the present value of $1 after one year is $0.935, after two years is $0.873, after three years is $0.816 when the discount rate is 7 percent). We then total those discounted cash flows. The option having the highest total will have the greatest net present value. We do not discount initial costs, of course, because they occur at a time when the present value of $1 is $1.

What discount rate to use is a valid question. In larger organizations, the chief financial officer will dictate that discount rate. Absent guidance, add 2 to 3

Exhibit E-2. Simple life-cycle cost for regular carpet (in dollars).

| | Initial costs | Annual costs | Year | | | | | | |
			1	2	3	4	5	6	7
Purchase	6,000	Labor	1,000	1,000	1,000	1,000	1,000	1,000	1,000
Installation	2,000	Materials	250	250	250	250	250	250	250
Other	—	None	—	—	—	—	—	—	—
Subtotal	8,000		1,250	1,250	1,250	1,250	1,250	1,250	1,250
Total cost:	$16,750								

percent for administration to the rate that the company borrows funds for capital projects on the open market. The present values for each discount rate are available in a book of discount tables or are resident in financial calculators.

The two analyses for computing the net present value of the life cycles of costs for the high-quality and regular carpets are shown in Exhibits E-3 and E-4.

Since we are comparing options with two different life cycles, however, we need to take one more step. We create an equivalent average annual cost. In the case of the high-quality carpet, we divide the net present value of its costs by 10; for the regular carpet, we divide by the service life of 7 years:

$17,024/10 = $1,702.40 average annual cost for the high-quality carpet
$14,737/7 = $2,105.28 average annual cost for the regular carpet

Using this analysis, we can recommend to management that we install the high-quality carpet.

If this carpet project had to compete with others for limited funds, we would take one additional step and compute the internal rate of return to determine which among competing projects gives our company the "greatest bang for the

Exhibit E-3. Net present value for high-quality carpet (in dollars).

	Initial costs	Annual costs	Year 1	2	3	4	5	6	7	8	9	10
Purchase	8,000	Labor	800	800	800	800	800	800	800	800	800	800
Installation	2,000	Materials	200	200	200	200	200	200	200	200	200	200
Other	—	None	—	—	—	—	—	—	—	—	—	—
Subtotal	10,000		1,000	1,000	1,000	1,000	1,000	1,000	1,000	1,000	1,000	1,000
Annual Present Value	10,000		935	873	816	763	713	666	623	582	544	508

Exhibit E-4. Net present value for regular carpet (in dollars).

	Initial costs	Annual costs	Year 1	2	3	4	5	6	7
Purchase	6,000	Labor	1,000	1,000	1,000	1,000	1,000	1,000	1,000
Installation	2,000	Materials	250	250	250	250	250	250	250
Other	—	None	—	—	—	—	—	—	—
Subtotal	8,000		1,250	1,250	1,250	1,250	1,250	1,250	1,250
Annual Present Value	8,000		1,168	1,092	1,020	954	891	833	778

Net present value: $14,737

buck" or which should be rejected because it does not generate a high enough return on our investment.

Note

1. John Preston, "Life Cycle Cost Analysis for the Beginner," in *Proceedings of the Fourteenth Annual Conference of the International Facility Management Association* (Houston: IFMA, 1993), pp. 115–124.

Appendix F

Backup Documents

F-1

The Facility Plan

This is a sample mid-range facility plan for a large law firm that has two office buildings (one owned, one leased) in one city. The firm plans continued growth through the period and desires to be in all owned buildings by year 5. Note: All material in brackets is editorial. Estimate approximately twelve hours to compile such a "first-ever" plan.

ANNEX G   June 4, 1990
                                                              Rev 1

Facility Plan
Mid-Range Business Plan (1992–1994)
Smith, Miller, Allen, Richardson and Tucker (SMART)

Approved By   Reviewed By

_____   _____
Sandra J. Lloyd   Gerald S. Gruen
Facility Manager   Controller and Planning Director

I. Introduction

    A. Introduction—The purpose of this plan is to present the impact of the SMART business plan (1992–1994) on facilities and the facilities department. In addition, the plan will highlight significant facility issues for SMART management.

    This plan considers the work plan currently in execution for 1990 and under consideration for 1991. In turn, it is the basis for the strategic facility plan 1995–1999.

II. Environment

    1. The business environment is appropriate for SMART to continue to grow during the period. [From business plan.]
    2. SMART, during the period, will phase out its tax practice, reduce its criminal practice substantially, but expand rapidly its international practice. [From the business plan.]
    3. The local environment is mixed. The manufacturing sector continues to decline, but internationally-oriented firms are the most rapidly expanding part of the economy. [From business plan.]
    4. SMART is viewed locally as highly competent but somewhat overly bureaucratic. Clients seek us for our name but not for our creativity. [From business plan.]
    5. SMART is committed to owning its operating space to control its image and the quality of its surrounding.
    6. The facilities department, during the period, must move from caretaker approach and organization to a full-service department.

III. Assumptions

    1. SMART will continue to grow during the period at a rate of 10% annually. [From business plan.]
    2. Space and furnishing standards will be approved, as written, by the end of this year.
    3. All staff will be in owned space by 1994, i.e., the newly planned headquarters will be ready for occupancy by November 1993. [From business plan.]
    4. New leased costs will be constant through 1992 but will increase \$2/gsf in 1993. All new lease costs will absorb the cost of tenant build-out.
    5. No "rent" is charged for owned space.
    6. Av Tech Inc., will sublease space (approx. 8,000 gsf) for 1991–1992.

IV. Constraints

    1. Administrative expenses [less capital] will be constrained at 5% growth throughout the term. [From business plan.]
    2. There will be resistance to increasing staff size; consultants and contractors must be maximized.

V. Discussion

    A. Presentation of Scenarios

    1. Most Probable—In this scenario, the business will continue to grow

throughout the period. Staff will increase at approximately 10% per year.

Initially these staff increases will have to be met by leasing space in near proximity to the headquarters. Current leasing rates average $22/gsf until 1993, when the current overbuilt condition should dry up. Commencing in 1991 the company will be capable and desirous of subletting some space.

During the period, the department will attempt to impose a 280 gsf/person space standard for all space, owned or leased.

The new building will be available for occupancy late in 1993. Some lease space will be available for release or sublet late in 1993, but it is assumed to be a trade-off for leases which will extend 1–2 months into 1994 as the new building is occupied.

Maintenance in existing owned space will be reduced to minimum essential, commencing with 1993.

Moves and alteration projects will be limited to those 1) needed to accommodate acknowledged growth and 2) those necessary to occupy the new building.

Utility costs during the period are extremely difficult to predict. The Public Service Commission is likely to approve a moderate (3–4%) increase in the electric rate effective January 1, 1990. Energy management initiatives will continue to dampen the upward pressure on utility costs. The thermal storage built into the new building should reduce the utility costs approximately 8%.

2. Best Case (from a facilities viewpoint)—In this case, SMART will construct two new buildings: the new headquarters plus an approximate 150,000 gsf building contiguous to it, to be complete for occupancy in 1995. This smaller building will be used for two purposes 1) gradually absorbing the long-term growth of the firm and 2) generating income through leases. While it is estimated that this scenario will require two additional staff, this building should pay for itself in four years (occupancy rate = 85%) and assist in paying for the new headquarters.

3. Worst Case (from a facilities viewpoint)—The worst case (which is still credible) would be a failure to get management agreement on imposing a space standard, a corporate headquarters growth rate of 15%, and slippage of the completion of the headquarters for one year. Each or any of these situations, while not probable, is possible.

B. Impacts on/of Programs for Each Scenario

1. Most Probable Case
   a. Financial display at Appendix A-2.
   b. Implementation of this scenario will have several very *positive impacts* upon SMART and the facilities department.
      1) Implementation of space standards
      2) Elimination of leasing
      3) Provision of adequate space plus room for growth
      4) Ability to provide workplace standards to increase productivity
      5) Ability to eliminate asbestos and radon concerns

6) Ability to better accommodate office technology
7) Continuing to implement energy management, particularly thermal storage
8) Reduction in long-range churn

C. Negative Impacts
    1) Capital expenditure
    2) Higher than average short-term churn

1. Best Case
  a. Positive Impacts
    1) Same as Most Probable Case
    2) Capital costs will be offset by lease income
    3) Long-term space needs met
  b. Negative Impacts
    1) Slight increase in staff
    2) Company is into the landlord business

2. Worst Case
  a. Positive Impacts—None
  b. Negative Impacts
    1) Lease costs will be both higher and longer lasting
    2) Capital costs likely to be higher
    3) Space will continue to be inconsistently assigned
    4) Expansion space, built into the new headquarters, will disappear 50% faster than planned
    5) Possible difficulties in getting current leases extended without paying a penalty

VI. Conclusion—Despite the advantages of the Best Case Scenario, there is a strong sense within the corporation 1) to stop any growth in non-legal staff and 2) not to become a major landlord.

VII. Recommendation—Implement the Most Probable Scenario.

Facility Plan, 1992–1994

Financial Display
Most Probable Scenario

	1992	*1993*	*1994*
a. Capital ($K)	15,000	12,000	——
b. Annually Funded Nondiscretionary ($K)	767	791	3,455
c. Annually Funded Discretionary ($K)	850	975	350
d. Lease Costs ($K)	3,934	4,740	——
e. Lease Income ($K)	(56)	——	——
f. Overhead Costs ($K)	1,600	1,700	1,900
g. Space Needs (GSF)	388,800	422,400	408,800

Capital Budget Request

PROJECT JUSTIFICATION & SCOPE OF WORK

FUND: NAME & CODE	CAPITAL (300)	AGENCY: NAME & CODE	RECREATION (HA)

PROJECT NAME	PROJECT NUMBER	PROJECT LOCATION
Outdoor Lighting Improvements	RIG	Various Locations

PROJECT JUSTIFICATION

The Department of Recreation is requesting $600,000 in additional authority to renovate and replace outdoor lighting at its recreation centers. This project will continue work started in fiscal year 1986. Some of the department's most popular evening activities are severely handicapped because outdoor lighting systems are obsolete and in some cases inoperative for long periods of time. The lack of adequate outdoor lighting because of deteriorating fixtures and breakage causes many evening activities to be cancelled. When play is attempted on badly lighted fields, players are in danger of injury. The department's lighting system includes a great variety of types and sizes of lighting fixtures, making standardization of purchase of parts and repairs impossible.

A survey of the lighting system undertaken in 1986 has revealed that previous estimates of renovation and replacement costs are too low. This project will supplement the FY 1986 authorization for field lights and permit its extension to security and playcourt lights, as well.

OPERATING BUDGET IMPACT

This project will result in operating budget savings as more energy-efficient fixtures are installed and as maintenance and replacement procedures can be standardized.

IMPACT ON THE COMMUNITY

This project will not displace homes or businesses. Benefits to the community will be increased safety and security at recreation centers, by having better lighting for evening activities. Redesign of lighting fixtures will also, in some cases, reduce the impact of field lights on adjacent residential areas by directing light away from residences

more efficiently. The project is consistent with two goals of the 1981 Comprehensive Recreation Plan: "to provide the highest level of service for the least possible cost" and "to achieve and maintain efficient use of energy . . ."

SOURCES OF REVENUE FOR THE REQUESTED PROJECT

The project will be funded by general obligation bonds to be issued by the City government.

SCOPE OF WORK

This project will allow the continuation of the installation of fully efficient and standardized system of outdoor lighting at all Recreation Department properties. Based on the survey and lighting plan being prepared in FY 1986, field, playcourt, and security lights will be renovated or replaced with the most effective and cost-effective lighting available. Whenever possible, existing wiring systems and light standards will be used. Highest priority will be given to sites with the highest level of activity and the highest potential for continued or increased activity.

CAP

FUND
NAME & CODE: CAPITAL (300)

AGENCY
NAME & CODE: RECREATION (HA)

PROJECT NAME: Outdoor Lighting Improvements
PROJECT NUMBER: R1G

PROJECT LOCATION: Various Locations
WARD(S): DW

PROJECT IS: [ ] NEW CONSTRUCTION [X] RENOVATION [ ] REPAIRS
ESTIMATED COMPLETION DATE: 1992
NUMBER OF SQUARE FEET: NA
USEFUL LIFE (YEARS): 15

PROJECT BUDGET AUTHORITY

PHASE	FY 1987 City Request	FY 1987 Federal Grant(s)	Prior City Authority	Prior Federal Grant(s)	Future City Request	Future Federal Grant(s)	Total City Authority	Total Federal Grants	Estimated Total Authority (City + Federal)
Site	---						---		---
Design	72						72		72
Project Management	48						48		48
Construction	480						480		480
Equipment	---						---		---
TOTAL AUTHORITY	600						600		600

Allocations of Expenditures Based on FY 1987 Total Capital Authority

FISCAL YEAR	GENERAL FUND	BONDS/LOANS	GRANTS	TOTAL
FY 1987		100		100
FY 1988		100		100
FY 1989		100		100
FY 1990		100		100
FY 1991		100		100
FY 1992		100		100
FY 1993		---		---
FY 1994		---		---
FY 1995		---		---
TOTAL		600		600

Supplementary Project Information

If grant funded, name the grantor:

Project is related to:
[ ] Infrastructure
[X] Public Facilities
[ ] Institutions
[ ] Land Acquisition
[ ] Major Equipment

Objective of project is to:
[ ] Restore Service
[ ] Expand Service
[X] Enhance Service
[ ] Comply with Court Order or Statute
[ ] Stimulate Economic Development
[ ] Other

Land ownership:
[ ] Private
[ ] Federal
[X] City
[ ] Not Applicable

Will the project cause the relocation of individuals or businesses?
[ ] Yes
[X] No
Number: _____

See CAP 4 for further information

F-3

Comparison of Outcomes Using Different Capital Project Analysis Alternatives

The type of capital project analysis used will influence the outcome. Here are the different project rankings possible using various analysis tools. The cases are hypothetical alternative uses of an enterprise's capital.

Example Projects for Comparison of Analysis Alternatives

Net investment	Project A $120,000		Project B $75,000		Project C $75,000	
Year	Profit	Cash Flow	Profit	Cash Flow	Profit	Cash Flow
1	$ 20,000	$ 44,000	$ 30,000	$ 45,000	$ 10,000	$ 25,000
2	30,000	54,000	30,000	45,000	20,000	35,000
3	70,000	94,000	30,000	45,000	40,000	55,000
4	100,000	124,000	30,000	45,000	60,000	75,000
5	100,000	124,000	30,000	45,000	85,000	100,000
Totals	$320,000	$440,000	$150,000	$225,000	$215,000	$290,000
Averages	$ 64,000	$ 88,000	$ 30,000	$ 45,000	$ 43,000	$ 58,000

The following summary of various analysis alternatives applied to the three projects shown above illustrate the sometimes conflicting results you might obtain:

		Project	
	A	B	C
Net investment	$120,000	$ 75,000	$75,000
Average annual:			
Profit	64,000	30,000	43,000
Cash flow	88,000	45,000	58,000
Project total:			
Profit	320,000	150,000	215,000
Cash flow	440,000	225,000	290,000

Analysis alternatives (ranking shown in parentheses):

	Project					
	A		B		C	
Average rate of return	107%	(2)	80%	(3)	115%	(1)
Average payback period	1.36 yrs	(2)	1.67 yrs	(3)	1.29 yrs	(1)
Actual payback period	2.23 yrs	(2)	1.67 yrs	(1)	2.27 yrs	(3)
Net present value with:						
Cost of capital 15%	$153,446	(1)	$75,847	(3)	$101,967	(2)
Cost of capital 20%	$118,197	(1)	$59,578	(3)	$78,324	(2)
Internal rate of return	50.9%	(3)	52.8%	(1)	51.0%	(2)

If your criteria are:

		Select	
	A	B	C
(1) Getting invested cash back as quickly as possible	Second	First	Third
(2) Containing the highest net present value of future cash flows	First	Third	Second
(3) Getting invested cash back within 1.5 years	(No project meets criteria)		

As the examples illustrate, the criteria used dictate the selection and the analysis technique. In most companies, both the method of analysis and the time period (three, five, ten years) is set by the CFO or controller.

F-4

Moving Instructions for Staff

I. Preface

The following information and instructions have been prepared to assist staff members in preparation for their move to new offices.

II. General Information
  A. Cartons—Packing cartons may be obtained through the Move Management Office by submitting Form 17 a week prior to the move.
  B. Moving Labels—Labels for tagging cartons, office machines, and all loose items to be moved may also be secured by telephoning the Move Management Office, ext. 72346, or by requesting them on Form 17 a week prior to the move.
  C. Office Layout Drawing—It would be most helpful to the facilities staff and moving contractor if each staff member would complete a rough sketch of their new individual office layout and affix it to their office door in the new office area prior to the move. Please note layouts must adhere to existing room conditions in regard to telephone and electrical outlets. If in doubt, contact your Facilities Project Manager. The drawing need not be exact. Movers will be available on the first workday after the move to rearrange furniture as directed by staff members.
  D. Packing and Unpacking Services—It is the responsibility of staff members being relocated to pack and unpack their offices and work stations. Moving services will provide movers to assist with packing and unpacking services only in connection in special instances where approval is obtained from the Move Manager. Examples are information centers, etc.

III. Packing Instructions
  A. Personal Items—Neither Moving Services nor our moving contractor will assume responsibility for personal items.

B. Cartons—Be sure each carton is assembled properly. The carton supplied does not require sealing tape.

A two-inch space left at the top of the box is required in order to close the inter-locking flap properly. Cartons should be tagged or marked in space provided on each end of box.

If instruction in assembling or marking cartons is needed, contact your Move Coordinator.

C. Contents (All Items)—Pack all contents from drawers and top of desk. Small items—pens, paper clips, pencils, and rubber bands are best placed in envelopes, and packed in the box.

All items should be in boxes. Any items which will not be in boxes but must be moved should be reported to the Move Coordinator before the move.

D. File Cabinets, Uprights—These types of files DO NOT have to be emptied. (Remove all breakables from drawers). The drawer "backup plate" should be pulled forward in order to compress contents and hold in place. Cabinets will be moved in an upright position. Lock cabinets if possible and remove key. IBM Card File cabinets should be locked or the drawer taped.

E. Lateral File Cabinets—This type of cabinet must be emptied of all contents. (Cabinet construction—false bottom, sliding tracks, thin metal fronts and sides, etc., do not permit moving contents intact).

F. Bookcase—Pack all contents, drop shelves to bottom of bookcase, and remove pegs or clips. (Pack in envelopes and place in carton).

G. Storage or Supply Cabinets—Pack all contents in cartons. Cabinet doors should be locked or taped closed.

H. Coat Racks—Remove hangers and pack in carton.

I. Office Machines—Do not pack typewriters, desk-size adding machines, and calculators. Remove cover and pads and pack these in carton. Unplug and center carriage. Wrap cord around carriage. Tag machines on front surface. Small calculators and dictating machines should be packed carefully in carton.

J. Pictures, Maps, Chalk or Bulletin Boards—Wherever possible pack pictures in cartons back to back and on end (do not lay flat in cartons). Each items should be tagged. Consolidation of pictures within an office is encouraged. Leave carton opened. Bank maintenance staff will be available the day following the move to re-hang pictures and maps.

Large items—tag and leave in place. Movers will handle as is. Tag plastic chair mats. (These items should be reported to the Move Coordinator prior to the move).

K. Map or Plan or Special File Cabinets—Contact the Move Management Office (ext. 72346) for special instructions.

L. Office Technology Equipment—It is the responsibility of all staff to transfer files to a diskette prior to the move. In general this equipment can be moved without further servicing. If you have a question contact User Services at 32121. Contact Copying Services, ext. 73738, to move all copiers.

Notify Moving Services for advice on making appropriate arrangements for all special equipment (CPUs printing equipment, etc.).

M. Plants (live or artificial)—Moving contractors are not responsible for transporting staff members personal plants.

Plant for common areas will, in general, remain there. If they are to be moved, the Project Manager will make the arrangements.

IV. Tagging and Marking

Your Move Coordinator has layouts of the assigned new office space—names, floors, room numbers, etc. Check drawings for your particular room or area.

Each item to be moved must be tagged with a properly color-coded tag. A crayon or magic marker should be used for marking on the tags. Do not type or use ballpoint pen or pencil in marking tags. Print clearly and as large as possible.

All items of furniture, equipment, and cartons should be marked with same information. Show name, letter prefix followed by room number for the principal room in which items are to be placed (i.e., A-800). The prefix "O" will designate area outside principal office, such as secretarial or reception area (i.e., O/A-800).

A. Location of Tags—A uniform tagging systems is most important to the movers locating various offices and placing items in them.

B. Please refer to attachment "A," where to place tags on furniture, boxes, and equipment.

C. Certain items, such as metal shelving, conference tables, "L" units from secretarial desks, need to be dismantled for moving. Be sure to tag each piece. For shelving, tag at least 10 pieces of shelving and all uprights ends or posts.

V. After the Move

Packing boxes should be broken down flat, and stacked in central locations (near elevators, if possible) for removal from the floors by the movers. Please note that these cartons are re-usable, and should not be taken from Bank premises for personal use.

VI. Information or Advice

All requests for information or advice regarding moving procedures should be addressed through your Move Coordinator to the Moving Management Office.

F-5

A Maintenance and Repair Program

Management Function	Maintenance and Repair (M&R) Element

Planning and Programming	• Inventory of facilities (input)
	  —By category
	  —By condition
	  —Highlight critical deficiencies
	  —Pickup "new finds"
	• Categorization of work (input)
	• Standards (input)
	  —Timeliness
	  —Quality
	  —Work
	• Condition assessment (input)
	  —Trends
	  —Critical deficiency trends
	  —Adverse impacts
	• Priorities (input)
	  —By activity
	  —By class
	  —By critical deficiency
	• Annual work plan (product)
	• Mid-term plan (product)

Budgeting	• Budget guidance sets the tone
	• Flows from the work plan
	• Budget process
	• Cost accounting must initially be considered
	• Impact of capital budget
	  —Design to maintain
	  —Life-cycle costs to be optimized; not simply
	    capital costs

Management Function	*Maintenance and Repair (M&R) Element*

	• Comparison to target range of percentage of current replacement value (CPV)
	• Historical trend comparison
	• Comparison to current budget year
	• Impact statements if inadequate
	• Definition of requirements
	  —By activity
	  —By criticality
	• Eliminate leakage of funds
	  —By definition
	  —By migration
	• Submission often "banded" to meet multiple funding scenarios

Organizing	• Organizational models are available • Lines of responsibility must be clear • Placement of program is important • Material management has an impact • Analysis capability needed in large organizations • "Submeter" facilities for comparison
Staffing	• Quality, technical competence • Quantity • Contract vs. in-house mix • Training • Leadership • Inspection

Directing	• Priorities set in budget cycle
	• Work management and coordination (the key)
	• Appropriate level of design needed
	• Rapid response to crises
	• Some provision for necessity to react
	• Allocation of budgets to subactivities
	  —Ability to execute
	  —Criticality
	  —Provide specific guidance
	• Contracting strategy
	• Condition assessment
	• Commissioning periods/procedures for new buildings to reduce maintenance
	• Automate diagnostics

Management Function	*Maintenance and Repair (M&R) Element*

Controlling

- Approval levels
- Control of budget
- Control of finances
- Management information systems (MIS)
- Accountability
- Ability to react to crises, new priorities, or end-of-year windfalls
- Documentation

Evaluating

- Comparators
- Condition assessment
  —Critical deficiency trends
  —Total deficiency trends
- Work management system
- Comparison with historical data
- Field assessment
- Customer feedback

F-6

Maintenance Schedule

Interior PM

	Inspection	Repair	Comments
Cafeterias/Dining Rooms	Weekly	IROAN	
President's Dining Room	Weekly	IROAN	Major cleaning done annually in coordination with his office.
Carpet	Quarterly	IROAN	Cleaning done by custodial services; carpet in common areas inspected weekly.
Major Conference Rooms/ Auditoriums	Weekly	IROAN	
Elevator Interiors	Weekly	IROAN	Replace carpet annually.
Exterior of Building	Annually	IROAN	Clean building every five years; plan to recaulk every 10 years.
Floors	Quarterly	IROAN	
Hallways and Stairs	Weekly	IROAN	
Lobbies	Weekly	IROAN	
Occupied Areas (3)	Quarterly	IROAN	Priority to owned space.
Restrooms	Weekly	IROAN	
Roofs, Patios, Sidewalks, Garages, Exteriors	Semi-Annually	IROAN	Plan roof replacement every 15 years.
Venetian Blinds	Quarterly	IROAN	

Note: IROAN = Inspect repair only as necessary.

Fire/Life Safety PM

	Inspection	Repair	Comments
Aiphone System	Annually	IROAN	
Fire Alarm System	Quarterly	IROAN	
Smoke Detectors	Semi-Annually	IROAN	
Pull Stations/Bells	Annually	IROAN	
P.A. System	Semi-Annually	IROAN	
Access Control	Semi-Annually	IROAN	
Door Guard	Semi-Annually	IROAN	There is also a weekly check by security.
Duress Alarm	Monthly	IROAN	
Laser System	Semi-Annually	IROAN	
Security Video Equipment	Semi-Annually	IROAN	
Surveillance Cameras	Semi-Annually	IROAN	
Transponder Cabinet	Semi-Annually	IROAN	
Autoterms	Semi-Annually	IROAN	
Motion Detectors	Quarterly	IROAN	
Temperature Sensors	Quarterly	IROAN	

Furniture PM

	Inspection	Cleaned	Repair	Comments
Lobbies	Weekly	Quarterly	IROAN	
Cafeterias/Dining Rooms	Weekly	Monthly	IROAN	Cleaned daily by food service contractor.
Board Room	Weekly	Quarterly	IROAN	
Executive Directors' Offices	Quarterly	Quarterly	IROAN	
Office and Systems	Quarterly	Quarterly	IROAN	

Note: All furniture is replaced only as necessary.

Electrical PM

	Inspection	Repair	Comments
Disconnects	Annually	IROAN	Thermograph.
Floor Panels	Annually	IROAN	Thermograph.
Main Panels	Annually	IROAN	Thermograph.
Service Units	Annually	IROAN	This includes copy rooms, print shop, computer rooms, etc.

	Inspection	*Repair*	*Comments*
Switchboards	Three Years	IROAN	Thermograph, cleaning, testing.
Transformers	Quarterly	IROAN	Thermograph, grounding, ventilation cleaning.

F-7

Space Forecasting Survey Form

Senior Management Overview
(To be completed prior to the interview)

I. Business Plan
   A. Is the Association likely to grow?
      1. Five-year percentage _____
      2. Ten-year percentage _____
      3. By year 2000 _____
      4. Comments _____
   B. What services or markets will be added?

   C. What are the market forces that will:
      1. Encourage growth?
      2. Limit growth?

II. Organization Structure
   A. What new organizational units will be needed?

   B. What current organizational units:
      1. Will grow?
      2. Will become less important?
   C. What new types of personnel will be required?

   D. Will the current personnel skills mix change substantially?

   E. Comments.

III. Strategic Facility Outlook
    A. Describe what image our facilities should project.
        1. To outsiders, particularly our client.
        2. To our staff.
    B. How comfortable are you with the image of our current facilities, particularly your own?

    C. As we grow, ownership of our facilities is an option that we must consider. On a rating of 0 (do not favor ownership) to 7 (strongly favor ownership), where do you rate us? _____ Comments: _____

IV. Special Facilities. On the basis of 0 (oppose) to 7 (strongly favor), how do you rate the importance and desirability of the following commonly desired corporate special facilities?
    A. Auditorium _____
    B. Training facilities _____
    C. Medical facility _____
    D. Newstand or bookstore _____
    E. Coffee stations _____
    F. Take-out food facilities _____
    G. Employee cafeterias _____
    H. Employee dining rooms with table service _____
    I. Reserved dining rooms for client business _____
    J. Lounges _____
    K. Fitness center with shower facilities _____
    L. Swimming pool _____
    M. Jogging or walking track _____
    N. Library _____
    O. Free parking _____
    P. Guaranteed parking on a pay deduction or commercial basis _____
    Q. High-tech conference room(s) _____
    R. A main lobby that "makes a statement" _____
    S. An art program _____
    T. Other (Specify) _____
    U. Other (Specify) _____
    V. Other (Specify) _____
    W. Comments: _____

V. Location
    A. Should we remain in the metro area?

    B. Will regionalization occur?

    C. Must some element of the headquarters remain in a downtown location? Is so, what and where?

D. If we moved totally, or in part to a suburban location, rank-order (0—not important; 7—extremely important) the following factors concerning location:
Current employee home locations _____
Closeness to the Metro system (bus or rail) _____
Rental/construction site _____
Parking _____
Local amenities _____
Other (Specify) _____
Other (Specify) _____
Which of these factors do you consider the most important?

E. If we relocate, what will be the triggering event?
When do you feel it will occur?

F. Do you favor relocation in the near future? Ever?

G. Comments:

F-8

Real Estate Tracking System

Owned Property—Pages 1–2
Leased Property—Pages 3–6

This form was developed by Edmond P. Rondeau and is representative of the type of automated real estate tracking systems available.

OWNED PROPERTY INPUT SHEET

R.E. FILE NO: PAGE 1

SECTOR -------- |__|
COMPANY NO. ------------ |__|__|__| IS THIS A
STATE ---------- |__|__| PERMANENT
EXCHANGE NO. ----------- |__|__|__|__| DATE SUBMITTED: SURPLUS APPROVAL: EASEMENT?
BLDG. NO. --- |__|__|__|__|
PARCEL NO. ----------------- |__|__| |__|__|/|__|__|/|__|__| (Y/N) |__| (Y/N) |__|

●●

PROPERTY INFORMATION

LOCATION
NAME: |__|__|__|__|__|__|__|__|__|__|__|__|__|__|__|__|__|__|__|__|__|__|__|__|__|__|__|__|__|__|__|__|__|__|__|__|__|__|__|__|
SECTOR/
DIVISION: |__|__|__|__|__|__|__|__|__|__|__|__|__|__|__|__|__|__|__|__|__|__|__|__|__|__|__|__|__|__|__|__|__|__|__|
PROPERTY
ADDRESS: |__|__|__|__|__|__|__|__|__|__|__|__|__|__|__|__|__|__|__|__|__|__|__|__|__|__|__|__|__|__|__|__|__|__|

            |__|__|__|__|__|__|__|__|__|__|__|__|__|__|__|__|__|__|__|__|__|__|__|__|__|__|__|__|__|__|__|

CITY: |__|__|__|__|__|__|__|__|__|__|__|__|__|__|__|__|__|__|__|__|__| STATE: |__|__| ZIP: |__|__|__|__|__|

COUNTY: |__|__|__|__|__|__|__|__|__|__|__|__|__|__|__|__|__|__|__|__|__| COUNTRY: |U|S|A|__|__|__|__|__|__|

NUMBER OF FLOORS: |__|__| (COUNTRY DEFAULT IS <u>USA</u>)

LOCATION MANAGER: |__|__|__|__|__|__|__|__|__|__|__|__|__|__|__|__|__|__|__|__|__|__|__|__|__|__|__|__|__|__|__|__|__|__|__|

          AREA CODE: |__|__|__| TELEPHONE: |__|__|__| - |__|__|__|__| EXTENSION: |__|__|__|__|

LEGAL REVIEW BY: |__|__|__|__|__|__|__|__|__|__|__|__|__|__|__|__|__|__|__|__|__| DATE: |__|__|/|__|__|/|__|__|

FINANCIAL REVIEW BY: |__|__|__|__|__|__|__|__|__|__|__|__|__|__|__|__|__|__|__|__|__| DATE: |__|__|/|__|__|/|__|__|

A/R REQUIRED (Y/N) |__|;   A/R APPROVED (Y/N) |__|;   IL ONLY (Y/N) |__|;   IF Y, DATE: |__|__|/|__|__|/|__|__|
TOTAL ACREAGE:
LAND: |__|__|__|__|__|__|__|__|__| . |__|__| BUILDING: |__|__|__|__|__|__|__|__|SQ. FT.   OTHER: |__|__|__|__|__|__|__|__|

TYPE OF FACILITY: |__|__|__|__|__|__|__|__|__|__|__|__|__|__|__|__|__|__|__|__|__|__|__|__|__|__|__|__|__|
                                              SURVEY/PLOT
TOPO AVAILABLE (Y/N) |__| DATE: |__|__|/|__|__|/|__|__| PLAN AVAILABLE (Y/N) |__| DATE: |__|__|/|__|__|/|__|__|

APPRAISED VALUE: $ |__|__|__|__|__|__|__|__|__|__| . |__|__| APPRAISAL DATE: |__|__|/|__|__|/|__|__|
PICTURES   ZONING
AVAILABLE (Y/N) |__| JURISDICTION: |__|__|__|__|__|__|__|__|__|__|__|__|__|__| ZONED: |__|__|__|__|__|__|__|__|

INSURANCE COVERAGE: |__|__|__|__|__|__|__|__|__|__|__|__|__|__|__|__|__|__|__|__|__|__|__|__|__|__|__|__|__|__|__|

                    |__|__|__|__|__|__|__|__|__|__|__|__|__|__|__|__|__|__|__|__|__|__|__|__|__|__|__|__|__|__|__|

PROPERTY TAXES: LAST YEAR |__|__|/|__|__|/|__|__| $ |__|__|__|__|__|__|__| . |__|__|

                   LAST YEAR |__|__|/|__|__|/|__|__| $ |__|__|__|__|__|__|__| . |__|__|

                   LAST YEAR |__|__|/|__|__|/|__|__| $ |__|__|__|__|__|__|__| . |__|__|

continued . . .

R.E. FILE NO: **OWNED PROPERTY INPUT SHEET** PAGE 2

|__| - |__|__|__| - |__|__| - |__|__|__|__| - |__|__|__|__| - |__|__|

....

TITLE INFORMATION

DEED DEED BOOK
DATED: |__|__|/|__|__|/|__|__| RECORDED: |__|__|/|__|__|/|__|__| VOLUME: |__|__|/|__|__|/|__|__| PAGE: |__|__|__|__|

TOTAL PURCHASE PRICE: $ |__|__|__|__|__|__|__|__|__|__| . |__|__| PURCHASE DATE: |__|__|/|__|__|/|__|__|

BOOK VALUE: LAND: $ |__|__|__|__|__|__|__|__|__|__| . |__|__|

IMPROVEMENTS: $ |__|__|__|__|__|__|__|__|__|__| . |__|__| DATE: |__|__|/|__|__|/|__|__|

GENERAL WARRANTY: (Y/N) |__|; SPECIAL WARRANTY: (Y/N) |__|; QUITCLAIM: (Y/N) |__|; GRANT: (Y/N) |__|

TITLE INSURANCE: (Y/N) |__| AMOUNT: $ |__|__|__|__|__|__|__|__|__|__|__| . |__|__|

PURCHASER: |__|__|__|__|__|__|__|__|__|__|__|__|__|__|__|__|__|__|__|__|__|__|__|__|__|__|__|__|__|__|__|__|__|__|__|__|__|__|__|__|__|__|

|__|__|__|__|__|__|__|__|__|__|__|__|__|__|__|__|__|__|__|__|__|__|__|__|__|__|__|__|__|__|__|__|__|__|__|__|__|__|__|__|__|__|

SELLER: |__|__|__|__|__|__|__|__|__|__|__|__|__|__|__|__|__|__|__|__|__|__|__|__|__|__|__|__|__|__|__|__|__|__|__|__|__|__|__|__|__|__|

|__|__|__|__|__|__|__|__|__|__|__|__|__|__|__|__|__|__|__|__|__|__|__|__|__|__|__|__|__|__|__|__|__|__|__|__|__|__|__|__|__|__|

EASEMENT(S) AT PURCH. (Y/N) |__| IF YES, SEE DEED; EASEMENTS AFTER PURCH. (Y/N) |__| IF YES, SEE FILE.

....

GENERAL INFORMATION

GENERAL
COMMENTS: |__|__|__|__|__|__|__|__|__|__|__|__|__|__|__|__|__|__|__|__|__|__|__|__|__|__|__|__|__|__|__|__|__|__|__|__|__|__|__|__|__|__|

|__|__|__|__|__|__|__|__|__|__|__|__|__|__|__|__|__|__|__|__|__|__|__|__|__|__|__|__|__|__|__|__|__|__|__|__|__|__|__|__|__|__|

|__|__|__|__|__|__|__|__|__|__|__|__|__|__|__|__|__|__|__|__|__|__|__|__|__|__|__|__|__|__|__|__|__|__|__|__|__|__|__|__|__|__|

|__|__|__|__|__|__|__|__|__|__|__|__|__|__|__|__|__|__|__|__|__|__|__|__|__|__|__|__|__|__|__|__|__|__|__|__|__|__|__|__|__|__|

|__|__|__|__|__|__|__|__|__|__|__|__|__|__|__|__|__|__|__|__|__|__|__|__|__|__|__|__|__|__|__|__|__|__|__|__|__|__|__|__|__|__|

|__|__|__|__|__|__|__|__|__|__|__|__|__|__|__|__|__|__|__|__|__|__|__|__|__|__|__|__|__|__|__|__|__|__|__|__|__|__|__|__|__|__|

|__|__|__|__|__|__|__|__|__|__|__|__|__|__|__|__|__|__|__|__|__|__|__|__|__|__|__|__|__|__|__|__|__|__|__|__|__|__|__|__|__|__|

|__|__|__|__|__|__|__|__|__|__|__|__|__|__|__|__|__|__|__|__|__|__|__|__|__|__|__|__|__|__|__|__|__|__|__|__|__|__|__|__|__|__|

....

DIV. APPROV/DATE: |__|__|__|__|__|__|__|__|__|__|__|__|__|__|__|__|__|__|__|__|__|__|__|__|__|__|__|__|__|__| , |__|__|/|__|__|/|__|__|;

SECT. APPROV/DATE: |__|__|__|__|__|__|__|__|__|__|__|__|__|__|__|__|__|__|__|__|__|__|__|__|__|__|__|__|__|__| , |__|__|/|__|__|/|__|__|;

CORP. APPROV/DATE: |__|__|__|__|__|__|__|__|__|__|__|__|__|__|__|__|__|__|__|__|__|__|__|__|__|__|__|__|__|__| , |__|__|/|__|__|/|__|__|.

....

USER DEFINED INFORMATION

(ONE HUNDRED TEN USER DEFINED FIELDS FOR USER CODES AND USER DEFINED INFORMATION HAVE BEEN PROVIDED)

R.E. FILE NO: **LEASED PROPERTY INPUT SHEET**   PAGE 3

SECTOR------|__|
COMPANY NO.----------|__|__|__|
STATE NO.-----|__|__| LEASE/   NEW LEASE/
EXCHANGE NO.------|__|__|__|__| DATE SUBMITTED: GROUND LEASE/   EXTENSION/   VACANCY   SUBLESSORS:
BLDG. NO.-----|__|__|__|__| EASEMENT: RENEWAL: APPROV.:
PARCEL NO.-------------------|__|__| |__|__|/|__|__|/|__|__| (L/G/E) |__| (L/E/R) |__| (Y/N) |__| (Y/N) |__|

• •

PROPERTY INFORMATION

LOCATION
NAME: |__|__|__|__|__|__|__|__|__|__|__|__|__|__|__|__|__|__|__|__|__|__|__|__|__|__|__|__|__|__|__|__|__|__|__|__|__|__|__|__|

SECTOR/
DIVISION
(LESSEE): |__|__|__|__|__|__|__|__|__|__|__|__|__|__|__|__|__|__|__|__|__|__|__|__|__|__|__|__|__|__|__|__|__|__|__|__|__|__|__|__|

PROPERTY
ADDRESS: |__|__|__|__|__|__|__|__|__|__|__|__|__|__|__|__|__|__|__|__|__|__|__|__|__|__|__|__|__|__|__|__| NUMBER OF FLOORS: |__|__|

|__|__|__|__|__|__|__|__|__|__|__|__|__|__|__|__|__|__|__|__|__|__|__|__|__|__|__|__|__|__|__|__|

CITY: |__|__|__|__|__|__|__|__|__|__|__|__|__|__|__|__|__|__|__|__| STATE: |__|__| ZIP: |__|__|__|__|__|

COUNTY: |__|__|__|__|__|__|__|__|__|__|__|__|__|__|__|__| COUNTRY (DEFAULT IS): |U|S|A|__|__|__|__|__|__|__|__|

LOCATION MANAGER: |__|__|__|__|__|__|__|__|__|__|__|__|__|__|__|__|__|__|__|__|__|__|__|__|__|__|__|__|

AREA CODE: |__|__|__| TELEPHONE: |__|__|__| - |__|__|__|__| EXTENSION: |__|__|__|__|

LANDLORD
(LESSOR): |__|__|__|__|__|__|__|__|__|__|__|__|__|__|__|__|__|__|__|__|__|__|__|__|__|__|__|__|__|__|__|__|__|__|__|__|__|

|__|__|__|__|__|__|__|__|__|__|__|__|__|__|__|__|__|__|__|__|__|__|__|__|__|__|__|__|__|__|__|__|__|__|

ADDRESS: |__|__|__|__|__|__|__|__|__|__|__|__|__|__|__|__|__|__|__|__|__|__|__|__|__|__|__|__|__|__|__|__|__|

|__|__|__|__|__|__|__|__|__|__|__|__|__|__|__|__|__|__|__|__|__|__|__|__|__|__|__|__|__|__|__|__|

|__|__|__|__|__|__|__|__|__|__|__|__|__|__|__|__|__|__|__|__|__|__|__|__|__|__|__|__|__|__|__|__|

CITY: |__|__|__|__|__|__|__|__|__|__|__|__|__|__|__|__|__|__|__|__| STATE: |__|__| ZIP: |__|__|__|__|__|

AREA CODE: |__|__|__| TELEPHONE: |__|__|__| - |__|__|__|__| EXTENSION: |__|__|__|__|

TYPE OF FACILITY: |__|__|__|__|__|__|__|__|__|__|__|__|__|__|__|__|__|__|__|__|__|__|__|__|__|__|__|__|__|

LEGAL REVIEW BY: |__|__|__|__|__|__|__|__|__|__|__|__|__|__|__|__|__|__|__|__|__| DATE: |__|__|/|__|__|/|__|__|

FINANCIAL REVIEW BY: |__|__|__|__|__|__|__|__|__|__|__|__|__|__|__|__|__|__|__|__|__| DATE: |__|__|/|__|__|/|__|__|

A/R REQUIRED (Y/N) |__|;   A/R APPROVED (Y/N) |__|;   IL ONLY (Y/N) |__|;   IF Y, DATE: |__|__|/|__|__|/|__|__|

OWNERS REPRESENTATIVE: |__|__|__|__|__|__|__|__|__|__|__|__|__|__|__|__|__|__|__|__|__|__|__|__|__|__|__|__|__|__|

AREA CODE: |__|__|__| TELEPHONE: |__|__|__| - |__|__|__|__| EXTENSION: |__|__|__|__|

LEASING AGENT: |__|__|__|__|__|__|__|__|__|__|__|__|__|__|__|__|__|__|__|__|__|__|__|__|__|__|__|__|

AGENT'S REPRESENTATIVE: |__|__|__|__|__|__|__|__|__|__|__|__|__|__|__|__|__|__|__|__|__|__|__|__|__|__|__|__|__|

AREA CODE: |__|__|__| TELEPHONE: |__|__|__| - |__|__|__|__| EXTENSION: |__|__|__|__|

R.E. FILE NO: **LEASED PROPERTY INPUT SHEET** PAGE 4

|_| - |_|_|_| - |_|_| - |_|_|_|_| - |_|_|_|_| - |_|_|

••

RENT
PAYMENT
PAYABLE TO: |_|_|_|_|_|_|_|_|_|_|_|_|_|_|_|_|_|_|_|_|_|_|_|_|_|_|_|_|_|_|_|_|_|_|_|_|_|_|_|_|_|_|_|_|_|

|_|_|_|_|_|_|_|_|_|_|_|_|_|_|_|_|_|_|_|_|_|_|_|_|_|_|_|_|_|_|_|_|_|_|_|_|_|_|_|_|_|_|_|_|

RENT |_|_|_|_|_|_|_|_|_|_|_|_|_|_|_|_|_|_|_|_|_|_|_|_|_|_|_|_|_|_|_|_|_|_|_|_|_|_|_|_|_|_|_|_|
PAYMENT
ADDRESS: |_|_|_|_|_|_|_|_|_|_|_|_|_|_|_|_|_|_|_|_|_|_|_|_|_|_|_|_|_|_|_|_|_|_|_|_|_|_|_|_|_|_|_|_|

|_|_|_|_|_|_|_|_|_|_|_|_|_|_|_|_|_|_|_|_|_|_|_|_|_|_|_|_|_|_|_|_|_|_|_|_|_|_|_|_|_|_|_|_|

|_|_|_|_|_|_|_|_|_|_|_|_|_|_|_|_|_|_|_|_|_|_|_|_|_|_|_|_|_|_|_|_|_|_|_|_|_|_|_|_|_|_|_|_|

CITY: |_|_|_|_|_|_|_|_|_|_|_|_|_|_|_|_|_|_|_|_|_|_|_| STATE: |_|_| ZIP: |_|_|_|_|_|
CORRESPONDENCE
NOTIFICATION
ADDRESS: |_|_|_|_|_|_|_|_|_|_|_|_|_|_|_|_|_|_|_|_|_|_|_|_|_|_|_|_|_|_|_|_|_|_|_|_|_|_|_|_|

|_|_|_|_|_|_|_|_|_|_|_|_|_|_|_|_|_|_|_|_|_|_|_|_|_|_|_|_|_|_|_|_|_|_|_|_|_|_|_|_|

|_|_|_|_|_|_|_|_|_|_|_|_|_|_|_|_|_|_|_|_|_|_|_|_|_|_|_|_|_|_|_|_|_|_|_|_|_|_|_|_|

CITY: |_|_|_|_|_|_|_|_|_|_|_|_|_|_|_|_|_|_|_|_|_|_|_| STATE: |_|_| ZIP: |_|_|_|_|_|

••

LEASE TERMS

LEASE DATES
EFFECTIVE: |_|_|/|_|_|/|_|_| OCCUPANCY: |_|_|/|_|_|/|_|_| TERMINATION: |_|_|/|_|_|/|_|_|
TOTAL
INITIAL TERM: YEARS: |_|_| MONTHS: |_|_|_|_| DAYS: |_|_|_|_| HOLDOVER: |_|_|_|_|_|_|_|_|

OPTIONS? (Y/N) |_|; IF YES, NUMBER OF OPTION PERIODS: |_|_| FOR YEARS PER OPTION: |_|_|
OF DAYS NOTICE PURCHASE
REQUIRED: |_|_|_|_|; OPTION FOR OTHER SPACE? (Y/N) |_| IF Y, SEE LEASE; OPTION? (Y/N) |_|

OPTION BEGINS: OPTION ENDS: OPTION EXERCISE NOTIFICATION SENT TO LANDLORD:

1. |_|_|/|_|_|/|_|_| |_|_|/|_|_|/|_|_| (Y/N) ? |_|; IF YES, DATE: |_|_|/|_|_|/|_|_|

2. |_|_|/|_|_|/|_|_| |_|_|/|_|_|/|_|_| (Y/N) ? |_|; IF YES, DATE: |_|_|/|_|_|/|_|_|

3. |_|_|/|_|_|/|_|_| |_|_|/|_|_|/|_|_| (Y/N) ? |_|; IF YES, DATE: |_|_|/|_|_|/|_|_|

4. |_|_|/|_|_|/|_|_| |_|_|/|_|_|/|_|_| (Y/N) ? |_|; IF YES, DATE: |_|_|/|_|_|/|_|_|

OPTION INFORMATION: |_|_|_|_|_|_|_|_|_|_|_|_|_|_|_|_|_|_|_|_|_|_|_|_|_|_|_|_|_|_|_|_|_|_|_|_|_|_|

|_|_|_|_|_|_|_|_|_|_|_|_|_|_|_|_|_|_|_|_|_|_|_|_|_|_|_|_|_|_|_|_|_|_|_|_|_|_|_|_|

|_|_|_|_|_|_|_|_|_|_|_|_|_|_|_|_|_|_|_|_|_|_|_|_|_|_|_|_|_|_|_|_|_|_|_|_|_|_|_|_|

|_|_|_|_|_|_|_|_|_|_|_|_|_|_|_|_|_|_|_|_|_|_|_|_|_|_|_|_|_|_|_|_|_|_|_|_|_|_|_|_|

|_|_|_|_|_|_|_|_|_|_|_|_|_|_|_|_|_|_|_|_|_|_|_|_|_|_|_|_|_|_|_|_|_|_|_|_|_|_|_|_|

|_|_|_|_|_|_|_|_|_|_|_|_|_|_|_|_|_|_|_|_|_|_|_|_|_|_|_|_|_|_|_|_|_|_|_|_|_|_|_|_|

|_|_|_|_|_|_|_|_|_|_|_|_|_|_|_|_|_|_|_|_|_|_|_|_|_|_|_|_|_|_|_|_|_|_|_|_|_|_|_|_|

R.E. FILE NO: **LEASED PROPERTY INPUT SHEET** PAGE 5

|__| - |__|__|__| - |__|__| - |__|__|__|__| - |__|__|__|__| - |__|__|

•••

RENT/PENALTY: |__|__|__|__|__|__|__|__|__|__|__|__|__|__|__|__|__|__|__|__|__|__|__|__|__|__|__|__|__|__|__|
CANCELLATION
PENALTY: |__|__|__|__|__|__|__|__|__|__|__|__|__|__|__|__|__|__|__|__|__|__|__|__|__|__|__|__|__|__|__|

DEPOSIT ? (Y/N) |__|, IF YES, AMOUNT $ |__|__|__|__|__|__| . |__|__| PARKING PER 1000 SQ.FT. |__|__|.|__|__|

UPFIT ALLOWANCE ? (Y/N) |__|, IF YES, AMOUNT $ |__|__|__|__|__|__|__|__|

FLOORS LEASED: |__|__|__|__|__|__|__|__|__|__|__|__|__|__| DATE OF AGREEMENT: |__|__|/|__|__|/|__|__|__|__|

•••

RENTAL INFORMATION

TOTAL
LEASE COMMITMENT: $ |__|__|__|__|__|__|__|__|__| . |__|__| RATE PER RENTABLE SQ.FT./YR: $ |__|__|__| . |__|__|
BASE RENT
PAYMENT PER MO.: $ |__|__|__|__|__|__|__| . |__|__| OPERATING EXPENSE PER MO.: $ |__|__|__|__|__| . |__|__|
COMMON AREA
MAINT. PER MO.: $ |__|__|__|__|__| . |__|__| OPTION PERIOD COST: $ |__|__|__|__|__|__|__|__| . |__|__|

OPTION PERIOD COST INFO.: |__|__|__|__|__|__|__|__|__|__|__|__|__|__|__|__|__|__|__|__|__|__|__|__|
AREAS (SQ.FT.)
    TOTAL: |__|__|__|__|__|__|__| OFFICE: |__|__|__|__|__|__|__| WAREHOUSE: |__|__|__|__|__|__|__|

    PRODUCTION: |__|__|__|__|__|__|__| NET RENTABLE: |__|__|__|__|__|__|__| NET USABLE: |__|__|__|__|__|__|__|
COMMON
AREA FACTOR: |__|__|% PROPERTY AREA: |__|__|__|__|__|__|__|__| SQ. FT. OR |__|__|__|__|__|__|__| ACRES

ADDITIONAL AREA AFFECTED BY: OPTION: |__|__|__|__|__|__|__|__|__| SQ. FT.; LAND: |__|__|__|__|__|__|__|__|__| ACRES

ESCALATION CLAUSE ? (Y/N) |__|

ESCALATION TERMS: |__|__|__|__|__|__|__|__|__|__|__|__|__|__|__|__|__|__|__|__|__|__|__|__|__|__|__|__|__|__|__|

                 |__|__|__|__|__|__|__|__|__|__|__|__|__|__|__|__|__|__|__|__|__|__|__|__|__|__|__|__|__|__|__|

                 |__|__|__|__|__|__|__|__|__|__|__|__|__|__|__|__|__|__|__|__|__|__|__|__|__|__|__|__|__|__|__|

                 |__|__|__|__|__|__|__|__|__|__|__|__|__|__|__|__|__|__|__|__|__|__|__|__|__|__|__|__|__|__|__|

                 |__|__|__|__|__|__|__|__|__|__|__|__|__|__|__|__|__|__|__|__|__|__|__|__|__|__|__|__|__|__|__|

                 |__|__|__|__|__|__|__|__|__|__|__|__|__|__|__|__|__|__|__|__|__|__|__|__|__|__|__|__|__|__|__|

                 |__|__|__|__|__|__|__|__|__|__|__|__|__|__|__|__|__|__|__|__|__|__|__|__|__|__|__|__|__|__|__|

ESCALATION PERIODS:

BEGINS: 1. |__|__|/|__|__|/|__|__| ENDS: |__|__|/|__|__|/|__|__| RENT PER MO.: $ |__|__|__|__|__|__|__|__| . |__|__|

        2. |__|__|/|__|__|/|__|__| |__|__|/|__|__|/|__|__| $ |__|__|__|__|__|__|__|__| . |__|__|

        3. |__|__|/|__|__|/|__|__| |__|__|/|__|__|/|__|__| $ |__|__|__|__|__|__|__|__| . |__|__|

        4. |__|__|/|__|__|/|__|__| |__|__|/|__|__|/|__|__| $ |__|__|__|__|__|__|__|__| . |__|__|

continued . . .

R.E. FILE NO: **LEASED PROPERTY INPUT SHEET** PAGE 6

|__| - |__|__|__| - |__|__| - |__|__|__|__| - |__|__|__|__| - |__|__|

•••

BEGINS: 5. |__|__|/|__|__|/|__|__| ENDS: |__|__|/|__|__|/|__|__| RENT $ |__|__|__|__|__|__|__|__|__| . |__|__|
PER MO.

6. |__|__|/|__|__|/|__|__| |__|__|/|__|__|/|__|__| $ |__|__|__|__|__|__|__|__|__| . |__|__|

7. |__|__|/|__|__|/|__|__| |__|__|/|__|__|/|__|__| $ |__|__|__|__|__|__|__|__|__| . |__|__|

8. |__|__|/|__|__|/|__|__| |__|__|/|__|__|/|__|__| $ |__|__|__|__|__|__|__|__|__| . |__|__|

9. |__|__|/|__|__|/|__|__| |__|__|/|__|__|/|__|__| $ |__|__|__|__|__|__|__|__|__| . |__|__|

10. |__|__|/|__|__|/|__|__| |__|__|/|__|__|/|__|__| $ |__|__|__|__|__|__|__|__|__| . |__|__|

•••

LESSEE RESPONSIBILITIES

PROPERTY TAXES BY LESSEE ? (Y/N) |__| INSURANCE BY LESSEE ? (Y/N) |__|

IF YES: LAST YEAR |__|__|/|__|__|/|__|__| $ |__|__|__|__|__|__|__| . |__|__| IF YES, COVERAGE: |__|__|__|__|__|__|__|__|

THIS YEAR |__|__|/|__|__|/|__|__| $ |__|__|__|__|__|__|__| . |__|__| |__|__|__|__|__|__|__|__|__|__|__|__|__|

NEXT YEAR |__|__|/|__|__|/|__|__| $ |__|__|__|__|__|__|__| . |__|__| UTILITIES BY LESSEE ? (Y/N) |__|

SERVICES INCLUDED IN LEASE: |__| |__| |__| |__| |__| |__| |__| |__| |__| |__| IF YES: |__|__|__|__|__|__|__|__|__|__|__|

SERVICE CODES:
 0 - NO SERVICES INCLUDED 4 - PLUMBING 7 - SIGNAGE |__|__|__|__|__|__|__|__|__|__|__|__|__|__|
 1 - JANITORIAL 5 - GROUNDS/C.A.M. 8 - LIGHTING
 2 - HVAC 6 - ROOFING 9 - EXTERIOR
 3 - ELECTRICAL

GENERAL |__|__|__|__|__|__|__|__|__|__|__|__|__|__|__|__|__|__|__|__|__|__|__|__|__|__|__|__|__|__|__|__|__|__|__|__|__|__|__|
COMMENTS:
|__|__|__|__|__|__|__|__|__|__|__|__|__|__|__|__|__|__|__|__|__|__|__|__|__|__|__|__|__|__|__|__|__|__|__|__|__|__|__|

|__|__|__|__|__|__|__|__|__|__|__|__|__|__|__|__|__|__|__|__|__|__|__|__|__|__|__|__|__|__|__|__|__|__|__|__|__|__|__|

|__|__|__|__|__|__|__|__|__|__|__|__|__|__|__|__|__|__|__|__|__|__|__|__|__|__|__|__|__|__|__|__|__|__|__|__|__|__|__|

|__|__|__|__|__|__|__|__|__|__|__|__|__|__|__|__|__|__|__|__|__|__|__|__|__|__|__|__|__|__|__|__|__|__|__|__|__|__|__|

|__|__|__|__|__|__|__|__|__|__|__|__|__|__|__|__|__|__|__|__|__|__|__|__|__|__|__|__|__|__|__|__|__|__|__|__|__|__|__|

|__|__|__|__|__|__|__|__|__|__|__|__|__|__|__|__|__|__|__|__|__|__|__|__|__|__|__|__|__|__|__|__|__|__|__|__|__|__|__|

|__|__|__|__|__|__|__|__|__|__|__|__|__|__|__|__|__|__|__|__|__|__|__|__|__|__|__|__|__|__|__|__|__|__|__|__|__|__|__|

•••

DIV.APPROV/DATE: |__|__|__|__|__|__|__|__|__|__|__|__|__|__|__|__|__|__|__|__|__|__|__|__|__|__|__| , |__|__|/|__|__|/|__|__|;

SECT.APPROV/DATE: |__|__|__|__|__|__|__|__|__|__|__|__|__|__|__|__|__|__|__|__|__|__|__|__|__|__|__| , |__|__|/|__|__|/|__|__|;

CORP.APPROV/DATE: |__|__|__|__|__|__|__|__|__|__|__|__|__|__|__|__|__|__|__|__|__|__|__|__|__|__|__| , |__|__|/|__|__|/|__|__|.

•••

USER DEFINED INFORMATION

(ONE HUNDRED TEN USER DEFINED FIELDS FOR USER CODES AND USER DEFINED INFORMATION HAVE BEEN PROVIDED)

F-9

Service Evaluation Questionnaire

In order to improve the quality of our service, we would appreciate you spending a few minutes completing this form.

1. Our record shows that you requested service on ___/___/___ at ___:___
    Date   Time

2. The service or repair was completed on ___/___/___ at ___:___
    Date   Time

3. Was the repair time acceptable to you?
    a) Extremely   b) Very   c) Satisfied   d) Somewhat   e) Not
       satisfied   satisfied   satisfied   satisfied

4. Was the response time acceptable to you?
    a) Extremely   b) Very   c) Satisfied   d) Somewhat   e) Not
       satisfied   satisfied   satisfied   satisfied

5. Did the technician fix the problem to your satisfaction?
    a) Extremely   b) Very   c) Satisfied   d) Somewhat   e) Not
       satisfied   satisfied   satisfied   satisfied

6. Did the technician leave the working area neat and clean?
    Yes ____ No ____ Explain _____

7. Did the technician answer your questions satisfactorily?
    a) Extremely   b) Very   c) Satisfied   d) Somewhat   e) Not
       satisfied   satisfied   satisfied   satisfied

8. If not, did the technician refer you to another person?
    Yes ____ No ____ Explain _____

9. Which of the following best describes the technician's performance?
    a) Excellent   b) Very good   c) Good   d) Poor   e) Unacceptable

10. Are there any suggestions for improving our services?

Name: _____ Ext.: _____ Service Order Number: _____

Please return to Service Evaluation, Room _____

(This form can easily be automated to evaluate overall shop or individual qualitative performance.)

F-10

Bidder Qualification Questionnaire

Bidder: _____

By: _____

1. What year was your company incorporated? _____
   In what state or country is your company incorporated? _____
   What were your (year) _____ annual Sales? $_____
   What were your _____ annual Sales? $_____
   Is your company publicly held? Yes _____ No _____
   (If publicly held, attach your (year) _____ annual report. If privately held, attach your (year) _____ audited financial statements.)
   Has your company ever filed or petitioned for bankrutpcy? Yes _____ No _____. If yes, explain in detail the reasons why, filing date, and current status.
2. Provide the number of *full-time* employees, by category, from your local office. If no local office, list the office that would support this requirement. Enclose a work résumé of your proposed superintendent and other key personnel.
3. If your employees are represented by a collective bargaining unit, list the name of the unit and expiration date of the current agreement, and give a brief explanation of past labor problems, if any.
4. What is the average length of service your *full-time* managers have within the industry? _____ years; in your company? _____ years
5. What is the average length of service your *full-time* carpenters have within the industry? _____ years; in your company? _____ years
6. Provide three major (over $2 million annual) projects of a same or similar nature you are currently engaged in or will be by (year) _____, including project description, location, client, contact, phone number, and dollar amount.
7. Provide the two largest projects of a same or similar nature that you have

accomplished in the last five years, including project description, location, client, contact, phone number, and dollar amount.

8. Provide any and all exceptions and/or variances to the specifications that your firm requests and/or is restricted from complying with.

9. Do you currently have any contracts or agreements for building supplies? Yes _____ No _____. If yes, list manufacturers and expiration dates.

10. Describe *in detail* what training you currently have in-house or under contract for your employees.

11. Describe *in detail* what experience your company had or has with _____ and include any reason(s) for termination.

12. Have you ever been terminated on a contract? Yes _____ No _____. If yes, describe *in detail*.

13. Do you currently, or within the last two years, have any staff "on-site" at a customer's facility performing similar services? Yes _____ No _____. If yes, list the number of personnel, company, services performed, and annual dollar scope of each.

14. Does your company have 24-hour emergency service? Yes _____ No _____. If yes, describe what services are provided?

15. Provide all current (last three years) customer references with contact and phone number, noting contracts of a same or similar nature.

16. Provide your financial reference with contact and phone number.

17. Provide your insurance reference with contact and phone number.

18. Provide your bonding reference with contact and phone number. What is your maximum bonding limit and your current available amount?

19. Describe *in detail* what your company's greatest strength is.

F-11

Contractor/Consultant Evaluation (Two-Step; Most Qualified Accepted)

Typical Phase I (Written Material)
Evaluation of Contractor/Consultant[1]

		Points
1.0	Project Manager Evaluation	<u>20</u>
	1.1 Experience in project management and construction industry	10
	1.2 Size, scope, and complexity of previous projects assigned	7
	1.3 Experience in local area	3
2.0	Key Staff Qualifications	<u>10</u>
	2.1 Qualifications of key staff	6
	2.2 Stability of key staff	4
3.0	Project Experience	<u>20</u>
	3.1 Current workload	5
	3.2 Size of recent projects	5
	3.3 Customer references	5
	3.4 Similar types of projects	5
4.0	Experience and Technical Capabilities	<u>20</u>
	4.1 Stability and breadth of company	6
	4.2 Ability to perform requirements	10
	4.3 Relevant experience	4
5.0	Approach of Terms of Reference	<u>15</u>
	5.1 Anticipated approach	10
	5.2 Proposed schedule and team	5

6.0	Financial and Insurance Capabilities	15[2]
	6.1 Sales history	7
	6.2 Financial reference	4
	6.3 Insurance reference	4
	Total	100

Notes: 1. Items evaluated and weights vary from bid to bid.
2. Normally done by procurement specialist.

Typical Phase II (Short-List)
Evaluation (Written Material, Price, and Presentation)[1]

Points

1.0	Project Manager Evaluation	10
	1.1 Experience in project management and construction industry	5
	1.2 Size, scope, and complexity of previous projects assigned	4
	1.3 Experience in local area	1
2.0	Project Experience	15
	2.1 Project similar to Bank's	5
	2.2 Phased projects	5
	2.3 Minimizing staff disturbance	5
3.0	Experience and Technical Capabilities	10
	3.1 Stability and breadth of firm	5
	3.2 Customer references	3
	3.3 Relevant experience	2
4.0	Approach of Terms and Reference	10
	4.1 Anticipated approach	5
	4.2 Proposed schedule and team	5
5.0	Presentation	20
	5.1 Cohesiveness of firm	5
	5.2 Commitment	5
	5.3 Understanding of complex organization	5
	5.4 Understanding of role	5
6.0	Price	35[2]
	Total	100

Notes: 1. Items evaluated and weights vary from bid to bid.
2. Points are calculated, normally by the procurement specialist, according to the following formula (low bidder gets 35 points):

$$\text{Contractor score (points)} = \text{Max score (points)} - \text{max score} \times \frac{(.5)(TS - LC)}{LC}$$

where:
TS = Price of contractor being evaluated
LC = Price of lowest contractor

F-12

Checklist for Rating Your Facilities Management Department

The checklist has eight principal facility management activities. Beneath each is a breakdown of specific functions. According to the following definitions, place check marks in the appropriate columns to indicate where the responsibility for that function falls:

1 = **Facilities Management Department**

2 = **Sister Department**—reporting to the same senior executive as does the facility management department.

3 = **Remote Department**—not reporting to the same senior executive

4 = **No Department**—no provision is made for specific functions

	1	2	3	4
A. Real Property Management				
1. Maintenance long-term property acquisition/lease program.				
2. Purchase of buildings and land.				
3. Leasing of non-owned premises for corporate use.				
4. Marketing and leasing of corporate owned or leased premises to others.				
5. Lease management.				
6. Service and management for tenants of the corporation.				
7. Cost control and financial reports.				

	1	2	3	4
B. Building Design and Construction				
1. General contracting.				
2. Construction management.				
3. Project management (for all new construction and all renovation of leasehold improvements).				
4. Architectural design.				
5. Landscape and site design.				
6. Specification of building operating systems.				
7. Upgrade programs.				
8. Engineering design.				
9. Estimating.				
10. Preparation of contract drawings and specifications.				
11. Preparation of bid packages.				
12. Bid supervision and contract award.				
13. Code compliance and contract supervision.				
14. Field supervision.				
15. Cost control and financial reports.				
C. Building Operations				
1. Operation of building operations systems.				
2. Building maintenance and repairs.				
3. Carpentry and minor renovation.				
4. Grounds maintenance.				
5. Cleaning, housekeeping, porter service.				
6. Inspection of premises.				
7. OSHA compliance.				
8. Maintaining files (plans, licenses, inspections).				
9. Security systems.				
10. Security staff.				
11. Life safety systems.				
12. Cost control and financial reports.				
D. Office Facility Planning				
1. Determining work place area standards.				
2. Determining work place furniture and equipment standards.				

	1	2	3	4
3. Specifying the common facilities.				
4. Programming long-term office space needs (2 years or longer).				
5. Programming short-term office space needs (less than 2 years).				
6. Programming future office furniture and equipment needs.				
7. Maintain office space inventory.				
8. Monitor quality of workplace environment.				
9. Space allocation to user-groups and to individuals.				
10. Project management for interior layout and design.				
11. Project management for interior furniture and layout changes (non-leasehold improvements).				
12. Planning moves.				
13. Supervising moves.				
E. Interior Layout and Design				
1. Stacking and blocking plans.				
2. Layout plans.				
3. Furniture and furnishings specifications.				
4. Art program.				
5. Determine decorative standards (colors, materials, finishes).				
6. Interior design (color, finish, graphics, signage, flooring, furniture selection, fabrics, accessories).				
F. Interior Architecture and Construction				
1. Interior architecture (leasehold improvements).				
2. Estimating.				
3. Preparation of contract drawings and specifications.				
4. Preparation of bid packages and purchase orders.				
5. Bid supervision, contract award, contract supervision.				
6. Field supervision.				
7. Cost control and financial reports.				
8. Updating of building plans following construction / renovation				
G. Office Furniture and Furnishings				

	1	2	3	4
1. Purchasing.				
2. Expediting.				
3. Installation of workstations, furniture, equipment.				
4. Furniture storage.				
5. Furniture repair and maintenance.				
6. Maintaining furniture inventory records.				
7. Cost control and financial reports.				
H. Telecommunications Planning & Control				
1. Plan individual user needs and features for telephones, data terminals, other information devices.				
2. Coordinate installation.				
3. Order required electrical or other leasehold work.				
4. Maintain telephone/terminal location plans.				
5. Cost control and financial reports.				

Source: "Checklist for Rating Your Facilities Management Department," *Facilities Design & Management,* November/December 1984, pp. 114–115.

F-13

The Facility Management Checklist

Themes

Because we think they're so important, we repeat themes that seem to be essential to public or private sector facility management in organizations—small or large.

Recurring Themes

• *Business issues.* We must understand not only our business but, in detail, how we affect the company/agency that we support. We must know the language of business and be able to use capital budget evaluation tools.

• *The cost of ownership.* There are initial and ongoing costs of the ownership of facilities. Management must understand and provide for those costs from planning through disposal.

• *Life-cycle costing.* As a general rule, all economic analyses and comparisons should be based on life-cycle costs. Comparison leading to bad decisions are often made by considering capital or initial costs only.

• *Integration of services.* Consider one example: Interior illumination design may be based solely on appearance and violate the principles of a good energy management program simply because no one bothered to integrate the two services of design and operations.

• *Design for operations and maintenance.* Operators and maintainers, even if they are contractors, must be actively involved in the design review process.

• *Responsibility.* Facility management functions should be grouped into budget programs, with a manager responsible and accountable for each.

• *Cost-effectiveness.* The key is to properly identify and compare costs; comparison must be made over time.

• *Constant efficiency improvement.* Efficiency should be judged through comparators, through user feedback, and through MBWA (management by walking around).

- *In-house vs. contracting out.* There is, and will continue to be, strong support for contracting out facility management services. Each facility manager should have clearly defined in his or her own mind what functions must be controlled in-house. The manager must be willing to fight for the resources to perform those functions. Those functions are generally managerial, not technical, in nature.

- *Quality of life.* The facility manager must actively promote and protect the quality of life of the company's employees. A safe and healthful workplace is the minimum; a workplace where the facility promotes individual and group productivity should be the goal.

Philosophy

We present here a listing of short themes that are particularly applicable to facility management.

- Safety is always the first concern; legality is a close second.
- Someone should be directly responsible for every physical asset and function.
- Service, service, and service!
- Quality, quality, quality!
- There is a cost of ownership of facilities; it is your task to ensure that your management understands that cost in its entirety.
- Your responsibility to management is well known; concentrate on your responsibility to the employees.
- Be cost-effective in everything you do, but capture all costs in your analyses.
- If something looks like a good idea, use it on a trial basis. If it doesn't work out, change it.
- No one is right 100 percent of the time. A good, commonsense decision beats "paralysis by analysis" every time. Excessive dependence on quantitative measurement can be the downfall of a facility department.
- A budget is a management tool. Put personal effort into its preparation and format; monitor its execution.
- Don't mind being compared, but insist upon true comparators (quantity, quality, time).
- Every physical asset should be under life-cycle maintenance.
- When an outside consultant is used, you must define the requirement or you have lost control.
- As the design-construct cycle proceeds, changes become costlier and less effective. Contractors and consultants bring special talents to the facility department, but the facility manager must retain control.
- In the planning of major projects, engineering requirements are nearly always understated. They are also the most costly to meet through changes at a later date. Plan for flexibility and redundancy.
- Plan with care, but always retain the capability to react.

• Cultivate lasting and long-term relationships. Develop them carefully. Any successful facility management organization is a team (staff, suppliers, contractors, consultants) and needs stronger bonding than what is provided in a least-cost contract.

FM Checklist

By now you know that we are great believers in evaluation. We evaluate constantly and expect to be evaluated. Fair, accurate, and continuous evaluation is the basis for improvement.

We provide you with a checklist that we have found valuable when giving a department an initial evaluation or the 30,000 mile checkup. Use it in good health—for yourself and for your department.

• Is there a clearly defined (regardless of name) facilities department?
• Is the department manager no further than two echelons from the CEO/ agency head?
• Does the department (manager) have sufficient control over the fourteen functions of facility management?
• Is there a facilities plan to support all long- and short-range business plans? Is there an annual facilities work plan?
• Is at least one person focused on strategic facilities planning?
• Does a *knowledgeable* person make buy/lease decisions?
• Is work centrally received, coordinated, and controlled?
• Is there a preventive maintenance program in place that extends beyond the physical plant?
• Is there any energy management program in place?
• Is there a close tie between the information management, communications, and facilities department?
• Is there good asset accountability?
• Does the department's organization reflect the need for both planning and design (proactive) and operations and maintenance (reactive)?
• Can someone in the department perform the economic analyses necessary to "sell" capital projects within the organization?
• Is there a close working relationship with the purchasing department?
• Do design, space, and engineering standards exist?
• Does the facilities budget format support good management information?

Glossary

Attempting to provide a glossary for a profession is a daunting task, particularly for facility management, with its many dimensions. I have limited this Glossary to the building functions and the financial aspects of facility management. The terms listed here have been drawn from many sources, and most are defined as commonly used in practice.

above building standard   Services and materials provided by a landlord that exceed those provided under the base rent and are therefore reimbursable to the landlord.

acceleration   The situation in which a contractor is forced to increase his work effort and speed in order to meet the contract completion date and avoid the assessment of liquidated damages.

access floor   A floor structure, normally raised over the floor slab, that allows almost unlimited access for below-floor cabling.

accessibility   A determination of the capability of a facility to permit disabled people to enter and use the room or building.

adapt   In building, to make suitable for a particular purpose by means of change or structure.

add   In building, to extend by means of new construction or by enclosing an existing structure.

adjacency diagram   A diagram documenting critical physical proximities or organizational groups, equipment, or support functions.

administrative approval   Approval that a work request has been processed correctly and that funding or level-of-effort floors or ceilings have been met.

administrative services   In facility management, services that are not building related (e.g., transportation, food service, security, reprographics).

A-E   Architectural-engineering firm. Such firms traditionally have enough in-house design capability to be the principal designers of major facilities.

AIA   American Institute of Architects

allocate   To set aside funds for a purpose.

allocations   *See* Chargeback System

allowance items   Items of materials and/or labor that the owner has the option to delete from the contract and procure directly, or allow to remain in the contract to be provided by the contractor. Alternatively, an item for which a budget amount only is specified.

alterations   Work required to change the interior arrangements or other physical characteristics of an existing facility or installed equipment, so that it may be more effectively used for its currently designed purpose, or adapted to a changed use as a result of a programmatic requirement. May include work referred to as improvements, conversion, rehabilitation, remodeling, and modernization.

ambient lighting   Surrounding light, such as that reaching an object in a room from all light sources in the room.

amortization of tenant allowances   The return to the landlord over the term of the lease of those costs included in the landlord's building standard work letter and any other costs that the landlord has agreed to assume or amortize.

amortization of tenant improvements   An agreement by the landlord to pay for above-building-standard improvements and amortize those improvements as a defined interest rate over a fixed term as additional rent.

annual plan   A plan that projects programs for twelve to eighteen months. Normally, at any one time, a facility manager will be gaining approval of next year's plan and formulating one for the out-years.

APPA   Association of Higher Education Facilities Officers

approved vendor list   A current list of vendors providing the owner with goods and services.

APWA   American Public Works Association.

arbitration   The settlement of a contract dispute by selecting an impartial third party to hear both sides and reach a decision.

area   *See* Building Area.

as-built drawing   Construction drawing revised to show changes made during the construction process, usually based on marked-up prints, drawings, and other data furnished by the contractor.

ASCE   American Society of Civil Engineers.

ASHRAE   American Society of Heating, Refrigeration and Air-Conditioning.

ASID   American Society of Interior Designers.

asset   Something, such as a building or piece of equipment, that retains value for a period of time after it is purchased and therefore has both an economic life and a residual value.

asset management   (1) The process of maximizing value to a property or portfolio of properties from acquisition to disposition within the objectives defined by the owner. (2) Management of real property, installed equipment, and furniture, furnishings, and equipment using automated and inventory techniques.

ASTM   American Society for Testing and Materials.

background noise   Noise in a work environment at a level low enough not to interfere with the normal conduct of business and conversation.

balance sheet   An accounting statement listing a company's total assets, total liabilities, and net worth. Capital assets are included, but operating expenses are not.

ballasts   The common term for the starting and regulating mechanism in a fluorescent light fixture.

base building   The basic building structure, including roof and exterior walls, basic mechanical and electrical systems, and the service core.

base-level services   In facilities operations, those services required to support occupancy of a facility.

base power feeds   Electricity supplied via junction boxes in the floor of a building.

base rental   The initial rental rate, normally identified as the annual rent in a gross lease.

base year   The year of building operation, normally a calendar year, in which the landlord fixes or identifies the operating costs included in a gross or semi-net lease. Any increase in operating expenses over the base year is "passed through" to the tenant on a pro rata share of rentable area.

benefit-cost ratio   Benefits divided by costs, where both are discounted to a present value or equivalent uniform annual value.

bid   A written response to an invitation for bid.

blanket purchase order (BPO)   An agreement, normally for a fixed time, for a purchase of low-dollar-value goods and services from a single vendor. BPOs are designed to fill anticipated repetitive needs for small quantities of goods and/or services.

block allocation plan   A drawing showing the location of each employee group relative to other groups and the associated support areas. The block plan should be approved primarily for group locations on the floor.

BOMA Building Owners and Managers Association.

BOMA standard measurement A defined way of measuring space by the Building Owners and Managers Association (BOMA). Landlords may choose their own method to measure space, normally by increasing the amount of common areas added to the usable area.

BOMI Institute A nonprofit organization devoted to providing education for property professionals.

book value The value of an asset at a given point in its economic life based on its value on the date when first placed into service, minus any accumulated depreciation since that date.

break-even analysis A technique for determining the value of a variable that results in savings just even to the costs.

bubble diagram *See* Adjacency Diagram

budget A financial plan for allocating funds during a specific time period.

building A shelter comprising a partially or totally enclosed space, erected by means of a planned process of forming and combining materials.

building area (floor area) A generic term referring to some aspect of the size measurement of a building. One method to characterize the subdivisions of this area is as follows:

> **amenity area** Any area in a facility used by employees for nonwork activity, such as dining rooms, vending areas, lounges, day care centers, and fitness and health centers.

> **area of penetration** The sum of the area of those physical objects that vertically penetrate the space serving more than one floor (e.g., elevator shafts).

> **assignable area** Floor areas of a facility designed to or available for assignment to occupant groups of functions, including interior walls, building columns, and building projections and excluding circulation.

> **circulation area** That portion of the gross area of a building required for physical access to various divisions and subdivisions of space.

> **common area** That area with common access to all users within a gross space (e.g. public corridors). Common area = Rentable area − usable area.

> **core and service area** Floor area of a facility necessary for the general operation that is not available for general occupancy, including primary circulation areas; mechanical, electrical, telephone, and custodial rooms serving individual floors; toilet rooms; building lobbies and atriums, stairways, elevators, vertical shafts, and chases; loading docks; and also central, mechanical, electrical, telephone, and custodial spaces and penthouses, but excluding the interstitial area.

> **gross area** The sum of floor areas within the outside faces of the exterior walls for all building levels that have floor surfaces.

> **leased rentable area** That area to which the base lease rate applies.

> **mechanical area** That portion of the gross area of a building designated to house mechanical equipment and utility services.

> **net assignable area** The sum of the floor areas available for assignment to a program occupant. By definition this excludes custodial, circulation, core, and mechanical areas.

> **net floor area** That part of the gross floor area located within occupiable space.

> **open space** The floor space inside a workstation for furniture, equipment, and internal circulation.

> **primary circulation area** That portion of a building that is a public corridor, lobby, or atrium; or is required for access by all occupants on a floor to stairs, elevators, toilet room, or building entrances.

> **secondary circulation area** That portion of a building required for access to some

subdivisions of space, whether bounded by walls or not, that does not serve all occupants on a floor and is not defined as primary circulation area.

support space Part of the usable area not assigned or dedicated to a specific task or function (e.g., meeting rooms, waiting areas, storage, lounges, computer rooms, copy areas, libraries).

usable area The floor area of a facility assigned to, or available for assignment to, occupant groups or functions, including the interior walls, building columns and projections, and secondary circulation.

workplace Part of the usable area intended for the individual or group to work in.

workspace Part of the usable area intended for a specific function or type of work.

workstation All or part of a workplace, suitable for carrying out one function or type of work.

building component A building element using industrial products that are manufactured as independent units capable of being joined with other elements.

building construction (1) The act or process of making or forming a building by assembly or combining elements, components, or systems. (2) The structure or part thereof so formed.

building economics The application of economic analysis to the design, financing, engineering, construction, management, operation, or ownership of buildings.

building efficiency rate The usable area divided by the rentable area multiplied by 100.

building envelope Perimeter elements of a building, both above and below ground, that divide the external from the internal environment.

building maintenance *See* Maintenance.

building module Standard dimensions within the usable area dictated by window mullion or column spacing (e.g., a five-foot module dictates spaces dimensioned in multiples of five feet).

building operating expense (BOE) Expenses incident to occupying buildings and grounds that are not repair, improvement, or maintenance. Includes rent payments under leases of less than ten years; custodial services; the salaries of building operating staff; service contracts; fuel and utilities; taxes; and fire and comprehensive insurance.

building performance The behavior in service of a building as a whole or of the building components. Often measured in terms of durability and serviceability.

building permit A permit issued by the local government authorizing construction of a project according to plans found to comply with that government's codes.

building projection Pilaster, convector, baseboard heating unit, radiator, or other building element located in the interior of a building wall that prevents the use of that space for furniture, equipment, circulation, or other functions.

building renewal A term referring to the complete reworking of an entire building or of a major, discrete portion to develop a facility equivalent to a new one. It involves the complete upgrading of systems, such as heating and ventilating; it usually includes element replacement, such as a new roof or new sashes; and it may involve program and occupancy changes. At the completion of a building renewal project, the expected useful life of the building should approximate that of an entirely new facility.

building services Services provided to ensure that the building is operable, such as heating, cooling and ventilation, and elevator services.

building standard Standard building materials and quantities provided by the landlord at no cost to the tenant to improve tenant premises.

building standard work letter A document that delineates the type and quality of materials and quantities to be furnished by the landlord as building standard.

building subsystem Complete, integrated set of parts that function as a unit within the finished building.

building system Collection of equipment, facilities, and software designated to perform a specific function.

building team The group of managers and professionals responsible for developing a board project definition of owner's criteria and conceptual design and implementing it into a completed structure. Such teams necessarily include the owner, in varying degrees of involvement depending on his own expertise: the architect-engineer, which may be made up of one or more design consultants; and a builder, who may be a general contractor or a construction manager. The team may also include one or more construction consultants. Building teams vary in makeup principally because of variation in the required services in that portion of the project that are overlapped by the design and construction phases.

build-to-suit An approach to real estate development that enables a corporation to assume ownership by having a developer hold ownership until the project is complete and ready for occupancy. It is a form of delayed ownership.

built-up roof A roof constructed of successive layers of waterproof material sealed with a sealer such as bitumen.

CADD Computer-assisted design and drawing.

CAFM Computer-assisted facility management. Integrated facility management hardware and software to manage diverse facility management functions—most commonly space management, design, inventory management, work management, building operations, lease management, and financial management.

capital costs *See* Costs.

cash flow The stream of dollar values, costs, and savings resulting from an investment decision.

CBX A telephone switchboard that switches data and voice.

ceiling (financial) A level of funding that must not be exceeded.

ceiling plenum The space between the suspended ceiling and the floor slab above.

centrex A centralized switch controlled by the local phone company.

CERCLC Comprehensive Environmental Response, Compensation and Liability Act.

certificate of occupancy A certificate issued by a local government authorizing occupancy of a space that has been found to meet building code requirements and is considered safe for the function for which it was designed.

Certified Facility Manager (CFM) The professional designation of someone who has passed a comprehensive exam administered by the International Facility Management Association.

change order A written order from the contracting officer to the contractor modifying the quantity, quality, or method of work required in the contract.

charge A financial obligation incurred pursuant to a valid contract.

chargeback system A system of cost control that requires the requesting business unit to pay for work done in its area or for work done over and above a standard.

churn The ratio of the number of employees moved annually compared to the total employees of the organization.

CIFM (computer integrated facility management) *See* CAFM.

classes of buildings Buildings categorized by selected attributes concerning facility serviceability and performance.

clean circuit A circuit that has only one technology device connected.

clerestory A window in a wall, often extending from door top to the ceiling to allow light into the interior of a space.

closed plan An approach to designing workspace with a predominance of full-height walls and few or no panels or modular furniture.

code compliance trigger Events that necessitate the compliance of a building to current codes.

code requirements Building code requirements that must be satisfied by the tenant or the landlord in preparing space or a building for tenant occupancy. Examples are seismic, life safety, energy, hazardous/toxic materials, and handicapped code requirements.

commissioning The orderly turnover of a building or major project from the contractor to the owner. Involves completing the operating tests on all major systems, the passing of all user manuals, material safety data sheets, and warranties, the passing of the as-built drawings, training for all operational personnel, agreeing on the satisfaction of all punch list items, and, in some cases, clearing the building of off-gases and ensuring initial air quality.

common area factor (rentable/usable ratio)   The factor used to determine a tenant's pro rata share of the common area. CAF = rentable area/usable area.

compartmentalization   A code requirement to divide large floor plates into smaller units to meet fire code requirements.

competitive range   In procurement, the range of proposal bids that will be considered responsive so that other factors of the bid will be considered.

complex   An organized group of two or more facilities designed to operate as a unit to achieve some programmatic end (e.g., a laboratory and a hospital).

computer-assisted drawing and drafting (CADD) system   An automated drawing system that can manage space, furniture, and equipment as well as produce drawings.

computer-assisted facility management (CAFM) system   A system that automates facility management functions. It commonly contains a computer-assisted drawing and drafting system, a work management system, a project management system, and an asset management system.

concessions   Those inducements offered by a landlord to a tenant to sign a lease. Common concessions are free rent, extra tenant improvement allowances, payment of moving costs, and lease pickups.

concurrent delay   A delay attributable to the actions of both the contractor and the owner. Because there is joint responsibility for a concurrent delay, the contractor is generally not entitled to recover damages for the delay, and the owner is not entitled to assess liquidated damages for delayed completion of the project.

constant dollars   Dollars of uniform purchasing power exclusive of general inflation or deflation.

construction   The erection, installation, or assembly of a new facility; the addition, expansion, alteration, conversion, or replacement of an existing facility; or the relocation of a facility from one installation to another. Includes equipment installed and made a part of such facilities, and related site preparation, excavation, filling, landscaping, or other land improvements.

construction consultant   One who provides specialized professional services to the owner, architect-engineer, or general contractor. Consultant services include such broad areas as budget costing, cost estimating, major purchasing, and scheduling control or more specialized services relating to particular project needs, such as architectural concrete design, foundation construction techniques, and curtain wall specifications.

construction documents (CDs)   Drawings and specifications for a building project, along with the applicable bid and administrative documents.

construction management (CM)   The process of applying management techniques to the design and construction of a project. Generally involves coordinating the overlap of the project's design and construction phases and the activities of multiple prime building contractors.

construction manager   One who furnishes all the services of a general contracting organization, as well as all the construction consulting services necessary from the inception of project planning. As such, the construction manager has a professional services contract with the owner and provides consulting and managerial functions. He is the construction professional of the building team and is responsible for design liaison, the proper selection of materials and methods of construction, and cost and scheduling information and control. In managing the construction activities, he contracts with subcontractors and suppliers on behalf of the owner.

contingency funds   Funds allotted to cover unexpected costs that may be incurred throughout the term of a project.

contract   A consensual relationship based on the willingness of the parties (owner and vendor) to be bound by its terms. It is a promise or a set of promises, the breach of which the law gives a remedy, or the performances of which the law recognizes as a duty. An annual contract is for a twelve-month period, normally one calendar or fiscal year.

cooling load   The amount of heat that must be removed to maintain a structure at a given temperature during cooling.

contract architect   The outside design professional retained by the owner to prepare a project design—normally an architectural-engineering firm for major projects.

contract change proposal   An offer by the contractor to perform work different in quantity, quality, or method from that required by the contract. Typically includes the price of the changed work and an estimate of the time necessary to complete it.

contractor   A vendor who has entered into a contract with the owner for the construction, modification, or rehabilitation of a project.

contracts officer   A staff member of the owner's purchasing department legally responsible for the contracting of services.

contracts officer's representative (COR)   Facility staff member appointed in writing as responsible for monitoring completion of contracts according to the terms and conditions stated therein.

corporate real estate   The owned or leased real property used by a corporation in support of its business mission.

cost

  capital costs   The costs of acquiring, substantially improving, expanding, changing the functional use of, or replacing a building or building system. Capitalization rules are driven by tax laws, so they vary between locations.

  operations costs   Total costs associated with the day-to-day operation of a facility. Includes all maintenance and repair (both fixed and variable); administrative costs; labor costs; janitorial, housekeeping, and other cleaning costs; all utility costs; management fees; and all costs associated with roadways and grounds.

  ownership costs   The cost to the owner to own the building, service existing debt, or receive a return on equity. Also includes costs of capital improvements, repair, and upkeep, which would not be considered standard operating costs.

cost avoidances   Projected or actual costs avoided by an initiative.

cost center   An organizational unit in which budgetary funding is used to sustain operations.

cost-effectiveness   Getting best value for funds expended, not necessarily lowest cost.

cost savings   Money saved by a proposed or actual initiative that can be used for other business purposes.

costs of providing the fixed asset   Capital costs, mortgage costs, capital improvements, taxes, insurance, and depreciation charges. Does not include lease costs, security costs, or relocation or rearrangement costs.

critical path method (CPM)   A project management method using a chart that shows the minimum amount of time required to complete a project and which tasks must be completed before subsequent ones can commence (the critical path).

crossover floor   A floor in which one bank of elevators connects to another bank of elevators, allowing tenants to have access to floors in other elevator banks without returning to the lobby of the building.

CSI   Construction Specification Institute.

current dollars   Dollars of purchasing power in which actual prices are stated, including inflation or deflation.

custodial services   Commonly used to mean janitorial services, window cleaning, rodent and pest control, and waste management.

custody   Condition of items procured in connection with or for use on a project, which are stored at the site or, if stored off-site, marked in such a manner as to indicate their intended use on the project.

customer satisfaction index (CSI)   An index whereby a service organization's customer service performance is measured against an established baseline.

customer service agreements   Informal minicontracts between the facility department and its customers.

day porter services   Miscellaneous services, normally custodial in nature, provided during hours that the facility is occupied (e.g., cleaning up spills, light moving, setting up meeting spaces, lobby tidying).

delegated contracting authority   The act of a contracting officer's giving limited contracting authority (e.g., a $5,000 limit) to an authorized line manager.

demising walls   The walls between one tenant's area and another, as well as walls between tenant areas and public corridors.

demolition plan   A construction drawing that delineates all demolition for an alteration project.

demountable partition   A prefabricated modular wall assembly that can be installed, removed, and reinstalled.

depreciation   The loss in value of a capital asset over its economic life.

design-build   A construction approach in which the owner buys both design and construction services from the same provider.

design development   The phase of a project consisting of preparing the drawings and specifications to fix and describe the size and character of the building systems, materials, and elements.

design program   Document specifying what facilities will be provided to the occupants and confirming to the owner the requirements of the facility.

direct charge of operating expenses   On a gross or seminet lease where the tenant does not pay costs directly, the pro rata share of occupancy costs that the landlord directly bills tenants. In most instances, this will be done on a good-faith, best-estimate, advanced-payment basis, whereby the landlord bills the tenant for estimated operating expense costs during the lease term.

discount rate   That rate of interest reflecting the investor's time value of money; used to determine discount factors for converting benefits and costs occurring at different times to a base time.

discounting   A technique for converting cash flows that occur over time to equivalent amounts at a common time.

drawings   *See* Plans.

due diligence survey   A facility survey taken before a major acquisition to validate building condition, regulatory compliance, the presence or absence of environment hazards, financial value, and other risks.

durability   The capability of a building, assembly, component, product, or construction to maintain serviceability for at least a specified period of time.

dwelling   Building designed or occupied as the living quarters for one or more families or households.

economic life   That period of time over which an investment is considered to be the least-cost alternative for meeting a particular objective.

efficiency   The percentage of rentable area that is usable area.

efficient rent   The dollar amount per square foot per year that the tenant pays on an average over the term of the lease. This would be the average of specified rents in a stair-stepped lease, as well as the average of a lease with substantial free rent period. *Example:* A five-year lease with six months' free rent offers a 10 percent discount from the face rate.

enclosed space   The floor area inside the enclosed space, measured to the inside surface of walls, major protrusions, or other surfaces that define the limit of functionally usable floor surface. Does not include the area of freestanding columns that inhibit functional use of the space or include circulation area outside the space.

engineering economics   Application of engineering, mathematical, and economic techniques to the economic evaluation of engineering alternatives.

EPA   Environmental Protection Agency.

equity An owner's right in a property after all claims against the property have been settled.

ergonomics Applying biologic and engineering data and techniques to solve the problems of the interface of the worker and his workplace.

errors and omissions insurance Insurance taken by design professionals to protect themselves from liability claims arising from mistakes made in design and construction documents.

estimate Short-form proposal from a prospective vendor for the provision of certain services.

estimating The process of determining the cost and/or duration of an item of work. Also refers to quantity determination for materials.

evaluate To assess the capability of a facility to perform the function(s) for which it is designed, used, or required to be used.

excess currency contract A contract in connection with which payments are to be made solely in excess of local currency held by the government.

excusable delay An unforeseeable delay that results from one of a number of causes specified in the contract. Since an excusable delay is not considered to be the fault of the contractor, he is entitled to a time extension for the period of the excusable delay.

expense stop An identified dollar amount, on either a dollar per square foot per year basis or a pro rata share basis of the total operating expense cost, that the landlord is responsible to pay. Any increase over the expense stop will be allocated to the tenant.

extension of time A period of time that extends the contractor's performance period beyond the contract completion date specified in the contract. Time extensions are granted by the contracting officer upon written request by the contractor when he has experienced an excusable delay.

fabric of a building All the elements, components, parts, and materials of a building, at any scale and of any age.

face rate The identified rental rate in a lease that is subsequently discounted by concessions offered by the landlord. Also called the *contract rate.*

facility Something that is built, installed, or established to serve a purpose.

facility audit (building audit) Identifying the physical condition, functional performance, and maintenance deficiencies of a facility to assist in long-term capital renewal and maintenance and operations planning.

facility evaluation Comparison of the qualitative and quantitative results of judgment, observations, measurements, analyses, or other tests against performance criteria established for a specified purpose and to a specified precision and reliability.

facility-in-service Facility as completed and operational.

facility management (FM) The practice of coordinating the physical workplace with the people and work of the organization; integrates the principles of business administration, architecture, and the behavioral and engineering services.

Facility Management Administrator (FMA) The professional designation conferred by the BOMI Institute for those who have successfully completed the FMA curriculum.

facility operator Organization or agency having a contract with the owner or investor to operate a facility.

facility performance Behavior in the service of a facility for a specified use; for example, how effectively could an architectural firm use a renovated warehouse as a principal office?

fair market value The rental value of space similar to the leased premises for comparison purpose in rental adjustments.

fast track Overlapping the phases of a project to save as much time as possible.

feasibility study Study of a planned scheme or development, the practicality of its achievement, and its projected financial outcome.

feature of a facility A building, building element, building component, or aspects of design, arrangement, form, or color that helps or hinders the satisfaction of a requirement for serviceability.

FFE   Furniture, furnishings, and equipment.

finish plan   A construction drawing that shows all new finishes keyed to the applicable specifications.

final acceptance date   The date, as determined by the project manager, in writing, and confirmed by the contracting officer, on which all items of work required by the contract have been satisfactorily completed.

final inspection date   The date on which the project manager makes a detailed inspection of the contractor's work to determine if it complies with contract requirements. During this inspection, the project manager compiles a punch list of incomplete or unsatisfactory items, which is transmitted to the contractor. This date normally coincides with the substantial completion date.

fire corridors   Special corridors with partitioning designed to create escape routes in time of fire.

fire rated   A designation for special building materials such as partitioning and doors that have been manufactured and tested to provide greater fire resistance than normal building-standard material.

first cost   Costs incurred in placing a building or system in place.

fiscal approval   The approval that verifies funds are available to complete the project.

fit-up (or fitout)   Alterations and improvements to the base building and to the building systems, including demolition, where required, to prepare the accommodation for occupancy.

flat cable   Cable designed to be used under carpet.

floor   A level of funding that must be exceeded.

floor area   *See* Building Area.

floor plate   A common term for floor size.

formal competitive bidding   A written solicitation in the form of an invitation for bid or request for proposal for procurements that are other than a telephonic solicitation or sole-source solicitation.

footprint   The working square footage required to support a particular function; often includes space for furniture as well as chair movement and circulation.

free rent   Period of time in which the tenant occupies the premises under the lease but does not pay rent.

functional program   The document that specifies functional facility serviceability requirements of the occupants and owner.

fungible   The ability to move funds from one account to another with no restrictions.

future value   The value of a benefit or a cost at some point in the future considering the time value of money.

Gantt chart   A form of bar chart used extensively to show schedules, time frames, and time sequences.

general contractor   The traditional builder who engages in the complete on-site management of the actual construction project. He performs the work by contracting on his own behalf with subcontractors and suppliers.

Global FM   The worldwide network of six facility management associations.

gross lease rate   A rental rate that includes normal building standard services as provided by the landlord within the base-year rental.

guarantee (warranty) period   A period of time from the date of acceptance of goods or services in which the contractor or supplier is obligated to repair or replace goods or work done by him that proves unsatisfactory because of defective material or workmanship.

handicapped requirement   Code-required features designed to accommodate those with disabilities. Typical areas affected are rest rooms, signage, hardware, stairs, and doors.

hard costs   In a project, the costs associated directly with construction.

hardwiring Physically connecting using cable or wire.

heat load The amount of heat that must be added to a structure to bring it to a certain temperature during heating.

hours of operation

> **active hours** Times when a facility is normally fully occupied and operational.
>
> **silent hours** Period when a facility is essentially unoccupied and only security and building operations staff are present.
>
> **transitional hours** Times in the morning after the first workers normally arrive, until a facility is fully operational and, in the evening, from the end of the normal workday until the occupants have left.

HVAC Heating, ventilating, and air-conditioning systems. Those systems that control and maintain the temperature, humidity, and air quality.

IDSA Industrial Designers Society of America.

IFMA International Facility Management Association.

improvement A valuable or useful addition or alteration that increases the value or changes the use of a building or property; something more than mere maintenance, repair, or restoration to the original condition.

improvement allowance The estimated or dollar value of the building-standard work letter being offered by the landlord.

individual job order (IJO) A category of work that is more than a work order but less than a project.

infrastructure The basic framework for building—for example, utilities, roads, and access.

installed equipment Equipment affixed to the owner's buildings, the maintenance of which is the responsibility of the facility manager, not a business unit manager.

internal rate of return (IRR) The compound rate of interest that, when used to discount the terminal values of costs and benefits of a project over a given period, will make the costs equal the benefits when cash flows are reinvested at a specific rate.

intraoffice The common area between departments and sections used for corridors, aisles, or walkways.

invitation for bid (IFB) A written solicitation for bids normally used when the requirement is clearly and completely specified and the basis for award is principally price.

IREM Institute of Real Estate Management.

ISFE International Society of Facilities Executives.

job order contracting Contracting for the reception, prioritization, and execution of work orders and small alteration projects.

key plan Small-scale floor plans designed to show room locations, occupant room numbers, and occasionally telephone numbers.

land use control measures In real estate management, plans and capital improvement budgets, zoning ordinances and master land use plans, subdivision regulations, mandatory dedications, development or impact fees, and construction codes.

landlord One who leases rights of use of real property to a tenant.

layout A space plan showing the locations of tenant improvements and the utilization of space by the tenant.

layout efficiency Efficiency of the usable area to meet the tenant's work requirements, office design, employees, and so forth. Efficiency of usable area is dictated by building shape, core location, floor size, corridors, and similar other factors.

lease A contract between the owner of real property (lessor) and another party (lessee) for the possession and use of the property for a specified term in return for rent or other income.

> **net lease** Base rent plus tenant pays directly a share of real estate taxes.
>
> **triple net lease** Base rent plus tenant pays directly a share of real estate taxes, insurance, maintenance, repair, and operating costs.

gross lease   One payment in which the owner has included estimated costs of operations.

long-term lease   A lease of real property of not less than ten years.

lease buyout   A cash inducement offered by a landlord to a tenant's previous landlord or by the tenant to the current landlord to cancel the remaining term of the tenant's lease.

lease pickup   The landlord's commitment to assume the costs associated with paying a tenant's rent in premises to be vacated that are still under lease.

license agreement   A means of legalizing and formalizing the terms of a temporary occupancy of property without creating a leasehold right to occupy property for a specified period of time.

life-cycle costing   Process of determining (in present-value terms) all costs incident to the planning, design, construction, operation, and maintenance of a structure over time.

life safety regulations   Regulation and code requirements for buildings relative to seismic, fire, and handicapped requirements.

liquidated damages   An amount of damages on a daily basis specified in the contract. This amount will be assessed against the contractor for each day beyond the contract completion date that the project remains uncompleted.

load factor   A method of allocating common areas among tenants. That percentage of the building in which common area is allocated to tenants to increase their usable area to rentable area.

local area network (LAN)   Assemblages of cable and switches that provide an interconnecting path for the flow of information among computer, terminals, word processors, facsimile, and other office machines within a building office complex.

lump-sum contract   A contract under which the contractor agrees to do the specified work for a single, fixed price.

maintainability   Capability of a system or facility to be maintained to a specified level of reliability at a specified measure of cost or economy.

maintenance   Work necessary to maintain the original, anticipated useful life of a fixed asset. It is the upkeep of property and equipment. Includes periodic or occasional inspection, adjustment, lubrication, cleaning (nonjanitorial), painting, replacement of parts, minor repairs, and other actions to prolong service and prevent unscheduled breakdown. Does not prolong the life of the property or equipment or add to its value.

> **corrective maintenance**   Maintenance activities performed because of equipment or system failure. Activities are directed toward the restoration of an item to a specified level of performance. Sometimes called *breakdown maintenance.*

> **cyclical maintenance**   Maintenance that can be predicted and scheduled on a regular basis (cycle).

> **deferrable maintenance**   A formal or informal listing of unaccomplished maintenance tasks. Such situations arise because of shortages of funds, personnel, or specific management practices.

> **emergency maintenance**   Corrective maintenance that requires immediate action because of impending danger to the occupants, the building, or a building system.

> **normal maintenance**   Maintenance activities that occur on a reasonably regular basis.

> **predictive maintenance**   Maintenance performed as a result of testing, such as oil or vibration analysis. Partially replaces preventive maintenance for some equipment.

> **preventive maintenance (PM)**   Planned actions undertaken to retain an item at a specified level of performance by providing repetitive scheduled tasks that prolong system operation and useful life: inspection, cleaning, lubrication, and part replacement.

> **special maintenance**   Maintenance activities that, because of cost, size, and/or infrequency of occurrence, tend to fall outside the normal frame of reference.

management of real property   Space allocation that is in the best interest of the owner with regard to representation, function, and economy; the economic organization of building operation and protection services; and control of property condition through timely maintenance and repair.

master plan A technical plan showing the proposed development of a particular piece of real property for a specific period of time, often twenty years.

midrange plan A facility business plan that projects programs three to five years into the future.

millwork Special architectural construction (e.g., cupboards, shelving, special wood trim).

modernize In building, to adapt to current needs, tastes, or usage by remodeling or repair.

modular furniture Furniture designed as a set of dimensionally standardized components. May be free-standing or systems furniture.

moves

> **to existing workspace (box move)** No furniture is moved, and no wiring or new telecommunications systems are required. Files and supplies are moved.

> **furniture/workstation move** Existing furniture is reconfigured and/or furniture is moved or purchased; no major new wiring or telecommunications installation is required.

> **moves requiring construction** New walls, new or additional wiring or telecommunications system are required, or other construction is needed to complete the move.

moving allowance An offer by a landlord to pay all or part of a tenant's moving costs.

MSDS (material safety data sheet) A document required by the Occupational Safety and Health Administration to be included with certain chemicals or products that could adversely affect the environment or human health or safety.

mullion The vertical member of a window frame. The mullion often determines the placement of full-height interior partitions that connect to the outside wall of a building.

multiyear agreements Agreements made with vendors for goods or services for a period exceeding one year (often three years) in order to obtain favorable pricing.

NACORE International Association of Corporate Real Estate Executives.

NFPA National Fire Protection Association.

notice to proceed A written notice from the contracting officer to the contractor that authorizes the contractor to incur obligations and proceed with work on the project.

noise reduction coefficient (NRC) The average of sound absorption coefficients for a material tested at 250, 500, 1,000, and 2,000 cycles per second; this average gives the general effectiveness of a material as a sound absorber and is expressed as a decimal. Example: A .95 NRC indicates that about 95 percent of the average sound energy striking a tested material is absorbed.

occupancy cost The total cost incurred by a company or organization to provide space for operations. Includes all costs of operating the facility, plus the costs of providing the fixed asset.

occupancy permit The permit that allows a facility to be used for the designed purpose.

occupant The department, agency, corporation, or a part thereof that is or will be occupying space. An occupant has certain rights to, possession of, or control over the premises occupied.

office plans

> **private offices** Offices enclosed by floor-to-ceiling walls.

> **open-plan offices** Offices divided by movable partitions.

> **bullpen-style offices** Offices are open with no partitions.

office space utilization rate The number of office workers divided by the facility's total number of work spaces and multiplied by 100.

operating costs (expenses) *See* Costs.

operating drawings Information drawings for use in the operation of erected and installed equipment.

operational test   A test designed by the owner or representative to test major mechanical or electrical items.

operations   Work to keep the facility performing the function for which it is currently classified. Commonly includes the cost of utilities; heating, ventilation, and air-conditioning; work reception and coordination; moving; and work associated with building systems.

OSHA   Occupational Safety and Health Administration of the U.S. Department of Labor.

outsourcing   The provision of a bundle or a full range of services by a single contractor so that the facilities staff is responsible only for managing the contractor relationship and monitoring its performance.

outtasking   The provision of individual services by a service provider.

overhead   Administrative and indirect costs for both job site and home office incurred by the contractor in connection with work on a project. Does not include the cost of direct labor and materials.

ownership costs   *See* Costs.

panels   Modular furniture sections used to define the limits of a workstation. Panels do not extend floor to ceiling.

partitions   Inside floor-to-ceiling structures not otherwise meeting the criteria of walls. Partitions are movable and removable.

partnering   An outsourcing technique in which the owner establishes a long-term relationship with a single or small group of high-performance contractors.

pass-through costs   Costs that can be directly associated with a particular project, program, or cost center.

pay request   The contractor's periodic request for payment that covers work completed and materials stored at the site during the pay period.

payback method   A technique of economic evaluation that determines the time required for the cumulative benefits from an investment to recover the investment cost and other accrued costs.

payback period   The length of time it takes an investor to recoup the costs of a capital investment.

PBX   A voice telephone switch.

performance criterion   A quantitative statement of the level of performance needed to satisfy a serviceability requirement.

performance specification   A document in which results are described precisely but methods to achieve them are left to the discretion of the contractor.

PERT chart   *See* Gantt Chart.

physical protection   Barriers that will delay or deter someone attempting unauthorized physical access to assets at a specific location.

plans (drawings/construction drawings)
>   **architectural: finish, millwork, partition**
>   **datacommunications**
>   **demolition**
>   **electrical: lighting, power**
>   **furniture**
>   **mechanical**
>   **reflected ceiling plan**
>   **telecommunications**

POE (postoccupancy evaluation)   A survey taken after project completion to assess end users' level of satisfaction with the various aspects of the new working environment, as well as to check on the performance against specifications of the major systems.

portfolio   Group of securities, buildings, or other properties held by an individual or institutional investor.

power poles   Poles suspended from a ceiling or extended to the ceiling that supply electricity or communications via internal cabling.

prebid conference   A meeting held after the contractors have been provided the bid package but before bids are due to brief contractors on the project and to answer their questions.

prelease   Leasing of premises in a building under construction that is not yet ready for occupancy.

preproposal conference   An open forum for the resolution of vendor questions concerning the solicitation; chaired by the assigned procurement officer.

present value   The concept that the value of money changes over time and that a dollar today is worth more than a dollar sometime in the future.

procurement officer   A purchasing department staff member acting as a purchasing officer or contracts officer.

profit center   An organizational unit that generates income.

project closeout   Completion of all paperwork, final payments, assembly of operating instructions, and other administrative details at the end of a project.

program   (1) A grouping of like work under single management. (2) The sum total of user requirements for a project.

programmed work   Work done in annual "slices" normally in all facilities.

project   The work category for the largest category of work. Used to achieve a specific set of objectives within a specified time schedule. Normally requires design.

project architect   The architect responsible to the owner for space planning and design for a project. Could be an in-house architect or an outsourced firm.

project coordinator   The individual authorized to present user requirements to the project developer. In space move projects, the occupant's single point of contact furnished to the space planner.

project designer   The individual who takes gross space requirements, refines them with the project coordinator, designs interior space, and obtains occupant approval.

project manager   (1) The contracting officer's representative at the site of a major project who has responsibility for that project. (2) The individual responsible for the total coordination of all aspects of a number of small projects.

projected operating expense increase   A "good-faith" estimate by the landlord as to the current operating expense increase over a base year, which is billed to the tenant as additional rent.

projected completion date   The date when the project will be completed, without reference to the contract completion date.

property management   The process of maintaining and creating value in real property consistent with the owner's objectives through the efficient balance of tenant and owner relations, budgeting and expense control, risk management, and all other operational aspects of the property in compliance with the highest standard of professional ethics.

proposal   A written response to a request for proposal.

pro rata share   The ratio between the tenant's percentage of occupancy of the rentable square footage of the building and the entire building rentable area.

provisional sum   An amount specified by the department for a particular contract item included in the contractor's lump-sum price. This amount is subject to adjustment once the actual cost of the item is determined.

punch list   A list of deficiencies and incomplete or unacceptable work items compiled by the project manager during the project, particularly during the final inspection (final punch list).

purchase order (PO)   A written contract between the owner and a vendor using a standard form.

purchasing officer   A staff member of the purchasing department who primarily procures goods.

rate of return   The percentage yield on an investment per unit time.

real estate   *See* Real Property.

real property   A parcel of land and any structures annexed thereto.

Real Property Administrator (RPA)   A professional designation conferred by the BOMI Institute for those who successfully complete an RPA curriculum.

rebuild   An alteration to return a building to its previous state or condition.

recapture   The billing to tenants of their pro rata share of increased operating expenses after those expenses have been incurred and paid for by the landlord.

reliability   The probability of performing without failure a specified function under normal conditions for a specified period of time.

remodel   An alteration to return a building to its previous state or condition.

rent   The cost charged per rentable square foot on a monthly or annual basis for a leased area.

repair   Work to restore damaged or worn-out property to a normal operating condition. As a basic distinction, repairs are curative, and maintenance is preventive. Repair can be classified as minor or major. Major repair commonly exceeds one to two man-days of effort or exceeds the in-house capability to perform.

replacement   Work to replace an item of equipment or a building component. It is the exchange or substitution of one fixed asset for another having the capacity to perform the same function. The replacement may arise from obsolescence, wear and tear, or destruction of the item to be replaced. In general, as distinguished from repair, replacement involves a complete, identifiable item.

replacement cost   Building component replacement and related costs, included in the capital budget, that are expected to be incurred during the period studied.

request for proposal (RFP)   A written solicitation used when the owner wants the option of making an award on initial proposals or conducting discussions with the offerors.

responsive bid   A bid that meets all the terms and conditions of a solicitation.

retrofit   In building, alterations to add new materials or equipment not provided at the time of original construction.

ROA (return on assets)   The net profit after taxes divided by the total value of assets employed to generate income.

ROE (return on equity)   The net profit after taxes divided by the net worth yielding the total percentage of equity gained through an investment.

ROI (return on investment)   The total profit divided by the total amount originally invested to gain a profit.

sale-leaseback   A combination ownership-lease development method in which a company develops and completes a project and then sells it to a third party, usually a developer or property manager. The developer then executes a lease with the same company that it purchased the building from. The company, now the developer's tenant, rents and occupies the facility for the lease term.

schematic plans (schematics)   Drawings to scale that show all basic design features of a space or building but no construction details or dimensions.

serviceability   The capability of a building, assembly, component, product, or construction to perform the function(s) for which it is designed or used, or both.

service contract   Agreement for the performance of various labor-oriented services, funded on a fiscal-year basis.

service evaluation   An evaluation of service to include customer service (effectiveness and responsiveness) and efficiency.

service order   The work category of the smallest category of work. Normally no design is required.

serviceability requirement   A qualitative statement of the serviceability required from a facility.

serviceability requirements profile (SRP)   A listing of the levels of serviceability required in a facility.

shared tenant services   Services provided by a building to allow tenants to share the costs and benefits of sophisticated telecommunication and other technical services.

shop drawings   Drawings prepared by the contractor and/or subcontractors that show the proposed method for fabricating and erecting in order to achieve the end result outlined in the contract drawings.

short-term lease   A lease with a basic term of less than ten years.

short list   A list of vendors selected for further consideration following initial review of all bids.

simple payback period   The time required for the cumulative benefits from an investment to pay back the investment cost and other accrued costs, not considering the time value of money.

smart building   A building that has additional technical capabilities to provide enhanced building management and operating efficiency.

soft costs   Costs related to the management of a project (e.g., overhead, fees, management time).

sole-source procurement   A procurement awarded to a single vendor without competition.

solicitation   A formal competitive procurement package consisting of applicable documents to obtain bids and proposals.

sound transmission class (STC)   A single-number rating determined by comparing the measured transmission loss in decibels through a partition against a standard STC contour. Denotes the reduction of intensity that occurs when sound energy passes through a barrier such as a partition (e.g., STC 40 indicates that about 40 decibels of energy are lost when a sound passes through the tested barrier).

source selection   Selecting a contractor or vendor through negotiations.

space   The generic definition of a particular enclosed area. May be a building, floor, or any other defined area. As a practical matter, a space is defined as that area defined by the drawing for that area.

space allocation   Assigning space, normally by rank or by function.

space limits   A limit, normally physical, that defines a space (e.g., are walls, partitions, panels).

space planner   The individual responsible to plan, manage, and document the space holdings of an agency or company.

specification   A precise statement of a set of requirements to be satisfied by a material, product, system, or service.

sprinklers   A fire-suppression system, usually water, designed into many buildings to reduce compartmentalization of space and provide additional fire protection.

stacking plans   Plans showing multiple floors of the same building, the departments occupying space, and the spaces they occupy.

staging area   Space for uncrating, assembly, and temporary storage during a project.

stair-stepped rent   A rental rate that increases by fixed amounts during the period of the lease term.

standards   The level of service or product that management is willing to fund and expects to be provided as basic.

statement of work   A document describing services to be provided by the design consultant (architect, engineer, or interior designer) for a facility in detail sufficient for the design to proceed.

stop-work order   A written order issued by the contracting officer to direct the contractor to suspend all or any part of the work.

strategic plan   The facility business plan that projects programs five to ten years for most businesses. Some facility strategic plans project three to five years.

subcontractor   A firm that enters into an agreement with the contractor to assume responsibility for a portion of the work covered by the contract.

sublease   Leasing of premises by the current tenant to another party for the remaining balance of an existing lease term.

submittal   An item that the contractor is required by the contract to submit to the project manager.

substantial completion date   The date, as determined by the project manager and confirmed by the contracting officer, on which the project is suitable for the use for which it was intended. Normally coincides with the final inspection date.

substitution and credits   The ability to substitute nonstandard or nonspecified materials as specified in a work letter or contract, or to receive dollar credits for the differential cost versus the standard or specified materials.

supplier   A firm that enters into an agreement with the department, the contractor, or a subcontractor to provide materials and/or equipment for use on a project.

support equipment environment (SEE)   The support surroundings to meet the specific needs for the operation of equipment (e.g., printers, modems, controllers).

suspension of work   A temporary work stoppage ordered by the contracting officer for the convenience of the owner.

swing space   Space in which occupants of space under construction can temporarily reside.

task lighting   A localized light or light system to accommodate the specific visual task or work area needs.

technical approval   Approval that a work request has received the appropriate technical review and design.

technical evaluation team   A team that includes a procurement officer, the contract officer's representative (COR), and other knowledgeable staff as may be determined by the COR and the purchasing department. This team is responsible for establishing the technical evaluation weights and criteria included in a solicitation, and reviews and evaluates the technical proposals of each fully responsive bidder in accordance with preestablished evaluation criteria.

technical operation   The operations that support the design and construction process (e.g., scheduling, cost engineering, value engineering).

technology unit   The organization that supports electronically augmented office work, terminals, modems, controllers, and so forth.

tenant   An organization that has rights and obligations of occupancy in a facility as specified in a lease or occupancy agreement.

tenant improvements   Construction alterations made to make a space suitable for occupancy by a specific tenant.

terminal use environment (TUE)   The support surrounding of a terminal designed to meet a specific purpose and function.

> **cluster**   A terminal with arm's reach of two users.
> **dedicated**   A terminal with arm's reach of one user.
> **regional**   A self-contained room with four terminals servicing an average of seven intermittent users.
> **satellite**   Two terminals within close proximity to four users for quick and sporadic access of information.

time and materials method   A retroactive method of change order pricing based on the contractor's verified accounting of direct costs collected as the work is actually being done.

time value of money   The time-dependent value of money stemming from both changes in the purchasing power of money (inflation/deflation) and the real earning potential of alternative investments over time.

TQM (total quality management)   Meeting or exceeding customer expectations and the system to measure performance toward that goal.

turnkey   (1) A complete build-out of tenant's premises to the tenant's specifications. (2) A project totally managed outside the owner or occupant's organization but to meet their program.

two-step bidding   A variation on formal bidding used most often when price is the dominant but not the only award factor. The first step is to establish technical acceptability. In the second step, bids reveal the lowest-priced, technically acceptable offer.

underfloor ducts A system of ducts permanently located within the floor structure to assist in the installation of telephone, datacommunications, and electrical wiring.

unit price (unit cost) The contractor's bid or proposal price for performing a specified quantity or unit of work. Normally includes the cost of labor, material, and equipment, plus an amount of overhead and profit.

unprogrammed costs Costs not anticipated or included in a budget but incurred, such as for an emergency repair.

useful life The period of time over which an investment is considered to meet its original objective.

user The generic definition of the occupant of a space. May be a tenant or a company department or an owner.

U.S. Green Buildings Council A nonprofit consensus coalition of the building industry promoting the understanding of, development, and accelerated implementation of environmentally efficient buildings.

utilization rate Net assignable area/gross area.

vacancy rate The current vacant square footage in a facility divided by the total usable area.

value analysis The procedure for developing and evaluating alternatives to a proposed economical design that best fulfills the needs and requirements of the owner/user of a building.

value engineering Evaluation of construction methods and/or materials to determine which have the net result of reducing cost, consistent with specified performance, reliability, maintainability, aesthetic, safety, and security criteria.

VAV system Variable air volume system. A system that allows great flexibility for controlling how air is distributed within a building.

vendor evaluation report A written document for a specific vendor detailing the satisfactory or unsatisfactory performance area ratings calculated in the vendor evaluation system.

vendor evaluation system A system that evaluates vendor performance in the areas of delivery, quality, and compliance with contract provisions.

video display terminal (VDT) The screen and keyboard, often detachable, of a computer.

visitor A person present who is not an occupant of a facility.

white noise Background, random-frequency noise used to mask high-frequency sounds, such as the consonants in human speech.

work The completed construction required by the contract. In a multiple prime contractor situation, the work will not be synonymous with the project.

work letter A written attachment to the lease that specifies the types, quantities, and qualities of fixtures and finishes that will be provided as standard by the landlord.

work order *See* service order.

workplace (office) solutions

> **flexspace** A combination of dedicated offices and shared team space. The offices are laid out to stress privacy or openness and flexible work arrangements.

> **floating office** An office whose location is determined by the changing location of its occupant. A floating office is the antithesis of assigned office space.

> **free address** Offices exist but are available on a first come–first served basis. Communications are wireless, and storage is mobile and limited.

> **name-based and shared offices** Offices are reduced in size, and more space is devoted to team space.

> **just-in-time space** Shared office or group space whose use must be scheduled.

> **shared/assigned space** Office and group space is assigned but its use is unscheduled. Lack of scheduling allows conflicts over space to occur.

work reception center The facilities department unit responsible for receiving, organizing, and prioritizing work requests. It is the place that customers call for facility services. Should also be the center of customer service evaluation.

zero-based budgeting   A budgeting approach whereby each budget is prepared as if the current year were the first year such a budget was prepared. Each line and requirement must be justified from a zero base.

zones   The identified portions of a building served by the heating, ventilation, and air-conditioning system that have separate controls.

Index